MINOR COUNTIES LIST A CRICKETERS

compiled by

Richard V. Isaacs

First published in Great Britain by
Association of Cricket Statisticians and Historians
Cardiff CF11 9XR

British Library Cataloguing-in-Publication Data.
A catalogue record for this book is available from the British Library.

ISBN: 978 1 905138 77 7
Typeset by Limlow Books

INTRODUCTION

It was a sad day on 4 May 2005 when, alongside my father Victor, we left Heath Road in Whitchurch knowing that the days of coming to quaint club cricket grounds like this were over. It was the ECB's decision to reformat the Cheltenham and Gloucester Trophy, as it was called at the time, the following season to a two-division north and south set-up which meant that minor counties, like Shropshire on that pleasant day, would no longer have a chance to pit their wits against the first-class opposition and put on a big occasion like this one.

To the first-class counties, they had nothing to gain. For their opponents, they had everything to gain. More often than not, the sides were made up by former county pros, upcoming promising youngsters, the odd overseas player, drafted in to bolster the side but mainly, the traditional good standard club players, who can regularly be found plying their trade every Saturday afternoon in the local leagues up and down the country.

Of course, the first-class county side came and comfortably conquered in the vast majority of cases, putting the challengers in their place by peppering the makeshift stands or proving to be too good or quick on the club wickets. But there was also the occasions when the minor county players got their chance to play 'away' and appear on fully fledged county or even Test grounds.

It wasn't always plain sailing for the professionals. Who can forget 1987 when Buckinghamshire stopped Somerset, containing Martin Crowe, Vic Marks and Neil Mallender – international cricketers all – at High Wycombe. Or Cheshire beating a powerpacked Northamptonshire team by 1 wicket at Chester a year later. And more recently, Devon prevailing over Leicestershire at Exmouth in 2004 by losing fewer wickets in a fairly low scoring encounter. These are just a handful of occasions but sadly, these days are unlikely to return as the days of knockout cricket seem to have passed.

This book is a tribute to all those players who have represented their minor county or representative county board teams in the Gillette Cup, NatWest Trophy, Cheltenham & Gloucester Trophy and the Benson and Hedges Cup. I have decided not to include Scotland, Ireland, the Netherlands, Denmark or the Universities for the purposes of this book but have included the county board XI's who were added for a brief period to the C&G Trophy.

This is my first step into producing a book for the Association of Cricket Statisticians and Historians, an organisation I have been a member of since I was a 'slip of a lad'. Many a meeting I attended alongside my dad, although in my very early days of 'involvement', I was more interested in collecting conkers from the outer at Worcester than listening in to the Association matters! I believe that, while still just 36, I am still regarded as one of the younger members we have! But I hope this book, featuring players and statistics for a competition still being fought out – even if it is in a different guise – will be of interest to the membership.

As always with a book of this type, I have a number of people to thank. First of all, to Peter Griffiths and Philip Bailey at CricketArchive, who helped me greatly with the player profiles and have produced this book for the Association. To Andrew Samson, whose outstanding database of cricket matches has been the source of much of the statistics. To High Wycombe Cricket Club for providing the picture of a memorable moment in the competition history. To Mike Davage, who not only assisted me with my Norfolk queries but used his excellent detective skills to trace a number of others. Also thanks must be passed to Michael Weeks (Cornwall), Kevin Beaumont and Douglas Miller (Buckinghamshire), Julian Lawton Smith (Oxfordshire), Harold Shaw (Devon), Kevin Clement (Huntingdonshire), Gilbert Johnstone (Cumberland), Andrew Hignell (Wales Minor Counties), Tony Percival, the Minor Counties cricket guru and the cast of many from various clubs and counties who have begun puzzled by my odd requests for biographical details for this book but pointed me in the right direction to find the players.

I also wonder if this is the first book ever produced by the Association of Cricket Statisticians and Historians where some of the information has been gained by contact made through the social networking site, Facebook! The wonders of modern technology creeping into this world of reams of paper and multitudes of pens.

Finally, and how could I complete a book without doing so, I have to pay tribute to my Dad, Victor, for whom I owe a lot, none more so than getting me into this mad world of statistics in the first place and his influence upon me to take up this fascinating path of interest. And, of course, to the ACS – an association I have great respect for, now being led very well by David Kendix's chairmanship.

Long may it continue.

Richard V. Isaacs
Helmshore, Rossendale
April 2009

Abbreviations

CB Cricket Board
CU Cambridge University
MC Minor Counties
OU Oxford University

THE PLAYERS

Jhangir Abbas (Cheshire 1999 NWT 1). Born 17.12.1970, Longsight, Manchester, Lancashire. RHB OB.

Ranil Gemunu Abeynaike (Bedfordshire 1982 NWT 1). Born 12.2.1955, Mount Lavinia, Sri Lanka. RHB SLA. FC for Sinhalese (1989/90). Also ListA for Sinhalese (1989/90).

John Abrahams (Shropshire 1989-91 NWT 3). Born 21.7.1952, Salt River, Cape Town, Cape Province, South Africa. LHB OB. FC for Lancashire (1973-88), MC (1974). Also ListA for Lancashire (1973-88), MC (1974). Father: C.J. (Western Province).

Andre Ryan Adams (Herefordshire 2001 C&G 2). Born 17.7.1975, Auckland, New Zealand. RHB RFM. 1 Test (2001/02) for New Zealand. 42 ODIs (2000/01-06/07) for New Zealand. 4 Int2020s (2004/05-06/07) for New Zealand. FC for Auckland (1997/98-07/08), Essex (2004-06), Nottinghamshire (2007-08). Also ListA for Auckland (1997/98-07/08), Essex (2004-06), Nottinghamshire (2007-08).

James Clive Adams (Berkshire 2003 C&G 1, Wiltshire 2004 C&G 1). Born 9.1.1968, Port Maria, St Mary, Jamaica. LHB SLA Occ WKT. 54 Tests (1991/92-00/01) for West Indies. 127 ODIs (1992/93-00/01) for West Indies. FC for Jamaica (1984/85-00/01), Nottinghamshire (1994), MCC (2001), Free State (2001/02-02/03). Also ListA for Jamaica (1984/85-00/01), Nottinghamshire (1994), MCC (2001), Free State (2001/02-02/03).

Kristian Adams (Lincolnshire 2002 C&G 1). Born 26.11.1976, Cleethorpes, Lincolnshire. RHB LMF. FC for Kent (2000). Also ListA for Kent (2000).

Nicholas Jack Adams (Cambridgeshire 1987-01 C&G 1, MC 1993 B&H 1, Norfolk 1997 NWT 1, Huntingdonshire 2002 C&G 1). Born 1.3.1967, Bedford. RHB RM.

Timothy William Adcock (Northumberland 1994 NWT 1). Born 25.5.1972, Wegberg, Germany. RHB WKT.

Jonathan Paul Addison (Staffordshire 1987-91 NWT 3, MC 1988 B&H 1). Born 14.11.1965, Leek, Staffordshire. RHB SLA. FC for Leicestershire (1983). Also ListA for Leicestershire (1983).

Steven Robert Ades (Sussex CB 2000-01 C&G 3 NWT 2). Born 1.3.1982, Brighton, Sussex. RHB OB.

Stephen Keith Adlard (Lincolnshire 1976 GC 1). Born 23.10.1950, Lincoln. RHB RFM.

Mohammad Adnan Akram (Essex CB 2002-03 C&G 2). Born 17.11.1983, Leytonstone, Essex. RHB RM. FC for Cambridge UCCE (2003-05). Also ListA for Cambridge UCCE (2003-05). Twin brother: Arfan Akram (Cambridge UCCE, Essex CB).

Adnan Saleem (Buckinghamshire 2002-05 C&G 5). Born 18.12.1976, Islamabad, Punjab, Pakistan. LHB LFM.

Stephen John Adshead (Herefordshire 1999 NWT 2, Leicestershire CB 2001 C&G 1, Shropshire 2003 C&G 1). Born 29.1.1980, Redditch, Worcestershire. RHB WKT. FC for Leicestershire (2000), Worcestershire (2003), Gloucestershire (2004-08). Also ListA for Leicestershire (2000), Worcestershire (2003), Gloucestershire (2004-08).

Aquib Shaffi Afzaal (Nottinghamshire CB 2001 C&G 1). Born 2.2.1985, Nottingham. LHB OB. Brothers: U. (MCC, Northamptonshire, Nottinghamshire, Nottinghamshire CB, Surrey) and K. (Derbyshire CB).

Kamran Afzaal (Derbyshire CB 1999 NWT 1). Born 31.12.1973, Rawalpindi, Punjab, Pakistan. RHB. Brothers: U. (MCC, Northamptonshire, Nottinghamshire, Nottinghamshire CB, Surrey) and A.S (Nottinghamshire CB).

Andrew Charles Agar (Norfolk 1983-84 NWT 2). Born 19.2.1956, Sanderstead, Surrey. RHB RM.

Agha Zahid (Devon 1983-85 NWT 3). Born 7.1.1953, Lahore, Punjab, Pakistan. RHB RM. 1 Test (1974/75) for Pakistan. FC for Punjab University (1970/71-71/72), Punjab (1971/72-75/76), Pakistan Universities (1972/73-74/75), Lahore Blues (1973/74), Lahore A (1974/75-75/76), Habib Bank (1975/76-92/93), Punjab A (1975/76). Also ListA for Punjab University (1970/71-71/72), Punjab (1971/72-75/76), Pakistan Universities (1972/73-74/75), Lahore Blues (1973/74), Lahore A (1974/75-75/76), Habib Bank (1975/76-92/93), Punjab A (1975/76).

James Robert Airey (Lincolnshire 1990 NWT 1). Born 28.3.1959, Barnsley, Yorkshire. RHB RM.

Stuart James Airey (Lincolnshire 2003 C&G 1). Born 18.3.1983, Cleethorpes, Lincolnshire. RHB RMF. FC for Oxford UCCE (2003-05). Also ListA for Oxford UCCE (2003-05).

Karachi Whites (1996/97-97/98). Also ListA for Pakistan Universities (1988/89), Karachi Blues (1989/90-95/96), Karachi (1990/91), Karachi Whites (1996/97-97/98).

Michael Rod Barfoot (Worcestershire CB 1999 NWT 1). Born 18.7.1980, Cheltenham, Gloucestershire. RHB RFM.

Andrew Hunter Barker (Wiltshire 1969-73 GC 3, MC South 1972-73 B&H 3). Born 7.8.1945, Salisbury, Wiltshire. LHB SLA. FC for OU (1964-67). Also ListA for OU (1964-67).

Philip David Barker (Suffolk 1981-88 NWT 5). Born 22.9.1951, Edmonton, Middlesex. RHB LM,SLA. FC for OU (1974). Also ListA for OU (1974).

Richard Guy Ross Barlow (Herefordshire 1997 NWT 1, Middlesex CB 2001 C&G 1). Born 28.6.1972, Epsom, Surrey. RHB LB.

Andrew Simon Barnard (Shropshire 1978-92 GC 1 NWT 9, MC 1985 B&H 3). Born 3.7.1957, Gloucester. RHB RFM. Father: M.R. (Shropshire).

Aaron Craig Barnes (Herefordshire 2003 C&G 1). Born 21.12.1971, Turangi, Waikato, New Zealand. RHB RM. FC for Auckland (1993/94-04/05). Also ListA for Auckland (1993/94-04/05).

David Edward Barnes (Cumberland 2003 C&G 1). Born 27.9.1982, Whitehaven, Cumberland. RHB RM.

Stuart Neil Barnes (Wiltshire 1993 NWT 1, Gloucestershire CB 2000-01 C&G 3 NWT 2). Born 27.6.1970, Bath, Somerset. RHB RM. FC for Gloucestershire (1990-91). Also ListA for Gloucestershire (1990-91).

Terence Harold Barnes (Lincolnshire 1971-76 GC 5, MC North 1974 B&H 1, Norfolk 1982 NWT 1, Wiltshire 1983-84 NWT 2). Born 22.10.1945, Grantham, Lincolnshire. LHB LM.

Alexander Anthony Barnett (Berkshire 1996 NWT 1). Born 11.9.1970, Malaga, Spain. RHB SLA. FC for Middlesex (1988-91), Lancashire (1992-94). Also ListA for Middlesex (1988-91), Lancashire (1992-94). Great-uncle: C.J. (Gloucestershire, MCC).

Kim John Barnett (Staffordshire 2003-05 C&G 3). Born 17.7.1960, Stoke-on-Trent, Staffordshire. RHB RM,LB Occ WKT. 4 Tests (1988-89) for England. 1 ODI (1988) for England. FC for Derbyshire (1979-98), Boland (1982/83-87/88), MCC (1989), Gloucestershire (1999-02). Also ListA for Derbyshire (1979-98), Boland (1982/83-87/88), MCC (1989), Gloucestershire (1999-02).

William Charles Peter Barnicoat (Cornwall 1970 GC 1). Born 19.6.1932, Truro, Cornwall. RHB RM.

Craig Jonathan Barnsley (Wales MC 2002 C&G 1). Born 28.2.1983, Durban, Natal, South Africa. RHB RM.

Alexander John Lewington Barr (Wales MC 1998-01 C&G 1 NWT 3). Born 4.12.1973, Marlborough, Wiltshire. RHB RM.

David James Barr (Warwickshire CB 2001-02 C&G 4, Buckinghamshire 2003-05 C&G 2). Born 23.7.1970, Coventry, Warwickshire. LHB.

Terry Barratt (Northamptonshire CB 2001 C&G 1). Born 23.2.1971, Rothwell, Northamptonshire. LHB RMF.

John Barrett (Norfolk 1982 NWT 1). Born 12.11.1946, Norwich, Norfolk. LHB OB.

Kevin Andrew Owen Barrett (Devon 1998-02 C&G 1 NWT 1). Born 16.11.1975, Swansea, Glamorgan, Wales. LHB RM.

Christopher Matthew Barrow (Lancashire CB 2001 C&G 1). Born 6.2.1982, Bolton, Lancashire. LHB SLA.

James Keith Barrow (Berkshire 1994-01 C&G 2 NWT 7). Born 16.12.1964, Haslemere, Surrey. RHB RFM.

Timothy James Barry (Buckinghamshire 1990-93 NWT 4). Born 12.12.1964, Chalfont St Giles, Buckinghamshire. RHB RM.

Terence Ian Barwell (MC South 1972 B&H 3, Wiltshire 1972-73 GC 2). Born 29.4.1937, Bloemhof, Transvaal, South Africa. RHB Occ WKT. FC for Somerset (1959-68), MC (1973). Also ListA for Somerset (1959-68), MC (1973).

Stephen Royston Barwick (Wales MC 1998-01 C&G 2, NWT 6). Born 6.9.1960, Neath, Glamorgan, Wales. RHB RM. FC for Glamorgan (1981-96). Also ListA for Glamorgan (1981-96).

Paul Robert Bates (Wiltshire 2001 C&G 2). Born 9.5.1974, Chippenham, Wiltshire. RHB RMF. Brother: R.J. (Wiltshire).

Richard John Bates (Wiltshire 1999-05 C&G 5 NWT 4). Born 2.3.1972, Chippenham, Wiltshire. LHB SLA. Brother: P.R. (Wiltshire).

Richard Terry Bates (Lincolnshire 1990 NWT 1, Nottinghamshire CB 2002 C&G 1). Born 17.6.1972, Stamford, Lincolnshire. RHB OB. FC for Nottinghamshire (1993-99). Also ListA for Nottinghamshire (1993-99).

Christopher James Batt (Berkshire 2001 C&G 2). Born 22.9.1976, Taplow, Buckinghamshire. LHB LMF. FC for Sussex (1997), Middlesex (1998-00). Also ListA for Sussex (1997), Middlesex (1998-00).

Ian Nicholas Battelley (Norfolk 1970 GC 1). Born 19.1.1944, Dereham, Norfolk. RHB RM. Brother: B.L. (Norfolk).

Andrew John Batterley (Cheshire 2002 C&G 1). Born 27.11.1976, Leigh, Lancashire. RHB OB.

Gareth Jon Batty (Surrey CB 2000 NWT 1). Born 13.10.1977, Bradford, Yorkshire. RHB OB. 7 Tests (2003/04-05) for England. 7 ODIs (2002/03-05/06) for England. FC for Yorkshire (1997), Surrey (1999-01), Worcestershire (2002-08). Also ListA for Yorkshire (1997), Surrey (1999-01), Worcestershire (2002-08). Brother: J.D. (Buckinghamshire, Cheshire, MCC, Shropshire, Somerset, Yorkshire, Yorkshire CB).

Jeremy David Batty (Yorkshire CB 1999 NWT 1, Buckinghamshire 2000-03 C&G 7 NWT 1). Born 15.5.1971, Bradford, Yorkshire. RHB OB. FC for Yorkshire (1989-94), Somerset (1995-96). Also ListA for Yorkshire (1989-94), Somerset (1995-96). Brother: G.J. (Surrey, Surrey CB, Worcestershire, Yorkshire).

Jonathan Neil Batty (MC 1996 B&H 5, Oxfordshire 1996 NWT 1). Born 18.4.1974, Chesterfield, Derbyshire. RHB WKT. FC for OU (1996), Surrey (1997-08). Also ListA for OU (1996), Surrey (1997-08).

Michael Edward Beale (Dorset 1968-73 GC 2). Born 7.4.1947, Sturminster Newton, Dorset. RHB WKT.

Jonathan Dobing Bean (Cheshire 1992-99 NWT 8). Born 20.8.1964, Altrincham, Cheshire. RHB Occ WKT.

Malcolm Beaty (MC East 1978 B&H 4). Born 11.1.1939, Carlisle, Cumberland. RHB WKT.

Thomas Beck (Bedfordshire 1970 GC 1).

David Beckett (Oxfordshire 1980 GC 1). Born 25.10.1954, Oxford. LHB LM.

Douglas Keith Beckett (MC North 1979 B&H 1). Born 29.8.1959, Hampton Court, Middlesex. RHB RM.

Richard Denison Bedbrook (Wiltshire 2001-05 C&G 4). Born 29.7.1978, Bury, Lancashire. RHB RMF.

Paul Beech (Cumberland 1996-99 NWT 4). Born 2.10.1965, Hailsham, Sussex. RHB RFM.

Ronald Neave Beeson (Lincolnshire 1966-67 GC 2). Born 23.10.1936, Grimsby, Lincolnshire. Died 8.8.1995, Grimsby, Lincolnshire. RHB WKT.

Andrew John Bell (Dorset 2001 CG 1). Born 22.1.1982, High Wycombe, Buckinghamshire. RHB.

Ian Ronald Bell (Warwickshire CB 1999 NWT 1). Born 11.4.1982, Walsgrave, Coventry, Warwickshire. RHB RM. 45 Tests (2004-08/09) for England. 79 ODIs (2004/05-08/09) for England. 5 Int2020s (2006-08) for England. FC for Warwickshire (1999-08), MCC (2004). Also ListA for Warwickshire (1999-08), MCC (2004).

Kristian Martin Bell (Wales MC 1993-01 C&G 2 NWT 6). Born 15.4.1972, Cardiff, Glamorgan, Wales. RHB LB.

T Alan Bell (Hertfordshire 1966 GC 1).

Michael Ramsay Bellhouse (Oxfordshire 2000-01 C&G 1 NWT 1). Born 11.10.1976, Wandsworth, London. RHB RFM.

Richard James Belmont (Norfolk 1991 NWT 1). Born 17.5.1965, Dronfield, Derbyshire. RHB RMF.

Christopher Charles Benham (Hampshire CB 2001 C&G 1). Born 24.3.1983, Frimley, Surrey. RHB OB. FC for Hampshire (2004-08), Loughborough UCCE (2004). Also ListA for Hampshire (2004-08), Loughborough UCCE (2004).

Joseph Emmanuel Benjamin (Staffordshire 1986-87 NWT 2). Born 2.2.1961, Christ Church, St Kitts. RHB RMF. 1 Test (1994) for England. 2 ODIs (1994/95) for England. FC for Warwickshire (1988-91), Surrey (1992-99). Also ListA for Warwickshire (1988-91), Surrey (1992-99).

Jonathon Andrew Benn (Northumberland 1992 NWT 1). Born 24.6.1967, Rawtenstall, Lancashire. RHB RM.

Gary Mark Bennett (Somerset CB 1999-00 NWT 2). Born 10.12.1971, Taunton, Somerset. RHB RM.

Matthew Robert Martin Bennett (Kent CB 2002-03 C&G 2). Born 2.9.1982, Epsom, Surrey. RHB WKT.

James Graham Edward Benning (Buckinghamshire 2001 C&G 2). Born 4.5.1983, Mill Hill, London. RHB RM. FC for Surrey (2003-08). Also ListA for Surrey (2003-08).

Justin David Ramsay Benson (Cambridgeshire 1986 NWT 1). Born 1.3.1967, Dublin, Ireland. RHB RM Occ WKT. FC for Leicestershire (1988-93), Ireland (1997). Also ListA for Leicestershire (1988-93), Ireland (1997).

James Richard Benstead (Derbyshire CB 2000-02 C&G 4 NWT 2, Staffordshire 2005 C&G 1). Born 8.3.1979, Burton-on-Trent, Staffordshire. RHB RM.

Paul Francis Berrill (Huntingdonshire 2000 NWT 2). Born 17.12.1964, Cambridge. RHB RM WKT. Father: D.R. (Huntingdonshire).

Paul James Berry (Cumberland 1995 NWT 1). Born 21.12.1968, Salford, Lancashire. RHB OB WKT.

Kenneth Paul Berryman (Cornwall 1995-02 C&G 2 NWT 1). Born 15.2.1970, Truro, Cornwall. RHB RMF.

Andrew John Bethel (Yorkshire CB 1999-02 C&G 6 NWT 4). Born 18.7.1967, Sheffield, Yorkshire. LHB OB.

Ian Robert Beven (Hertfordshire 1981 NWT 1). Born 27.11.1958, Hobart, Tasmania, Australia. LHB OB. FC for Tasmania (1980/81-83/84), Scotland (1993). Also ListA for Tasmania (1980/81-83/84), Scotland (1993).

Stuart Roy Bevins (Herefordshire 1995-97 NWT 2). Born 8.3.1967, Solihull, Warwickshire. RHB WKT. FC for Worcestershire (1989-91). Also ListA for Worcestershire (1989-91).

Peter William Bichener (Bedfordshire 1971 GC 1). Born 22.2.1941, Bedford. RHB RM.

Donald Albert Bick (Hertfordshire 1971 GC 1). Born 22.2.1936, Hampstead, London. Died 24.1.1992, Ware, Hertfordshire. RHB OB. FC for Middlesex (1954-67), MCC (1967). Also ListA for Middlesex (1954-67), MCC (1967).

Kenneth David Biddulph (Durham 1964-72 GC 5). Born 29.5.1932, Chingford, Essex. Died 7.1.2003, Oxfordshire. RHB RFM. FC for Somerset (1955-61). Also ListA for Somerset (1955-61).

Kenneth Robert James Bingham (Kent CB 2002 C&G 2). Born 20.9.1980, Oxford. RHB WKT.

Travis Binnion (Nottinghamshire CB 2002 C&G 1). Born 10.11.1986, Derby. LHB WKT.

Shaun David Birbeck (Durham CB 1999-00 NWT 6). Born 26.7.1972, Easington Lane, Co Durham. LHB RM. FC for Durham (1994-96). Also ListA for Durham (1994-96). Brother: A. (Durham).

Peter Cresswell Birtwisle (Durham 1968-83 GC 8 NWT 3, MC East 1977 B&H 1). Born 2.8.1946, Sunderland, Co Durham. RHB RM. Son: S.J. (Durham CB, Northumberland).

Simon Jonathan Birtwisle (Durham CB 2002-03 C&G 2). Born 24.7.1979, Sunderland, Co Durham. RHB SLA. Father: P.C. (Durham, MC East).

Ian Emlyn Bishop (Devon 1998-04 C&G 4 NWT 1, Surrey CB 1999 NWT 1). Born 26.8.1977, Taunton, Somerset. RHB RF. FC for Somerset (1996), Surrey (1999-00). Also ListA for Somerset (1996), Surrey (1999-00).

Justin Edward Bishop (Suffolk 2000 NWT 1). Born 4.1.1982, Bury St Edmunds, Suffolk. LHB LMF. FC for Essex (1999-05), Durham UCCE (2002-04). Also ListA for Essex (1999-05), Durham UCCE (2002-04). Father: K.C. (Suffolk).

Keith Charles Bishop (Suffolk 1979-80 GC 2). Born 11.3.1949, Bury St Edmunds, Suffolk. RHB RM. Son: J.E. (Devon, Durham UCCE, Essex, Suffolk).

Gary Raymond Black (Buckinghamshire 1985-93 NWT 8). Born 11.5.1954, Hammersmith, London. RHB RM.

Marlon Ian Black (Cheshire 2003 C&G 1). Born 7.6.1975, Dow, California, Trinidad. RHB RFM. 6 Tests (2000/01-01/02) for West Indies. 5 ODIs (2000/01-01/02) for West Indies. FC for Trinidad and Tobago (1993/94-03/04). Also ListA for Trinidad and Tobago (1993/94-03/04).

Geoffrey James Blackburn (Cheshire 1987-88 NWT 3). Born 13.11.1950, Liverpool, Lancashire. LHB SLA.

Kevin Richard Blackburn (Somerset CB 1999-01 C&G 1 NWT 2). Born 19.8.1968, Doncaster, Yorkshire. RHB RM.

Trevor George Blades (Lincolnshire 1974 GC 2). Born 22.6.1947, Peterborough. RHB WKT.

Richard George Blair (Bedfordshire 1994 NWT 1). Born 6.3.1967, Stanstead, Suffolk. LHB.

Paul Malcolm Blakeley (Shropshire 1993 NWT 1). Born 27.5.1964, Dewsbury, Yorkshire. RHB RM.

Ian Paul Corbett Blakemore (Herefordshire 1997 NWT 1). Born 13.5.1965, Ironbridge, Shropshire. LHB SLA.

Ian Neale Blanchett (Cambridgeshire 2001 C&G 2). Born 2.10.1975, Melbourne, Victoria, Australia. RHB RFM. FC for Middlesex (1998-99). Also ListA for Middlesex (1998-99).

Tony Gordon Bland (Norfolk 1968 GC 1). Born 19.7.1941, Ranworth, Suffolk. RHB RFM.

David Clifford Blank (Staffordshire 1984-90 NWT 7). Born 9.12.1959, Stoke-on-Trent, Staffordshire. RHB RFM.

Darren Andrew Blenkiron (Durham 1991 NWT 1). Born 4.2.1974, Solihull, Warwickshire. LHB RM. FC for Durham (1994-96). Father: W. (Durham, MCC, Warwickshire).

Henry Calthorpe Blofeld (Norfolk 1965 GC 1). Born 23.9.1939, Hoveton Home Farm, Norfolk. RHB WKT. FC for CU (1958-59). Also ListA for CU (1958-59). Uncle: F.S.G.Calthorpe (CU, MCC, Sussex, Warwickshire).

Stephen Michael Bloyce (Berkshire 2004 C&G 1). Born 11.11.1980, Reading, Berkshire. RHB RMF.

David Jonathan Peter Boden (Staffordshire 1998-00 NWT 4, Shropshire 2001 C&G 1). Born 26.11.1970, Eccleshall, Staffordshire. RHB RMF. FC for Middlesex (1989), Essex (1992-93), Gloucestershire (1995-96). Also ListA for Middlesex (1989), Essex (1992-93), Gloucestershire (1995-96).

Iain Anthony Bond (Devon 1999 NWT 2). Born 7.11.1973, Barnstaple, Devon. RHB RFM.

Raymond Ernest Bond (Buckinghamshire 1969-79 GC 5, MC South 1973-74 B&H 4). Born 7.9.1944, Burnham, Buckinghamshire. LHB RMF. FC for MC (1973). Also ListA for MC (1973).

Richard John Bond (Suffolk 1983 NWT 1). Born 8.2.1948, Beck Row, Mildenhall, Suffolk. RHB RM.

Christopher Derek Booden (Buckinghamshire 1987-93 NWT 5). Born 22.6.1961, Newport Pagnell, Buckinghamshire. RHB RM. FC for Northamptonshire (1980-81). Also ListA for Northamptonshire (1980-81).

Stuart Brian Boon (Hertfordshire 1964 GC 1). Born 25.2.1934, Stafford. Died 13.8.1989, Stoke-on-Trent, Staffordshire.

Timothy James Boon (Norfolk 1996-97 NWT 2). Born 1.11.1961, Balby, Doncaster, Yorkshire. RHB RM. FC for Leicestershire (1980-95). Also ListA for Leicestershire (1980-95).

Paul Antony Booth (Yorkshire CB 2000-01 C&G 2 NWT 1). Born 5.9.1965, Crossland Moor, Huddersfield, Yorkshire. LHB SLA. FC for Yorkshire (1982-89), Warwickshire (1990-93). Also ListA for Yorkshire (1982-89), Warwickshire (1990-93).

Richard Boothroyd (Staffordshire 1975-76 GC 2). Born 25.11.1944, Huddersfield, Yorkshire. RHB RFM.

Ravinder Singh Bopara (Essex CB 2001 C&G 1). Born 4.5.1985, Forest Gate, London. RHB RM. 3 Tests (2007/08) for England. 33 ODIs (2006/07-08/09) for England. 1 Int2020 (2008) for England. FC for Essex (2002-08), MCC (2006-08). Also ListA for Essex (2002-08), MCC (2006-08).

Christopher William Boroughs (Herefordshire 1998-04 C&G 8 NWT 4). Born 21.4.1975, Stourbridge, Worcestershire. RHB RM.

Christopher Richard Borrett (Norfolk 2001-03 C&G 5). Born 2.12.1979, North Walsham, Norfolk. RHB RFM. Father: P.C. (Norfolk).

Paul Clarke Borrett (Norfolk 1970 GC 1). Born 1.2.1944, Martham, Norfolk. RHB LB. Son: C.R. (Norfolk).

David Borthwick (Northumberland 1994 NWT 1). Born 2.2.1963, Sunderland, Co Durham. RHB WKT. Nephew: S.G. (Durham).

Timothy Jon Bostock (Cheshire 1992-96 NWT 4). Born 21.1.1962, Widnes, Lancashire. RHB OB.

William Neil Boustead (Cumberland 1984-86 NWT 3). Born 13.8.1953, Carlisle, Cumberland. LHB WKT.

James Noel Bruce Bovill (Buckinghamshire 1998-99 NWT 3). Born 2.6.1971, High Wycombe, Buckinghamshire. RHB RFM. FC for Hampshire (1993-97). Also ListA for Hampshire (1993-97).

John Daniel Peter Bowden (Kent CB 1999-03 C&G 7 NWT 5). Born 25.7.1973, Sidcup, Kent. LHB LM.

David Michael Bowen (Middlesex CB 1999-00 NWT 3). Born 3.10.1971, Enfield, Middlesex. RHB.

Richard Brian Bowers (Surrey CB 2001-02 C&G 4). Born 16.6.1976, Redhill, Surrey. RHB RMF.

Duncan John Bowett (Shropshire 1997-05 C&G 2 NWT 1). Born 7.12.1971, Perth, Western Australia, Australia. RHB RM.

Matthew Bowyer (Buckinghamshire 1997-03 C&G 4 NWT 1). Born 25.7.1973, Eastbourne, Sussex. RHB.

Matthew Kavan Leslie Boyden (Norfolk 1997-99 NWT 3). Born 24.2.1979, King's Lynn, Norfolk. RHB WKT.

Cedric Nigel Boyns (Shropshire 1983 NWT 1). Born 14.8.1954, Starbeck, Harrogate, Yorkshire. RHB RM. FC for CU (1976), Worcestershire (1976-79). Also ListA for CU (1976), Worcestershire (1976-79).

Ian Justin Boyton (Middlesex CB 2001 C&G 1). Born 19.8.1974, Barking, Essex. RHB RM.

Peter Lulham Bradbury (Oxfordshire 1980 GC 1). Born 12.3.1950, Pill, Bristol. RHB OB.

Carl Crispin Bradfield (Huntingdonshire 2001 C&G 3). Born 18.1.1975, Grahamstown, Cape Province, South Africa. LHB RM. FC for Eastern Province B (1993/94-97/98), Eastern Province (1996/97-03/04), Border (2004/05-06/07), Warriors (2004/05-05/06). Also ListA for Eastern Province B (1993/94-97/98), Eastern Province (1996/97-03/04), Border (2004/05-06/07), Warriors (2004/05-05/06).

Robert Leslie Bradford (Norfolk 1984 NWT 1). Born 29.4.1952, Swardeston, Norfolk. RHB.

Stephen Alvin Bradford (Lincolnshire 1996-99 NWT 3). Born 15.7.1963, Lincoln. LHB SLA. Brother: T.J.Bradford (Lincolnshire).

Peter Bradley (MC North 1973-75 B&H 11, Shropshire 1974 GC 1, MC East 1976 B&H 4). Born 3.3.1937, Gee Cross, Hyde, Cheshire. LHB RM. FC for MC (1973-74). Also ListA for MC (1973-74).

Paul John Bradshaw (Norfolk 1997-03 C&G 6 NWT 5). Born 1.5.1978, Chelmsford, Essex. RHB RFM.

William David Bragg (Wales MC 2005 C&G 1). Born 24.10.1986, Newport, Monmouthshire, Wales. LHB WKT. FC for Glamorgan (2007). Also ListA for Glamorgan (2007).

Brian Maurice Brain (MC 1982 B&H 1). Born 13.9.1940, Worcester. RHB RFM. FC for Worcestershire (1959-75), Gloucestershire (1976-81). Also ListA for Worcestershire (1959-75), Gloucestershire (1976-81).

Stephen Bramhall (Cheshire 1994-01 C&G 1 NWT 7). Born 26.11.1967, Warrington, Lancashire. RHB WKT. FC for Lancashire (1990), Nottinghamshire (1992-93). Also ListA for Lancashire (1990), Nottinghamshire (1992-93).

Andrew Richard Bray (Kent CB 2000-01 C&G 4 NWT 1). Born 16.11.1979, Westminster, London. RHB RFM.

Kevin George Bray (Warwickshire CB 1999-01 C&G 2 NWT 2). Born 24.9.1968, Sydney, New South Wales, Australia. RHB RFM.

David Hilton Breakwell (Shropshire 1974-76 GC 2). Born 16.6.1946, Bridgnorth, Shropshire. RHB RFM. Son: A.D. (Shropshire).

Alastair Nigel Bressington (Gloucestershire CB 1999-00 NWT 3). Born 28.11.1979, Bristol. LHB RM. FC for Gloucestershire (2000-04). Also ListA for Gloucestershire (2000-04). Brother: N.S. (Gloucestershire CB).

Nathan Stewart Bressington (Gloucestershire CB 2000 NWT 2). Born 7.2.1981, Cheltenham, Gloucestershire. LHB RM. Brother: A.N. (Gloucestershire, Gloucestershire CB).

Noel Adrian Brett (Surrey CB 2002 C&G 2). Born 8.9.1975, Aldershot, Hampshire. RHB OB.

Christopher Trevor Brice (Yorkshire CB 2001-02 C&G 3). Born 5.1.1983, Leeds, Yorkshire. LHB SLA.

Graeme David Bridge (Durham CB 1999-02 C&G 1 NWT 3). Born 4.9.1980, Sunderland, Co Durham. RHB SLA. FC for Durham (1999-06). Also ListA for Durham (1999-06).

Mark Paul Briers (Herefordshire 1998 NWT 1). Born 21.4.1968, Loughborough, Leicestershire. RHB LB. FC for Durham (1992-93). Also ListA for Durham (1992-93).

Patrick David Briggs (Cheshire 1968 GC 2, Bedfordshire 1970-71 GC 2). Born 24.8.1940, Timperley, Cheshire. RHB RM. FC for CU (1963-64). Also ListA for CU (1963-64).

David Stephen Brignull (Leicestershire CB 1999-01 C&G 1 NWT 1). Born 27.11.1981, Forest Gate, London. RHB RMF. FC for Leicestershire (2003-05). Also ListA for Leicestershire (2003-05).

Tony Robert Bristow (Bedfordshire 2001-02 C&G 3). Born 23.6.1965, Newcastle, New South Wales, Australia. LHB RM occ WKT.

Daniel Peter Britton (Dorset 2001 C&G 1). Born 25.9.1981, Salisbury, Wiltshire. RHB RFM.

Daniel Louis Broadbent (Yorkshire CB 2002 C&G 1). Born 22.1.1985, Leeds, Yorkshire. LHB OB.

Robert Gillespie Broadbent (Hertfordshire 1964 GC 1). Born 21.6.1924, Beckenham, Kent. Died 26.4.1993, Bromyard, Herefordshire. RHB RFM. FC for Worcestershire (1950-63). Also ListA for Worcestershire (1950-63).

Denton John Brock (Staffordshire 1996-99 NWT 3, Cheshire 2000 NWT 1). Born 10.7.1971, Newcastle-under-Lyme, Staffordshire. RHB RFM. Father: D.J. (Staffordshire).

Stephen Michael Brogan (Herefordshire 1995 NWT 1, Nottinghamshire CB 1999-00 NWT 2). Born 24.9.1969, Worksop, Nottinghamshire. RHB.

Gary Brook (Yorkshire CB 2000-01 C&G 2 NWT 2). Born 25.11.1968, Leeds, Yorkshire. RHB WKT.

Mervyn Edward William Brooker (Staffordshire 1984 NWT 1). Born 24.3.1954, Burton-on-Trent, Staffordshire. RHB RM. FC for CU (1974-76). Also ListA for CU (1974-76).

Andrew Phillip Brookes (Warwickshire CB 1999 NWT 1). Born 31.7.1969, Solihull, Warwickshire. RHB OB.

Charles Edward William Brooks (Berkshire 1965-66 GC 3). Born 17.2.1927, Epsom, Surrey. Died 18.5.2002, Abingdon, Oxfordshire. RHB LB.

Kevin Graham Brooks (Lincolnshire 1983 NWT 1, Suffolk 1986-87 NWT 2). Born 15.10.1959, Caversham, Reading, Berkshire. RHB RM. FC for Derbyshire (1980). Also ListA for Derbyshire (1980).

Robert David Brooks (Oxfordshire 2000-01 C&G 1 NWT 1). Born 14.9.1970, Truro, Cornwall. LHB WKT.

Alan Brown (Northumberland 1971-77 GC 3, MC North 1974 B&H 4). Born 1.4.1933, Seaton Delaval, Northumberland. RHB RM.

Adrian Desmond Brown (Suffolk 1984-99 NWT 8). Born 18.5.1962, Clacton-on-Sea, Essex. RHB WKT. FC for CU (1986), Essex (1988-92). Also ListA for CU (1986), Essex (1988-92).

Alexander Gordon Brown (Northumberland 2003 C&G 1). Born 10.2.1967, Stockfield, Northumberland. LHB RMF.

Andrew Mark Brown (Suffolk 2001-02 C&G 7). Born 6.11.1964, Heanor, Derbyshire. LHB OB. FC for Derbyshire (1985-92). Also ListA for Derbyshire (1985-92).

Christopher Brown (Norfolk 2001-03 C&G 6). Born 16.8.1974, Oldham, Lancashire. RHB OB. FC for Badureliya (2005/06). Also ListA for Badureliya (2005/06).

Gregg Brown (Somerset CB 1999 NWT 1). Born 20.12.1972, Bath, Somerset. RHB RM.

Gary Kevin Brown (Durham 1989-90 NWT 2, MC 1989-91 B&H 12, Durham CB 1999-01 C&G 1 NWT 5). Born 16.6.1965, Welling, Kent. RHB OB. FC for Middlesex (1986), MC (1990), Durham (1992). Also ListA for Middlesex (1986). Brother: K.R. (MCC, Middlesex).

Jason Fred Brown (Staffordshire 1995 NWT 1). Born 10.10.1974, Newcastle-under-Lyme, Staffordshire. RHB OB. FC for Northamptonshire (1996-08). Also ListA for Northamptonshire (1996-08).

Mark Brown (Cambridgeshire 1982-83 NWT 2). Born 3.9.1958, Bangor, Caernarvonshire, Wales. RHB RFM.

Paul Anthony Brown (Devon 1986-90 NWT 3). Born 13.5.1965, Crediton, Devon. RHB RM.

Simon John Emmerson Brown (Durham 1991 NWT 1). Born 29.6.1969, Cleadon, Co Durham. RHB LMF. 1 Test (1996) for England. FC for Northamptonshire (1987-90), Durham (1992-02). Also ListA for Northamptonshire (1987-90), Durham (1992-01).

Barrington St Aubyn Browne (Cheshire 2004 C&G 1). Born 16.9.1967, New Amsterdam, West Bank, Berbice, Guyana. RHB RF. 4 ODIs (1994/95) for West Indies. FC for Demerara (1987/88-88/89), Guyana (1987/88-96/97), MCC (1996). Also ListA for Demerara (1987/88-88/89), Guyana (1987/88-96/97), MCC (1996). Brother: R.E. (Demerara, Guyana).

James Thomas Anthony Bruce (Cumberland 2001 C&G 1). Born 17.12.1979, Hammersmith, London. RHB RMF. FC for Durham UCCE (2001-02), Hampshire (2003-07). Also ListA for Durham UCCE (2001-02), Hampshire (2003-07). Brother: E.C.A. (Durham UCCE).

Iain Brunnschweiler (Hampshire CB 2002 C&G 1). Born 10.12.1979, Southampton, Hampshire. RHB WKT. FC for Hampshire (2000-03). Also ListA for Hampshire (2000-03).

Andrew Paul Bryan (Worcestershire CB 2001 C&G 3). Born 31.7.1964, Birmingham, Warwickshire. RHB.

Russell Barnaby Bryan (Devon 1999-03 C&G 1 NWT 1). Born 14.2.1981, Maidstone, Kent. RHB RFM.

Paul Robert John Bryson (Cheshire 1995-02 C&G 3 NWT 6). Born 6.7.1968, Welton, Liverpool, Lancashire. RHB OB.

Anthony C Buck (Oxfordshire 1967 GC 1). Born 18.8.1944, Oxford.

Christopher Richard John Budd (Gloucestershire CB 1999-01 C&G 2 NWT 3, Wiltshire 2002-05 C&G 3). Born 26.12.1978, Bristol. RHB OB.

Matthew Paul Leonard Bulbeck (Somerset CB 2001 C&G 1). Born 8.11.1979, Taunton, Somerset. LHB LMF. FC for Somerset (1998-02). Also ListA for Somerset (1998-02).

David Alfred Bulfield (Dorset 1973 GC 1). Born 15.1.1938, Lancaster, Lancashire. RHB LB.

James Jonathan Bull (Leicestershire CB 2001 C&G 1). Born 22.12.1976, Leicester. RHB OB. FC for OU (1996-99). Also ListA for OU (1996-99).

Christopher Keith Bullen (Bedfordshire 1994-97 NWT 2, Surrey CB 1999-01 C&G 3 NWT 3). Born 5.11.1962, Clapham, London. RHB OB. FC for Surrey (1982-91), MC (1994). Also ListA for Surrey (1982-91), MC (1994). Cousin: D.J.Roberts (Bedfordshire, Cornwall, Northamptonshire, Northamptonshire CB).

Guy Bulpitt (Staffordshire 2001-04 C&G 7). Born 16.4.1968, Stafford. RHB SLA.

Rodney Alan Bunting (Norfolk 1985-95 NWT 5, MC 1987 B&H 4). Born 25.4.1965, East Winch, Norfolk. RHB RFM. FC for Sussex (1988-91). Also ListA for Sussex (1988-91). Brother: S.J. (Norfolk).

Andrew John Burch (Suffolk 2001 C&G 1). Born 24.2.1963, Ipswich, Suffolk. RHB WKT.

Oliver Edward Burford (Lincolnshire 2001-04 C&G 8). Born 23.7.1980, Lincoln. RHB WKT.

Graham Iefvion Burgess (MC 1981-82 B&H 3). Born 5.5.1943, Glastonbury, Somerset. RHB RM. FC for Somerset (1966-79). Also ListA for Somerset (1966-79).

James Burgoyne (Worcestershire CB 1999 NWT 1). Born 21.2.1980, Wordsley, Stourbridge, Worcestershire. RHB RM.

William Arthur Burgoyne (Berkshire 1976 GC 1). Born 28.10.1942, Windsor, Berkshire. RHB RMF.

Roger Mark Burley (Cornwall 2001 C&G 1). Born 1.10.1970, Redruth, Cornwall. RHB WKT.

Paul Burn (Durham 1985-91 NWT 6, Northumberland 1992 NWT 1, Durham CB 1999 NWT 2). Born 31.10.1963, Sacriston, Co Durham. RHB RM. FC for MC (1990). Also ListA for MC (1990).

Mark Ian Burns (Cumberland 2002 C&G 2). Born 18.9.1967, Bury, Lancashire. RHB RM WKT.

Neil David Burns (Buckinghamshire 1997-99 NWT 4). Born 19.9.1965, Chelmsford, Essex. LHB SLA WKT. FC for Western Province B (1985/86), Essex (1986), Somerset (1987-93), MCC (1989), Leicestershire (2000-02). Also ListA for Western Province B (1985/86), Essex (1986), Somerset (1987-93), MCC (1989), Leicestershire (2000-02).

Alan James Burridge (Durham 1964-72 GC 6, MC North 1972-74 B&H 10, MC South 1975 B&H 4, Hertfordshire 1976-77 GC 4, MC West 1976-78 B&H 12). Born 8.10.1936, Sunderland, Co Durham. LHB RS. FC for MC (1973). Also ListA for MC (1973).

Stephen Burrow (Berkshire 1983 NWT 1, Buckinghamshire 1985-93 NWT 7, MC 1988 B&H 2, Hertfordshire 1999-00 NWT 4). Born 13.1.1958, Wokingham, Berkshire. RHB RM.

Thomas George Burrows (Berkshire 2003 C&G 1). Born 5.5.1985, Wokingham, Berkshire. RHB WKT. FC for Hampshire (2005-08). Also ListA for Hampshire (2005-08).

Michael Timothy Burt (Somerset CB 2001 C&G 1). Born 2.1.1972, Bletchley, Buckinghamshire. RHB WKT.

Anthony William Burton (Yorkshire CB 1999 NWT 1). Born 15.4.1975, Ripon, Yorkshire. RHB RFM.

Martin Arthur Edward Burton (Cambridgeshire 1995 NWT 1, Huntingdonshire 1999-02 C&G 4 NWT 3). Born 6.7.1973, Cambridge. LHB SLA.

Robert Lingen Burton (Shropshire 1974-78 GC 3). Born 20.4.1943, Pointe-a-Pierre, Trinidad. RHB RM. Son: R.P.L. (Shropshire).

Richard Leslie Burton (MC North 1974 B&H 1, Lincolnshire 1983-88 NWT 2). Born 29.1.1955, Thealby, Lincolnshire. RHB RM.

Richard Peter Lingen Burton (Shropshire 2001 C&G 1). Born 24.8.1976, Shrewsbury, Shropshire. LHB RM. Father: R.L. (Shropshire).

Roger Neil Busby (Oxfordshire 1975-87 GC 3 NWT 6, MC 1987-88 B&H 3). Born 18.9.1946, Oxford. RHB RFM.

John Edgar Bush (Oxfordshire 1967 GC 1). Born 20.8.1928, Oxford. RHB. FC for OU (1950-52). Also ListA for OU (1950-52).

William John Bushby (Bedfordshire 1967-73 GC 6). Born 26.9.1935, Southwick, Sussex. RHB RM.

David Neil Butcher (Devon 1992 NWT 1). Born 2.10.1969, Colchester, Essex. RHB SLA.

Gary Paul Butcher (Hertfordshire 2003 C&G 1). Born 11.3.1975, Clapham, London. RHB RM. FC for Glamorgan (1994-98), Surrey (1999-01). Also ListA for Glamorgan (1994-98), Surrey (1999-01). Father: A.R. (Glamorgan, MCC, Surrey), brother: M.A. (Surrey), uncle: I.P. (Gloucestershire, Leicestershire), M.S.Butcher (Surrey).

Keith Andrew Butler (Suffolk 1993 NWT 1). Born 20.1.1971, Camden Town, London. RHB RM. FC for Essex (1989). Also ListA for Essex (1989).

Norman Victor Butler (Buckinghamshire 1965 GC 1). Born 6.5.1930, Chippenham, Wiltshire. Died 1.4.2007, Slough, Buckinghamshire. LHB.

Paul Richard Butler (Lincolnshire 1983-88 NWT 2). Born 26.6.1963, Sleaford, Lincolnshire. RHB RM.

Trevor Butler (Buckinghamshire 1987-90 NWT 4). Born 6.12.1958, Northampton. RHB.

Adam Bramley Byram (Shropshire 1990-02 C&G 4 NWT 9). Born 17.3.1971, Wellington, Shropshire. LHB SLA. Brother: G.J. (MC, Shropshire).

Gavin James Byram (Shropshire 1997-01 C&G 3 NWT 5). Born 15.2.1974, Shrewsbury, Shropshire. RHB RFM. Brother: A.B. (MC, Shropshire, Staffordshire).

Adrian Mark Cade (Cambridgeshire 1991-92 NWT 2, Huntingdonshire 1999 NWT 1). Born 23.9.1961, Peterborough. RHB RM. Brother: J (Huntingdonshire).

Jonathan Richard Cade (Huntingdonshire 2001 C&G 1). Born 27.1.1981, Peterborough, Cambridgeshire. RHB RM. Uncles: A.M. (Cambridgeshire, Huntingdonshire), C.J. (Huntingdonshire), J.L. (Huntingdonshire).

John Frank Cadman (Suffolk 1966 GC 1). Born 27.3.1934, Colchester, Essex. RHB RF.

Bernard Lance Cairns (Durham 1979-88 GC 3 NWT 2, MC 1980-81 B&H 4). Born 10.10.1949, Picton, Marlborough, New Zealand. RHB RMF. 43 Tests (1973/74-85/86) for New Zealand. 78 ODIs (1973/74-84/85) for New Zealand. FC for Central Districts (1972/73-75/76), Otago (1976/77-79/80), Northern Districts (1981/82-84/85). Also ListA for Central Districts (1972/73-75/76), Otago (1976/77-79/80), Northern Districts (1981/82-84/85). Son: C.L. (Canterbury, MCC, Northern Districts, Nottinghamshire), brother-in-law: B.L.Roberts (Northern Districts, Taranaki).

Lee Brian Caldicott (Herefordshire 1999 NWT 1). Born 26.6.1969, Stourport-on-Severn, Worcestershire. RHB LFM.

Philip John Caley (Suffolk 1983-05 C&G 9 NWT 13). Born 18.10.1962, Harwich, Essex. RHB OB.

David John Callaghan (Suffolk 1999-01 C&G 5 NWT 2). Born 1.2.1965, Queenstown, Cape Province, South Africa. RHB RM. 29 ODIs (1992/93-99/00) for South Africa. FC for Eastern Province B (1983/84-91/92), Eastern Province (1984/85-02/03), Griqualand West (1985/86), Nottinghamshire (1988), MCC (2000). Also ListA for Eastern Province B (1983/84-91/92), Eastern Province (1984/85-02/03), Griqualand West (1985/86), Nottinghamshire (1988), MCC (2000). Uncle: R.T.D.Kemp (Border).

Ian Wayne Callen (Northumberland 1977 GC 2). Born 2.5.1955, Alexandra, Victoria, Australia. LHB RFM. 1 Test (1977/78) for Australia. 5 ODIs (1977/78-82/83) for Australia. FC for Victoria (1976/77-82/83), Boland (1985/86). Also ListA for Victoria (1976/77-82/83), Boland (1985/86).

Graeme Stuart Calway (Dorset 1987-93 NWT 6, MC 1992 B&H 3). Born 16.12.1965, Yeovil, Somerset. RHB RM.

James Cameron (Nottinghamshire CB 2000 NWT 1). Born 20.9.1979, Johannesburg, Transvaal, South Africa. RHB RFM.

Peter Camm (Derbyshire CB 1999-01 C&G 2 NWT 1). Born 19.7.1980, Chesterfield, Derbyshire. RHB RM.

George Richard Angus Campbell (Sussex CB 2000-02 C&G 5 NWT 2). Born 9.2.1979, Hammersmith, London. LHB Occ WKT.

Hugh James Campbell-Ferguson (Cambridgeshire 1965-67 GC 2). Born 8.2.1940, Royston, Hertfordshire. RHB WKT.

George Brian Camplin (Lincolnshire 1966-67 GC 2). Born 27.8.1939, Grimsby, Lincolnshire. RHB RMF.

Mark Christopher Cannons (Oxfordshire 1994 NWT 1). Born 31.8.1963, Chipping Norton, Oxfordshire. LHB OB.

David John Capel (Northamptonshire CB 2001-02 C&G 3). Born 6.2.1963, Northampton. RHB RMF. 15 Tests (1987-89/90) for England. 23 ODIs (1986/87-89/90) for England. FC for Northamptonshire (1981-98), Eastern Province (1985/86-86/87), Eastern Province B (1985/86), MCC (1988). Also ListA for Northamptonshire (1981-98), Eastern Province (1985/86-86/87), Eastern Province B (1985/86), MCC (1988).

Stephen John Caple (Gloucestershire CB 2002 C&G 1). Born 7.6.1984, Hereford. RHB OB WKT.

Ian James Capon (Wales MC 2003 C&G 1). Born 23.1.1977, Haverfordwest, Pembrokeshire, Wales. RHB RFM.

Michael Alexander Carberry (Surrey CB 1999 NWT 2). Born 29.9.1980, Croydon, Surrey. LHB OB. FC for Surrey (2001-02), Kent (2003-05), Hampshire (2006-08), MCC (2008). Also ListA for Surrey (2001-02), Kent (2003-05), Hampshire (2006-08), MCC (2008).

Christopher Stephen Carey (Norfolk 2001 C&G 2). Born 3.4.1973, Chelmsford, Essex. RHB LFM.

Nicholas Carlier (Essex CB 1999-00 NWT 3). Born 22.3.1968, Belper, Derbyshire. RHB.

Iain David Carr (Staffordshire 2000 NWT 2). Born 25.3.1977, Newcastle-under-Lyme, Staffordshire. RHB RFM.

John Donald Carr (Hertfordshire 1991 NWT 1). Born 15.6.1963, St John's Wood, London. RHB OB,RM. FC for Middlesex (1983-96), OU (1983-85), MCC (1987-89). Also ListA for Middlesex (1983-96), OU (1983-85), MCC (1987-89). Father: D.B. (Derbyshire, MCC, OU), grandfather: J.L. (Berkshire, MCC).

John Richard Carruthers (Yorkshire CB 1999-01 C&G 2 NWT 4). Born 13.4.1970, Barnsley, Yorkshire. RHB RMF.

Graeme John Carsberg (Lincolnshire 1988 NWT 1). Born 21.8.1957, Grimsby, Lincolnshire. RHB.

Darrell Morris Carter (Suffolk 1995 NWT 1). Born 28.10.1967, Welling, Kent. RHB RF.

John Ronald Carter (Norfolk 1985 NWT 1). Born 9.8.1963, Brundall, Norfolk. RHB.

Nicholas Anthony Carter (Cornwall 2002 C&G 2). Born 29.9.1978, Truro, Cornwall. RHB RM.

Timothy Jolyon Carter (Surrey CB 1999-01 C&G 2 NWT 2). Born 21.9.1969, Tiverton, Devon. RHB LB.

David Cartledge (Staffordshire 1984-95 NWT 9). Born 11.7.1956, Stoke-on-Trent, Staffordshire. RHB OB.

Neil David John Cartmel (Berkshire 1992-94 NWT 2). Born 15.7.1968, Harrow, Middlesex. RHB WKT.

Colin Casemore (Berkshire 1976 GC 1). Born 21.2.1940, St Mellons, Cardiff, Glamorgan, Wales. RHB LB.

George Rodney Cass (Shropshire 1976-78 GC 2). Born 23.4.1940, Overton, Wakefield, Yorkshire. LHB WKT. FC for Essex (1964-67), Worcestershire (1969-75), Tasmania (1970/71-72/73). Also ListA for Essex (1964-67), Worcestershire (1969-75), Tasmania (1970/71-72/73).

Julian Cassell (Dorset 1995-99 NWT 2). Born 24.10.1967, Salisbury, Wiltshire. RHB RM.

Matthew Duncan Catley (Suffolk 2001-02 C&G 3). Born 11.2.1975, Huntingdon. RHB RM,LB. Brothers: R.J. (Suffolk) and T.M. (Suffolk).

Russell James Catley (Suffolk 1996-03 C&G 6 NWT 3). Born 11.5.1973, Cambridge. RHB LB. Brothers: M.D. (Suffolk) and T.M. (Suffolk).

Timothy Mark Catley (Suffolk 2005 C&G 1). Born 15.9.1977, Newmarket, Suffolk. RHB OB,LB WKT. Brothers: R.J. (Suffolk) and M.D. (Suffolk).

Duncan Neil Catterall (Shropshire 2003-05 C&G 3). Born 19.9.1978, Preston, Lancashire. RHB RMF. FC for Worcestershire (1998-00). Also ListA for Worcestershire (1998-00).

Stuart Colin Catterall (Lancashire CB 2000-02 C&G 3 NWT 1). Born 9.4.1975, Southampton, Hampshire. RHB OB.

Clifford Neil Cavener (Hertfordshire 1993-01 C&G 1 NWT 1). Born 30.4.1967, Edmonton, Middlesex. RHB RM.

Brian Andrew Chambers (Sussex CB 1999 NWT 1). Born 1.4.1965, Melbourne, Victoria, Australia. RHB LFM.

John Edward Chambers (Essex CB 2001 C&G 1). Born 23.10.1971, Barking, Essex. RHB RMF.

Laurence John Champniss (Buckinghamshire 1972-74 GC 2). Born 20.2.1939, Harrow, Middlesex. LHB LBG. FC for MCC (1973/74). Also ListA for MCC (1973/74).

Christopher Robert McNairn Chaplin (Cornwall 1970-77 GC 3). Born 13.12.1938, Calcutta (now Kolkata), Bengal, India. RHB OB.

Nigel John Chapman (Oxfordshire 1975 GC 1). Born 31.5.1945, Bishop's Stortford, Hertfordshire. LHB WKT.

Robert James Chapman (Lincolnshire 2000-03 C&G 5 NWT 3). Born 28.7.1972, Nottingham. RHB RFM. FC for Nottinghamshire (1992-96), Worcestershire (1996/97-98). Also ListA for Nottinghamshire (1992-96), Worcestershire (1996/97-98).

Steven Chapman (Durham CB 2000 NWT 3, Northumberland 2001-03 C&G 4). Born 2.10.1971, Crook, Co Durham. RHB SLA. FC for Durham (1998-99). Also ListA for Durham (1998-99).

Daniel Martin Chard (Gloucestershire CB 2001 C&G 1, Wiltshire 2002 C&G 1). Born 1.6.1980, Bristol. RHB RM.

Brian Eldon Frederick Cheesman (Berkshire 1965-66 GC 3). Born 14.6.1929, Shefford Woodlands, Berkshire. RHB OB.

Gordon Edward James Child (Berkshire 1976-85 GC 2 NWT 3). Born 7.11.1939, Mumbles, Glamorgan, Wales. RHB WKT.

Anthony Basil Chivers (Wiltshire 1964 GC 1). Born 31.12.1939, Devizes, Wiltshire. RHB.

David Anthony Christmas (Lincolnshire 1991-04 C&G 7 NWT 7). Born 1.4.1969, Bourne, Lincolnshire. RHB RM.

Andrew John Churchill (Essex CB 1999-01 C&G 1 NWT 3). Born 27.11.1970, Hornchurch, Essex. RHB LM.

Dominic Adrian Clapp (Sussex CB 2000 NWT 2). Born 25.5.1980, Southport, Lancashire. RHB RM. FC for Sussex (2002), Hampshire (2003). Also ListA for Sussex (2002), Hampshire (2003).

Steven George Clark (Yorkshire CB 2002 C&G 2). Born 17.11.1982, Doncaster, Yorkshire. RHB RMF. FC for Loughborough UCCE (2005), Leicestershire (2006). Also ListA for Loughborough UCCE (2005), Leicestershire (2006).

Andrew John Clarke (Essex CB 2001 C&G 1). Born 9.11.1975, Brentwood, Essex. LHB RM. FC for Essex (2002-04). Also ListA for Essex (2002-04).

Andrew Russell Clarke (Buckinghamshire 1997-03 C&G 6 NWT 3, Norfolk 2000 NWT 2). Born 23.12.1961, Patcham, Sussex. RHB LB. FC for Sussex (1988-89). Also ListA for Sussex (1988-89).

Douglas Peter Clarke (Bedfordshire 1977 GC 1). Born 27.4.1948, Denmark. RHB RFM.

David Robert Clarke (Bedfordshire 1994-03 C&G 9 NWT 5). Born 26.6.1967, Kettering, Northamptonshire. RHB OB.

Grahame Jeffrey Clarke (Cumberland 1985-97 NWT 7). Born 1.8.1965, Lancaster, Lancashire. RHB.

James Clarke (Lincolnshire 1999-03 C&G 5 NWT 3). Born 7.5.1979, Lincoln. RHB RM.

Rikki Clarke (Surrey CB 2001 C&G 1). Born 29.9.1981, Orsett, Essex. RHB RFM. 2 Tests (2003/04) for England. 20 ODIs (2003-06) for England. FC for Surrey (2002-07), MCC (2006), Derbyshire (2008), Warwickshire (2008). Also ListA for Surrey (2002-07), MCC (2006), Derbyshire (2008), Warwickshire (2008).

John Alan Claughton (Berkshire 1983-85 NWT 3, MC 1983 B&H 1, Dorset 1989-91 NWT 2). Born 17.9.1956, Guiseley, Leeds, Yorkshire. RHB SLA. FC for OU (1976-79), Warwickshire (1979-80). Also ListA for OU (1976-79), Warwickshire (1979-80). Nephew: J.A. (Oxford Universities, OU), great-uncle: H.M. (Yorkshire).

Oliver James Clayson (Bedfordshire 2000-001 C&G 4 NWT 1). Born 25.4.1980, Bedford. RHB OB.

Christopher Jonathan Clements (Oxfordshire 1980-87 GC 1 NWT 2). Born 25.10.1954, Wheatley, Oxfordshire. RHB.

Simon Mark Clements (Suffolk 1978-96 GC 3 NWT 10, MC 1983 B&H 1). Born 29.4.1956, Felixstowe, Suffolk. LHB RM. FC for OU (1976-79). Also ListA for OU (1976-79).

Jeffrey Ian Clifford (Warwickshire CB 2001-02 C&G 2). Born 12.10.1982, Birmingham, Warwickshire. RHB WKT. FC for Warwickshire (2002). Also ListA for Warwickshire (2002).

Paul Robert Clifford (Wiltshire 1999 NWT 2). Born 19.9.1976, Swindon, Wiltshire. RHB RM.

John Lawrence Clinch (Suffolk 1995 NWT 1). Born 14.2.1967, Carshalton, Surrey. RHB SLA. Brother: M.L. (Suffolk).

Roger Ian Clitheroe (Wales MC 1998-01 C&G 2 NWT 1). Born 18.11.1966, Radcliffe, Manchester, Lancashire. RHB WKT. FC for CU (1987-91). Also ListA for CU (1987-91). Brother: P.A. (Wales MC).

Thomas Lawson Clough (Hertfordshire 1964-71 GC 5). Born 1.1.1926, Lynesack, Co Durham. RHB Occ WKT.

James Clutterbuck (Surrey CB 1999 NWT 1). Born 18.8.1973, Sandown, Isle of Wight. RHB RM.

Nigel George Cock (Cornwall 1975-80 GC 2). Born 24.11.1946, Penzance, Cornwall. RHB WKT.

Ian Cockbain (Cheshire 1985-01 C&G 2 NWT 15, MC 1993-97 B&H 14). Born 19.4.1958, Bootle, Lancashire. RHB SLA. FC for Lancashire (1979-83), MC (1994). Also ListA for Lancashire (1979-83). Father: R.G. (Cheshire).

Kyle James Coetzer (Durham CB 2003 C&G 1). Born 14.4.1984, Aberdeen, Scotland. RHB RMF. 1 ODI (2008) for Scotland. 3 Int2020s (2008) for Scotland. FC for Durham (2004-08), Scotland (2004). Also ListA for Durham (2004-08), Scotland (2004).

Adam Peter Cole (Norfolk 1993-94 NWT 2, Buckinghamshire 1998 NWT 1). Born 4.5.1974, Norwich, Norfolk. RHB RFM.

Derek Henry Cole (Devon 1969 GC 1). Born 9.3.1925, Dawlish, Devon. Died 7.4.2006, Calne, Wiltshire. RHB RFM,OB. FC for MC (1959-67). Also ListA for MC (1959-67).

Robert Cole (Durham 1964-73 GC 7). Born 27.11.1938, Ferryhill Station, Co Durham. RHB WKT.

Christopher Philip Coleman (Middlesex CB 2002 C&G 1). Born 1.6.1980, Ashford, Middlesex. RHB WKT.

Jason Coleman (Huntingdonshire 2001 C&G 3). Born 21.8.1974, Sydney, New South Wales, Australia. RHB RM.

Timothy Edward Coleman (Northamptonshire CB 1999-02 C&G 3 NWT 1). Born 19.6.1971, Wellingborough, Northamptonshire. RHB OB.

Michael Stuart Coles (Somerset CB 2000-02 C&G 3 NWT 1, Wiltshire 2004-05 C&G 2). Born 11.9.1981, Bristol. RHB RM.

Nicholas Coles (Bedfordshire 2001 C&G 1). Born 14.9.1974, Kettering, Northamptonshire. RHB RM.

Douglas Christopher Collard (Cambridgeshire 1975-89 GC 1 NWT 4). Born 26.9.1952, Barnet, Hertfordshire. RHB RMF.

Andrew James Collins (Wiltshire 1999 NWT 2). Born 24.7.1972, Andover, Hampshire. Died 25.12.1999, London. RHB RM.

Brian George Collins (Hertfordshire 1969-87 GC 8 NWT 2, MC South 1973-79 B&H 11, MC West 1976-78 B&H 9, MC 1980-81 B&H 7). Born 11.8.1941, Enfield, Middlesex. RHB RFM. FC for MC (1979).

Roy Collins (Cheshire 1964-66 GC 2). Born 10.3.1934, Clayton, Manchester, Lancashire. RHB OB. FC for Lancashire (1954-62), MC (1960). Also ListA for Lancashire (1954-62), MC (1960). Brother-in-law: J.Cumbes (Lancashire, MCC, Surrey, Warwickshire, Worcestershire).

Barry John Collis (Oxfordshire 1980 GC 1). Born 14.8.1947, Walmer, Kent. RHB RMF.

Francis Edward Collyer (Hertfordshire 1969-86 GC 8 NWT 5, MC South 1972-79 B&H 18, MC West 1976-78 B&H 12, MC 1980-84 B&H 15). Born 4.2.1947, Brentford, Middlesex. RHB WKT. FC for CU (1967-69), MC (1973-79). Also ListA for CU (1967-69).

Matthew Stuart Compton (Hampshire CB 1999-00 NWT 4). Born 4.2.1979, Newport, Monmouthshire, Wales. LHB LM.

Ian Edward Conn (Durham 1986-89 NWT 4, MC 1989-92 B&H 9, Northumberland 1992-94 NWT 2). Born 16.4.1962, Sunderland, Co Durham. RHB RFM.

Alastair Nathan Cook (Essex CB 2003 C&G 1). Born 25.12.1984, Gloucester. LHB OB Occ WKT. 36 Tests (2005/06-08/09) for England. 23 ODIs (2006-08/09) for England. 2 Int2020s (2007) for England. FC for Essex (2003-08), MCC (2004-07). Also ListA for Essex (2003-08), MCC (2004-07).

Adam Philip Cook (Oxfordshire 1999-03 C&G 5 NWT 2). Born 13.11.1979, Oxford. LHB OB. Brother: S.J. (Kent, MCC, Middlesex).

Geoffrey Cook (Durham 1991 NWT 1). Born 9.10.1951, Middlesbrough, Yorkshire. RHB SLA Occ WKT. 7 Tests (1981/82-82/83) for England. 6 ODIs (1981/82-82/83) for England. FC for Northamptonshire (1971-90), MCC (1978-82), Eastern Province (1978/79-80/81). Also ListA for Northamptonshire (1971-90), MCC (1978-82), Eastern Province (1978/79-80/81).

Jeffrey William Cook (Northamptonshire CB 1999 NWT 1). Born 2.2.1972, Sydney, New South Wales, Australia. LHB RM. FC for Northamptonshire (2000-04). Also ListA for Northamptonshire (2000-04).

Nigel Dennis Cook (Norfolk 1982-85 NWT 3). Born 10.5.1954, Swanton Morley, Norfolk. RHB.

Simon Hewitt Cook (Worcestershire CB 2002 C&G 2). Born 29.1.1972, Hastings, Victoria, Australia. LHB RFM. 2 Tests (1997/98) for Australia. FC for Victoria (1992/93-94/95), New South Wales (1995/96-00/01). Also ListA for Victoria (1992/93-94/95), New South Wales (1995/96-00/01).

Robert Michael Oliver Cooke (MC North 1972-79 B&H 8, MC East 1978 B&H 1, Cheshire 1981-83 NWT 3). Born 3.9.1943, Adlington, Cheshire. LHB LBG Occ WKT. FC for MC (1972-76), Essex (1973-75). Also ListA for MC (1972-76), Essex (1973-75).

Norman Sidney Cooley (Bedfordshire 1967-73 GC 5). Born 16.1.1941, Meppershall, Bedfordshire. RHB WKT.

Patrick Arthur Coombe (Cornwall 1980 GC 1). Born 16.7.1950, St Austell, Cornwall. LHB RM.

Mark Andrew Coombes (Gloucestershire CB 1999-02 C&G 1 NWT 1). Born 19.4.1978, Bristol. LHB LM.

Kevin Edwin Cooper (Herefordshire 1997-02 C&G 4 NWT 4). Born 27.12.1957, Sutton-in-Ashfield, Nottinghamshire. LHB RFM. FC for Nottinghamshire (1976-92), Gloucestershire (1992/93-96). Also ListA for Nottinghamshire (1976-92), Gloucestershire (1992/93-96).

Lee Anthony Cooper (Somerset CB 2000 NWT 1). Born 1.9.1979, Taunton, Somerset. RHB OB.

Leonard Michael Gordon Cooper (Hertfordshire 2001 C&G 2). Born 9.6.1981, Barnet, Hertfordshire. RHB LMF.

Richard Andrew Cooper (Staffordshire 2001-03 C&G 6). Born 7.8.1972, Stoke-on-Trent, Staffordshire. RHB RFM.

Richard Claude Cooper (MC South 1975 B&H 4, MC West 1976 B&H 1, Wiltshire 1983-89 NWT 4). Born 9.12.1945, Malmesbury, Wiltshire. Died 14.3.1990, Crudwell, Wiltshire. RHB RM. FC for Somerset (1972). Also ListA for Somerset (1972).

Geoffrey Alan Cope (Lincolnshire 1983 NWT 1). Born 23.2.1947, Burmantofts, Leeds, Yorkshire. RHB OB. 3 Tests (1977/78) for England. 2 ODIs (1977/78) for England. FC for Yorkshire (1966-80), MCC (1976/77). Also ListA for Yorkshire (1966-80), MCC (1976/77).

Wendell Ricardo Coppin (Norfolk 1999 NWT 1). Born 8.8.1966, Barbados. RHB RF.

Kevin Corby (Northumberland 1984-89 NWT 4). Born 12.7.1959, Newcastle upon Tyne, Northumberland. RHB WKT. Son: N. (Northumberland).

Terence Michael Cordaroy (Buckinghamshire 1979 GC 1). Born 26.5.1944, Hampstead, London. RHB. FC for Middlesex (1968). Also ListA for Middlesex (1968).

Stephen Geoffrey Cordingley (Hertfordshire 2001-03 C&G 3). Born 19.12.1981, Hertford. RHB. Brother: R.J. (Hertfordshire).

Paul Gregory Cormack (Northumberland 1986-89 NWT 3). Born 15.4.1962, Blyth, Northumberland. RHB.

Andrew Richard Cornford (Sussex CB 2001-02 C&G 3). Born 8.10.1970, Crowborough, Sussex. RHB RM.

Andrew Colin Cottam (Devon 1993-98 NWT 4). Born 14.7.1973, Northampton. RHB SLA. FC for Somerset (1992-96), Derbyshire (1995). Also ListA for Somerset (1992-96), Derbyshire (1995). Father: R.M.H. (Devon, Hampshire, MCC, Northamptonshire).

Michael Andrew Cottam (Devon 1988 NWT 1). Born 23.9.1966, Southampton, Hampshire. RHB RMF.

Robert Michael Henry Cottam (Devon 1978 GC 1). Born 16.10.1944, Cleethorpes, Lincolnshire. RHB RFM. 4 Tests (1968/69-72/73) for England. FC for Hampshire (1963-71), MCC (1964-73), Northamptonshire (1972-76). Also ListA for Hampshire (1963-71), MCC (1964-73), Northamptonshire (1972-76). Son: A.C. (Derbyshire, Devon, Somerset).

Thomas Paul Cotterell (Gloucestershire CB 2000 NWT 1). Born 9.3.1977, Hounslow, Middlesex. LHB SLA. FC for Gloucestershire (1999-00). Also ListA for Gloucestershire (1999-00). Brother: J.F. (Herefordshire).

Philip James Cottrell (Cheshire 1999 NWT 1). Born 3.1.1972, Birkenhead, Cheshire. RHB RMF.

David Graeme Court (Devon 2001-05 C&G 6). Born 1.11.1980, Plymouth, Devon. RHB RMF.

Denis Charles Cousins (Cambridgeshire 1972 GC 1). Born 29.3.1939, Cambridge. RHB RMF. Son: D.M. (Cambridgeshire, Essex, MCC, MC, Northamptonshire, Surrey).

Darren Mark Cousins (Cambridgeshire 1999 NWT 1). Born 24.9.1971, Cambridge. RHB RMF. FC for Essex (1993-98), Northamptonshire (2000-02). Also ListA for Essex (1993-98), Northamptonshire (2000-02). Father: D.C. (Cambridgeshire).

Paul Stephen Coverdale (Northamptonshire CB 2001-02 C&G 3). Born 24.7.1983, Harrogate, Yorkshire. RHB OB. FC for Northamptonshire (2007). Also ListA for Northamptonshire (2007). Father: S.P. (CU, Northamptonshire, Yorkshire).

Ian Cowap (Cheshire 1981 NWT 1). Born 10.6.1950, Nantwich, Cheshire. RHB RM.

Darren James Cowley (Dorset 2004 C&G 1). Born 30.10.1976, Winchester, Hampshire. LHB SLA. Father: N.G.C. (Devon, Dorset, Glamorgan, Hampshire).

Simon Thomas John Cowley (Gloucestershire CB 2000 NWT 1). Born 8.11.1979, Welwyn Garden City, Hertfordshire. RHB OB.

Dennis Frank Cox (Cheshire 1964-66 GC 2). Born 21.12.1925, Bermondsey, London. Died 22.2.2001, Chislehurst, Kent. RHB RFM. FC for Surrey (1949-57). Also ListA for Surrey (1949-57).

Ian Cox (Sussex CB 1999 NWT 1). Born 24.2.1967, Heathfield, Sussex. RHB RM.

Roger Cox (Bedfordshire 1968-73 GC 5). Born 27.4.1947, Luton, Bedfordshire. RHB RM. FC for MC (1971). Also ListA for MC (1971).

Mark David Coxon (Wiltshire 2001-02 C&G 2). Born 24.1.1978, Salisbury, Wiltshire. RHB RM.

Julian Michael Cradick (Cornwall 1986 NWT 1). Born 27.11.1947, St Dominick, Cornwall. RHB.

Stuart Cradock (Hertfordshire 1976 GC 1). Born 14.9.1949, Hertford. RHB RMF.

Edward John Craig (Cambridgeshire 1967 GC 1). Born 26.3.1942, Formby, Lancashire. RHB OB. FC for CU (1961-63), Lancashire (1961-62). Also ListA for CU (1961-63), Lancashire (1961-62).

Peter John Crane (Durham 1973-80 GC 2). Born 15.3.1950, South Shields, Co Durham. RHB OB.

Thomas Paul Cranston (Hertfordshire 2001 C&G 1). Born 21.11.1983, Aylesbury, Buckinghamshire. RHB RM.

Graham Andrew Crawford (Surrey CB 1999 NWT 2). Born 16.10.1967, Windlesham, Surrey. RHB OB.

James Michael Crawhall (Northumberland 1971-77 GC 3, MC North 1972 B&H 1). Born 21.2.1938, Newcastle upon Tyne, Northumberland. RHB.

Mark Andrew Crawley (Middlesex CB 1999 NWT 1). Born 16.12.1967, Newton-le-Willows, Lancashire. RHB RM. FC for OU (1987-90), Lancashire (1990), Nottinghamshire (1991-94). Also ListA for OU (1987-90), Lancashire (1990), Nottinghamshire (1991-94). Brothers: J.P. (CU, Hampshire, Lancashire) and P.M. (CU).

Stephen Thomas Crawley (Cheshire 1986-93 NWT 7). Born 16.9.1962, Bebington, Cheshire. RHB RFM.

Murray Wayne Creed (Nottinghamshire CB 2001-02 C&G 3). Born 5.3.1979, Port Elizabeth, Cape Province, South Africa. RHB RFM. FC for Eastern Province B (1997/98-98/99), Eastern Province (1998/99-00/01). Also ListA for Eastern Province B (1997/98-98/99), Eastern Province (1998/99-00/01).

Nicholas John Keyworth Creed (Sussex CB 2000-02 C&G 1 NWT 2). Born 28.8.1980, Cuckfield, Sussex. RHB RFM.

Matthew Leonard Creese (Middlesex CB 2001-02 C&G 2). Born 13.2.1982, Enfield, Middlesex. LHB SLA. FC for Middlesex (1999), Durham UCCE (2002). Also ListA for Middlesex (1999), Durham UCCE (2002).

Steven John Croft (Lancashire CB 2002 C&G 2). Born 11.10.1984, Blackpool, Lancashire. RHB RMF. FC for Lancashire (2005-08), Auckland (2008/09). Also ListA for Lancashire (2005-08), Auckland (2008/09).

Michael Richard Cronin (Shropshire 1992 NWT 1). Born 21.10.1961, Bromyard, Herefordshire. LHB OB.

Geoffrey David Crook (Staffordshire 2002 C&G 1). Born 30.10.1978, Cambridge. LHB LFM.

Ian Malcolm Crosby (Oxfordshire 2002 C&G 1). Born 18.12.1981, Aldershot, Hampshire. RHB RAB.

Brett Lyle Crosdale (Wiltshire 2000 NWT 2). Born 30.5.1973, Waratah, New South Wales, Australia. RHB RM.

Gareth David Cross (Lancashire CB 2002 C&G 2). Born 20.6.1984, Bury, Lancashire. RHB RMF WKT. FC for Lancashire (2005-08). Also ListA for Lancashire (2005-08).

Neil David Cross (Cheshire 1998-03 C&G 4 NWT 4). Born 19.9.1972, Wallasey, Cheshire. RHB OB.

Alan Crossley (Oxfordshire 1972-87 GC 3 NWT 6). Born 14.5.1941, Oldham, Lancashire. RHB WKT.

Maurice Alfred Crouch (Cambridgeshire 1964 GC 1). Born 9.8.1917, Wisbech, Cambridgeshire. Died 19.3.2001, Morocco. RHB. FC for MCC (1950-52), MC (1951). Also ListA for MCC (1950-52), MC (1951). Son-in-law: D.H.R.Fairey (Cambridgeshire, MCC, MC).

Carl Daniel Crowe (Berkshire 2004-05). Born 25.11.1975, Leicester. RHB OB. Matches: C&G 2. FC for Leicestershire (1995-02). Also ListA for Leicestershire (1995-02). Brother: C.P. (Berkshire, Leicestershire CB).

Craig Piers Crowe (Leicestershire CB 2000-02 C&G 3 NWT 1). Born 18.11.1979, Leicester. RHB RM. Brother: C.D. (Berkshire, Leicestershire, Leicestershire CB).

Stephen Christopher Crowley (Norfolk 1993-96 NWT 4). Born 18.12.1961, Hillingdon, Middlesex. RHB WKT.

Lee James Crozier (Northumberland 1999-05 C&G 4 NWT 4). Born 16.10.1973, Newcastle upon Tyne, Northumberland. RHB OB.

Roger Cruttenden (Berkshire 1979 GC 1). Born 5.10.1944, Hastings, Sussex. RHB RFM.

Efren Pablioto Cruz (Surrey CB 2001-02 C&G 5). Born 27.5.1981, Hammersmith, London. RHB WKT.

Jeffrey Cullip (Wiltshire 1987-88 NWT 2). Born 4.2.1950, Mitcham, Surrey. RHB WKT.

Stuart Cummings (Cheshire 1986-87 NWT 2). Born 17.11.1960, Whitehaven, Cumberland. RHB WKT.

John William James Cundle (Hertfordshire 1964 GC 1). Born 6.8.1939, Welwyn Garden City, Hertfordshire. RHB.

Clifford James Cunnell (Suffolk 1966 GC 1). Born 31.8.1944, Ipswich, Suffolk. RHB. Brother: R.E. (Suffolk).

Robert Edmund Cunnell (Suffolk 1966-79 GC 4). Born 16.7.1942, Ipswich, Suffolk. RHB OB. Brother: C.J. (Suffolk).

Neil Stephen Curnow (Cornwall 2001-02 C&G 3). Born 29.4.1982, Truro, Cornwall. RHB LB.

Mark Robert Currie (Cheshire 2001-02 C&G 3). Born 22.9.1979, Manchester, Lancashire. RHB OB. FC for Lancashire (2002-03). Also ListA for Lancashire (2002-03).

Ian James Curtis (Oxfordshire 1986-96 NWT 10). Born 13.5.1959, Purley, Surrey. LHB SLA. FC for OU (1980-82), Surrey (1983-84). Also ListA for OU (1980-82), Surrey (1983-84).

Barnaby James Cutbill (Cheshire 2002 C&G 2). Born 21.3.1973, Halifax, Yorkshire. RHB RM.

Andrew David Cuthill (Cambridgeshire 1987 NWT 1). Born 2.11.1961, Great Wilbraham, Cambridgeshire. RHB WKT.

Charles Edward Dagnall (Cumberland 1998 NWT 1). Born 10.7.1976, Bury, Lancashire. RHB RFM. FC for Warwickshire (1999-01), Leicestershire (2002-04). Also ListA for Warwickshire (1999-01), Leicestershire (2002-04).

Adrian Dalby (Northumberland 1989 NWT 1). Born 16.9.1957, Malton, Yorkshire. RHB RM.

John Ronald Dale (Lincolnshire 1974-76 GC 3, MC North 1974 B&H 1). Born 24.10.1930, Cleethorpes, Lincolnshire. SLA. FC for Kent (1958). Also ListA for Kent (1958).

Mark Adam Paul Dale (Worcestershire CB 2001-02 C&G 2). Born 16.3.1982, Nottingham. RHB. FC for Durham UCCE (2003-05). Also ListA for Durham UCCE (2003-05).

Daniel Anthony Thomas Dalton (Warwickshire CB 1999-02 C&G 6 NWT 2). Born 31.1.1974, Oxford. RHB LM.

Richard Neil Dalton (Bedfordshire 1994-99 NWT 4, MC 1997-98 B&H 7). Born 11.8.1965, Portsmouth, Hampshire. RHB RM.

Paul Antony John Dancy (Middlesex CB 2001 C&G 1). Born 26.9.1978, Farnborough, Kent. RHB RMF.

Richard Dandy (Warwickshire CB 2001 C&G 1). Born 30.11.1977, Birmingham, Warwickshire. RHB.

Andrew David Daniels (Northamptonshire CB 2002 C&G 1). Born 11.3.1983, Kettering, Northamptonshire. RHB LB WKT.

David Michael Daniels (Dorset 1968 GC 1, MC South 1972 B&H 4, Bedfordshire 1977-82 GC 1 NWT 1, MC West 1977 B&H 4). Born 29.3.1942, Bexleyheath, Kent. RHB. FC for CU (1964-65). Also ListA for CU (1964-65).

Simon Antony Brewis Daniels (Durham 1980-83 GC 1 NWT 1). Born 23.8.1958, Darlington, Co Durham. RHB RFM. FC for Glamorgan (1981-82). Also ListA for Glamorgan (1981-82).

Thomas Oliver Dann (Northamptonshire CB 2000-01 C&G 3 NWT 1). Born 30.1.1981, Cambridge. RHB WKT.

Ian John Darlington (Derbyshire CB 1999-02 C&G 3 NWT 3). Born 2.11.1977, Derby. RHB RM.

D. A. Dass (Bedfordshire 2001 C&G 1). WKT.

Jack Davey (Devon 1983-85 NWT 2). Born 4.9.1944, Tavistock, Devon. LHB LFM. FC for Gloucestershire (1966-78). Also ListA for Gloucestershire (1966-78).

Michael Joseph Davidson (Shropshire 1992-93 NWT 2). Born 18.10.1970, Penrith, Cumberland. RHB WKT.

Adam James Davies (Wales MC 2005 C&G 1). Born 26.10.1980, Cardiff, Glamorgan, Wales. RHB RMF. Father: H.D. (Glamorgan).

Gareth Rhys Davies (Wales MC 2001 C&G 2). Born 16.2.1975, Gorsenion, Glamorgan, Wales. LHB SLA.

Jonathan Davies (Wales MC 1998-02 C&G 1 NWT 3). Born 23.2.1980, Maesteg, Glamorgan, Wales. RHB LM.

Jonathan Richard Davies (Lincolnshire 2002-04 C&G 4). Born 9.3.1976, Burnley, Lancashire. RHB RM.

Mark Davies (Wales MC 1998-01 C&G 1 NWT 6). Born 18.4.1969, Neath, Glamorgan, Wales. RHB SLA. FC for Glamorgan (1990), Gloucestershire (1992-95). Also ListA for Glamorgan (1990), Gloucestershire (1992-95). Brothers: B. (Wales MC) and B. (Wales MC).

Mark Davies (Durham CB 2000-01 C&G 1 NWT 3). Born 4.10.1980, Stockton-on-Tees, Co Durham. RHB RM. FC for Durham (2002-08), Nottinghamshire (2007). Also ListA for Durham (2002-08), Nottinghamshire (2007).

Mark Robert Davies (Shropshire 1985-00 NWT 10). Born 24.9.1962, Shrewsbury, Shropshire. RHB RM.

Nicholas Mark Davies (Herefordshire 2001-04 C&G 8). Born 30.4.1975, Bromsgrove, Worcestershire. RHB RM.

Peter George Thomas Davies (Derbyshire CB 2000 NWT 1). Born 1.9.1976, Derby. RHB WKT.

Richard John Davies (Berkshire 1979 GC 1). Born 11.2.1954, Selly Oak, Birmingham, Warwickshire. RHB RM. FC for Warwickshire (1976). Also ListA for Warwickshire (1976).

Steven Michael Davies (Worcestershire CB 2002-03 C&G 2). Born 17.6.1986, Bromsgrove, Worcestershire. LHB WKT. FC for Worcestershire (2005-08), MCC (2006-07). Also ListA for Worcestershire (2005-08), MCC (2006-07).

William Oliver Davies (Shropshire 1999 NWT 1). Born 29.12.1972, Shrewsbury, Shropshire. LHB WKT.

Anthony Tilton Davis (Berkshire 1965-66 GC 3). Born 14.8.1931, Reading, Berkshire. Died 20.11.1978, Reading, Berkshire. RHB SLA. FC for MCC (1967), MC (1967). Also ListA for MCC (1967), MC (1967).

Edward Davis (Cambridgeshire 1967 GC 1). Born 8.3.1922, Brackley, Northamptonshire. RHB. FC for Northamptonshire (1947-56). Also ListA for Northamptonshire (1947-56). Brother: C.P. (Northamptonshire).

Keith Davis (Cornwall 1970 GC 1). Born 5.12.1935, St Germans, Cornwall. LHB RSM.

Mark Richard Davis (Wiltshire 1989 NWT 1). Born 26.2.1962, Kilve, Somerset. LHB LFM. FC for Somerset (1982-87). Also ListA for Somerset (1982-87).

Richard Peter Davis (Berkshire 2001 C&G 3). Born 18.3.1966, Westbrook, Margate, Kent. Died 29.12.2003, Blean, Canterbury, Kent. RHB SLA. FC for Kent (1986-93), Warwickshire (1993/94-95), Gloucestershire (1996-97), Leicestershire (2001). Also ListA for Kent (1986-93), Warwickshire (1993/94-95), Gloucestershire (1996-97), Leicestershire (2001). Brother-in-law: R.Sharma (Derbyshire).

Simon David Linghorn Davis (Bedfordshire 1991 NWT 1). Born 23.4.1965, Kempston, Bedford. RHB RM.

Simon Peter Davis (Durham 1982-83 NWT 2, MC 1982-83 B&H 3). Born 8.11.1959, Brighton, Victoria, Australia. RHB RFM. 1 Test (1985/86) for Australia. 39 ODIs (1985/86-87/88) for Australia. FC for Victoria (1983/84-87/88). Also ListA for Victoria (1983/84-87/88).

Ian Joseph Davison (Bedfordshire 1967-68 GC 3). Born 4.10.1937, Hemel Hempstead, Hertfordshire. RHB RMF. FC for Nottinghamshire (1959-66). Also ListA for Nottinghamshire (1959-66).

Owen Alun Dawkins (Wales MC 2001-04 C&G 5). Born 23.11.1978, Cheltenham, Gloucestershire. RHB LB.

Ismail Dawood (Herefordshire 2000-04 C&G 8 NWT 1). Born 23.7.1976, Dewsbury, Yorkshire. RHB WKT. FC for Northamptonshire (1994), Worcestershire (1996-97), Glamorgan (1998-99), Yorkshire (2004-05). Also ListA for Northamptonshire (1994), Worcestershire (1996-97), Glamorgan (1998-99), Yorkshire (2004-05).

Geoffrey Dawson (Bedfordshire 1967 GC 1). Born 24.2.1940, Dunstable, Bedfordshire.

John Peter Dawson (Shropshire 1974-84 GC 3 NWT 3). Born 22.8.1946, Chester, Cheshire. RHB OB.

Robert Ian Dawson (Devon 1990-05 C&G 9 NWT 4). Born 29.3.1970, Exmouth, Devon. RHB RM,LB. FC for Gloucestershire (1992-99). Also ListA for Gloucestershire (1992-99).

Richard Kevin James Dawson (Devon 1999-00 NWT 3). Born 4.8.1980, Doncaster, Yorkshire. RHB OB. 7 Tests (2001/02-02/03) for England. FC for Yorkshire (2001-06), MCC (2002), Northamptonshire (2007), Gloucestershire (2008). Also ListA for Yorkshire (2001-06), MCC (2002), Northamptonshire (2007), Gloucestershire (2008).

Ashley Christopher Day (Durham CB 2001-02 C&G 2). Born 26.3.1969, Hartlepool, Co Durham. RHB RMF.

Alan Richard Day (Hertfordshire 1966-74 GC 5). Born 12.11.1938, Muswell Hill, Middlesex. RHB. FC for MCC (1968). Also ListA for MCC (1968).

Peter James Deakin (Dorset 1999-04 C&G 3 NWT 3). Born 9.12.1970, Liverpool, Lancashire. RHB OB. FC for CU (1996). Also ListA for CU (1996).

Alan Dean (Bedfordshire 1991 NWT 1). Born 2.4.1962, Potton, Bedfordshire. RHB LM.

Michael Matthew Dean (Warwickshire CB 2002 C&G 1). Born 7.6.1972, Sutton Coldfield, Warwickshire. RHB RM.

Stephen Anthony Dean (Hertfordshire 1983-87 NWT 3). Born 15.5.1964, Welwyn Garden City, Hertfordshire. RHB.

Steven John Dean (Staffordshire 1986-02 C&G 5 NWT 16, MC 1992-98 B&H 27). Born 16.11.1960, Cosford, Staffordshire. RHB. FC for MC (1994), MCC (2000). Also ListA for MCC (2000).

Stephen Edward Dearden (Lancashire CB 1999-02 C&G 4 NWT 3). Born 1.2.1968, Walshaw, Lancashire. RHB RM.

Christopher John Debenham (Hertfordshire 1977 GC 1). Born 4.4.1953, St Albans, Hertfordshire. RHB.

Pierre de Bruyn (Norfolk 2003 C&G 1). Born 31.3.1977, Pretoria, Transvaal, South Africa. RHB RFM. FC for Northern Transvaal (1995/96), Northern Transvaal B (1995/96), Northerns (1997/98-06/07), Northerns B (1997/98-98/99), Easterns (1999/00-04/05), Titans (2004/05-07/08), Dolphins (2008/09). Also ListA for Northern Transvaal (1995/96), Northern Transvaal B (1995/96), Northerns (1997/98-06/07), Northerns B (1997/98-98/99), Easterns (1999/00-04/05), Titans (2004/05-07/08), Dolphins (2008/09). Twin brother: E.de Bruyn (Northerns B).

Zander de Bruyn (Surrey CB 2000-01 C&G 2 NWT 1). Born 5.7.1975, Johannesburg, Transvaal, South Africa. RHB RFM. 3 Tests (2004/05) for South Africa. FC for Transvaal B (1995/96-96/97), Transvaal (1996/97), Gauteng (1997/98-00/01), MCC (2000), Easterns (2002/03-05/06), Titans (2004/05-05/06), Worcestershire (2005), Warriors (2006/07-08/09), Somerset (2008). Also ListA for Transvaal B (1995/96-96/97), Transvaal (1996/97), Gauteng (1997/98-00/01), MCC (2000), Easterns (2002/03-05/06), Titans (2004/05-05/06), Worcestershire (2005), Warriors (2006/07-08/09), Somerset (2008).

Shane Alan Deitz (Lincolnshire 2002-04 C&G 4). Born 4.5.1975, Bankstown, New South Wales, Australia. LHB LBG Occ WKT. FC for South Australia (1998/99-07/08). Also ListA for South Australia (1998/99-07/08).

Robert Oliver Demming (Bedfordshire 1973-77 GC 2). Born 5.5.1949, Trinidad. RHB RFM.

Anthony Charles Denness (Berkshire 1965-66 GC 3). Born 23.9.1936, Hampton, Middlesex. Died 15.5.2008, Grainville, France. RHB RFM.

Nicholas Alexander Denning (Berkshire 2001-05 C&G 5). Born 3.10.1978, Ascot, Berkshire. RHB RFM.

Matthew John Dennington (Kent CB 2003 C&G 1). Born 16.10.1982, Durban, Natal, South Africa. RHB RFM. FC for Kent (2004-06). Also ListA for Kent (2004-06).

Philip John Densham (Oxfordshire 1980-83 GC 1 NWT 2). Born 7.4.1957, Banbury, Oxfordshire. LHB RM.

Peter Hugh de Prez (Cheshire 1987 NWT 1). Born 9.11.1951, Warrington, Lancashire. Died 9.7.2008, Warrington, Cheshire. RHB OB. Grandfather: G.Duckworth (Cheshire, Lancashire, MCC).

John Derrick (MC 1993 B&H 1, Wales MC 1993-00 NWT 3). Born 15.1.1963, Cwmaman, Glamorgan, Wales. RHB RM. FC for Glamorgan (1983-91). Also ListA for Glamorgan (1983-91).

Dandeniyage Somachandra de Silva (Shropshire 1983 NWT 1). Born 11.6.1942, Galle, Sri Lanka. RHB LBG. 12 Tests (1981/82-84) for Sri Lanka. 41 ODIs (1975-84/85) for Sri Lanka. FC for Bloomfield (1994/95). Also ListA for Bloomfield (1994/95). Brothers: D.H. (Ceylon) and D.P. (Ceylon), son: N.S. (Shropshire).

Frank Rodney Dethridge (Bedfordshire 1982 NWT 1). Born 13.9.1961, Pembury, Kent. RHB RFM.

Roger Thomas de Ville (Staffordshire 1971-73 GC 2). Born 21.1.1935, Uttoxeter, Staffordshire. RHB LB. FC for Derbyshire (1963-64). Also ListA for Derbyshire (1963-64).

Ian Michael Dews (Yorkshire CB 1999 NWT 1). Born 24.6.1964, Wakefield, Yorkshire. LHB OB.

Richard Rockley Dibden (Hampshire CB 2001-02 C&G 3). Born 29.1.1975, Southampton, Hampshire. RHB OB. FC for Hampshire (1995). Also ListA for Hampshire (1995).

Philip John Dicks (Cambridgeshire 1988-89 NWT 2). Born 4.5.1962, Bristol. RHB OB.

Raymond John Digman (Cheshire 1964-66 GC 2). Born 14.11.1934, Liverpool, Lancashire. RHB RFM.

Mathew Dimond (Somerset CB 1999-02 C&G 3 NWT 2). Born 24.9.1975, Taunton, Somerset. RHB RFM. FC for Somerset (1994-97). Also ListA for Somerset (1994-97).

Nafees Ahmed Din (Cheshire 2002-04 C&G 4). Born 6.5.1981, Manchester, Lancashire. RHB LB.

Andrew Dindar (Berkshire 1983 NWT 1). Born 26.6.1942, Johannesburg, Transvaal, South Africa. RHB RM Occ WKT. FC for Gloucestershire (1962-63). Also ListA for Gloucestershire (1962-63).

John Henry Dixon (Wiltshire 1988 NWT 1). Born 3.3.1954, Westbourne, Bournemouth, Hampshire. RHB RMF. FC for Gloucestershire (1973-81). Also ListA for Gloucestershire (1973-81).

Stephen Brian Dixon (Norfolk 1990-93 NWT 3). Born 12.7.1958, Bolton, Lancashire. LHB SLA.

Carl Martin Doar (Derbyshire CB 2001 C&G 2). Born 5.7.1983, Derby. RHB RM.

Nigel Patrick Dobbs (Lincolnshire 1988-94 NWT 3). Born 8.5.1962, Scunthorpe, Lincolnshire. RHB WKT.

Martyn Colin Dobson (Northamptonshire CB 2001 C&G 1, Lincolnshire 2002-04 C&G 3). Born 28.5.1982, Scunthorpe, Lincolnshire. RHB OB.

Timothy Patrick Johnstone Dodd (Berkshire 1988-89 NWT 2). Born 21.4.1961, Hammersmith, London. RHB RMF.

David Henry Dodds (Derbyshire CB 2000-01 C&G 1 NWT 2). Born 27.11.1981, Manchester, Lancashire. RHB RM.

Christopher William Dodsley (Durham CB 2001 C&G 1). Born 4.4.1978, Gateshead, Co Durham. RHB RM.

Michael Edward Doggrell (Dorset 1968 GC 1). Born 1935, Salisbury, Wiltshire. Died 9.1988, Poole, Dorset. RHB RFM.

Matthew James Doidge (Yorkshire CB 1999-01 C&G 2 NWT 4). Born 2.7.1970, Horsforth, Yorkshire. LHB SLA. FC for Yorkshire (1990). Also ListA for Yorkshire (1990).

James Andrew Donaldson (Norfolk 1968-69 GC 2). Born 27.8.1943, Castle Rising, Yorkshire. LHB.

Richard Phillip Done (Suffolk 1979-80 GC 3). Born 5.8.1955, Ryde, Sydney, New South Wales, Australia. RHB RFM. FC for New South Wales (1978/79-85/86). Also ListA for New South Wales (1978/79-85/86).

Bradleigh Thomas Peter Donelan (Cambridgeshire 1995-99 NWT 5). Born 3.1.1968, Park Royal, Middlesex. RHB OB. FC for Sussex (1989-93), Somerset (1994). Also ListA for Sussex (1989-93), Somerset (1994).

Keith Donohue (Devon 1986-00 NWT 11). Born 11.10.1963, Chatham, Kent. RHB RMF.

Dilip Rasiklal Doshi (Hertfordshire 1976 GC 2). Born 22.12.1947, Rajkot, Gujarat, India. LHB SLA. 33 Tests (1979/80-83/84) for India. 15 ODIs (1980/81-82/83) for India. FC for Bengal (1968/69-84/85), Nottinghamshire (1973-78), Warwickshire (1980-81), Saurashtra (1985/86). Also ListA for Bengal (1968/69-84/85), Nottinghamshire (1973-78), Warwickshire (1980-81), Saurashtra (1985/86). Son: N.D. (Buckinghamshire, Derbyshire, Saurashtra, Surrey).

Nayan Dilip Doshi (Buckinghamshire 2001 C&G 1). Born 6.10.1978, Nottingham. RHB SLA. FC for Saurashtra (2001/02-06/07), Surrey (2004-07), Derbyshire (2008). Also ListA for Saurashtra (2001/02-06/07), Surrey (2004-07), Derbyshire (2008). Father: D.R. (Bengal, Hertfordshire, MCC, Northumberland, Nottinghamshire, Saurashtra, Warwickshire).

Paul Julian Douglas (Suffolk 1993 NWT 1). Born 12.10.1971, Barnstaple, Devon. RHB RFM.

Mathew Peter Dowman (Lincolnshire 2003-04 C&G 3). Born 10.5.1974, Grantham, Lincolnshire. LHB RMF. FC for Nottinghamshire (1994-99), Derbyshire (2000-02). Also ListA for Nottinghamshire (1994-99), Derbyshire (2000-02).

Richard Hugh Downend (Staffordshire 1971-75 GC 4, MC North 1972-75 B&H 5). Born 19.1.1945, Stoke-on-Trent, Staffordshire. RHB RM. FC for MC (1972). Also ListA for MC (1972).

Mark Anthony Downes (Shropshire 2001-05 C&G 5). Born 1.8.1974, Wellington, Shropshire. RHB RFM.

Paul Robert Draper (Wiltshire 1999-01 C&G 1 NWT 1). Born 19.5.1972, Southampton, Hampshire. RHB SLA.

Daniel Raymond Drepaul (Buckinghamshire 2001-02 C&G 5). Born 5.9.1975, Lambeth, London. RHB OB WKT.

John Stephen Drewett (Berkshire 1965 GC 1). Born 23.10.1932, Windsor, Berkshire. RHB WKT.

Jan Nicolaas Dreyer (Warwickshire CB 2000 NWT 1). Born 9.9.1976, Amanzimtoti, Natal, South Africa. RHB RM. FC for North West (1996/97-01/02), KwaZulu-Natal (1998/99), KwaZulu-Natal B (1998/99). Also ListA for North West (1996/97-01/02), KwaZulu-Natal (1998/99), KwaZulu-Natal B (1998/99).

Richard Dreyer (Northumberland 1986-87 NWT 2). Born 24.11.1960, Morpeth, Northumberland. RHB OB,RM.

Ryan Craig Driver (Cornwall 1996-03 C&G 2 NWT 1). Born 30.4.1979, Truro, Cornwall. LHB RM. FC for Worcestershire (1998-00), Lancashire (2001-02). Also ListA for Worcestershire (1998-00), Lancashire (2001-02).

David Brian Drury (Cumberland 1985 NWT 1). Born 1.5.1961, Blackpool, Lancashire. LHB WKT.

Nathan Robert Charles Dumelow (Derbyshire CB 1999-00 NWT 2). Born 30.4.1981, Derby. RHB OB. FC for Derbyshire (2001-04). Also ListA for Derbyshire (2001-04).

Jean-Paul Duminy (Devon 2003 C&G 1). Born 14.4.1984, Strandfontein, Cape Town, Cape Province, South Africa. LHB OB. 3 Tests (2008/09) for South Africa. 37 ODIs (2004-08/09) for South Africa. 8 Int2020s (2007/08-08/09) for South Africa. FC for Western Province (2001/02-03/04), Western Province Boland (2004/05), Cape Cobras (2005/06-08/09). Also ListA for Western Province (2001/02-03/04), Western Province Boland (2004/05), Cape Cobras (2005/06-08/09).

Alan Alexander Duncan (Buckinghamshire 2005 C&G 1). Born 9.3.1980, Kirkaldy, Fifeshire, Scotland. RHB RMF.

Philip John Dunkley (Cheshire 1981 NWT 1). Born 3.3.1951, Sandbach, Cheshire. RHB. Grandfather: J.Sharp (Lancashire), brother: F.D. (Cheshire).

Michael Thomas Dunn (Hertfordshire 1971-81 GC 6 NWT 1, MC South 1973 B&H 1, MC West 1976-77 B&H 8). Born 14.11.1940, Doncaster, Yorkshire. RHB RFM.

Malcolm Stephen Thomas Dunstan (Cornwall 1970-86 GC 4 NWT 1, MC West 1977-78 B&H 6, MC South 1979 B&H 1). Born 14.10.1950, Redruth, Cornwall. RHB RM. FC for Gloucestershire (1971-1974). Also ListA for Gloucestershire (1971-1974).

Cristian Dominic Durant (Cambridgeshire 1997-01 C&G 2 NWT 5). Born 23.1.1977, Leicester. RHB WKT.

Anthony William Durley (Bedfordshire 1967-73 GC 6). Born 30.9.1933, Ilford, Essex. Died 1.1.1993, Luton, Bedfordshire. RHB WKT. FC for Essex (1957). Also ListA for Essex (1957).

Wesley John Durston (Somerset CB 2000-2002 C&G 1 NWT 1). Born 6.10.1980, Taunton, Somerset. RHB OB Occ WKT. FC for Somerset (2002-08). Also ListA for Somerset (2002-08).

Anthony John Dutton (Staffordshire 1988-96 NWT 6). Born 11.6.1963, Stoke-on-Trent, Staffordshire. RHB RM.

Paul Nicholas Symon Dutton (Northumberland 1987-94 NWT 4). Born 6.8.1965, Manchester, Lancashire. RHB RM.

Simon Michael Dutton (Cumberland 1987-01 C&G 1 NWT 14). Born 17.3.1964, Barrow-in-Furness, Lancashire. RHB WKT.

Robert John Dyer (Staffordshire 1990-92 NWT 2). Born 21.4.1959, Birmingham, Warwickshire. RHB OB.

Simon Dyson (Cheshire 1989 NWT 1). Born 14.2.1948, Guildford, Surrey. RHB LB.

Raymond Eric East (Suffolk 1993 NWT 1). Born 20.6.1947, Manningtree, Essex. RHB SLA. FC for Essex (1965-84), MCC (1973). Also ListA for Essex (1965-84), MCC (1973). Son: J.P. (Suffolk), J.R. (Suffolk).

Stewart Mark Eaton (Cheshire 2001-02 C&G 3). Born 28.7.1979, Crewe, Cheshire. RHB RM.

Giles William Ecclestone (Cambridgeshire 1992-02 C&G 1 NWT 5, MC 1997 B&H 1, Essex CB 1999-01 C&G 2 NWT 3). Born 17.10.1968, Lambeth, London. LHB RM. Brother: S.C. (Cambridgeshire, MCC, OU, Somerset).

Simon Charles Ecclestone (Cambridgeshire 1992 NWT 1). Born 16.7.1971, Great Dunmow, Essex. LHB RM. FC for OU (1994), Somerset (1994-98). Also ListA for OU (1994), Somerset (1994-98). Brother: G.W. (Cambridgeshire, Essex CB, MCC, MC, Natal Country Districts).

James Luke Ede (Derbyshire CB 2002 C&G 1). Born 19.9.1984, Burton-on-Trent, Staffordshire. RHB RM.

Russell Stuart Edmonds (Lancashire CB 2000 NWT 2). Born 9.9.1977, Blackburn, Lancashire. RHB WKT.

Peter Wilson Edmondson (Oxfordshire 1970 GC 1). Born 24.10.1941, Brighouse, Yorkshire. Died 26.6.1993, Lanzarote, Canary Islands. LHB RM.

Geoffrey Edmunds (Shropshire 1988-93 NWT 5). Born 2.9.1954, Stoneleigh. RHB SLA.

Brian Robert Edrich (Oxfordshire 1967-70 GC 2). Born 18.8.1922, Cantley, Norfolk. LHB OB. FC for Kent (1947-53), Glamorgan (1954-56), MC (1967). Also ListA for Kent (1947-53), Glamorgan (1954-56), MC (1967). Brothers: W.J. (MCC, Middlesex, MC, Norfolk), E.H. (Huntingdonshire, Lancashire, MC, Norfolk) and G.A. (Cumberland, Lancashire, Norfolk), cousin: J.H. (MCC, Norfolk, Surrey), nephew: J.W. (Suffolk).

Justin Wells Edrich (Suffolk 1983-90 NWT 5). Born 17.1.1961, Islington, London. RHB. Father: W.J. (MCC, Middlesex, MC, Norfolk), uncles: B.R. (Glamorgan, Kent, MC, Oxfordshire), E.H. (Huntingdonshire, Lancashire, MC, Norfolk) and G.A. (Cumberland, Lancashire, Norfolk).

William John Edrich (Norfolk 1965-70 GC 4). Born 26.3.1916, Lingwood, Norfolk. Died 24.4.1986, Whitehill Court, Chesham, Buckinghamshire. RHB RFM,OB Occ WKT. 39 Tests (1938-54/55) for England. FC for MCC (1934-58), MC (1934-36), Middlesex (1937-58). Also ListA for MCC (1934-58), MC (1934-36), Middlesex (1937-58). Cousin: J.H. (MCC, Norfolk, Surrey), brothers: B.R. (Glamorgan, Kent, MC, Oxfordshire), E.H. (Huntingdonshire, Lancashire, MC, Norfolk) and G.A. (Cumberland, Lancashire, Norfolk), son: J.W. (Suffolk).

Andrew Nicholas Edwards (Gloucestershire CB 1999-00 NWT 3, Herefordshire 2001 C&G 3). Born 12.11.1978, Delft, Netherlands. RHB OB. G.Edwards (Nottinghamshire).

Christopher James Edwards (Devon 1985 NWT 1). Born 18.5.1958, Torquay, Devon. LHB.

David James Edwards (Staffordshire 2001-02 C&G 2). Born 6.6.1980, Stoke-on-Trent, Staffordshire. RHB RFM.

Gavin Derek Edwards (Cornwall 2000-03 C&G 6 NWT 1). Born 14.4.1979, Penzance, Cornwall. RHB WKT.

Gareth Ian Edwards (Berkshire 1999 NWT 1). Born 30.11.1973, Exeter, Devon. RHB RFM.

John Hiley Edwards (Devon 1985-91 NWT 6). Born 10.3.1951, Newton Abbot, Devon. LHB.

John Keith Sheridan Edwards (Buckinghamshire 1972-79 GC 5, MC South 1973-74 B&H 8, MC West 1976 B&H 4). Born 26.8.1951, Brampton, Cumberland. RHB RM.

Stephen James Edwards (Buckinghamshire 1987-92 NWT 3, MC 1988 B&H 1). Born 23.6.1951, Highgate, Middlesex. RHB LM,SLA.

Timothy Edwards (Cornwall 2001 C&G 2). Born 24.6.1974, Penzance, Cornwall. RHB WKT. FC for Worcestershire (1993-94). Also ListA for Worcestershire (1993-94).

William Gerwyn Edwards (Wales MC 1993-94 NWT 2). Born 22.6.1953, Glanamman, Carmarthenshire, Wales. LHB LM.

William Jeffrey Edwards (Cornwall 1975 GC 1). Born 12.10.1938, Goldsithney, Cornwall. LHB.

Peter James Eele (Devon 1969 GC 1). Born 27.1.1935, Taunton, Somerset. LHB WKT. FC for Somerset (1958-65). Also ListA for Somerset (1958-65).

John Bernard Elleray (Cumberland 1985-86 NWT 2). Born 13.5.1946, Windermere, Westmorland. RHB RMF.

Edward Thomas Elliot-Square (Dorset 1999 NWT 1). Born 7.5.1978, Winchester, Hampshire. RHB RM.

James Anthony Elliot-Square (Dorset 2001 GC 1). Born 22.5.1983, Salisbury, Wiltshire. RHB RMF.

David John Ellis (Durham 1964 GC 2). Born 13.4.1934, Middlesbrough, Yorkshire. RHB.

Mark Thomas Ellis (Norfolk 1990-91 NWT 2). Born 19.5.1962, Castle Acre, Norfolk. RHB RFM.

Richard Gary Peter Ellis (Hertfordshire 1993 NWT 1). Born 20.12.1960, Paddington, London. RHB OB. FC for OU (1981-83), Middlesex (1982-84), Gloucestershire (1985). Also ListA for OU (1981-83), Middlesex (1982-84), Gloucestershire (1985). Father: P.M. (MCC, Scotland).

Scott William Kenneth Ellis (Shropshire 1999 NWT 1, Worcestershire CB 2001 C&G 2). Born 3.10.1975, Newcastle-under-Lyme, Staffordshire. RHB RMF. FC for Worcestershire (1996-98). Also ListA for Worcestershire (1996-98).

Bruce Charles Aurelius Ellison (Oxfordshire 1996 NWT 1). Born 10.12.1969, King's Lynn, Norfolk. RHB RMF. FC for OU (1993). Also ListA for OU (1993).

Christopher John Ellison (Cornwall 1999 NWT 1). Born 12.4.1979, Sheffield, Yorkshire. RHB SLA. Brother: S.J. (Cornwall).

David Rory Ellison (Essex CB 2001 C&G 1). Born 22.10.1980, Belfast, Ireland. RHB OB.

Richard Ellwood (Cumberland 1989-95 NWT 4). Born 6.4.1965, Penrith, Cumberland. RHB SLA.

John Ernest Emburey (Berkshire 2000 NWT 2). Born 20.8.1952, Peckham, London. RHB OB. 64 Tests (1978-95) for England. 61 ODIs (1979/80-92/93) for England. FC for Middlesex (1973-95), MCC (1978-87), Western Province (1982/83-83/84), Northamptonshire (1996-97). Also ListA for Middlesex (1973-95), MCC (1978-87), Western Province (1982/83-83/84), Northamptonshire (1996-97).

Justin Marc Engelke (Hertfordshire 2000 NWT 1). Born 3.4.1976, Cape Town, Cape Province, South Africa. RHB RMF. FC for Transvaal B (1996/97), Gauteng (1998/99). Also ListA for Transvaal B (1996/97), Gauteng (1998/99).

Richard John English (Suffolk 1966 GC 1). Born 23.8.1942, Holme Hale, Norfolk. RHB OB.

Robert Entwistle (Cumberland 1984 NWT 1). Born 20.10.1941, Burnley, Lancashire. RHB. FC for Lancashire (1962-66), MC (1976). Also ListA for Lancashire (1962-66), MC (1976).

David Ewart Essenhigh (Wiltshire 1965-69 GC 2). Born 31.7.1936, Folkestone, Kent. RHB RM.

Roderick Orville Estwick (Lincolnshire 1983 NWT 1). Born 28.6.1961, Christ Church, Barbados. RHB RFM. FC for Barbados (1982/83-86/87), Transvaal (1987/88-89/90). Also ListA for Barbados (1982/83-86/87), Transvaal (1987/88-89/90).

Stephen Paul Eva (Cornwall 1986 NWT 1). Born 17.7.1967, Redruth, Cornwall. RHB WKT.

Alun Wyn Evans (Wales MC 2003-05 C&G 3). Born 20.8.1975, Glanamman, Dyfed, Wales. RHB RM. FC for Glamorgan (1996-01), Northern Districts (2004/05-06/07). Also ListA for Glamorgan (1996-01), Northern Districts (2004/05-06/07).

Brian Gordon Evans (Hertfordshire 1983-91 NWT 4). Born 23.5.1964, Preston, Lancashire. RHB.

Craig Evans (Wales MC 1994 NWT 1). Born 15.11.1971, Neath, Glamorgan, Wales. RHB OB.

David John Evans (Hertfordshire 1969 GC 2). Born 23.4.1935, North London. Died 21.10.2008, Boston, Massachusetts, USA. RHB.

Geoffrey Rossall Evans (Devon 1978 GC 1). Born 28.4.1939, Exeter, Devon. RHB WKT.

Ian James Evans (Oxfordshire 2001 C&G 3). Born 30.3.1982, Oxford. RHB OB. Twin brother: P.J. (Oxfordshire).

John Brian Evans (Lincolnshire 1966-71 GC 4). Born 9.11.1936, Clydach, Glamorgan, Wales. RHB RFM Occ WKT. FC for Glamorgan (1958-63), MC (1969). Also ListA for Glamorgan (1958-63), MC (1969).

Kevin Paul Evans (Shropshire 2000-01 C&G 2 NWT 2). Born 10.9.1963, Nottingham. RHB RMF. FC for Nottinghamshire (1984-99). Also ListA for Nottinghamshire (1984-99). Brother: R.J. (Lincolnshire, MC, Nottinghamshire).

Matthew Robert Evans (Hertfordshire 1999-02 C&G 1 NWT 3). Born 27.11.1974, Gravesend, Kent. RHB RFM.

Philip Julian Evans (Oxfordshire 2001 C&G 1). Born 30.3.1982, Oxford. RHB RFM. Twin brother: I.J. (Oxfordshire).

Rupert Arnold Evans (Oxfordshire 1983-96 NWT 10, MC 1988-95 B&H 18). Born 24.2.1954, Kingston, Jamaica. RHB OB. FC for MC (1990).

Russell John Evans (Lincolnshire 1994-97 NWT 3, MC 1995-96 B&H 7). Born 1.10.1965, Calverton, Nottinghamshire. RHB RM. FC for Nottinghamshire (1987-90), MC (1994). Also ListA for Nottinghamshire (1987-90). Brother: K.P. (MCC, Nottinghamshire, Shropshire).

William Vincent Evans (Durham 1964 GC 1). Born 19.2.1935, Stockton-on-Tees, Co Durham. RHB WKT.

Mark Andrew Everett (Hertfordshire 1999-02 C&G 3 NWT 1). Born 11.11.1967, Harlow, Essex. LHB SLA.

Carl Dennis Eyden (Derbyshire CB 2001 C&G 3). Born 9.11.1980, Burton-on-Trent, Staffordshire. RHB RMF.

Matthew James Eyles (Buckinghamshire 2001-03 C&G 2). Born 1.5.1979, Amersham, Buckinghamshire. LHB SLA.

Damian Richard Eyre (Lancashire CB 1999-01 C&G 1 NWT 3). Born 8.10.1967, Glossop, Derbyshire. RHB SLA. Father: J.R. (Derbyshire).

David Harold Richardson Fairey (Cambridgeshire 1964-75 GC 6). Born 17.8.1940, Linton, Cambridgeshire. RHB LM. Father-in-law: M.A.Crouch (Cambridgeshire, MCC, MC, Northamptonshire).

Robert John Falconer (Surrey CB 1999 NWT 1). Born 26.12.1962, Hampton Court, Middlesex. RHB OB.

Richard Edward Falkner (Northamptonshire CB 1999-01 C&G 2 NWT 2). Born 13.8.1982, Northampton. RHB Occ WKT.

Wayne Falla (Northumberland 1992-00 NWT 5). Born 18.12.1970, North Shields, Northumberland. RHB RM.

Ian James Fantham (Bedfordshire 1998-00 NWT 3). Born 13.10.1964, Hemel Hempstead, Hertfordshire. LHB RM.

Neil James Farnsworth (Surrey CB 2000 NWT 1). Born 8.1.1977, Ashford, Middlesex. RHB OB.

Aamir Farooque (Warwickshire CB 1999 NWT 1, Herefordshire 2000-02 C&G 5 NWT 1). Born 5.11.1968, Karachi, Sind, Pakistan. RHB OB.

Jonathan Colin Farrow (Cheshire 2002 C&G 2). Born 22.2.1984, Stockport, Cheshire. RHB RFM.

Nigel Ward Farrow (Buckinghamshire 1992 NWT 1). Born 24.11.1963, Cookham, Berkshire. RHB.

Richard Daniel Ellis Farrow (Norfolk 1992-93 NWT 2). Born 31.8.1972, Grays, Essex. LHB.

Richard Anthony Fay (Middlesex CB 2000 NWT 2). Born 14.5.1974, Kilburn, Middlesex. RHB RM. FC for Middlesex (1995-96). Also ListA for Middlesex (1995-96).

Charles Duncan Fearnley (Lincolnshire 1971 GC 2). Born 12.4.1940, Pudsey, Yorkshire. LHB OB Occ WKT. FC for Worcestershire (1962-68). Also ListA for Worcestershire (1962-68). Brother: M.C. (Yorkshire).

Matthew Ross Featherstone (Kent CB 1999-00 NWT 6). Born 5.7.1970, Bromley, Kent. RHB.

Mark Andrew Fell (MC 1986-98 B&H 10, Lincolnshire 1988-03 C&G 6 NWT 9). Born 17.11.1960, Newark, Nottinghamshire. RHB SLA. FC for Nottinghamshire (1982-83), Derbyshire (1985). Also ListA for Nottinghamshire (1982-83), Derbyshire (1985).

Gary Matthew Fellows (Shropshire 2005 C&G 1). Born 30.7.1978, Halifax, Yorkshire. RHB RM. FC for Matabeleland (1996/97), Yorkshire (1998-03). Also ListA for Matabeleland (1996/97), Yorkshire (1998-03).

Jonathan Payn Fellows-Smith (Hertfordshire 1966 GC 1). Born 3.2.1932, Berea, Durban, Natal, South Africa. RHB RM. 4 Tests (1960) for South Africa. FC for OU (1953-55), MCC (1956), Northamptonshire (1957), Transvaal (1958/59-59/60). Also ListA for OU (1953-55), MCC (1956), Northamptonshire (1957), Transvaal (1958/59-59/60). Father: H. (Natal), uncles: C.Payn (Natal) and G.Payn (Natal), son: C.H. (MCC).

Christopher Glen Feltham (Staffordshire 1996-97 NWT 2). Born 8.9.1972, Sydney, New South Wales, Australia. RHB OB.

Simon Alexander Ross Ferguson (Suffolk 1984 NWT 1). Born 13.5.1961, Lagos, Nigeria. RHB RM. FC for Somerset (1985). Also ListA for Somerset (1985).

Robert Steven Ferley (Kent CB 2001-02 C&G 2). Born 4.2.1982, Norwich, Norfolk. RHB SLA. FC for Durham UCCE (2001-03), Kent (2003-06), Nottinghamshire (2007-08). Also ListA for Durham UCCE (2001-03), Kent (2003-06), Nottinghamshire (2007-08).

Nicholas John Ferraby (Leicestershire CB 2002 C&G 2). Born 31.5.1983, Market Harborough, Leicestershire. RHB RM.

Lloyd Douglas Ferreira (Dorset 1998 NWT 1). Born 6.5.1974, Parktown, Johannesburg, Transvaal, South Africa. RHB LM. FC for Boland (1993/94-96/97), Western Province (1997/98-03/04), Western Province B (1997/98-98/99). Also ListA for Boland (1993/94-96/97), Western Province (1997/98-03/04), Western Province B (1997/98-98/99).

Quentin Ferreira (Surrey CB 1999 NWT 2). Born 28.12.1972, East London, Cape Province, South Africa. RHB RFM. FC for Eastern Province (1996/97-97/98), Eastern Province B (1996/97-97/98), Northerns (1998/99), Northerns B (1998/99). Also ListA for Eastern Province (1996/97-97/98), Eastern Province B (1996/97-97/98), Northerns (1998/99), Northerns B (1998/99). Brother: D. (Orange Free State, Orange Free State B).

Jonathan Mark Fielding (Cumberland 1996-01 C&G 3 NWT 8, MC 1997-98 B&H 6). Born 13.3.1973, Bury, Lancashire. RHB SLA. FC for Lancashire (1994). Also ListA for Lancashire (1994).

Jason Michael Finch (Sussex CB 2001-02 C&G 3). Born 27.9.1969, Hastings, Sussex. RHB Occ WKT.

Christopher Charles Finegan (Cheshire 1999-02 C&G 2 NWT 3). Born 4.11.1971, Liverpool, Lancashire. RHB RM.

Roger John Finney (Norfolk 1990-94 NWT 5). Born 2.8.1960, Darley Dale, Derbyshire. RHB LM,SLA. FC for Derbyshire (1982-88). Also ListA for Derbyshire (1982-88).

Paul Gavin Breedon Fisher (Leicestershire CB 1999-01 C&G 1 NWT 2). Born 19.5.1977, Leicester. RHB SLA.

Robin William Fisher (Cheshire 2001-04 C&G 3). Born 24.11.1970, Chester, Cheshire. RHB SLA.

John Dexter Fitton (Cumberland 1994 NWT 1). Born 24.8.1965, Littleborough, Lancashire. LHB OB. FC for Lancashire (1987-92). Also ListA for Lancashire (1987-92).

Simon David Fitzgerald (Essex CB 1999-01 C&G 1 NWT 3). Born 6.12.1966, Ilford, Essex. LHB WKT.

Shawn Martin Fitzgerald (Dorset 1990 NWT 1). Born 21.8.1962, Bridport, Dorset. RHB WKT.

Ian Nicholas Flanagan (Essex CB 2001 C&G 1, Cambridgeshire 2002-04 C&G 2). Born 5.6.1980, Colchester, Essex. LHB OB. FC for Essex (1997-00). Also ListA for Essex (1997-00).

Robert Leonard Fleck (Suffolk 1966 GC 1). Born 7.2.1943, Cambridge. LHB LM.

Iain Fletcher (Hertfordshire 1990-03 C&G 3 NWT 1). Born 31.8.1971, Sawbridgeworth, Hertfordshire. RHB RM. FC for Somerset (1991-94). Also ListA for Somerset (1991-94).

Stuart David Fletcher (Lincolnshire 1994 NWT 1). Born 8.6.1964, Keighley, Yorkshire. RHB RMF. FC for Yorkshire (1983-91), Lancashire (1992-93). Also ListA for Yorkshire (1983-91), Lancashire (1992-93).

Grant William Flower (Cheshire 1998 NWT 1). Born 20.12.1970, Salisbury (now Harare), Zimbabwe. RHB SLA Occ WKT. 67 Tests (1992/93-03/04) for Zimbabwe. 219 ODIs (1992/93-03/04) for Zimbabwe. FC for Mashonaland Under-24s (1993/94-94/95), Mashonaland (1994/95-03/04), Young Mashonaland (1995/96), MCC (1996-97), Mashonaland A (2001/02), Leicestershire (2002), Essex (2005-08). Also ListA for Mashonaland Under-24s (1993/94-4/95), Mashonaland (1994/95-03/04), Young Mashonaland (1995/96), MCC (1996-97), Mashonaland A (2001/02), Leicestershire (2002), Essex (2005-08). Brother: A. (Essex, MCC, Mashonaland, South Australia).

John Ernest Flower (Berkshire 1965 GC 1). Born 7.11.1938, Chislehurst, Kent. RHB RMF.

Russell William Flower (MC 1982 B&H 2, Staffordshire 1984-88 NWT 4). Born 6.11.1942, Stone, Staffordshire. LHB SLA. FC for Warwickshire (1978). Also ListA for Warwickshire (1978).

Geoffrey Ian Foley (Cheshire 2000 NWT 1). Born 11.10.1967, Jandowae, Queensland, Australia. LHB RM. FC for Queensland (1989/90-99/00), MCC (1996-97). Also ListA for Queensland (1989/90-99/00), MCC (1996-97).

Nicholas Arthur Folland (Devon 1984-01 C&G 1 NWT 15, MC 1989-92 B&H 17). Born 17.9.1963, Bristol. LHB RM. FC for MC (1990), Somerset (1992-94). Also ListA for Somerset (1992-94). Brother: N.G. (Bedfordshire, Devon, MCC).

Neil Geoffrey Folland (Devon 1986 NWT 1, Bedfordshire 1991 NWT 1). Born 27.6.1960, Bristol. RHB. Brother: N.A. (Devon, MCC, MC, Somerset).

David Follett (Staffordshire 2000-05 C&G 6 NWT 1). Born 14.10.1968, Newcastle-under-Lyme, Staffordshire. RHB RFM. FC for Middlesex (1995-96), Northamptonshire (1997-99). Also ListA for Middlesex (1995-96), Northamptonshire (1997-99).

Anthony John Foot (Dorset 1989 NWT 1). Born 10.12.1957, Shaftesbury, Dorset. RHB.

Mark Harold Alan Footitt (Nottinghamshire CB 2001 C&G 1). Born 25.11.1985, Nottingham. RHB LFM. FC for Nottinghamshire (2005-07), MCC (2006). Also ListA for Nottinghamshire (2005-07), MCC (2006).

Geoffrey Charles Ford (Oxfordshire 1984-91 NWT 8). Born 26.9.1961, Oxford. RHB RM.

Martin David Ford (Dorset 2004 C&G 1). Born 13.12.1978, Bournemouth, Hampshire. RHB RMF.

Damian Joseph Forder (Gloucestershire CB 1999-01 C&G 1 NWT 2). Born 11.3.1979, Bristol. RHB LM.

Steven Mark Forshaw (Dorset 1998-02 C&G 1 NWT 4). Born 19.6.1974, Temple Combe, Somerset. RHB RM.

Richard Chalmers Gordon Fortin (Berkshire 1966 GC 2). Born 12.4.1941, Singapore. RHB WKT. FC for OU (1963). Also ListA for OU (1963). Uncle: D.J.W.Bridge (Dorset, Northamptonshire, OU).

Charles Heaton Forward (Hampshire CB 2002 C&G 1). Born 13.6.1969, Romsey, Hampshire. LHB.

Daren Joseph Foster (Berkshire 1995 NWT 1). Born 14.3.1966, Tottenham, Middlesex. RHB RFM. FC for Somerset (1986-89), Glamorgan (1991-92). Also ListA for Somerset (1986-89), Glamorgan (1991-92).

John Foster (Shropshire 1983-91 NWT 8). Born 2.11.1955, Oldham, Lancashire. RHB. Son: EJ Foster (Leicestershire, Loughborough UCCE, MCC, Shropshire), Son: R.J. (Shropshire).

Michael James Foster (Warwickshire CB 2000 NWT 1). Born 24.12.1979. LHB.

Neil Alan Foster (Norfolk 1995 NWT 1). Born 6.5.1962, Colchester, Essex. RHB RFM. 29 Tests (1983-93) for England. 48 ODIs (1983/84-89) for England. FC for Essex (1980-93), Transvaal (1991/92). Also ListA for Essex (1980-93), Transvaal (1991/92).

Stephen John Foster (Yorkshire CB 1999-02 C&G 4 NWT 2, Northumberland 2000 NWT 3). Born 21.2.1968, Rotherham, Yorkshire. RHB RM.

Andrew Robert Fothergill (Durham 1983-91 NWT 7, MC 1989-91 B&H 9). Born 10.2.1962, Newcastle upon Tyne, Northumberland. RHB WKT. FC for MC (1990), Durham (1992-93).

Roger James Fouhy (Wiltshire 1999 NWT 1). Born 25.3.1972, Hamilton, Waikato, New Zealand. RHB RMF. FC for Wellington (2005/06). Also ListA for Wellington (2005/06).

Brenden Craig Fourie (Northamptonshire CB 2001-02 C&G 4). Born 13.4.1970, East London, Cape Province, South Africa. RHB RFM. FC for Border (1988/89-97/98), Border B (1993/94), Leicestershire (1994). Also ListA for Border (1988/89-97/98), Border B (1993/94), Leicestershire (1994). Brother: S.E. (Border, Border B).

Paul Albert Fowler (Oxfordshire 1981-87 NWT 4). Born 12.6.1954, Wigan, Lancashire. LHB.

Mitchell Graham Fowles (Herefordshire 1995-97 NWT 2). Born 18.12.1970, Worcester. RHB RM.

Andrew Fox (Cheshire 1987-89 NWT 4). Born 7.11.1962, Holmfirth, Yorkshire. RHB RMF.

Neil Fox (Norfolk 1993-00 NWT 8). Born 10.2.1962, Norwich, Norfolk. RHB OB.

Darron Townley Foy (Lancashire CB 1999-00 NWT 2). Born 8.3.1971, Bury, Lancashire. RHB RFM.

Kevin Nigel Foyle (Wiltshire 1988-93 NWT 3). Born 19.6.1962, Hammersmith, London. RHB LB.

Benjamin John France (Suffolk 2003 C&G 1). Born 14.5.1982, Brunei, Malaysia. LHB RM. FC for Derbyshire (2004-05). Also ListA for Derbyshire (2004-05).

Gavin David Franklin (Staffordshire 2002-03 C&G 2). Born 9.1.1978, Wolverhampton, Staffordshire. RHB OB Occ WKT.

Jonathan Guy Franks (Lincolnshire 1983-88 NWT 2). Born 23.9.1962, Stamford, Lincolnshire. RHB WKT. FC for OU (1983-85). Also ListA for OU (1983-85).

Alastair Gregory James Fraser (Middlesex CB 1999-02 C&G 2 NWT 3). Born 17.10.1967, Edgware, Middlesex. RHB RFM. FC for Middlesex (1986-88), Essex (1991-92). Also ListA for Middlesex (1986-88), Essex (1991-92). Brother: A.R.C. (MCC, Middlesex, Wellington).

Thomas David Fray (Berkshire 1999-05 C&G 5 NWT 1). Born 20.9.1979, Epping, Essex. RHB.

Benjamin James Frazer (Hertfordshire 2001-03 C&G 5). Born 2.4.1981, Truro, Cornwall. RHB OB.

Peter John Free (Norfolk 2000-01 C&G 2 NWT 2). Born 6.12.1971, Norwich, Norfolk. RHB RM.

Gary David Freear (Cambridgeshire 2001-04 C&G 4). Born 4.5.1982, King's Lynn, Norfolk. RHB.

Alexander Niall French (Wales MC 2001-02 C&G 2). Born 1.12.1980, Hong Kong. RHB OB. 2 ODIs (2004) for Hong Kong.

Neil French (Lincolnshire 1988-94 NWT 3). Born 18.7.1964, Warsop, Nottinghamshire. RHB RM. Brother: B.N.French (MCC, Nottinghamshire), C.C.French (Nottinghamshire CB).

Mark Frost (Wales MC 1994 NWT 1). Born 21.10.1962, Barking, Essex. RHB RMF. FC for Surrey (1988-89), Glamorgan (1990-93). Also ListA for Surrey (1988-89), Glamorgan (1990-93).

John Arthur William Fry (Surrey CB 1999-02 C&G 3 NWT 2). Born 13.11.1961, Streatham, London. RHB.

Daniel William Furnival (Leicestershire CB 2001 C&G 1). Born 25.10.1978, Ashford, Kent. RHB LB.

Godfrey Ronald Furse (Cornwall 1986-96 NWT 3). Born 27.8.1960, Launceston, Cornwall. LHB RM.

Neil Andrew Fusedale (Berkshire 1992-00 NWT 4). Born 11.11.1967, Hendon, Middlesex. RHB SLA. FC for Transvaal B (1994/95-96/97), Easterns (1997/98), Gauteng (2000/01). Also ListA for Transvaal B (1994/95-96/97), Easterns (1997/98), Gauteng (2000/01).

Charles Brian Gadsby (Cambridgeshire 1964-72 GC 5). Born 30.6.1933, Wimpole, Cambridgeshire. RHB SLA. Son: N.T. (Cambridgeshire, MC).

Nigel Timothy Gadsby (Cambridgeshire 1982-04 C&G 6 NWT 16). Born 1.2.1961, Wimpole, Cambridgeshire. RHB LB. Father: C.B. (Cambridgeshire).

Nathan Ashley Gage (Wales MC 2001-02 C&G 6). Born 9.2.1974, Perth, Western Australia, Australia. LHB RM.

Andrew William Gale (Yorkshire CB 2001-02 C&G 3). Born 28.11.1983, Dewsbury, Yorkshire. LHB LB. FC for Yorkshire (2004-08). Also ListA for Yorkshire (2004-08).

Stephen Clifford Gale (Shropshire 1976-85 GC 2 NWT 3). Born 3.6.1952, Shrewsbury, Shropshire. RHB LB. Son: J.S.J. (Shropshire).

Derek Anthony Gallop (Oxfordshire 1980-84 GC 1 NWT 2). Born 26.6.1951, Bristol. RHB LFM.

Devang Jayant Gandhi (Essex CB 2001 C&G 2). Born 6.9.1971, Bhavnagar, Gujarat, India. RHB RM. 4 Tests (1999/00) for India. 3 ODIs (1999/00) for India. FC for Bengal (1994/95-05/06). Also ListA for Bengal (1994/95-05/06).

Nicholas John Charles Gandon (Lincolnshire 1990-91 NWT 2). Born 7.7.1956, Leicester. RHB OB. FC for OU (1979). Also ListA for OU (1979).

David Denis Gardner (Wiltshire 1965-69 GC 2). Born 11.9.1940, Swindon, Wiltshire. RHB.

Leslie Robin Gardner (Hertfordshire 1964-66 GC 2). Born 23.2.1934, Ledbury, Herefordshire. RHB RM. FC for Leicestershire (1954-62). Also ListA for Leicestershire (1954-62).

Paul Lawrence Garlick (Dorset 1993-95 NWT 2). Born 2.8.1964, Chiswick, Middlesex. RHB RFM. FC for CU (1984). Also ListA for CU (1984).

James Peter Garner (Norfolk 2000-02 C&G 4 NWT 2). Born 27.1.1972, Tittleshall, Norfolk. RHB WKT.

Phillip John Garner (Oxfordshire 1975-94 GC 3 NWT 13, MC 1985 B&H 2). Born 26.3.1946, Liverpool, Lancashire. RHB OB.

Edward Stewart Garnett (Cheshire 1996 NWT 1). Born 2.6.1965, Lancaster, Lancashire. LHB RFM.

Michael Anthony Garnham (Cambridgeshire 1986-88 NWT 3, MC 1987-88 B&H 7). Born 20.8.1960, Johannesburg, Transvaal, South Africa. RHB WKT. FC for Gloucestershire (1979), Leicestershire (1980-88), Essex (1989-95). Also ListA for Gloucestershire (1979), Leicestershire (1980-88), Essex (1989-95).

Alasdair George Garnsworthy (Somerset CB 2002 C&G 1). Born 30.12.1983, Marlborough, Wiltshire. RHB WKT.

Alan Robert Garofall (Hertfordshire 1971-89 GC 6 NWT 6, MC South 1972-74 B&H 9). Born 1.6.1946, Kingston-upon-Thames, Surrey. RHB RM. FC for OU (1966-68). Also ListA for OU (1966-68).

Rex Alan Gautrey (Cambridgeshire 1964-67 GC 4). Born 6.1.1928, Tottenham, Middlesex. Died 12.2001, Ely, Cambridgeshire. RHB WKT.

Nicholas Richard Gaywood (Devon 1985-98 NWT 8, MC 1993-98 B&H 4). Born 30.4.1963, Newton Abbot, Devon. LHB SLA.

Carl Matthew Gazzard (Cornwall 1999 NWT 1). Born 15.4.1982, Penzance, Cornwall. RHB WKT. FC for Somerset (2002-08). Also ListA for Somerset (2002-08).

Michael Eric Gear (Bedfordshire 1970-82 GC 4 NWT 1, MC South 1973 B&H 3, Buckinghamshire 1984 NWT 1). Born 7.12.1945, Bath, Somerset. RHB LB.

Simon Gear (Warwickshire CB 2000 NWT 1). Born 2.10.1974, Pembury, Kent. RHB.

Karl Lewis Geary (Leicestershire CB 2001 C&G 2). Born 29.6.1982, Nuneaton, Warwickshire. RHB WKT.

Ian James Gemmell (MC North 1979 B&H 2, Cheshire 1981-83 NWT 3, MC 1981-82 B&H 5). Born 6.4.1953, Ashton-under-Lyne, Lancashire. RHB RFM.

Kevin Gentle (Bedfordshire 1985 NWT 1). Born 31.10.1959, Stotfold, Bedfordshire. LHB.

Mark Thomas George (Kent CB 2003 C&G 1). Born 22.12.1977, Ryde, Sydney, New South Wales, Australia. RHB RFM.

Nicholas Thomas Peter George (Cornwall 2001 C&G 2). Born 29.2.1972, Penzance, Cornwall. LHB RM. Brother: W.M. (Cornwall, MCC).

Philip Stanley George (Wales MC 1999-01 C&G 2 NWT 6). Born 16.9.1978, Swansea, Glamorgan, Wales. RHB RM.

Winston Mark George (Cornwall 2000 NWT 1). Born 8.7.1975, Penzance, Cornwall. LHB OB. Brother: N.T.P. (Cornwall).

Brian Dennis Gessner (Staffordshire 1978 GC 1). Born 20.6.1947, Durban, Natal, South Africa. LHB LFM. FC for Natal B (1970/71-76/77), Natal (1972/73-76/77). Also ListA for Natal B (1970/71-76/77), Natal (1972/73-76/77).

Craig Richard Gibbens (Wiltshire 2000-01 C&G 2 NWT 2). Born 14.10.1965, Bristol. RHB RM.

Peter John Keith Gibbs (MC North 1973 B&H 4, Staffordshire 1973 GC 2). Born 17.8.1944, Buglawton, Cheshire. RHB OB. FC for OU (1964-66), Derbyshire (1966-72). Also ListA for OU (1964-66), Derbyshire (1966-72).

Ottis Delroy Gibson (Staffordshire 2001 C&G 3). Born 16.3.1969, Sion Hill, St Peter, Barbados. RHB RF. 2 Tests (1995-98/99) for West Indies. 15 ODIs (1995-96/97) for West Indies. FC for Barbados (1990/91-97/98), Border (1992/93-94/95), Glamorgan (1994-96), Griqualand West (1998/99-99/00), Gauteng (2000/01), Leicestershire (2004-05), Durham (2006-07). Also ListA for Barbados (1990/91-97/98), Border (1992/93-94/95), Glamorgan (1994-96), Griqualand West (1998/99-99/00), Gauteng (2000/01), Leicestershire (2004-05), Durham (2006-07).

Alexander Peter Richard Gidman (Gloucestershire CB 2001 C&G 3). Born 22.6.1981, High Wycombe, Buckinghamshire. RHB RM. FC for Gloucestershire (2002-08), MCC (2004-07). Also ListA for Gloucestershire (2002-08), MCC (2004-07), Otago (2007/08). Brother: W.R.S. (Durham, Gloucestershire CB, MCC).

William Robert Simon Gidman (Gloucestershire CB 2002 C&G 1). Born 14.2.1985, High Wycombe, Buckinghamshire. LHB RM. FC for Durham (2007). Also ListA for Durham (2007). Brother: A.P.R. (Gloucestershire, Gloucestershire CB, MCC, Otago).

Christopher Robert Gilbert (Yorkshire CB 2002 C&G 1). Born 16.4.1984, Scarborough, Yorkshire. RHB OB. FC for Yorkshire (2007). Also ListA for Yorkshire (2007).

Nicholas Gilbert (Hertfordshire 1984-99 NWT 7). Born 14.6.1963, East Ham, Essex. RHB.

Neil Stuart Gill (Lincolnshire 1996 NWT 1, Yorkshire CB 2000-02 C&G 5 NWT 1). Born 22.9.1971, Bradford, Yorkshire. RHB LMF.

Peter Nigel Gill (Staffordshire 1971-84 GC 6 NWT 1, MC East 1976-78 B&H 12). Born 12.11.1947, Clayton, Newcastle-under-Lyme, Staffordshire. RHB OB. FC for MC (1976-79). Also ListA for MC (1976-79).

Ian Gillespie (Shropshire 2002 C&G 1). Born 3.11.1976, Shrewsbury, Shropshire. RHB RFM.

Stuart Ross Gillespie (Northumberland 1987 NWT 1). Born 2.3.1957, Wanganui, New Zealand. RHB RFM. 1 Test (1985/86) for New Zealand. 19 ODIs (1985/86-87/88) for New Zealand. FC for Northern Districts (1979/80-82/83), Auckland (1984/85-88/89). Also ListA for Northern Districts (1979/80-82/83), Auckland (1984/85-88/89).

David Edward Gillett (Lincolnshire 1996-00 NWT 2, Huntingdonshire 2001-02 C&G 4). Born 16.5.1969, Peterborough. LHB RM.

Mark Allan Gilliver (Yorkshire CB 1999-01 C&G 2 NWT 2). Born 18.6.1969, Upper Agbrigg, Yorkshire. RHB OB.

Matthew Thomas Gitsham (Somerset CB 2001 C&G 2). Born 1.2.1982, Truro, Cornwall. RHB LB. FC for Gloucestershire (2008). Also ListA for Gloucestershire (2008).

Christopher Gladwin (Suffolk 1988-90 NWT 2). Born 10.5.1962, East Ham, Essex. LHB RM. FC for Essex (1981-87), Derbyshire (1989). Also ListA for Essex (1981-87), Derbyshire (1989).

Neil Gladwin (Hertfordshire 2001 C&G 1). Born 23.8.1978, Harlow, Essex. RHB WKT.

Martin Jamie Glasson (Wiltshire 1999-04 C&G 1 NWT 4). Born 21.5.1973, Salisbury, Wiltshire. RHB RM.

John David Glendenen (Durham 1989-91 NWT 3, Cumberland 1999-00 NWT 5). Born 20.6.1965, Middlesbrough, Yorkshire. RHB RM. FC for Durham (1992-93).

Lee James Goddard (Yorkshire CB 2002 C&G 2). Born 22.10.1982, Dewsbury, Yorkshire. RHB WKT. FC for Loughborough UCCE (2003), Derbyshire (2004-06), Durham (2007). Also ListA for Loughborough UCCE (2003), Derbyshire (2004-06), Durham (2007).

Alan Frederick Gofton (Derbyshire CB 2000 NWT 1). Born 4.10.1979, Chesterfield, Derbyshire. RHB RM. FC for OU (1999-01), Oxford Universities (2000), Oxford UCCE (2002). Also ListA for OU (1999-01), Oxford Universities (2000), Oxford UCCE (2002).

Robert Paul Gofton (Suffolk 1995 NWT 1). Born 10.9.1968, Scarborough, Yorkshire. RHB RM. FC for Leicestershire (1992). Also ListA for Leicestershire (1992).

Christopher Frederick Evelyn Goldie (Middlesex CB 2001 C&G 1). Born 2.11.1960, Johannesburg, Transvaal, South Africa. RHB WKT. FC for CU (1981-82), Hampshire (1983-85). Also ListA for CU (1981-82), Hampshire (1983-85).

Andrew Kenneth Golding (Suffolk 1990-96 NWT 4). Born 5.10.1963, Colchester, Essex. RHB SLA. FC for Essex (1983), CU (1984-88). Also ListA for Essex (1983), CU (1984-88).

James Mathew Golding (Kent CB 1999 NWT 3, Wiltshire 2005 C&G 1). Born 19.7.1977, Canterbury, Kent. RHB RMF. FC for Kent (1999-02). Also ListA for Kent (1999-02).

David John Goldsmith (Buckinghamshire 1987-91 NWT 5). Born 11.9.1947, Romford, Essex. RHB WKT.

Steven Clive Goldsmith (Norfolk 1993-03 C&G 6 NWT 9, MC 1995-98 B&H 6). Born 19.12.1964, Ashford, Kent. RHB RM. FC for Kent (1987), Derbyshire (1988-92). Also ListA for Kent (1987), Derbyshire (1988-92).

Daniel Benton Goldstraw (Hampshire CB 2002 C&G 1). Born 17.6.1969, Sheffield, Yorkshire. LHB LFM.

Ian Gompertz (Devon 1999-00 NWT 3). Born 24.7.1975, Bideford, Devon. RHB RM.

Peter Anthony Gooch (MC West 1978 B&H 4, Buckinghamshire 1979 GC 1, MC South 1979 B&H 4). Born 2.5.1949, Timperley, Cheshire. LHB RFM. FC for Lancashire (1970). Also ListA for Lancashire (1970).

Antony John Good (MC East 1978 B&H 1, MC North 1979 B&H 4). Born 10.11.1952, Kumasi, Ghana. RHB RFM. FC for Lancashire (1973-76). Also ListA for Lancashire (1973-76).

Jeremy Richard Goode (Northamptonshire CB 1999 NWT 1, Wiltshire 2001 C&G 1). Born 2.6.1972, Northampton. LHB LB.

Paul Arnold Goodman (Cambridgeshire 1967 GC 1). Born 11.5.1943, Cambridge. RHB.

Andrew John Goodwin (Derbyshire CB 2001 C&G 2). Born 3.9.1982, Burton-on-Trent, Staffordshire. LHB LB.

Paul Samuel James Goodwin (Staffordshire 2004-05 C&G 2). Born 12.5.1978, Madeley Heath, Staffordshire. RHB WKT.

Robin Goodyer (Oxfordshire 1975 GC 1). Born 28.10.1951, Ventnor, Isle of Wight. RHB WKT.

David Brian Gorman (Berkshire 1984-88 NWT 4). Born 13.8.1955, Havant, Hampshire. RHB.

David Edward Gorrod (Surrey CB 2001-02 C&G 4). Born 10.11.1975, Wimbledon, Surrey. RHB RFM.

Christopher Stephen Gott (Yorkshire CB 1999 NWT 1). Born 5.8.1965, Calverley, Leeds, Yorkshire. RHB RMF.

Alan James Gough (Worcestershire CB 2001 C&G 1). Born 30.4.1972, Ashby-de-la-Zouch, Leicestershire. RHB.

Martyn John Goulding (Devon 1978-85 GC 4 NWT 3). Born 31.7.1954, Westminster, London. RHB RMF.

Mark Roger Gouldstone (Bedfordshire 1991 NWT 1, Hertfordshire 1993 NWT 1, Lincolnshire 1996-97 NWT 2). Born 3.2.1963, Bishop's Stortford, Hertfordshire. RHB RM. FC for Northamptonshire (1986-88). Also ListA for Northamptonshire (1986-88).

Paul Nicholas Gover (Hampshire CB 2001-02 C&G 3). Born 12.3.1968, Oxford. LHB.

Jonathan Peter Govett (Berkshire 1996 NWT 1). Born 22.6.1969, St Germans, Cornwall. RHB RFM.

Colin Charles Graham (Suffolk 1983-85 NWT 3). Born 5.8.1957, Wendover, Buckinghamshire. RHB RMF. Brother: I.D. (Suffolk).

David Alexander Graham (Herefordshire 1997-99 NWT 4). Born 21.5.1971, Moreton-in-Marsh, Gloucestershire. RHB RM.

Ian Douglas Graham (Suffolk 1990-01 C&G 5 NWT 6). Born 14.3.1968, Akrotiri, Cyprus. RHB RMF. Brother: C.C. (Suffolk).

John Alexander Graham (Northumberland 2001-05 C&G 4). Born 4.3.1978, Newcastle upon Tyne, Northumberland. RHB RM.

John Norman Graham (Northumberland 1984 NWT 1). Born 8.5.1943, Hexham, Northumberland. RHB RM. FC for Kent (1964-77), MCC (1968). Also ListA for Kent (1964-77), MCC (1968). Cousin: P.C. (MC, Northumberland, Yorkshire CB).

Peter Colin Graham (MC 1985-94 B&H 2, Northumberland 1986-94 NWT 5, Yorkshire CB 1999 NWT 1). Born 25.12.1954, Newcastle upon Tyne, Northumberland. RHB RFM. FC for MC (1994). Cousin: J.N. (Kent, MCC, Northumberland).

James Martin Hilary Graham-Brown (Dorset 1990-91 NWT 2). Born 11.7.1951, Thetford, Norfolk. RHB RM Occ WKT. FC for Kent (1974-76), Derbyshire (1977-78). Also ListA for Kent (1974-76), Derbyshire (1977-78). Great-uncle: L.B.Blaxland (Derbyshire).

Joseph Benjamin Grant (Cambridgeshire 2004 C&G 1). Born 17.12.1967, White House, St James, Jamaica. RHB RFM. FC for Jamaica (1990/91-95/96), Essex (2001-03). Also ListA for Jamaica (1990/91-95/96), Essex (2001-03).

Maurice Alric Grant (Suffolk 1978 GC 1). Born 11.3.1947, Barbados. RHB RFM.

Robert John Grant (Staffordshire 1989-90 NWT 2). Born 28.7.1965, Leamington, Warwickshire. RHB RM.

Jonathan David Gray (Cheshire 1993-95 NWT 3, Staffordshire 1999 NWT 1). Born 15.7.1967, Congleton, Cheshire. RHB.

Andrew David Greasley (Cheshire 1995-96 NWT 2). Born 23.3.1960, Leicester. RHB OB.

E. John Greatrex (Norfolk 1970 GC 1). Born 18.11.1936, Nuneaton, Warwickshire. RHB WKT.

Braddon Clive Green (Devon 1980 GC 2). Born 18.1.1958, Benalla, Victoria, Australia. RHB RM. FC for Victoria (1978/79-82/83). Also ListA for Victoria (1978/79-82/83).

Cameron Rufus Frederick Green (Cambridgeshire 1989 NWT 1). Born 25.10.1968, Harpley, Norfolk. RHB OB.

David John Green (Wiltshire 1964 GC 1). Born 18.12.1935, Burton-on-Trent, Staffordshire. RHB. FC for Derbyshire (1953-60), CU (1957-59). Also ListA for Derbyshire (1953-60), CU (1957-59).

Jonathan Adam Green (Bedfordshire 2002 C&G 2). Born 15.1.1980, Dunstable, Bedfordshire. RHB RMF.

James E. Green (Suffolk 1966 GC 1).

Michael Redvers Green (Staffordshire 1975-78 GC 4). Born 17.9.1951, Stafford. RHB WKT.

Paul Green (Lancashire CB 1999-02 C&G 3 NWT 3). Born 1.6.1976, Salford, Lancashire. RHB RM.

Russell Christopher Green (Suffolk 1983-90 NWT 7, MC 1987-91 B&H 11). Born 30.7.1959, St Albans, Hertfordshire. RHB RFM. FC for Glamorgan (1984). Also ListA for Glamorgan (1984).

Joseph Andrew Greenhalgh (Derbyshire CB 2001 C&G 1). Born 9.1.1985, Chesterfield, Derbyshire. RHB OB.

Trevor Francis Greenshields (Durham 1974-78 GC 4). Born 27.10.1941, Newcastle upon Tyne, Northumberland. LHB.

Stephen Greensword (Durham 1972-90 GC 9 NWT 11, MC North 1973 B&H 1, Northumberland 1977-92 GC 2 NWT 1, MC 1980-92 B&H 35). Born 6.9.1943, Gateshead, Co Durham. RHB RM. FC for Leicestershire (1963-66), MC (1973-90). Also ListA for Leicestershire (1963-66).

Christopher Herbert Millington Greetham (Devon 1969 GC 1). Born 28.8.1936, Wargrave, Berkshire. RHB RM. FC for Somerset (1957-66). Also ListA for Somerset (1957-66).

David James Greetham (Hampshire CB 2001-02 C&G 3). Born 10.7.1975, Liss, Hampshire. RHB RMF.

Mark Richard Gribble (Devon 2002 C&G 1). Born 24.7.1975, Bovey Tracey, Devon. RHB RFM.

Andrew Declan Griffin (Hertfordshire 1999-00 NWT 4). Born 9.1.1972, Hammersmith, London. RHB WKT.

Frank Alexander Griffith (Cambridgeshire 2000 NWT 1). Born 15.8.1968, Whipps Cross, Leytonstone, Essex. RHB RM Occ WKT. FC for Derbyshire (1988-96). Also ListA for Derbyshire (1988-96).

Alan Griffiths (MC 1981-85 B&H 7, Staffordshire 1984-88 NWT 5). Born 18.9.1957, Newcastle-under-Lyme, Staffordshire. RHB WKT. FC for MC (1981).

Adrian David Griffiths (Wales MC 1993-94 NWT 2). Born 27.11.1959, Carmarthen, Wales. RHB RFM. Brother: J.L.Griffiths (Wales, Wales MC).

Christopher James Griffiths (Leicestershire CB 1999-01 C&G 1 NWT 2). Born 20.11.1971, Bradford, Yorkshire. RHB RM.

Paul John Griffiths (Warwickshire CB 2002 C&G 1). Born 26.4.1979, Solihull, Warwickshire. RHB OB.

Mark Peter Guest (Gloucestershire CB 2002 C&G 1). Born 4.12.1983, Gloucester. RHB WKT.

Richard James Gulliver (Wiltshire 1969-83 GC 3 NWT 1, MC West 1976 B&H 3, MC South 1979 B&H 1). Born 20.11.1942, Bower Chalke, Wiltshire. LHB RM.

Neil Edward Lloyd Gunter (Berkshire 2001-05 C&G 2). Born 12.5.1981, Basingstoke, Hampshire. LHB RFM. FC for Derbyshire (2002-04). Also ListA for Derbyshire (2002-04).

Aftab Habib (Berkshire 1995 NWT 1). Born 7.2.1972, Reading, Berkshire. RHB RMF. 2 Tests (1999) for England. FC for Middlesex (1992), Leicestershire (1995-06), Essex (2002-04). Also ListA for Middlesex (1992), Leicestershire (1995-06), Essex (2002-04). Cousin: Z.A.Sadiq (Derbyshire, MCC, Surrey, Surrey CB).

Peter John Hacker (Lincolnshire 1983-94 NWT 2, Cheshire 1985 NWT 1). Born 16.7.1952, Lenton Abbey, Nottingham. RHB LFM. FC for Nottinghamshire (1974-81), Orange Free State (1979/80), Derbyshire (1982). Also ListA for Nottinghamshire (1974-81), Orange Free State (1979/80), Derbyshire (1982).

Nigel Paul Hackett (Staffordshire 1991-94 NWT 4, MC 1992 B&H 2). Born 22.8.1962, Stowbridge, Norfolk. RHB LMF.

Abdul Hafeez (Shropshire 2000 NWT 1, Worcestershire CB 2001-03 C&G 4). Born 21.3.1977, Moseley, Birmingham, Warwickshire. RHB RM. FC for Worcestershire (1998-99). Also ListA for Worcestershire (1998-99).

Stanley Thomas Hahn (Oxfordshire 1970-72 GC 2). Born 9.12.1945, Watford, Hertfordshire. Died 28.1.1991, Oxford. RHB WKT.

Robert John Hailey (MC 1982 B&H 1, Hertfordshire 1983-88 NWT 6). Born 25.7.1952, Gosforth, Newcastle upon Tyne, Northumberland. RHB SLA.

David Andrew Hale (Oxfordshire 1987-91 NWT 4, MC 1989 B&H 2). Born 20.3.1966, Oxford. RHB RFM.

Terrance Saville Hale (Cambridgeshire 1964-67 GC 4). Born 8.10.1936, Waterbeach, Cambridgeshire. LHB. FC for MC (1965). Also ListA for MC (1965).

Alan J. Halford (Norfolk 1969-70 GC 2). Born 1.11.1934, Leicester. RFM.

David John Halfyard (Durham 1972 GC 2, MC North 1972-73 B&H 2, Cornwall 1975-77 GC 2). Born 3.4.1931, Winchmore Hill, Middlesex. Died 23.8.1996, Northam, Devon. RHB RFM,RM. FC for Kent (1956-64), MCC (1959), Nottinghamshire (1968-70). Also ListA for Kent (1956-64), MCC (1959), Nottinghamshire (1968-70).

Andrew James Hall (Cheshire 1994-04 C&G 5 NWT 1). Born 12.3.1973, Gorton, Manchester, Lancashire. RHB RM.

Andrew James Hall (Durham CB 1999 NWT 3, Suffolk 2002 C&G 1). Born 31.7.1975, Johannesburg, Transvaal, South Africa. RHB RFM Occ WKT. 21 Tests (2001/02-06/07) for South Africa. 88 ODIs (1998/99-07) for South Africa. 2 Int2020s (2005/06) for South Africa. FC for Transvaal (1995/96-96/97), Transvaal B (1995/96-96/97), Gauteng (1997/98-00/01), Easterns (2001/02-03/04), Worcestershire (2003-04), Lions (2004/05-05/06), Kent (2005-07), Northamptonshire (2008). Also ListA for Transvaal (1995/96-96/97), Transvaal B (1995/96-96/97), Gauteng (1997/98-00/01), Easterns (2001/02-03/04), Worcestershire (2003-04), Lions (2004/05-05/06), Kent (2005-07), Northamptonshire (2008).

Christopher James Hall (Cheshire 1999-00 NWT 3). Born 28.11.1977, Bury, Lancashire. RHB OB.

Danny Charles Richard Hall (Berkshire 1976 GC 1). Born 3.11.1944, Penzance, Cornwall. RHB.

Harry Mark Hall (Berkshire 1996-00 NWT 6). Born 19.11.1970, Wokingham, Berkshire. RHB SLA.

Jonathan Roger Hall (Dorset 1989-91 NWT 3). Born 3.9.1962, Hampstead, London. RHB RM.

Matthew James Hall (Derbyshire CB 2000-01 C&G 1 NWT 3). Born 30.10.1981, Chesterfield, Derbyshire. RHB RM.

Maximillian Palmer Hall (Surrey CB 2001-02 C&G 3). Born 29.9.1975, Surrey. RHB OB.

Robert Henry Fosbroke Hall (Herefordshire 1997-98 NWT 2). Born 1.11.1963, Andover, Hampshire. RHB WKT.

Richard Jonathon Hall (Herefordshire 2004 C&G 1). Born 27.9.1978, Worcester. LHB SLA.

Timothy John Hall (Dorset 1973 GC 1). Born 25.7.1944, Bristol. RHB RS.

Thomas Leonard Hall (Berkshire 1996-02 C&G 1 NWT 1). Born 14.6.1969, Wokingham, Berkshire. RHB.

Dave Hallack (Derbyshire CB 2002 C&G 1). Born 22.1.1966, Bulawayo, Zimbabwe. RHB RM.

Graeme Hallam (Northumberland 1999-03 C&G 2 NWT 4). Born 6.1.1973, Wallsend, Northumberland. RHB RM.

Gordon Donald Halliday (Northumberland 1984-86 NWT 2). Born 11.11.1950, Edinburgh, Midlothian, Scotland. RHB RM.

Simon John Halliday (Suffolk 1987-95 NWT 5). Born 23.10.1958, Ipswich, Suffolk. RHB WKT.

Simon John Halliday (Dorset 1983-87 NWT 3). Born 13.7.1960, Haverfordwest, Pembroke, Wales. RHB. FC for OU (1980-82). Also ListA for OU (1980-82).

David Halliwell (Cumberland 1984-89 NWT 6). Born 11.12.1948, Leyland, Lancashire. LHB RFM.

Norman Richard Halsall (Cheshire 1964-68 GC 4). Born 9.10.1935, West Derby, Liverpool, Lancashire. RHB RMF.

Richard Grant Halsall (Sussex CB 2000-01 C&G 3 NWT 2). Born 1.10.1968, Salisbury (now Harare), Zimbabwe. RHB RFM. FC for Mashonaland Country Districts (1993/94), CU (1999). Also ListA for Mashonaland Country Districts (1993/94), CU (1999).

Greg Elliott Hames (Buckinghamshire 1999 NWT 1). Born 3.5.1980, Reading, Berkshire. RHB RM.

Neil Gregory Hames (Buckinghamshire 1984-91 NWT 7). Born 17.12.1949, Hampstead, London. LHB RM. Son: B.A. (Buckinghamshire).

Stephen William Hampson (Cheshire 1998 NWT 1). Born 14.6.1968, Ashton-under-Lyne, Lancashire. LHB SLA.

David Arthur Hancock (Staffordshire 1971-78 GC 6, MC North 1972-75 B&H 13, MC East 1977-78 B&H 5). Born 28.3.1940, Newcastle-under-Lyme, Staffordshire. LHB.

Neil David Hancock (Devon 1999-05 C&G 8 NWT 2). Born 13.4.1976, Casino, New South Wales, Australia. RHB RFM.

Frederick Lester Quorn Handley (Norfolk 1970-90 GC 1 NWT 5, MC North 1979 B&H 2, MC 1985 B&H 2). Born 11.8.1949, Kampala, Uganda. LHB.

James Michael Hands (Cornwall 1996-03 C&G 7 NWT 1). Born 9.10.1978, Truro, Cornwall. RHB SLA.

Michael Dennis Hands (Cornwall 1977 GC 1). Born 13.9.1951, Cheltenham, Gloucestershire. RHB.

Michael Hanna (Wiltshire 1964-65 GC 2). Born 6.6.1926, Camberwell, London. RHB WKT. FC for Somerset (1951-54). Also ListA for Somerset (1951-54).

Richard John Harding (Herefordshire 1995-98 NWT 3). Born 14.10.1966, Bristol. RHB OB.

Gerald Charles Hardstaff (Cheshire 1964-68 GC 4, MC North 1972 B&H 2). Born 4.2.1940, Crewe, Cheshire. RHB RM.

Mark Hardwicke (Dorset 1968 GC 1). Born 22.8.1936, Weymouth, Dorset. RHB RS.

Donald Wrightson Hardy (Durham 1964-67 GC 3). Born 24.3.1926, East Boldon, Co Durham. Died 16.1.1998, Felling, Co Durham. RHB RM. FC for MC (1965). Also ListA for MC (1965). Father: H.W. (Durham).

Jonathan James Ean Hardy (Dorset 1992-98 NWT 4). Born 2.10.1960, Nakuru, Kenya. LHB. FC for Hampshire (1984-85), Somerset (1986-90), Western Province (1987/88-90/91), Western Province B (1987/88-90/91), Gloucestershire (1991). Also ListA for Hampshire (1984-85), Somerset (1986-90), Western Province (1987/88-90/91), Western Province B (1987/88-90/91), Gloucestershire (1991).

John Michael Hargreaves (Suffolk 1966 GC 1). Born 25.2.1944, Gainsborough, Lincolnshire. LHB OB. Father: H.S. (MC, Suffolk, Yorkshire).

Darren Simon Harland (Yorkshire CB 2001-02 C&G 4). Born 15.10.1979, Whitby, Yorkshire. RHB.

Thomas Harland (Durham 1974-78 GC 4). Born 15.1.1942, Hetton-le-Hole, Co Durham. LHB WKT.

Nigel W. Harper (Oxfordshire 1975 GC 2). Born 17.1.1948, Wigginton, Oxfordshire. RHB.

Robert Frank Harriott (Devon 1978-80 GC 4). Born 30.11.1947, Birmingham, Warwickshire. RHB.

Andrew William Harris (Wales MC 1993-94 NWT 2). Born 2.2.1971, Newport, Monmouthshire. LHB WKT.

Frederick William Harris (Buckinghamshire 1965-75 GC 7). Born 12.11.1934, Chesham, Buckinghamshire. RHB RFM.

Gordon Andrew Robert Harris (Hertfordshire 1990-93 NWT 3). Born 11.1.1964, Tottenham, Middlesex. RHB RFM. FC for Leicestershire (1986), Middlesex (1994). Also ListA for Leicestershire (1986), Middlesex (1994).

Keith Rowland Harris (Cheshire 1982 NWT 1). Born 5.6.1957, St Helens, Lancashire. LHB.

Paul Roy Harris (Bedfordshire 1977 GC 1). Born 21.2.1955, Dagenham, Essex. RHB.

Jason Christian Harrison (Buckinghamshire 1998-05 C&G 1 NWT 1, Lincolnshire 1999-02 C&G 4 NWT 4). Born 15.1.1972, Amersham, Buckinghamshire. RHB OB. FC for Middlesex (1994-96). Also ListA for Middlesex (1994-96).

Michael Thomas Harrison (Sussex CB 2002 C&G 1). Born 25.8.1978, Cuckfield, Sussex. RHB RMF.

Tom William Harrison (Middlesex CB 1999-00 NWT 2). Born 11.12.1971, Peterborough. LHB LM. FC for Derbyshire (1995). Also ListA for Derbyshire (1995).

Jamie Paul Hart (Leicestershire CB 2001 C&G 2, Nottinghamshire CB 2001 C&G 2). Born 31.12.1975, Blackpool, Lancashire. RHB RM. FC for Nottinghamshire (1996). Also ListA for Nottinghamshire (1996).

David James Benedict Hartley (Berkshire 1988-97 NWT 7). Born 28.3.1963, Ruscombe, Reading, Berkshire. RHB LB.

Jonathan Samuel Hartley (Oxfordshire 1989-93 NWT 6). Born 8.1.1960, Burnley, Lancashire. RHB RM.

Jonathon David Harvey (Hertfordshire 1993 NWT 1, Lancashire CB 1999-01 C&G 1 NWT 1). Born 18.12.1969, Burnley, Lancashire. RHB WKT. Brother: M.E. (Berkshire, Lancashire).

John Frank Harvey (Cambridgeshire 1975 GC 1, MC North 1975 B&H 1, MC East 1976 B&H 3, Berkshire 1979-86 GC 1 NWT 4). Born 27.9.1939, Barnwell, Cambridge. Died 20.8.2003, Bradfield, Berkshire. RHB OB. FC for MCC (1961-67), Derbyshire (1963-72). Also ListA for MCC (1961-67), Derbyshire (1963-72).

Nicholas Paul Harvey (Berkshire 2001 C&G 1). Born 21.11.1973, Ascot, Berkshire. RHB WKT.

Richard Peter Harvey (Staffordshire 1998-05 C&G 7 NWT 4). Born 3.8.1974, Stoke-on-Trent, Staffordshire. LHB SLA. Father: P.R. (Staffordshire).

Stephen Robert Harvey (Norfolk 1995 NWT 1). Born 12.7.1964, Little Snoring, Norfolk. LHB.

Andrew Robert Harwood (Buckinghamshire 1984-92 NWT 7). Born 6.1.1964, Aylesbury, Buckinghamshire. LHB RM.

Paul James Harwood (Norfolk 1998 NWT 1). Born 16.2.1977, King's Lynn, Norfolk. LHB RFM.

Sheikh Jamil Hassan (Nottinghamshire CB 1999 NWT 1, Leicestershire CB 2001 C&G 1, Worcestershire CB 2002 C&G 2). Born 22.10.1980, Nottingham. RHB OB Occ WKT. Father: S.B. (Kenya, MCC, Nottinghamshire).

Saeed Ahmed Hatteea (Oxfordshire 1972 GC 1). Born 2.2.1950, Bombay (now Mumbai), Maharashtra, India. RHB RFM. FC for Bombay (1969/70-70/71). Also ListA for Bombay (1969/70-70/71).

Craig Arend Haupt (Oxfordshire 1999-01 C&G 2 NWT 2). Born 25.6.1972, Cape Town, Cape Province, South Africa. LHB RM. Nephew: D.L. (Western Province).

Andrew Charles Hawkins (Staffordshire 1987 NWT 1). Born 16.6.1967, Stoke-on-Trent, Staffordshire. LHB RM.

Richard William Hawkins (Oxfordshire 2002 C&G 1). Born 1.10.1979, Banbury, Oxfordshire. LHB.

Ian Anthony Hawtin (Oxfordshire 1999-03 C&G 5 NWT 1). Born 10.10.1966, Bicester, Oxfordshire. RHB WKT.

Geoffrey William Hayes (Shropshire 1974 GC 1). Born 13.8.1950, Burford, Shropshire. RHB WKT.

Kevin Anthony Hayes (Cumberland 1988-89 NWT 2). Born 26.9.1962, Thurnscoe, Yorkshire. RHB RM. FC for Lancashire (1980-86), OU (1981-84). Also ListA for Lancashire (1980-86), OU (1981-84).

Peter James Hayes (Suffolk 1981-89 NWT 6). Born 20.5.1954, Crowborough, Sussex. RHB RM. FC for CU (1974-77). Also ListA for CU (1974-77).

Derek Reginald Hayward (Dorset 1968-83 GC 2 NWT 1). Born 7.12.1940, Wyke Regis, Dorset. RHB RM.

Richard Edward Hayward (Buckinghamshire 1979-84 GC 1 NWT 1, MC South 1979 B&H 4, MC 1984 B&H 4). Born 15.2.1954, Ickenham, Middlesex. LHB LM Occ WKT. FC for MC (1979), Hampshire (1981-82), Central Districts (1982/83-85/86), Somerset (1985). Also ListA for Hampshire (1981-82), Central Districts (1982/83-85/86), Somerset (1985).

Marc Alexander Hazelton (Sussex CB 2001 C&G 1). Born 17.10.1980, Cuckfield, Sussex. RHB RMF. FC for Durham UCCE (2002). Also ListA for Durham UCCE (2002).

Gary Tyrone Headley (Berkshire 1990-94 NWT 3). Born 5.9.1966, Reading, Berkshire. RHB RM.

Robert Dennis Healey (Devon 1969 GC 1). Born 10.2.1934, Plymouth, Devon. RHB RFM.

Timothy Michael Heap (Staffordshire 1994-95 NWT 2). Born 2.3.1969, Wakefield, Yorkshire. RHB RM.

Adam Tom Heather (Northumberland 1999-05 C&G 1 NWT 4). Born 7.11.1972, Manchester, Lancashire. LHB.

Adrian John Hedley (Durham CB 1999 NWT 3). Born 8.12.1978, Durham. RHB RM.

Andrew Keith Hele (Devon 1998-01 C&G 1 NWT 5). Born 3.9.1967, Torquay, Devon. RHB WKT.

Timothy James Hemp (Wales MC 1999 NWT 1). Born 12.4.1974, Hamilton, Bermuda. RHB RM. Brother: D.L. (Bermuda, Free State, Glamorgan, Wales, Wales MC, Warwickshire).

Colin Ronald Hemsley (Shropshire 1976 GC 1). Born 11.8.1949, Highley, Shropshire. RHB RM. Brother: E.J.O. (Shropshire, Worcestershire).

Claude William Henderson (Worcestershire CB 2000-01 C&G 2 NWT 1). Born 14.6.1972, Worcester, Cape Province, South Africa. RHB SLA. 7 Tests (2001/02-02/03) for South Africa. 4 ODIs (2001/02) for South Africa. FC for Boland (1990/91-97/98), Western Province (1998/99-03/04), Western Province B (1998/99), Leicestershire (2004-08), Lions (2006/07-07/08), Cape Cobras (2008/09). Also ListA for Boland (1990/91-97/98), Western Province (1998/99-03/04), Western Province B (1998/99), Leicestershire (2004-08), Lions (2006/07-07/08), Cape Cobras (2008/09). Brother: J.M.Henderson (Boland, Boland B, Eagles, Free State, North West, South Western Districts, Transvaal B).

Henry Burton Henderson (Northumberland 1971 GC 1). Born 23.9.1923, Northumberland. Died 2.7.1997, Newcastle upon Tyne, Northumberland. RHB WKT.

Stephen Peter Henderson (Hertfordshire 1987-89 NWT 3, MC 1987-88 B&H 5). Born 24.9.1958, Headington, Oxfordshire. LHB RM Occ WKT. FC for Worcestershire (1977-81), CU (1982-83), Glamorgan (1983-85), MCC (1987). Also ListA for Worcestershire (1977-81), CU (1982-83), Glamorgan (1983-85), MCC (1987). Father: D. (OU).

Tyron Henderson (Berkshire 2002-03 C&G 2). Born 1.8.1974, Durban, Natal, South Africa. RHB RFM. 1 Int2020 (2006/07) for South Africa. FC for Border (1998/99-03/04), Warriors (2004/05-05/06), Kent (2006), Lions (2006/07), Boland (2007/08), Cape Cobras (2007/08). Also ListA for Border (1998/99-03/04), Warriors (2004/05-05/06), Kent (2006), Lions (2006/07), Boland (2007/08), Cape Cobras (2007/08), Middlesex (2008). Grandfather: J.K. (North Eastern Transvaal), great-uncle: W.A. (North Eastern Transvaal).

Douglas Henry Henson (Staffordshire 1971-73 GC 3). Born 27.5.1930, Shrewsbury, Shropshire. Died 6.6.2003, Stoke-on-Trent, Staffordshire. RHB RM.

Reuben Herbert (Suffolk 1984-86 NWT 3, MC 1986-87 B&H 8, Hertfordshire 1987 NWT 1). Born 1.12.1957, Lansdown, Cape Town, Cape Province, South Africa. RHB OB. FC for Essex (1976-80), MC (1985-86). Also ListA for Essex (1976-80).

Robert Stephen Herman (MC South 1979 B&H 2). Born 30.11.1946, Shirley, Southampton, Hampshire. RHB RFM. FC for Middlesex (1965-71), Hampshire (1972-77), Border (1972/73), Griqualand West (1974/75). Also ListA for Middlesex (1965-71), Hampshire (1972-77), Border (1972/73), Griqualand West (1974/75). Father: O.W. (Hampshire, Wiltshire).

Peter Anthony William Heseltine (Durham 1991 NWT 1). Born 5.4.1965, Barnsley, Yorkshire. RHB OB. FC for Sussex (1987-88). Also ListA for Sussex (1987-88). Brother: P.J. (Berkshire, Lincolnshire, OU).

Phillip John Heseltine (Berkshire 1989 NWT 1, Lincolnshire 1991 NWT 1). Born 21.6.1960, Skipton, Yorkshire. RHB RM,OB. FC for OU (1983). Also ListA for OU (1983). Brother: P.A.W. (Durham, MCC, Sussex).

Christopher Jon Hewison (Durham CB 1999 NWT 2, Northumberland 2002-03 C&G 2). Born 6.10.1979, Gateshead, Co Durham. RHB RM Occ WKT. FC for Nottinghamshire (2000). Also ListA for Nottinghamshire (2000). Father: N. (Durham).

David John Heyes (Lancashire CB 1999-00 NWT 3). Born 7.2.1967, Prescot, Lancashire. RHB RM.

James Hibberd (Hampshire CB 2001 C&G 1, Wiltshire 2002-05 C&G 3). Born 19.4.1981, Southampton, Hampshire. RHB RMF.

Andrew James Edward Hibbert (Essex CB 1999-01 C&G 1 NWT 3). Born 17.12.1974, Harold Wood, Essex. RHB RM Occ WKT. FC for Essex (1995-98). Also ListA for Essex (1995-98).

Thomas Leslie Hickling (Buckinghamshire 1970 GC 2). Born 4.1.1940, Roydon, Norfolk. LHB.

Thomas Charles Hicks (Dorset 2000 NWT 1). Born 28.8.1979, Farnborough, Kent. RHB OB. FC for OU (1999-02), Oxford Universities (2000), Oxford UCCE (2001-02). Also ListA for OU (1999-02), Oxford Universities (2000), Oxford UCCE (2001-02). Brother: G.D. (Dorset).

Mark Anthony Higgs (Lincolnshire 2003 C&G 1). Born 30.6.1976, Queanbeyan, New South Wales, Australia. LHB SLA,SLC. FC for New South Wales (1998/99-01/02), South Australia (2002/03-03/04). Also ListA for New South Wales (1998/99-01/02), South Australia (2002/03-03/04).

Richard Graeme Hignett (Cheshire 1993-03 C&G 6 NWT 8, MC 1995-98 B&H 5). Born 29.4.1972, Widnes, Lancashire. RHB RFM.

James Charles Hildreth (Somerset CB 2002 C&G 1). Born 9.9.1984, Milton Keynes. RHB RFM. FC for Somerset (2003-08). Also ListA for Somerset (2003-08).

Elliot Vernon Hill (Middlesex CB 2001 C&G 1). Born 9.11.1978, Birmingham, Warwickshire. LHB WKT.

Gregory Russell Hill (Devon 1992 NWT 1, Worcestershire CB 2000-03 C&G 4 NWT 1). Born 13.9.1972, Canterbury, Kent. RHB OB. Father: M. (Derbyshire, MCC, Nottinghamshire, Somerset).

Martin Richard Hill (Staffordshire 1978 GC 2). Born 1.4.1945, Quarry Bank, Staffordshire. RHB.

Ian Jack Hilsum (Hampshire CB 2000 NWT 1). Born 29.12.1981, Newport, Isle of Wight. RHB LB. FC for Oxford UCCE (2002). Also ListA for Oxford UCCE (2002).

Richard James Edward Hindley (Hampshire CB 2001-02 C&G 4). Born 25.4.1975, Portsmouth, Hampshire. LHB OB. FC for Hampshire (2003). Also ListA for Hampshire (2003).

James Edward Hindson (Nottinghamshire CB 2000-02 C&G 3 NWT 1). Born 13.9.1973, Huddersfield, Yorkshire. RHB SLA. FC for Nottinghamshire (1992-97). Also ListA for Nottinghamshire (1992-97).

Simon Graham Hinks (Gloucestershire CB 1999 NWT 1). Born 12.10.1960, Northfleet, Kent. LHB RM Occ WKT. FC for Kent (1982-91), Gloucestershire (1992-94). Also ListA for Kent (1982-91), Gloucestershire (1992-94).

Lionel Edward Hitchings (Buckinghamshire 1965 GC 1). Born 15.5.1936, Hereford. LHB WKT.

John Jeffrey Hitchmough (Cheshire 1985-92 NWT 7). Born 20.1.1962, Liverpool, Lancashire. RHB OB.

John Sutton Hitchmough (Cheshire 1982-89 NWT 4, MC 1985-86 B&H 5). Born 18.4.1958, Hale, Liverpool, Lancashire. RHB RM.

David John Frank Hoare (Bedfordshire 1967-70 GC 4). Born 14.1.1934, West Malling, Kent. Died 26.2.2002. LHB. Son: P.D.B. (Bedfordshire).

Philip David Baxter Hoare (Bedfordshire 1985-99 NWT 7). Born 29.11.1962, Bedford. RHB RM. Father: D.J.F. (Bedfordshire).

Graham Raymond Hobbins (Oxfordshire 1975-86 GC 1 NWT 3). Born 27.2.1946, Eastbourne, Sussex. RHB RFM.

Alan David Hobbs (Cambridgeshire 1965 GC 1). Born 11.3.1944, Cambridge. RHB RM. Father: E. (Cambridgeshire).

Robin Nicholas Stuart Hobbs (MC East 1976 B&H 3, Suffolk 1978 GC 1). Born 8.5.1942, Chippenham, Wiltshire. RHB LBG. 7 Tests (1967-71) for England. FC for Essex (1961-75), MCC (1963-70), Glamorgan (1979-81). Also ListA for Essex (1961-75), MCC (1963-70), Glamorgan (1979-81).

Anthony David Hobson (Staffordshire 1992 NWT 1). Born 10.9.1965, Eccleshall, Staffordshire. RHB OB.

Malcolm Ralph Hobson (Hampshire CB 2002 C&G 2). Born 5.6.1966, Graaff-Reinet, Cape Province, South Africa. RHB RFM. FC for Natal B (1985/86-88/89), Natal (1986/87), Eastern Province B (1989/90), Border (1990/91-92/93), Transvaal (1993/94-94/95), Transvaal B (1993/94-94/95), Northern Transvaal B (1995/96). Also ListA for Natal B (1985/86-88/89), Natal (1986/87), Eastern Province B (1989/90), Border (1990/91-92/93), Transvaal (1993/94-94/95), Transvaal B (1993/94-94/95), Northern Transvaal B (1995/96). Brother: I.B. (Natal, Natal B).

Andrew John Hodd (Sussex CB 2002 C&G 1). Born 12.1.1984, Chichester, Sussex. RHB WKT. FC for Sussex (2003-08), Surrey (2005). Also ListA for Sussex (2003-08), Surrey (2005).

Richard Hodgkinson (Nottinghamshire CB 2001 C&G 1). Born 9.12.1983, Mansfield, Nottinghamshire. RHB RFM. FC for Derbyshire (2007). Also ListA for Derbyshire (2007).

Mark Anthony Hodgkiss (Worcestershire CB 2001 C&G 2). Born 10.1.1977, Sandwell, Staffordshire. RHB.

Andrew Sabin Hodgson (Dorset 1973 GC 1). Born 16.9.1941, Auckland, New Zealand. RHB RM. FC for Western Province (1967/68). Also ListA for Western Province (1967/68).

Geoffrey Dean Hodgson (Cumberland 1986-87 NWT 2). Born 22.10.1966, Carlisle, Cumberland. RHB. FC for Gloucestershire (1989-95). Also ListA for Gloucestershire (1989-95).

James Hodgson (Berkshire 1997 NWT 1, Kent CB 2001-02 C&G 2). Born 28.3.1972, Reading, Berkshire. RHB LB.

Kenneth Ian Hodgson (Buckinghamshire 1984-88 NWT 5). Born 24.2.1960, Port Elizabeth, Cape Province, South Africa. RHB RM. FC for CU (1981-83). Also ListA for CU (1981-83).

Timothy Philip Hodgson (Surrey CB 2000-01 C&G 2 NWT 1). Born 27.3.1975, Guildford, Surrey. LHB. FC for Essex (1997-99). Also ListA for Essex (1997-99). Great-uncle: N.A.Knox (MCC, Surrey), brothers: J.S. (CU) and C.P.R. (Berkshire).

Edward Robert Hodson (Norfolk 1984 NWT 1). Born 16.8.1964, Lincoln. RHB.

Michael David Hodson (Lincolnshire 1976 GC 1, MC North 1979 B&H 2). Born 2.8.1942, Grimsby, Lincolnshire. RHB WKT.

Dean Stuart Hoffman (Cambridgeshire 1989 NWT 1). Born 13.1.1966, Erdington, Birmingham, Warwickshire. RHB RMF. FC for Warwickshire (1985), Northamptonshire (1988). Also ListA for Warwickshire (1985), Northamptonshire (1988).

Charlie Alan Holcomb (Dorset 1999 NWT 1). Born 4.3.1980, Oklahoma, USA. RHB OB.

Vanburn Alonzo Holder (MC 1981 B&H 2). Born 10.10.1945, Deans Village, St Michael, Barbados. RHB RFM. 40 Tests (1969-78/79) for West Indies. 12 ODIs (1973-77/78) for West Indies. FC for Barbados (1966/67-77/78), Worcestershire (1968-80), Orange Free State (1985/86). Also ListA for Barbados (1966/67-77/78), Worcestershire (1968-80), Orange Free State (1985/86).

Kenneth Frank Holding (Cheshire 1964-68 GC 4). Born 25.6.1915, Bolton, Lancashire. Died 14.6.1997, Chelford, Cheshire. RHB WKT.

Matthew Holland (Wiltshire 1989-90 NWT 2). Born 9.12.1971, Worcester. RHB SLA.

David Charles Holliday (Cambridgeshire 1983 NWT 1). Born 20.12.1958, Cambridge. RHB LB. FC for CU (1979-81). Also ListA for CU (1979-81).

Andrew Philip Hollingsworth (Surrey CB 2001-02 C&G 2). Born 11.10.1979, Chertsey, Surrey. RHB RM. FC for Durham UCCE (2002). Also ListA for Durham UCCE (2002).

Hugh Basil Hollington (Hertfordshire 1971-74 GC 2, MC South 1972-74 B&H 5). Born 14.8.1949, Harpenden, Hertfordshire. LHB. FC for MC (1972). Also ListA for MC (1972).

Kevin John Hollis (Derbyshire CB 2000-01 C&G 3 NWT 1). Born 5.1.1983, Derby. LHB WKT.

Patrick Walter Holman (Cambridgeshire 1975 GC 1). Born 26.3.1945, Downham Market, Norfolk. RHB.

Guy Leonard Home (Shropshire 2001-05 C&G 6). Born 13.9.1964, Shrewsbury, Shropshire. LHB. Father: J. (Shropshire), brother: E.L. (MCC, Shropshire).

Ronald William Hooker (Buckinghamshire 1970-75 GC 6). Born 22.2.1935, Lower Clapton, London. RHB RM. FC for Middlesex (1956-69). Also ListA for Middlesex (1956-69).

Owain Charles Hopkins (Wales MC 2001-02 C&G 2). Born 18.12.1980, Bridgend, Glamorgan, Wales. RHB OB.

Carl Daniel Hopkinson (Sussex CB 2001 C&G 2). Born 14.9.1981, Brighton, Sussex. RHB RM. FC for Sussex (2002-08). Also ListA for Sussex (2002-08).

Stuart William Horne (Cumberland 2001 C&G 1). Born 13.9.1979, Barrow-in-Furness, Lancashire. RHB OB.

Robert William Horner (Berkshire 1995 NWT 1). Born 20.1.1967, Liskeard, Cornwall. RHB WKT.

Ryan Horrell (Devon 1996-00 NWT 3). Born 7.4.1973, Barnstaple, Devon. LHB SLA.

Roland Edward William George Horridge (Lancashire CB 1999-01 C&G 2 NWT 3). Born 27.1.1963, Radcliffe, Lancashire. RHB RM.

Mark Horrocks (Herefordshire 2003-04 C&G 2). Born 13.1.1977, Hereford. RHB RM.

Simon Daniel Horsfall (Staffordshire 1997-98 NWT 2). Born 4.3.1976, Leeds, Yorkshire. LHB LB.

Paul James Horton (Lancashire CB 2002 C&G 2). Born 20.9.1982, Sydney, New South Wales, Australia. RHB RM. FC for Lancashire (2003-08). Also ListA for Lancashire (2003-08).

Philip Hough (Wiltshire 1965 GC 1). Born 31.8.1924, Macclesfield, Cheshire. RHB LBG.

Kenneth Henry House (Dorset 1973 GC 1). Born 7.4.1936, Sturminster Newton, Dorset. RHB RM.

John Stirling Howarth (MC East 1977 B&H 2). Born 26.3.1945, Stockport, Cheshire. RHB RFM. FC for Nottinghamshire (1966-67). Also ListA for Nottinghamshire (1966-67).

Christopher Robert Howell (Warwickshire CB 1999-02 C&G 4 NWT 1, Staffordshire 2005 C&G 1). Born 19.7.1977, Kingston-upon-Thames, Surrey. RHB RM.

Richard Thomas James Howell (Gloucestershire CB 2000-01 C&G 2 NWT 1). Born 2.1.1982, Gloucester. RHB RM Occ WKT.

Richard William John Howitt (Lincolnshire 1999-02 C&G 5 NWT 2, Berkshire 2003-04 C&G 2). Born 17.8.1977, Grantham, Lincolnshire. LHB RM. FC for CU (2000). Also ListA for CU (2000).

Roger Frederick Howlett (MC East 1978 B&H 1, Suffolk 1978-84 GC 2 NWT 3). Born 27.4.1948, Bury St Edmunds, Suffolk. RHB RM.

Tony Howorth (Cambridgeshire 1975 GC 1). Born 20.3.1938, Whittlesey, Cambridgeshire. RHB LB. Son: A. (Cambridgeshire, Huntingdonshire).

Brian James Hoyle (Somerset CB 2001 C&G 1). Born 25.8.1963, Worksop, Nottinghamshire. LHB.

Roger Douglas Hudson (Huntingdonshire 1999 NWT 1). Born 8.6.1967, Selly Oak, Birmingham, Warwickshire. RHB RM. FC for OU (1997). Also ListA for OU (1997).

Robin David Paul Huggins (Norfolk 1982-85 NWT 4). Born 28.4.1947, Coltishall, Norfolk. RHB.

Thomas Benjamin Huggins (Cambridgeshire 2001 C&G 1). Born 6.3.1983, Peterborough. RHB OB. FC for Northamptonshire (2003-05). Also ListA for Northamptonshire (2003-05). Brother: O.J. (Huntingdonshire).

John Gareth Hughes (Bedfordshire 1998-01 C&G 5 NWT 5). Born 3.5.1971, Wellingborough, Northamptonshire. RHB RM. FC for Northamptonshire (1990-97). Also ListA for Northamptonshire (1990-97).

Kevin John Hughes (Oxfordshire 1991-92 NWT 3). Born 14.3.1966, Banbury, Oxfordshire. RHB WKT.

Nicholas David Hughes (Hertfordshire 1999-00 NWT 2). Born 6.7.1978, Dublin, Ireland. RHB RM.

Quentin John Hughes (Durham CB 2000-02 C&G 3 NWT 1, Cumberland 2003 C&G 1). Born 17.10.1974, Durham. LHB OB. FC for CU (1997-00). Also ListA for CU (1997-00). Father: T.J. (Durham).

Robert David Hughes (Herefordshire 1999-04 C&G 4 NWT 3). Born 26.10.1973, Rugby, Warwickshire. LHB.

Timothy John Hughes (Durham 1974 GC 2). Born 25.9.1943, Escrick, York. LHB RM. Son: Q.J. (CU, Cumberland, Durham, Durham CB).

John Arthan Hulme (Shropshire 1983 NWT 1). Born 13.11.1950, Chirk, Denbighshire, Wales. LHB.

Stephen Humble (Durham CB 2001-02 C&G 2, Northumberland 2005 C&G 1). Born 3.1.1977, Hexham, Northumberland. RHB RM.

Neil Victor Humphrey (Warwickshire CB 2001-02 C&G 5). Born 2.4.1973, Kingston, Jamaica. RHB.

Richard Geoffrey Humphrey (Buckinghamshire 1984-85 NWT 2). Born 17.9.1936, Hampstead, London. RHB WKT. FC for Surrey (1964-70). Also ListA for Surrey (1964-70).

Edward Humphreys (Huntingdonshire 2000 NWT 1). Born 25.4.1968, Bedford. RHB RM.

Mark Ian Humphries (Staffordshire 1990-03 C&G 6 NWT 12, MC 1992-95 B&H 8). Born 4.10.1965, Highley, Shropshire. LHB WKT. FC for MC (1994). Brother: D.J. (Leicestershire, MCC, Shropshire, Worcestershire).

Paul Jonathan Humphries (Herefordshire 1998-01 C&G 1 NWT 4). Born 10.10.1965, Bromsgrove, Worcestershire. RHB RFM.

Christopher Andrew Hunkin (Somerset CB 2000-01 C&G 1 NWT 1, Cornwall 2001-03 C&G 4). Born 14.12.1980, St Austell, Cornwall. RHB RM.

Matthew Paul Hunt (Devon 2002-04 C&G 5). Born 10.6.1977, Newton Abbot, Devon. RHB RM.

Simon Alexander Hunt (Cornwall 1986 NWT 1). Born 26.5.1962, Guildford, Surrey. RHB RM.

Terence Anderson Hunte (Cumberland 1992-01 C&G 2 NWT 2). Born 4.4.1962, Thickets, St Philip, Barbados. RHB RM. FC for Barbados (1983/84-87/88). Also ListA for Barbados (1983/84-87/88).

Charles Michael Geoffrey Hunter (Dorset 1968-73 GC 2, MC South 1972 B&H 3). Born 11.9.1937, Windle, St Helens, Lancashire. RHB RM. FC for MC (1971). Also ListA for MC (1971).

Ian David Hunter (Durham CB 2001-03 C&G 2). Born 11.9.1979, Durham. RHB RMF. FC for Durham (2000-03), Derbyshire (2004-08). Also ListA for Durham (2000-03), Derbyshire (2004-08).

Ross Leslie Alan Hunter (Hampshire CB 2000 NWT 1). Born 27.1.1981, Frimley Park, Surrey. RHB WKT.

Richard Brian Hurd (Buckinghamshire 1997-98 NWT 2). Born 18.12.1970, Amersham, Buckinghamshire. RHB.

James Hurn (Wiltshire 1964 GC 1). Born 10.11.1926, Melksham, Wiltshire. LHB.

John Hurrell (Cornwall 1970 GC 1). Born 1.9.1947, Redruth, Cornwall. LHB RFM.

Graham Hurst (Durham 1982-86 NWT 4). Born 22.9.1960, Newcastle upon Tyne, Northumberland. RHB.

Mehriyar Hussain (Essex CB 2001 C&G 1). Born 17.10.1963, South Shields, Co Durham. RHB OB. FC for Worcestershire (1985). Also ListA for Worcestershire (1985). Brother: N. (Essex, MCC), father: R.Jawad Hussain (Madras).

David John Hussey (Sussex CB 2001 C&G 3). Born 15.7.1977, Morley, Western Australia, Australia. RHB OB. 5 ODIs (2008) for Australia. 4 Int2020s (2007/08-08/09) for Australia. FC for Victoria (2002/03-08/09), Nottinghamshire (2004-07). Also ListA for Victoria (2002/03-08/09), Nottinghamshire (2004-07). Brother: M.E.K. (Durham, Gloucestershire, Northamptonshire, Western Australia).

Richard Martin Hutchings (Leicestershire CB 1999-01 C&G 3 NWT 1). Born 6.5.1978, Leicester. RHB WKT.

Ian James Frederick Hutchinson (Shropshire 1985 NWT 1). Born 31.10.1964, Welshpool, Montgomeryshire, Wales. RHB RMF. FC for Middlesex (1988-91). Also ListA for Middlesex (1988-91). Brother: G.M. (CU).

Raymond William Hutchison (Buckinghamshire 1974-75 GC 2, MC South 1974-75 B&H 8). Born 21.7.1944, Dunedin, Otago, New Zealand. LHB SLA. FC for Otago (1965/66-71/72), Central Districts (1975/76). Also ListA for Otago (1965/66-71/72), Central Districts (1975/76).

John Iberson (Hertfordshire 1964-66 GC 2). Born 10.12.1923, Barrow-in-Furness, Lancashire. Died 10.1989, Bromley, Kent. RHB LBG.

Ijaz Ahmed (Durham 1991 NWT 1). Born 20.9.1968, Sialkot, Punjab, Pakistan. RHB LM. 60 Tests (1986/87-00/01) for Pakistan. 250 ODIs (1986/87-00/01) for Pakistan. FC for Gujranwala (1983/84-85/86), Pakistan Automobiles Corporation (1983/84-85/86), Habib Bank (1987/88-00/01), Islamabad (1992/93-00/01), Lahore City (1994/95), Rawalpindi (1998/99), Sialkot (2006/07). Also ListA for Gujranwala (1983/84-85/86), Pakistan Automobiles Corporation (1983/84-85/86), Habib Bank (1987/88-00/01), Islamabad (1992/93-00/01), Lahore City (1994/95), Rawalpindi (1998/99), Sialkot (2006/07). Brother-in-law: Saleem Malik (Essex, Habib Bank, Lahore City, Lahore City A, Lahore City Whites, Sargodha).

Michael John Ikin (Staffordshire 1971-78 GC 7, MC East 1977 B&H 2). Born 31.12.1946, Bignall End, Staffordshire. LHB OB. FC for MC (1972-79). Also ListA for MC (1972-79). Father: J.T. (Lancashire, MCC, MC, Staffordshire), grandfather: A.W. (Staffordshire).

Aamir Ikram (Wales MC 1993 NWT 1). Born 12.1.1960, Lahore, Punjab, Pakistan. RHB LB.

Richard Keith Illingworth (Worcestershire CB 2002 C&G 2). Born 23.8.1963, Greengates, Bradford, Yorkshire. RHB SLA. 9 Tests (1991-95/96) for England. 25 ODIs (1991-95/96) for England. FC for Worcestershire (1982-00), Natal (1988/89), Natal B (1988/89), MCC (1991), Derbyshire (2001). Also ListA for Worcestershire (1982-00), Natal (1988/89), Natal B (1988/89), MCC (1991), Derbyshire (2001).

Nigel John Ilott (Hertfordshire 1993 NWT 1). Born 22.8.1965, Watford, Hertfordshire. RHB. Brother: M.C. (Essex, Hertfordshire).

Mohammad Imran Tahir (Staffordshire 2004-05 C&G 2). Born 27.3.1979, Lahore, Punjab, Pakistan. RHB LBG. FC for Lahore City (1996/97-97/98), Water and Power Development Authority (1998/99), REDCO Pakistan (1999/00), Lahore Whites (2000/01), Sui Northern Gas Pipelines (2001/02-03/04), Sialkot (2002/03), Middlesex (2003), Lahore Blues (2004/05), Pakistan International Airlines (2004/05-06/07), Lahore Ravi (2005/06), Yorkshire (2007), Titans (2007/08-08/09), Hampshire (2008). Also ListA for Lahore City (1996/97-97/98), Water and Power Development Authority (1998/99), REDCO Pakistan (1999/00), Lahore Whites (2000/01), Sui Northern Gas Pipelines (2001/02-03/04), Sialkot (2002/03), Middlesex (2003), Lahore Blues (2004/05), Pakistan International Airlines (2004/05-06/07), Lahore Ravi (2005/06), Yorkshire (2007), Titans (2007/08-08/09), Hampshire (2008).

John Darling Inchmore (Wiltshire 1987 NWT 1). Born 22.2.1949, Ashington, Northumberland. RHB RFM. FC for Worcestershire (1973-86), Northern Transvaal (1976/77). Also ListA for Worcestershire (1973-86), Northern Transvaal (1976/77).

Michael John Ingham (Cumberland 1996 NWT 1). Born 20.2.1957, Accrington, Lancashire. RHB.

Peter Geoffrey Ingham (Northumberland 1984 NWT 1). Born 28.9.1956, Beauchief, Sheffield, Yorkshire. RHB OB. FC for Yorkshire (1979-81). Also ListA for Yorkshire (1979-81).

Russell Inglis (Durham 1964-73 GC 8). Born 13.6.1936, Blackhill, Consett, Co Durham. Died 28.4.1982, Gosforth, Newcastle upon Tyne, Northumberland. RHB RM. FC for MC (1965-69). Also ListA for MC (1965-69).

Lee Royston Ingram (Huntingdonshire 1999-00 NWT 3). Born 10.1.1965, Cambridge. RHB LFM.

Dale Lee Iniff (Northamptonshire CB 1999 NWT 1). Born 18.9.1977, Penrith, Cumberland. RHB LM.

Kevin John Innes (Bedfordshire 2005 C&G 1). Born 24.9.1975, Wellingborough, Northamptonshire. RHB RM. FC for Northamptonshire (1994-01), Sussex (2002-04). Also ListA for Northamptonshire (1994-01), Sussex (2002-04).

Richard Francis Innes (Norfolk 1983 NWT 1). Born 31.8.1953, Aberdeen, Scotland. RHB RMF.

Hesham Iqbal (Kent CB 1999-03 C&G 4 NWT 4). Born 19.1.1975, Farnborough, Kent. RHB RM. Father: Asif Iqbal (Hyderabad, Karachi, Karachi A, Karachi Blues, Karachi Whites, Kent, MCC, National Bank of Pakistan, Pakistan International Airlines, Pakistan International Airlines A, Pakistan International Airlines B, Sind).

Zahid Iqbal (Nottinghamshire CB 1999-02 C&G 1 NWT 1). Born 11.2.1981, Nottingham. RHB RFM.

John Jacklin (Cambridgeshire 1975 GC 1). Born 12.12.1947, Cambridge. RHB RFM.

Andrew Fitz Donald Jackman (Nottinghamshire CB 1999-02 C&G 2 NWT 2). Born 27.1.1963, Georgetown, Demerara, Guyana. RHB OB. FC for Demerara (1981/82-89/90), Guyana (1983/84-90/91). Also ListA for Demerara (1981/82-89/90), Guyana (1983/84-90/91).

Barry Scott Jackson (Berkshire 1986-94 NWT 4). Born 13.9.1966, Maidenhead, Berkshire. RHB RMF.

David Christopher Jackson (Durham 1983-85 NWT 4). Born 29.6.1953, Alnwick, Northumberland. RHB.

Richard Neville Jackson (Sussex CB 2001 C&G 4). Born 8.12.1979, Sittingbourne, Kent. RHB OB.

Charles Milne Jaggard (Buckinghamshire 1997 NWT 1). Born 22.5.1973, Chalfont St Peter, Buckinghamshire. LHB.

Kafeel Jahangir (Hertfordshire 1993-00 NWT 5, MC 1995 B&H 1). Born 22.5.1971, Karachi, Sind, Pakistan. RHB RFM.

Brian George James (Staffordshire 1973 GC 2). Born 21.3.1941, Wolverhampton, Staffordshire. Died 6.11.2002, Wolverhampton, Staffordshire. RHB RFM.

Gareth David James (Essex CB 2002-03 C&G 2). Born 1.12.1984, Walthamstow, Essex. RHB LB. FC for Cambridge UCCE (2004-07), Tamil Union (2005/06). Also ListA for Cambridge UCCE (2004-07), Tamil Union (2005/06). Brother: P.B.C. (Devon).

Martin Henry James (Hertfordshire 1993-02 C&G 4 NWT 5). Born 26.10.1963, Enfield, Middlesex. LHB Occ WKT. Brother: K.D. (Hampshire, Middlesex, Wellington).

Peter Martin James (Surrey CB 1999-00 NWT 3). Born 4.10.1971, Kensington, London. RHB WKT.

Imran Jamshed (Worcestershire CB 2002-03 C&G 3). Born 31.12.1973, Sialkot, Punjab, Pakistan. RHB RM.

David Allan Janes (Buckinghamshire 1965-72 GC 4). Born 15.1.1944, Beaconsfield, Buckinghamshire. Died 15.9.1987, London. LHB.

Graham Maurice Jarrett (Bedfordshire 1967-77 GC 7). Born 9.2.1937, Bedford. Died 4.2004, North Devon. RHB LB. FC for MC (1971-74). Also ListA for MC (1971-74).

Kevin Bertram Sidney Jarvis (Herefordshire 1995 NWT 1). Born 23.4.1953, Dartford, Kent. RHB RFM. FC for Kent (1975-87), Gloucestershire (1988-90). Also ListA for Kent (1975-87), Gloucestershire (1988-90).

Paul Anthony Jeacock (Oxfordshire 1999-01 C&G 2 NWT 2). Born 25.4.1963, Bicester, Oxfordshire. RHB OB.

Martin Jean-Jacques (Buckinghamshire 1984-85 NWT 2). Born 2.7.1960, Soufriere, Dominica. RHB RMF. FC for Derbyshire (1986-92), Hampshire (1993-94). Also ListA for Derbyshire (1986-92), Hampshire (1993-94).

Richard Ingleby Jefferson (Norfolk 1968-70 GC 3, MC North 1972 B&H 3). Born 15.8.1941, Frimley Green, Surrey. RHB RMF. FC for CU (1961), Surrey (1961-66), MCC (1963), MC (1969). Also ListA for CU (1961), Surrey (1961-66), MCC (1963), MC (1969). Son: W.I. (Durham UCCE, Essex, Norfolk, Nottinghamshire).

Brian Reginald Jeffries (Oxfordshire 1972-75 GC 3, MC South 1974-75 B&H 6, MC West 1978 B&H 2). Born 1.10.1946, Banbury, Oxfordshire. RHB RM.

Austin Cedric Jelfs (Lincolnshire 1991 NWT 1). Born 29.8.1949, Evesham, Worcestershire. RHB RM.

Martin Peter Jenkin (Cornwall 2002 C&G 1). Born 1.3.1975, Redruth, Cornwall. LHB.

Lewis James Philip Jenkins (Kent CB 2001 C&G 4). Born 15.11.1981, Canterbury, Kent. RHB SLA.

Paul Edward Jenkins (Wales MC 1999 NWT 1). Born 8.2.1972, Gloucester. RHB SLA.

Stefan Hefin Gravell Jenkins (Wales MC 1998-99 NWT 3). Born 17.4.1974, Carmarthen, Wales. RHB OB,RM.

Steven Paul Jenkins (Somerset CB 1999-00 NWT 2). Born 30.5.1978, Taunton, Somerset. RHB WKT.

Terrence James Jenner (Cambridgeshire 1972 GC 1). Born 8.9.1944, Mount Lawley, Perth, Western Australia, Australia. RHB LBG. 9 Tests (1970/71-75/76) for Australia. 1 ODI (1974/75) for Australia. FC for Western Australia (1963/64-66/67), South Australia (1967/68-76/77). Also ListA for Western Australia (1963/64-66/67), South Australia (1967/68-76/77).

Craig James Robert Jennings (Northamptonshire CB 2001 C&G 1). Born 13.11.1984, Rugeley, Staffordshire. RHB RFM. FC for Northamptonshire (2004). Also ListA for Northamptonshire (2004).

Robert Alan Jennings (Gloucestershire CB 2001 C&G 1). Born 28.2.1977, Bristol. RHB WKT.

Richard Simon Jerome (Hertfordshire 2000 NWT 1). Born 4.4.1968, Edgware, Middlesex. RHB OB.

Jamie Francis Jervis (Staffordshire 2001 C&G 1). Born 5.8.1980, Stoke-on-Trent, Staffordshire. LHB OB.

Richard Martin Jervis (Staffordshire 1999 NWT 1). Born 12.10.1976, Newcastle-under-Lyme, Staffordshire. RHB RFM.

Patrick Michael Jobson (Oxfordshire 1989-94 NWT 6). Born 4.4.1967, Oxford. RHB RM.

David Frank Victor Johns (Buckinghamshire 1965 GC 1). Born 27.6.1921, Paddington, London. Died 20.11.1979, High Wycombe, Buckinghamshire. LHB SLA. FC for MC (1953). Also ListA for MC (1953).

Philip Ivor Johns (Cornwall 1977-80 GC 2). Born 21.7.1956, Fowey, Cornwall. RHB RFM.

Robert Leslie Johns (Hertfordshire 1976-83 GC 3 NWT 2, MC West 1977 B&H 1, MC South 1979 B&H 3, MC 1980 B&H 1). Born 30.6.1946, Southampton, Hampshire. RHB OB. FC for OU (1970), Northamptonshire (1971). Also ListA for OU (1970), Northamptonshire (1971).

Anthony Alexander Johnson (Northumberland 1971-77 GC 3, Durham 1973 GC 1). Born 30.3.1944, Loughborough, Leicestershire. RHB RFM. FC for Nottinghamshire (1963-66), MC (1974). Also ListA for Nottinghamshire (1963-66), MC (1974).

Andy Neil Johnson (Shropshire 1989-01 C&G 1 NWT 7). Born 30.8.1964, Wolverhampton, Staffordshire. RHB.

David Johnson (Lincolnshire 1966-67 GC 2). Born 23.8.1944, Dowsby, Bourne, Lincolnshire. RHB.

Graham Johnson (Durham 1984-87 NWT 5). Born 1.5.1958, Hetton, Co Durham. LHB RFM.

John Stephen Johnson (Shropshire 1974-89 GC 3 NWT 4, MC East 1978 B&H 3, MC North 1979 B&H 4, MC 1980 B&H 2). Born 7.7.1944, Belle Vue, Doncaster, Yorkshire. RHB. FC for MC (1979).

Peter David Johnson (MC East 1978 B&H 1, MC 1980-82 B&H 8). Born 12.11.1949, Sherwood, Nottingham. RHB LBG. FC for CU (1970-72), Nottinghamshire (1970-77), MC (1979-81). Also ListA for CU (1970-72), Nottinghamshire (1970-77).

Richard Kurt Johnson (Surrey CB 2001-02 C&G 3). Born 4.7.1979, Croydon, Surrey. LHB RF.

Terry Johnson (Lincolnshire 1971-76 GC 5). Born 28.6.1941, Grantham, Lincolnshire. RHB.

William Johnson (Durham 1988 NWT 1). Born 27.2.1959, Sunderland, Co Durham. RHB OB.

William Robert Johnson (Wiltshire 1989 NWT 1). Born 7.10.1962, Iserlohn, Germany. RHB WKT.

David Johnston (MC South 1975 B&H 1, Berkshire 1976-79 GC 2, MC West 1976 B&H 3). Born 17.4.1943, Blackpool, Lancashire. RHB LB.

John Johnston (Durham 1977-89 GC 1 NWT 7). Born 15.2.1953, Chesterfield, Derbyshire. Died 2.6.2008, Stockton-on-Tees, Co Durham. RHB RMF.

Arwyn Jones (Oxfordshire 1996 NWT 1). Born 2.7.1971, Devizes, Wiltshire. LHB SLA.

Andrew James Jones (Wales MC 1993-05 C&G 5 NWT 8, MC 1998 B&H 3). Born 5.8.1972, Swansea, Glamorgan, Wales. RHB. Father: A. (Glamorgan, MCC, Natal, Northern Transvaal, Western Australia), uncle: E.W. (Glamorgan).

Andrew James Jones (Staffordshire 2000 NWT 1). Born 30.11.1977, Stoke-on-Trent, Staffordshire. RHB RFM.

Christopher Jones (Cambridgeshire 2001-04 C&G 3). Born 28.9.1973, Stamford, Lincolnshire. RHB SLA.

Charles Ian McMillan Jones (Hertfordshire 1969 GC 2). Born 11.10.1934, Woodhouse, Leeds, Yorkshire. RM. FC for CU (1959). Also ListA for CU (1959).

Craig Michael Parry Jones (Middlesex CB 2002 C&G 2). Born 13.4.1978, Tamworth, New South Wales, Australia. RHB RMF. FC for Middlesex (2005). Also ListA for Middlesex (2005).

Gwynne Auld Jones (Buckinghamshire 1972-79 GC 4, MC South 1975 B&H 1, MC West 1976 B&H 2). Born 23.4.1945, Zimbabwe. RHB RFM.

Huw Rhys Jones (Warwickshire CB 2001-02 C&G 2). Born 23.11.1980, Oxford. RHB LB. FC for Oxford UCCE (2001-03). Also ListA for Oxford UCCE (2001-03).

Ian Jones (Somerset CB 2001 C&G 1). Born 11.3.1977, Edmonton, Middlesex. RHB RFM. FC for Somerset (1999), Middlesex (2002). Also ListA for Somerset (1999), Middlesex (2002).

John Bryan Richardson Jones (Shropshire 1983-02 C&G 5 NWT 15). Born 21.5.1961, Shrewsbury, Shropshire. LHB RM. Brother: B.J.R. (Shropshire, Worcestershire).

Jefferson Harcourt Jones (Berkshire 1976-92 GC 2 NWT 9). Born 6.1.1954, Christ Church, Barbados. RHB RFM.

Keith Vaughan Jones (MC South 1975 B&H 4, MC West 1976-77 B&H 7, Bedfordshire 1977-82 GC 1 NWT 1). Born 28.3.1942, Park Royal, Middlesex. RHB RM. FC for Middlesex (1967-74), MC (1976). Also ListA for Middlesex (1967-74), MC (1976).

Lyndon Owain Jones (Wales MC 2000-02 C&G 3 NWT 2). Born 8.11.1976, Newport, Monmouthshire, Wales. RHB OB.

Peter Henry Jones (Suffolk 1978-81 GC 3 NWT 1). Born 19.6.1935, Woolwich, London. Died 29.12.2007, Tattenhall, Wolverhampton, Staffordshire. LHB SLA. FC for Kent (1953-67), MCC (1961). Also ListA for Kent (1953-67), MCC (1961).

Philip Steffan Jones (Wales MC 1994 NWT 1). Born 9.2.1974, Llanelli, Carmarthenshire, Wales. RHB RFM. FC for CU (1997), Somerset (1997-08), Northamptonshire (2004-05), Derbyshire (2006). Also ListA for CU (1997), Somerset (1997-08), Northamptonshire (2004-05), Derbyshire (2006).

Russell Jones (Devon 2001 C&G 1). Born 21.9.1980, Taunton, Somerset. RHB RM.

Robert Alexander Jones (Buckinghamshire 2002 C&G 1). Born 11.5.1981, Enfield, Middlesex. LHB OB.

Robin Owen Jones (Middlesex CB 1999-00 NWT 3). Born 4.10.1973, Crewe, Cheshire. RHB OB. FC for CU (1996-97). Also ListA for CU (1996-97). Brother: G.W. (CU).

Timothy David Jones (Essex CB 1999-00 NWT 3). Born 26.4.1978, North Shields, Northumberland. RHB RM.

Anthony Mervyn Jorden (Bedfordshire 1977 GC 1). Born 28.1.1947, Radlett, Hertfordshire. RHB RFM. FC for Essex (1966-70), CU (1968-70). Also ListA for Essex (1966-70), CU (1968-70).

John Richard Jordison (Derbyshire CB 2001 C&G 2). Born 18.6.1981, Nottingham. RHB RM. FC for Cambridge UCCE (2002). Also ListA for Cambridge UCCE (2002).

Bhavin Joshi (Warwickshire CB 2001 C&G 2). Born 9.11.1983, Coventry, Warwickshire. RHB LB.

Pierre Joubert (Suffolk 2003 C&G 1). Born 2.5.1978, Pretoria, Transvaal, South Africa. RHB RFM. FC for Northern Transvaal B (1995/96), Northern Transvaal (1996/97), Northerns (1997/98-06/07), Northerns B (1997/98-98/99), Titans (2006/07-08/09). Also ListA for Northern Transvaal B (1995/96), Northern Transvaal (1996/97), Northerns (1997/98-06/07), Northerns B (1997/98-98/99), Titans (2006/07-08/09).

Gary Steven Joyce (Kent CB 1999 NWT 3). Born 20.10.1964, Frome, Somerset. RHB WKT.

Sean Graham Joyner (Oxfordshire 1992-96 NWT 4). Born 2.3.1968, Banbury, Oxfordshire. RHB RFM.

Shane John Jurgensen (Sussex CB 1999 NWT 1). Born 28.4.1976, Redcliffe, Queensland, Australia. RHB RFM. FC for Western Australia (1998/99), Tasmania (2000/01-02/03),

Queensland (2003/04-06/07). Also ListA for Western Australia (1998/99), Tasmania (2000/01-02/03), Queensland (2003/04-06/07).

Gurdeep Singh Kandola (Worcestershire CB 2001-03 C&G 5). Born 6.3.1980, Forest Gate, London. RHB LB.

Rahim Karim (Nottinghamshire CB 2000 NWT 1). Born 8.4.1978, Nottingham. RHB RFM.

Kashif Ibrahim (Sussex CB 2000 NWT 2). Born 16.11.1977, Karachi, Sind, Pakistan. RHB RM. FC for Karachi Whites (1996/97-00/01), Karachi (1997/98), Karachi Blues (1998/99), Pakistan National Shipping Corporation (1999/00). Also ListA for Karachi Whites (1996/97-00/01), Karachi (1997/98), Karachi Blues (1998/99), Pakistan National Shipping Corporation (1999/00).

Richard Ian Kaufman (Northamptonshire CB 2000-01 C&G 1 NWT 1, Oxfordshire 2003 C&G 1). Born 25.12.1980, Kettering, Northamptonshire. RHB OB.

Michael John Kay (Huntingdonshire 2001-02 C&G 3). Born 30.10.1981, Bristol. LHB RM.

Reginald Leslie Keates (Dorset 2002-04 C&G 3). Born 27.6.1980, Johannesburg, Transvaal, South Africa. RHB OB.

Matthew Keech (Dorset 2001 C&G 1). Born 21.10.1970, Hampstead, London. RHB RM. FC for Middlesex (1991-93), Hampshire (1994-99). Also ListA for Middlesex (1991-93), Hampshire (1994-99).

Simon David Kelk (Lincolnshire 1988 NWT 1). Born 2.2.1966, Grimsby, Lincolnshire. RHB RM.

Martin Jon Kellaway (Yorkshire CB 2001-02 C&G 2). Born 12.8.1970, Southampton, Hampshire. RHB WKT.

Simon Andrew Kellett (Cambridgeshire 1996-03 C&G 5 NWT 6). Born 16.10.1967, Mirfield, Yorkshire. RHB RM. FC for Yorkshire (1989-95), Wellington (1991/92). Also ListA for Yorkshire (1989-95), Wellington (1991/92).

Patrick Arthur Charles Kelly (Cheshire 1964-68 GC 4). Born 1.1.1929, Ilford, Essex. Died 21.6.2002, Macclesfield, Cheshire. RHB LB.

Justin Miles Kemp (Worcestershire CB 2003 C&G 1). Born 2.10.1977, Queenstown, Cape Province, South Africa. RHB RFM. 4 Tests (2000/01-05/06) for South Africa. 6 ODIs (2005/06-07) for African XI, 79 ODIs (2000/01-07/08) for South Africa. 8 Int2020s (2005/06-07/08) for South Africa. FC for Eastern Province B (1996/97), Eastern Province (1997/98-02/03), Worcestershire (2003), Northerns (2003/04-04/05), Titans (2004/05-06/07), Kent (2005-08), Cape Cobras (2007/08). Also ListA for Eastern Province B (1996/97), Eastern Province (1997/98-02/03), Worcestershire (2003), Northerns (2003/04-04/05), Titans (2004/05-06/07), Kent (2005-08), Cape Cobras (2007/08). Grandfather: J.M. (Border), father: J.W. (Border).

Charles Peter Cartwright Kendall (Cornwall 1970-75 GC 2 GC 2). Born 29.12.1938, Penryn, Cornwall. LHB RFM.

Neil Michael Kendrick (Berkshire 1997 NWT 1, Surrey CB 1999 NWT 1). Born 11.11.1967, Bromley, Kent. RHB SLA. FC for Surrey (1988-94), Glamorgan (1994/95-96). Also ListA for Surrey (1988-94), Glamorgan (1994/95-96).

Stratford Garfield Kenlock (Surrey CB 1999-00 NWT 3). Born 16.4.1965, Portland, Jamaica. LHB LFM. FC for Surrey (1994-96). Also ListA for Surrey (1994-96).

Andrew Kennedy (Dorset 1983-87 NWT 3, MC 1983 B&H 3). Born 4.11.1949, Billinge End, Blackburn, Lancashire. LHB RM. FC for Lancashire (1970-82). Also ListA for Lancashire (1970-82).

Andrew Kennedy (Essex CB 2001-03 C&G 3). Born 10.1.1975, Colchester, Essex. RHB RMF.

James Kennedy (Durham 1967-68 GC 2). Born 31.8.1932, Hartlepool, Co Durham. Died 21.2.2007, Hartlepool, Co Durham. LHB SLA.

Jonathan Peter Kent (Cornwall 1995-03 C&G 7 NWT 4). Born 3.9.1973, St Colomb, Truro, Cornwall. LHB RM Occ WKT.

Richard Keith Kenway (Hampshire CB 2001 C&G 2). Born 17.7.1975, Southampton, Hampshire. RHB. Brother: D.A. (Hampshire, Hampshire CB).

Daniel Harry Kerry (Dorset 2002 C&G 1). Born 10.1.1982, Poole, Dorset. RHB RMF.

Richard Allan Kettleborough (Yorkshire CB 2000 NWT 2). Born 15.3.1973, Sheffield, Yorkshire. LHB RM. FC for Yorkshire (1994-97), Middlesex (1998-99). Also ListA for Yorkshire (1994-97), Middlesex (1998-99).

Aamer Ali Khan (Cambridgeshire 2001 C&G 2). Born 5.11.1969, Lahore, Punjab, Pakistan. RHB LB Occ WKT. FC for Rawalpindi (1987/88), Middlesex (1995), Sussex (1997-98), Leicestershire (1999). Also ListA for Rawalpindi (1987/88), Middlesex (1995), Sussex (1997-98), Leicestershire (1999).

Rawait Mahmood Khan (Derbyshire CB 2000 NWT 1). Born 5.3.1982, Birmingham, Warwickshire. RHB RM. FC for Derbyshire (2001-03), Pakistan Customs (2002/03-07/08). Also ListA for Derbyshire (2001-03), Pakistan Customs (2002/03-07/08). Brother: Z.M. (Derbyshire).

Wasim Gulzar Khan (Warwickshire CB 2002 C&G 1). Born 26.2.1971, Birmingham, Warwickshire. LHB LB. FC for Warwickshire (1995-97), Sussex (1998-00), Derbyshire (2001). Also ListA for Warwickshire (1995-97), Sussex (1998-00), Derbyshire (2001).

David Aaron Kidner (Dorset 2000-04 C&G 2 NWT 1). Born 13.3.1982, Bristol. RHB LF.

Paul Daniel King (Suffolk 2000-05 C&G 3 NWT 1). Born 25.2.1979, Ipswich, Suffolk. RHB RFM.

Robert David King (Staffordshire 2004 C&G 1). Born 10.7.1978, Stoke-on-Trent, Staffordshire. RHB OB.

Richard Eric King (Northamptonshire CB 2001-02 C&G 2). Born 3.1.1984, Hitchin, Hertfordshire. RHB LMF. FC for Loughborough UCCE (2003-08), Northamptonshire (2005), MCC (2007). Also ListA for Loughborough UCCE (2003-08), Northamptonshire (2005), MCC (2007).

Raymond Kingshott (Norfolk 1990-92 NWT 3). Born 13.1.1957, Merriwa, Australia. LHB SLA.

James Howard Kingstone (Berkshire 2004 C&G 1). Born 10.2.1982, Reading, Berkshire. RHB WKT.

Christopher Richard Granville Kippax (Cumberland 2002 C&G 1). Born 3.5.1969, Leeds, Yorkshire. RHB. Brother: S.A.J. (Cumberland), father: P.J. (Durham, MCC, MC, MC East, Northumberland, Yorkshire).

Peter John Kippax (MC East 1977 B&H 2, Northumberland 1977 GC 2, Durham 1978-87 GC 4 NWT 5). Born 15.10.1940, Huddersfield, Yorkshire. RHB LBG. FC for Yorkshire (1961-62), MCC (1987). Also ListA for Yorkshire (1961-62), MCC (1987). Sons: S.A.J. (Cumberland) and C.R.G. (Cumberland).

Simon Alexander Jonathan Kippax (Cumberland 1995-00 NWT 5). Born 8.5.1964, Leeds, Yorkshire. RHB LBG. Father: P.J. (Durham, MCC, MC, MC East, Northumberland, Yorkshire), brother: C.R.G. (Cumberland).

William Anthony Kirby (Nottinghamshire CB 2000 NWT 1). Born 2.6.1981, Hull, Yorkshire. RHB RM. FC for Durham UCCE (2002). Also ListA for Durham UCCE (2002).

Gary Michael Kirk (Suffolk 1999-02 C&G 7 NWT 2). Born 10.4.1961, Colchester, Essex. RHB RFM.

Christopher George Knight (Hampshire CB 2001 C&G 2). Born 1.12.1972, Taunton, Somerset. RHB RM.

Colin Richard Knight (Cumberland 1992 NWT 1). Born 24.5.1956, Barrow-in-Furness, Lancashire. RHB WKT.

Martin Joseph Knight (Cheshire 2002 C&G 1). Born 5.10.1984, Ashton-under-Lyne, Lancashire. RHB LM.

Roger David Verdon Knight (MC 1988 B&H 2). Born 6.9.1946, Streatham, London. LHB RM. FC for CU (1967-70), Surrey (1968-84), Gloucestershire (1971-75), MCC (1973/74-89), Sussex (1976-77). Also ListA for CU (1967-70), Surrey (1968-84), Gloucestershire (1971-75), MCC (1973/74-89), Sussex (1976-77).

Charles Stuart Knightley (Oxfordshire 1996-03 C&G 3 NWT 2). Born 3.2.1972, Cheltenham, Gloucestershire. LHB Occ WKT.

James Alan Knott (Bedfordshire 2001-05 C&G 9). Born 14.6.1975, Canterbury, Kent. RHB RM WKT. FC for Surrey (1995-98). Also ListA for Surrey (1995-98). Father: A.P.E. (Kent, MCC, Tasmania).

Graham Andrew Knowles (Lancashire CB 2000-02 C&G 4 NWT 2). Born 29.8.1973, Rossendale, Lancashire. RHB. Father: B. (MCC).

Steven Thomas Knox (Cumberland 1996-02 C&G 5 NWT 8). Born 16.2.1974, Barrow-in-Furness, Lancashire. RHB RM. FC for Scotland (2004-07). Also ListA for Scotland (2004-07). Brother: S.R. (Cumberland).

Shitanshu Hargovindbhai Kotak (Warwickshire CB 2002 C&G 1). Born 19.10.1972, Rajkot, Gujarat, India. LHB SLA. FC for Saurashtra (1992/93-08/09). Also ListA for Saurashtra (1992/93-08/09).

Ronald Kotkamp (Hertfordshire 2002 C&G 1). Born 15.4.1972, Dunedin, New Zealand. RHB RFM.

Pallav Kumar (Cumberland 2003 C&G 1). Born 13.7.1981, Patna, Bihar, India. RHB RMF. FC for Durham (2004). Also ListA for Durham (2004).

Abey Kuruvilla (Cheshire 2001 C&G 1). Born 8.8.1968, Mannar, Allepey (now Alappuzha), Kerala, India. RHB RFM. 10 Tests (1996/97-97/98) for India. 25 ODIs (1996/97-97/98) for India. FC for Bombay (1990/91-95/96), Mumbai (1996/97-99/00). Also ListA for Bombay (1990/91-95/96), Mumbai (1996/97-99/00).

Simon James Lacey (Derbyshire CB 2001 C&G 1). Born 9.3.1975, Nottingham. RHB OB Occ WKT. FC for Derbyshire (1997-00). Also ListA for Derbyshire (1997-00).

David James Laitt (Oxfordshire 1967-72 GC 3, MC South 1972-73 B&H 6). Born 3.5.1931, Oxford. Died 27.6.1998, Croydon, Surrey. RHB RM. FC for MC (1959-60). Also ListA for MC (1959-60).

Brian Laity (Cornwall 1970-77 GC 3). Born 20.10.1935, Penzance, Cornwall. Died 22.3.2007, Treliske Hospital, Truro, Cornwall. RHB OB.

Charles Stennett Lamb (Cheshire 1994-01 C&G 2 NWT 2). Born 16.9.1972, Macclesfield, Cheshire. RHB RFM.

Timothy Charles Zerrubabel Lamb (Dorset 1998-04 C&G 2 NWT 1). Born 18.11.1976, Bolton, Lancashire. RHB WKT.

Greg Andrew Lambert (Yorkshire CB 1999 NWT 1). Born 4.1.1980, Stoke-on-Trent, Staffordshire. RHB RM. FC for Yorkshire (2000). Also ListA for Yorkshire (2000).

Thomas Luke Lambert (Berkshire 2001-05 C&G 7). Born 9.5.1981, Ascot, Berkshire. RHB RM.

Stuart Richard Lampitt (Worcestershire CB 2003 C&G 1). Born 29.7.1966, Wolverhampton, Staffordshire. RHB RM. FC for Worcestershire (1985-01). Also ListA for Worcestershire (1985-01).

Peter Martin Lamsdale (Berkshire 1999 NWT 2). Born 11.3.1971, Shifnal, Shropshire. RHB RFM.

Roger Lancaster (Staffordshire 1976 GC 1). Born 4.2.1951, Biddulph, Staffordshire. RHB RFM.

Robert John Lanchbury (Wiltshire 1984-87 NWT 2, MC 1985 B&H 2). Born 11.2.1950, Evesham, Worcestershire. RHB Occ WKT. FC for Gloucestershire (1971), Worcestershire (1973-74), MC (1985). Also ListA for Gloucestershire (1971), Worcestershire (1973-74).

Brian Richard Lander (Durham 1972-82 GC 10 NWT 1, MC North 1973-74 B&H 3, MC East 1976-78 B&H 12). Born 9.1.1942, Bishop Auckland, Co Durham. RHB RM.

Derek Mark Lane (Hertfordshire 1999 NWT 2, Bedfordshire 2003 C&G 1). Born 7.10.1974, Wakefield, Yorkshire. RHB RFM.

Mark Geoffrey Lane (Berkshire 1996-01 C&G 2 NWT 6). Born 26.1.1968, Aldershot, Hampshire. RHB WKT.

Russell Paul Lane (Buckinghamshire 1998-05 C&G 7 NWT 6). Born 23.11.1973, Hayes, Middlesex. LHB RM.

James Howard Langworth (Wales MC 1999-00 NWT 6). Born 24.4.1973, Newport, Monmouthshire. RHB RM WKT.

Robert Derek Large (Northamptonshire CB 2001 C&G 1). Born 23.10.1981, Aylesbury, Buckinghamshire. RHB RM.

Wayne Larkins (Bedfordshire 1997-00 NWT 6, MC 1997 B&H 5, Huntingdonshire 2001 C&G 3). Born 22.11.1953, Roxton, Bedfordshire. RHB RM. 13 Tests (1979/80-90/91) for England. 25 ODIs (1979-90/91) for England. FC for Northamptonshire (1972-91), MCC (1978-89), Eastern Province (1982/83-83/84), Durham (1992-95). Also ListA for Northamptonshire (1972-91), MCC (1978-89), Eastern Province (1982/83-83/84), Durham (1992-95).

James Patrick Thomas Latham (Cambridgeshire 1998 NWT 1). Born 8.10.1975, Hexham, Northumberland. RHB RM. Father: M.E. (Gloucestershire, Northumberland, Somerset).

Michael Edward Latham (Northumberland 1971 GC 1). Born 14.1.1939, Birmingham, Warwickshire. RHB RFM. FC for Somerset (1961-62). Also ListA for Somerset (1961-62). Son: J.P.T. (Cambridgeshire).

Stewart Vernon Laudat (Oxfordshire 1991-02 C&G 3 NWT 7, MC 1996-97 B&H 7). Born 25.2.1971, Oxford. RHB RM.

Simon Allen Launder (Oxfordshire 2002-03 C&G 2). Born 2.12.1978, Swansea, Glamorgan, Wales. RHB RM.

Benjamin James Lawes (Dorset 2001-04 C&G 3). Born 5.4.1982, Weymouth, Devon. RHB.

Allan Lawrence (Cornwall 1977 GC 1). Born 6.2.1951, Penzance, Cornwall. RHB RFM.

Ian Seth Lawrence (Cambridgeshire 1986-89 NWT 4). Born 11.4.1963, Ely, Cambridgeshire. LHB.

John Lawrence (Lincolnshire 1966 GC 1). Born 29.3.1911, Carlton, Leeds, Yorkshire. Died 10.12.1988, Toulston, Tadcaster, Yorkshire. RHB LBG. FC for Somerset (1946-55). Also ListA for Somerset (1946-55). Sons: J.M. (Somerset) and S.T. (Cheshire, Lincolnshire).

William Justus Lawry (Cornwall 1970-80 GC 3). Born 24.4.1940, St Just, Cornwall. LHB WKT. FC for MC (1965-69). Also ListA for MC (1965-69).

Peter James Lawson (Cumberland 2001-02 C&G 3). Born 11.9.1981, Barrow-in-Furness, Lancashire. RHB RFM.

Stewart John Layton (Cambridgeshire 2004 C&G 1). Born 24.4.1981, Wisbech, Cambridgeshire. RHB WKT.

Paul Stuart Lazenbury (Gloucestershire CB 1999 NWT 1, Kent CB 2001 C&G 3, Herefordshire 2002 C&G 2). Born 10.8.1978, Bath, Somerset. LHB LB.

Clive William Leach (Durham 1964 GC 2, Buckinghamshire 1969-70 GC 3). Born 4.12.1934, Almudabad, Bombay (now Mumbai), Maharashtra, India. RHB SLA. FC for Warwickshire (1955-58). Also ListA for Warwickshire (1955-58).

David Leather (Cheshire 1999 NWT 1). Born 25.11.1977, Whiston, Lancashire. RHB RFM.

Daniel Norman Leech (Cheshire 2004 C&G 1). Born 13.4.1981, Crewe, Cheshire. RHB OB. Brother: D.R. (Cheshire).

Antony Orlando Frank le Fleming (Devon 1994-96 NWT 2). Born 7.7.1976, Birmingham, Warwickshire. RHB RM.

Simon Jonathan Legg (Dorset 1989 NWT 1). Born 24.6.1966, Yeovil, Somerset. RHB WKT.

Christopher Paul Lello (Cornwall 1996-00 NWT 3). Born 23.2.1971, Penzance, Cornwall. LHB RM.

Timothy Adam Lester (Oxfordshire 1989-93 NWT 4, MC 1990 B&H 3). Born 25.3.1964, Hampstead, London. RHB. FC for MC (1990).

Christopher Lethbridge (Cambridgeshire 1986-87 NWT 2). Born 23.6.1961, Castleford, Yorkshire. RHB RM. FC for Warwickshire (1981-85). Also ListA for Warwickshire (1981-85).

Colin Lever (Buckinghamshire 1965-75 GC 8). Born 4.8.1939, Todmorden, Yorkshire. RHB RM. FC for MC (1965). Also ListA for MC (1965). Brother: P. (Lancashire, MCC, MC, Tasmania).

Peter John Lewington (MC West 1978 B&H 1, Berkshire 1979-91 GC 1 NWT 5). Born 30.1.1950, Finchampstead, Berkshire. RHB OB. FC for Warwickshire (1970-82). Also ListA for Warwickshire (1970-82).

Andrew Stuart Lewis (Hertfordshire 2003 C&G 1). Born 6.7.1976, Enfield, Middlesex. RHB.

James Christopher Mansel Lewis (Norfolk 1990-92 NWT 2). Born 3.10.1967, Ditchingham, Norfolk. LHB RFM.

John Martin Lewis (Cumberland 1999-02 C&G 4 NWT 5). Born 29.9.1969, Barrow-in-Furness, Lancashire. RHB RM.

Richard Victor Lewis (MC West 1978 B&H 3, MC South 1979 B&H 3, MC 1980-83 B&H 7, Dorset 1983-86 NWT 2). Born 6.8.1947, Winchester, Hampshire. RHB LB. FC for Hampshire (1967-76), MC (1979-81). Also ListA for Hampshire (1967-76).

Victor Barry Lewis (Dorset 1983-92 NWT 6). Born 9.12.1952, Sherborne, Dorset. RHB WKT.

Martin Gregory Lickley (Berkshire 1983-92 NWT 9). Born 15.8.1957, Windsor, Berkshire. RHB RM.

David George Coutts Ligertwood (Hertfordshire 1991 NWT 1). Born 16.5.1969, Oxford. RHB WKT. FC for Surrey (1992), Durham (1995-96). Also ListA for Surrey (1992), Durham (1995-96).

David Graham Light (MC South 1974 B&H 1). Born 2.3.1944, Luton, Bedfordshire. RHB.

James Edward Guy Lincoln (Kent CB 2001-03 C&G 5). Born 29.10.1981, Ashford, Middlesex. RHB RMF.

Steven John Lines (Bedfordshire 1982-85 NWT 2). Born 16.3.1963, Luton, Bedfordshire. RHB RM. FC for Northamptonshire (1983). Also ListA for Northamptonshire (1983).

Stephen Geoffrey Lishman (Northumberland 1984 NWT 1). Born 21.3.1960, Corbridge, Northumberland. RHB RFM.

Luke Robert John List (Oxfordshire 1999-01 C&G 2 NWT 2). Born 15.2.1977, Banbury, Oxfordshire. RHB RM.

John Wilton Lister (Durham 1983-88 NWT 7). Born 1.4.1959, Darlington, Co Durham. RHB. FC for Derbyshire (1978-79). Also ListA for Derbyshire (1978-79).

John B. Livermore (Wiltshire 1969 GC 1). Born 29.10.1940, Greenford, Middlesex.

Stephen John Berry Livermore (Norfolk 1992-02 C&G 4 NWT 3). Born 8.9.1970, Chippenham, Wiltshire. LHB OB.

Nigel James Llong (Norfolk 2000 NWT 2). Born 11.2.1969, Ashford, Kent. LHB OB. FC for Kent (1990-98). Also ListA for Kent (1990-98).

Barry John Lloyd (Wales MC 1993 NWT 1). Born 6.9.1953, Neath, Glamorgan, Wales. RHB OB. FC for Glamorgan (1972-83). Also ListA for Glamorgan (1972-83). Daughter: H.J. (Central Districts Women, Diamonds, Somerset Women, West Women).

David Lloyd (Cumberland 1984-85 NWT 2). Born 18.3.1947, Accrington, Lancashire. LHB SLA. 9 Tests (1974-74/75) for England. 8 ODIs (1973-80) for England. FC for Lancashire (1965-83), MCC (1973-76). Also ListA for Lancashire (1965-83), MCC (1973-76). Son: G.D. (Cumberland, Lancashire).

Graham David Lloyd (Cumberland 2003 C&G 1). Born 1.7.1969, Accrington, Lancashire. RHB RM. 6 ODIs (1996-98/99) for England. FC for Lancashire (1988-02). Also ListA for Lancashire (1988-02). Father: D. (Cumberland, Lancashire, MCC).

Dennis Gordon Lock (Oxfordshire 1975 GC 2). Born 16.8.1950, Oxford. RHB RM.

Kelvin John Locke (Buckinghamshire 1999-03 C&G 3 NWT 3). Born 4.10.1980, Northampton. RHB SLA WKT.

Mark Christopher Lomas (Lancashire CB 1999-01 C&G 2 NWT 1). Born 14.5.1970, Blackburn, Lancashire. RHB.

Ian Raymond Lomax (Wiltshire 1965-69 GC 2). Born 30.7.1931, Fulham, London. Died 31.7.1996, Deane, Basingstoke, Hampshire. RHB RFM. FC for MC (1960), Somerset (1962), MCC (1963-65). Also ListA for MC (1960), Somerset (1962), MCC (1963-65).

Stephen Richard Lawsell Long (Suffolk 1979 GC 2). Born 19.1.1951, Bury St Edmunds, Suffolk. LHB LB.

Michael Colin Longmore (Staffordshire 2001-02 C&G 3). Born 19.9.1979, Stoke-on-Trent, Staffordshire. RHB.

Alexander Guy Rushworth Loudon (Kent CB 2001 C&G 1). Born 6.9.1980, Westminster, London. RHB OB. 1 ODI (2006) for England. FC for Durham UCCE (2001-03), Kent (2003-04), Warwickshire (2005-07), MCC (2006-07). Also ListA for Durham UCCE (2001-03), Kent (2003-04), Warwickshire (2005-07), MCC (2006-07). Brother: H.J.H. (Durham UCCE, Hampshire CB, Kent CB, MCC).

Hugo John Hope Loudon (Kent CB 2002-03 C&G 2). Born 11.12.1978, Westminster, London. RHB SLA. FC for Durham UCCE (2001). Also ListA for Durham UCCE (2001). Brother: A.G.R. (Durham UCCE, Kent, Kent CB, MCC, Warwickshire).

John Love (Oxfordshire 1967 GC 1). Born 11.3.1937. RHB.

James Derek Love (Lincolnshire 1990-91 NWT 2, MC 1991-92 B&H 6). Born 22.4.1955, Headingley, Leeds, Yorkshire. RHB RM. 3 ODIs (1981) for England. FC for Yorkshire (1975-89), MCC (1978), Scotland (1993). Also ListA for Yorkshire (1975-89), MCC (1978), Scotland (1993).

Gary Edward Loveday (Berkshire 1988-00 NWT 13). Born 15.4.1964, Eton Wick, Windsor, Buckinghamshire. RHB RM.

Christopher Charles Lovell (Cornwall 1986-96 NWT 3). Born 1.6.1967, St Austell, Cornwall. RHB RMF.

David John Lovell (Wales MC 1998-01 C&G 1 NWT 1). Born 16.2.1969, Adelaide, South Australia, Australia. RHB SLA.

Bryan Mellalieu Lowe (Cheshire 1964 GC 1). Born 5.11.1925, Worsley, Manchester, Lancashire. RHB.

David Lowe (Hertfordshire 2001 C&G 3). Born 12.1.1979, Harlow, Essex. RHB. Brother: S.J. (Hertfordshire, Oxford UCCE).

Leslie Lowe (Staffordshire 1975 GC 1). Born 4.2.1948, Knypersley, Staffordshire. RHB RM. Father: L. (Staffordshire).

Stephen James Lowe (Hertfordshire 2001 C&G 2). Born 7.5.1981, Welwyn Garden City, Hertfordshire. LHB LB WKT. FC for Oxford UCCE (2003). Also ListA for Oxford UCCE (2003). Brother: D. (Hertfordshire).

Mark John Lowrey (Middlesex CB 1999 NWT 1). Born 13.9.1971, Hampstead, London. RHB OB. FC for CU (1990-91). Also ListA for CU (1990-91).

David John Lupton (Cumberland 1984 NWT 1). Born 7.8.1948, Millom, Cumberland. RHB RFM.

Ross David Lupton (Herefordshire 2000 NWT 1). Born 6.1.1975, Warwick, Queensland, Australia. RHB RM.

David Frank Lye (Devon 2000-05 C&G 8 NWT 2). Born 11.4.1979, Exeter, Devon. RHB RM.

Richard Lynch (Oxfordshire 2002-03 C&G 2). Born 26.3.1967, Banbury, Oxfordshire. RHB RMF.

Stephen Giles Lynch (Buckinghamshire 1990 NWT 1). Born 2.1.1951, Hillingdon, Middlesex. LHB SLA.

Andrew Walker Lyon (Buckinghamshire 1979-88 GC 1 NWT 5). Born 18.12.1946, Poole, Dorset. RHB OB. Brother: D.W. (Buckinghamshire, Cambridgeshire).

David Walker Lyon (Cambridgeshire 1972 GC 1). Born 2.9.1943, Douglas, Isle of Man. RHB RFM. Brother: A.W. (Buckinghamshire, MCC, Middlesex, MC).

Keith Paul William James McAdam (Buckinghamshire 1969 GC 1). Born 13.8.1945, Edinburgh, Midlothian, Scotland. LHB RAB. FC for CU (1965-66), MCC (1967). Also ListA for CU (1965-66), MCC (1967).

Brendan Joseph McArdle (Staffordshire 1984-89 NWT 2). Born 2.3.1952, Preston, Melbourne, Victoria, Australia. RHB RMF. FC for Victoria (1976/77-78/79). Also ListA for Victoria (1976/77-78/79).

Martin John McCague (Herefordshire 2002-04 C&G 3). Born 24.5.1969, Larne, Co Antrim, Ireland. RHB RF. 3 Tests (1993-94/95) for England. FC for Western Australia (1990/91-91/92), Kent (1991-01). Also ListA for Western Australia (1990/91-91/92), Kent (1991-01).

Richard Charles Arthur Marum McCarthy (Yorkshire CB 2000 NWT 2). Born 21.12.1961, Geelong, Victoria, Australia. RHB RFM. FC for Victoria (1984/85-89/90). Also ListA for Victoria (1984/85-89/90).

Craig Macconacie (Leicestershire CB 2002 C&G 2). Born 10.11.1977, Leicester. RHB RMF.

Stephen McDonald (Warwickshire CB 1999-01 C&G 2 NWT 2). Born 2.10.1974, Birmingham, Warwickshire. RHB OB.

Gerald James McDougall (Cambridgeshire 2002-03 C&G 2). Born 17.1.1967, Manchester, Lancashire. RHB WKT.

Michael Stephen Anthony McEvoy (Cambridgeshire 1982 NWT 1, Suffolk 1985-90 NWT 6). Born 25.1.1956, Jorhat, Assam, India. RHB RM. FC for Essex (1976-81), Worcestershire (1983-84). Also ListA for Essex (1976-81), Worcestershire (1983-84).

Andrew Charles McGarry (Suffolk 2005 C&G 1). Born 8.11.1981, Basildon, Essex. RHB RFM. FC for Essex (1999-07). Also ListA for Essex (1999-07).

Stuart Charles Glyndwr MacGill (Devon 1997-98 NWT 2). Born 25.2.1971, Mount Lawley, Perth, Western Australia, Australia. RHB LBG. 44 Tests (1997/98-08) for Australia. 3 ODIs (1999/00) for Australia. FC for Western Australia (1993/94), New South Wales (1996/97-07/08), Somerset (1997), Nottinghamshire (2002-04). Also ListA for Western Australia (1993/94), New South Wales (1996/97-07/08), Somerset (1997), Nottinghamshire (2002-04). Grandfather: C.W.T. (Western Australia), father: T.M.D. (Western Australia).

Alex Machin (Cornwall 1980 GC 1). Born 17.4.1949, Plymouth, Devon. RHB RM.

Timothy James Machin (Bedfordshire 1977 GC 1). Born 3.12.1948, Godmanchester, Huntingdonshire. RHB.

Andrew James Mack (MC 1990-91 B&H 7). Born 14.1.1956, Aylsham, Norfolk. LHB LM. FC for Surrey (1976-77), Glamorgan (1978-80). Also ListA for Surrey (1976-77), Glamorgan (1978-80).

Andrew Nicholas Mackelworth (Staffordshire 1989 NWT 1, Shropshire 1997 NWT 1). Born 15.5.1963, Wolverhampton, Staffordshire. RHB WKT.

Anthony Edward McKenna (Yorkshire CB 1999-01 C&G 1 NWT 4). Born 19.1.1969, St Anne's-on-Sea, Lancashire. RHB RM.

Patrick Christopher McKeown (Cheshire 2001 C&G 1). Born 1.6.1976, Liverpool, Lancashire. RHB OB. FC for Lancashire (1996-00). Also ListA for Lancashire (1996-00).

Paul Dominic McKeown (Lincolnshire 1990-91 NWT 2). Born 3.5.1962, Oldham, Lancashire. RHB RFM.

Neal Alexander Scott Mackey (Leicestershire CB 2002 C&G 1). Born 10.2.1983, Leicester. RHB RMF.

Andrew Ian MacKinlay (Essex CB 1999-01 C&G 1 NWT 3). Born 21.9.1967, Durban, Natal, South Africa. RHB RFM.

David Stewart Mackintosh (Buckinghamshire 1972-75 GC 3, MC South 1973 B&H 1). Born 18.2.1947, Paisley, Renfrewshire, Scotland. RHB. FC for Scotland (1972). Also ListA for Scotland (1972).

Neil Ralph Charter MacLaurin (Hertfordshire 1989-91 NWT 3). Born 22.3.1966, Welwyn Garden City, Hertfordshire. RHB RM. FC for Middlesex (1988). Also ListA for Middlesex (1988). Father: I.C. (MCC).

Ross Alexander McLean (Northamptonshire CB 2000-02 C&G 1 NWT 1). Born 16.3.1981, Northampton. RHB RFM.

Colin Alan McManus (Norfolk 1968-69 GC 2, MC North 1975 B&H 1). Born 19.9.1943, Norwich, Norfolk. RHB WKT.

Bradley Edward McNamara (Middlesex CB 1999 NWT 1). Born 30.12.1965, Sydney, New South Wales, Australia. RHB RM Occ WKT. FC for New South Wales (1989/90-98/99). Also ListA for New South Wales (1989/90-98/99).

Norman Michael McVicker (Lincolnshire 1966-67 GC 2). Born 4.11.1940, Whitefield, Manchester, Lancashire. Died 19.11.2008, Cleethorpes, Lincolnshire. RHB RFM. FC for MC (1965-67), Warwickshire (1969-73), Leicestershire (1974-76). Also ListA for MC (1965-67), Warwickshire (1969-73), Leicestershire (1974-76).

Ivan Samuel Madray (Lincolnshire 1966-67 GC 2). Born 2.7.1934, Port Mourant, Berbice, Guyana. RHB LB. 2 Tests (1957/58) for West Indies. FC for British Guiana (1954/55-57/58). Also ListA for British Guiana (1954/55-57/58).

Keith Robert Maguire (Staffordshire 1984-86 NWT 3). Born 20.3.1961, Marston Green, Birmingham, Warwickshire. RHB RM. FC for Warwickshire (1982). Also ListA for Warwickshire (1982).

Don Jude Chaminda Mahadanaarachchi (Wales MC 1994 NWT 1). Born 31.10.1973, Colombo, Sri Lanka. RHB OB.

Sajid Iqbal Mahmood (Lancashire CB 2001 C&G 1). Born 21.12.1981, Bolton, Lancashire. RHB RFM. 8 Tests (2006-06/07) for England. 25 ODIs (2004-06/07) for England. 2 Int2020s (2006) for England. FC for Lancashire (2002-08), MCC (2005). Also ListA for Lancashire (2002-08), MCC (2005).

Alexander John Mahoney (Berkshire 1976 GC 1). Born 30.1.1947, Invercargill, Southland, New Zealand. RHB SLA.

Maisam Hasnain (Shropshire 2002 C&G 1). Born 3.2.1977, Karachi, Sind, Pakistan. RHB RM. FC for Pakistan National Shipping Corporation (1995/96-96/97), Karachi Whites (1996/97-04/05), Karachi Blues (1998/99-01/02), Pakistan International Airlines (1999/00-00/01), Karachi Port Trust (2003/04-04/05), Karachi Urban (2005/06). Also ListA for Pakistan National Shipping Corporation (1995/96-96/97), Karachi Whites (1996/97-04/05), Karachi Blues (1998/99-01/02), Pakistan International Airlines (1999/00-00/01), Karachi Port Trust (2003/04-04/05), Karachi Urban (2005/06). Father: Taj-ul-Hasnain (Karachi University).

Mark Makin (Cheshire 2002 C&G 1). Born 19.12.1980, Stockport, Cheshire. RHB WKT.

David John Makinson (Cumberland 1992-95 NWT 3). Born 12.1.1961, Eccleston, Lancashire. RHB LFM. FC for Lancashire (1984-88). Also ListA for Lancashire (1984-88).

Muhammad Nadeem Malik (Nottinghamshire CB 2000 NWT 1). Born 6.10.1982, Nottingham. RHB RMF. FC for Nottinghamshire (2001-07), Worcestershire (2004-07), Leicestershire (2008). Also ListA for Nottinghamshire (2001-07), Worcestershire (2004-07), Leicestershire (2008).

Peter James Malkin (Cambridgeshire 1983 NWT 1). Born 14.12.1951, Plymouth, Devon. RHB SLA.

Steven John Malone (Durham 1986 NWT 1, MC 1986 B&H 3, Dorset 1987 NWT 1, Wiltshire 1990 NWT 1). Born 19.10.1953, Chelmsford, Essex. RHB RFM. FC for Essex (1975-78), Hampshire (1980-84), Glamorgan (1985). Also ListA for Essex (1975-78), Hampshire (1980-84), Glamorgan (1985).

Christopher John Malton (Huntingdonshire 2000-01 C&G 3 NWT 2). Born 10.1.1969, Peterborough. RHB WKT.

James Manger (Oxfordshire 1983-84 NWT 2). Born 10.1.1958, Headington, Oxfordshire. RHB RM. Brother: A.S.W. (Oxfordshire).

Maninder Singh (Shropshire 1988 NWT 1). Born 13.6.1965, Poona (now Pune), Maharashtra, India. RHB SLA. 35 Tests (1982/83-92/93) for India. 59 ODIs (1982/83-92/93) for India. FC for Delhi (1980/81-93/94). Also ListA for Delhi (1980/81-93/94).

Christopher Mann (Durham CB 2001 C&G 1). Born 14.4.1981, South Shields, Co Durham. RHB RM.

John Paul William Mann (Northamptonshire CB 2000-01 C&G 1 NWT 1, Cambridgeshire 2004 C&G 1). Born 25.11.1983, Northampton. RHB LB.

David Manning (Worcestershire CB 1999-03 C&G 6 NWT 2). Born 9.3.1963, Wolverhampton, Staffordshire. RHB OB.

Richard James Mansfield (Surrey CB 2001-02 C&G 3). Born 21.1.1975, Madras (now Chennai), Tamil Nadu, India. RHB OB.

Michael Gerard Maranta (Suffolk 1981 NWT 1). Born 20.3.1961, South Brisbane, Queensland, Australia. RHB LM. FC for Queensland (1982/83-85/86). Also ListA for Queensland (1982/83-85/86).

Kervin Marc (Berkshire 1997 NWT 1, Middlesex CB 2000 NWT 2, Surrey CB 2001 C&G 2, Hertfordshire 2002 C&G 1). Born 9.1.1975, Mon Repos, St Lucia. RHB RF. FC for Middlesex (1994-95), Central Districts (1999/00). Also ListA for Middlesex (1994-95), Central Districts (1999/00).

John George March (Durham 1972-73 GC 4). Born 25.11.1932, Ushaw Moor, Co Durham. LHB SLA.

Christopher Peter Marks (Staffordshire 1971-73 GC 2). Born 17.7.1946, Hanley, Staffordshire. RHB RM. FC for Derbyshire (1967-69). Also ListA for Derbyshire (1967-69).

Paul Andrew Marks (Hampshire CB 2001 C&G 2). Born 30.8.1967, Southampton, Hampshire. RHB RM.

Lee John Marland (Warwickshire CB 2002 C&G 1). Born 21.9.1975, Withington, Manchester, Lancashire. RHB OB.

Christopher Marples (Derbyshire CB 1999-00 NWT 3). Born 3.8.1964, Chesterfield, Derbyshire. RHB OB WKT. FC for Derbyshire (1985-86). Also ListA for Derbyshire (1985-86).

Charles Vernon Lewis Marques (Hertfordshire 1964-66 GC 2). Born 2.10.1923, Enfield, Middlesex. RHB RF.

Joshua Phillip Marquet (Norfolk 2003 C&G 1). Born 3.12.1969, Melbourne, Victoria, Australia. RHB RF. FC for Tasmania (1994/95-97/98). Also ListA for Tasmania (1994/95-97/98).

Adrian John Marsh (Derbyshire CB 1999-01 C&G 1 NWT 3). Born 4.11.1978, Nottingham. LHB RM.

Andrew Michael Marsh (Dorset 1973 GC 1). Born 1.11.1952, Bridport, Dorset. RHB SLA.

Dean Marsh (Shropshire 1993 NWT 1). Born 3.12.1963, Bedworth, Warwickshire. RHB RM.

Paul Michael Marsh (Wiltshire 1993-01 C&G 1 NWT 1). Born 20.12.1966, Bradford-on-Avon, Wiltshire. RHB RM.

Anthony Granville Marshall (Wiltshire 1964-69 GC 3). Born 10.9.1932, Isleworth, Middlesex. Died 5.12.1988, Bristol. RHB RMF. FC for Kent (1950-54), MC (1967). Also ListA for Kent (1950-54), MC (1967).

David Marshall (Lincolnshire 1983-91 NWT 4). Born 18.5.1946, Flixborough, Lincolnshire. RHB SLA.

Hamish John Hamilton Marshall (Buckinghamshire 2003 C&G 1). Born 15.2.1979, Warkworth, Auckland, New Zealand. RHB RM Occ WKT. 13 Tests (2000/01-05/06) for New Zealand. 66 ODIs (2003/04-06/07) for New Zealand. 3 Int2020s (2004/05-05/06) for New Zealand. FC for Northern Districts (1998/99-06/07), Gloucestershire (2006-08). Also ListA for Northern Districts (1998/99-06/07), Gloucestershire (2006-08). Twin brother: J.A.H. (Buckinghamshire, MCC, Northern Districts).

James Andrew Hamilton Marshall (Buckinghamshire 2002-03 C&G 4). Born 15.2.1979, Warkworth, Auckland, New Zealand. RHB RM. 7 Tests (2004/05-08) for New Zealand. 10 ODIs (2004/05-08) for New Zealand. 3 Int2020s (2005/06-08) for New Zealand. FC for Northern Districts (1997/98-08/09). Also ListA for Northern Districts (1997/98-08/09). Twin brother: H.J.H. (Buckinghamshire, Gloucestershire, MCC, Northern Districts).

Paul Arthur Marshall (Staffordshire 1984-85 NWT 2). Born 6.11.1949, Dinnington, Yorkshire. RHB RM.

Simon James Marshall (Cheshire 2001-02 C&G 2). Born 20.9.1982, Birkenhead, Cheshire. RHB LB. FC for CU (2002-04), Cambridge UCCE (2002-04), Lancashire (2005-08). Also ListA for CU (2002-04), Cambridge UCCE (2002-04), Lancashire (2005-08).

Christopher Peter Martin (Shropshire 2005 C&G 1). Born 29.10.1972, Newcastle-under-Lyme, Staffordshire. LHB WKT.

Gary Robert E. Martin (Surrey CB 2002 C&G 2). Born 27.2.1968, Chessington, Surrey. RHB.

Michael Halton Martin (Wiltshire 1964-65 GC 2). Born 11.5.1926, Startley, Wiltshire. LHB RF.

Rajesh Jamandass Maru (Hampshire CB 1999-01 C&G 1 NWT 4). Born 28.10.1962, Nairobi, Kenya. RHB SLA. FC for Middlesex (1980-82), Hampshire (1984-98). Also ListA for Middlesex (1980-82), Hampshire (1984-98).

Marcus James Marvell (MC 1996 B&H 2, Shropshire 2002-03 C&G 3). Born 18.11.1970, Shrewsbury, Shropshire. RHB SLA.

Brian Leslie Marvin (Bedfordshire 1985 NWT 1). Born 21.1.1958, Stamford, Lincolnshire. RHB RMF.

Martin Maslin (Lincolnshire 1966-76 GC 7, MC North 1972-75 B&H 13, MC East 1976 B&H 4). Born 14.3.1942, Grimsby, Lincolnshire. RHB RM,LB. FC for MC (1967-74). Also ListA for MC (1967-74). Father: N. (Lincolnshire), brother: D. (Lincolnshire).

Andrew Mark Mason (Herefordshire 2001 C&G 1). Born 16.3.1979, Worcester. RHB OB.

John Mason (Cumberland 2001-02 C&G 2). Born 6.3.1984, Barrow-in-Furness, Cumbria. RHB RM.

Matthew Barry Mason (Wales MC 2003-05 C&G 3). Born 24.11.1984, Swansea, Glamorgan, Wales. LHB RFM.

Mark Jonathon George Mason (Cambridgeshire 2000-03 C&G 4 NWT 1). Born 12.9.1975, Leicester. RHB RFM.

Robert William Mason (Cumberland 2002-03 C&G 2). Born 19.12.1983, Whitehaven, Cumberland. LHB.

Timothy James Mason (Shropshire 2002-04 C&G 4). Born 12.4.1975, Leicester. RHB OB. FC for Leicestershire (1994-99), Essex (2000-01). Also ListA for Leicestershire (1994-99), Essex (2000-01).

Kevin David Masters (Cambridgeshire 1996 NWT 1, Kent CB 1999-02 C&G 6 NWT 6). Born 19.5.1961, Chatham, Kent. LHB RMF. FC for Kent (1983-84). Also ListA for Kent (1983-84). Son: D.D. (Essex, Kent, Kent CB, Leicestershire).

Barrie Lloyd Matthews (Devon 1969-84 GC 5 NWT 2, MC South 1974 B&H 1). Born 4.8.1943, Ashburton, Devon. RHB.

Robin Birkby Matthews (Oxfordshire 1967-70 GC 2). Born 30.1.1944, Stockton-on-Tees, Co Durham. RHB RM. FC for Leicestershire (1971-73). Also ListA for Leicestershire (1971-73).

Douglas Eric Mattocks (Norfolk 1969-91 GC 1 NWT 6). Born 5.7.1944, Norwich, Norfolk. Died 7.10.1999, Norwich, Norfolk. RHB WKT. FC for MC (1985). Also ListA for MC (1985).

John Kenneth Maunders (Middlesex CB 2001 C&G 1). Born 4.4.1981, Ashford, Middlesex. LHB RM. FC for Middlesex (1999), Leicestershire (2003-07), Essex (2008). Also ListA for Middlesex (1999), Leicestershire (2003-07), Essex (2008).

Andrew David Mawson (Cumberland 1996-98 NWT 3, Suffolk 2002-05 C&G 3). Born 27.10.1974, Workington, Cumberland. RHB LB Occ WKT.

Brian Mayes (Suffolk 1980 GC 1). Born 11.4.1950, Ramsgate, Kent. RHB LBG. Father: R. (Kent, Suffolk).

John Carl Maynard (Norfolk 1994 NWT 1). Born 18.5.1969, Hanleys Road, Gingerland, Nevis. RHB RF. FC for Leeward Islands (1991/92-98/99). Also ListA for Leeward Islands (1991/92-98/99).

Robert Gerald James Meale (Wiltshire 1983-84 NWT 2). Born 18.12.1947, Hammersmith, London. RHB WKT.

Keith Thomas Medlycott (Buckinghamshire 2005 C&G 1). Born 12.5.1965, Whitechapel, London. RHB SLA. FC for Surrey (1984-91), Northern Transvaal B (1988/89), MCC (1989). Also ListA for Surrey (1984-91), Northern Transvaal B (1988/89), MCC (1989).

Paul Meehan (Wiltshire 1972-88 GC 2 NWT 2). Born 12.3.1938, Liverpool, Lancashire. RHB SLA.

Thomas Mees (Worcestershire CB 1999 NWT 1, Warwickshire CB 2001 C&G 3). Born 8.6.1981, Wolverhampton, Staffordshire. RHB RMF. FC for Oxford UCCE (2001-03), Warwickshire (2005). Also ListA for Oxford UCCE (2001-03), Warwickshire (2005).

Christopher Alan Melhuish (Devon 1983 NWT 1). Born 6.1.1955, Exeter, Devon. RHB.

Mohammed Ahmed Meman (Shropshire 1978 GC 1). Born 26.6.1952, Lundazi, Zambia. RHB OB. 1 ODI (1987/88) for Zimbabwe.

Joseph Alan Mence (Berkshire 1965 GC 1). Born 21.4.1921, Hampstead, London. RHB LB. Son: M.D.Mence (Berkshire, Gloucestershire, MCC, MC South, Warwickshire).

Michael David Mence (MC South 1973-75 B&H 6, Berkshire 1976-79 GC 2). Born 13.4.1944, Newbury, Berkshire. LHB RM. FC for Warwickshire (1962-65), Gloucestershire (1966-67), MCC (1966). Also ListA for Warwickshire (1962-65), Gloucestershire (1966-67), MCC (1966). Father: J.A. (Berkshire).

Andrew James Mercer (Lancashire CB 2002 C&G 2). Born 31.5.1979, Blackburn, Lancashire. RHB RFM.

David Jeremy Matthew Mercer (Wiltshire 1983-88 NWT 3, Berkshire 1989-94 NWT 4, Bedfordshire 1998-01 C&G 5 NWT 5). Born 7.5.1962, Warrington, Lancashire. RHB OB Occ WKT.

Ian Pickford Mercer (Norfolk 1965-70 GC 4). Born 30.5.1930, Oldham, Lancashire. RHB RM. FC for MC (1965). Also ListA for MC (1965).

Richard Anthony David Mercer (Durham 1977-86 GC 4 NWT 5, MC North 1979 B&H 2). Born 14.1.1951, Stockholm, Sweden. Died 25.10.1996, Hexham, Northumberland. RHB WKT.

Richard Peter Merriman (Dorset 1986-90 NWT 3, Cambridgeshire 1991-97 NWT 2). Born 12.11.1958, Loughborough, Leicestershire. RHB LB Occ WKT.

William Gerald Merry (Hertfordshire 1977-91 GC 1 NWT 8, MC West 1978 B&H 2, MC 1984-87 B&H 11). Born 8.8.1955, Newbury, Berkshire. RHB RM. FC for Middlesex (1979-82), MC (1985-86). Also ListA for Middlesex (1979-82).

James Herbert Merryweather (Wiltshire 1964-73 GC 5, MC South 1972 B&H 4). Born 2.5.1929, Rowlands Gill, Co Durham. Died 19.2.2000, Bath, Somerset. RHB OB. Son: R.J. (Wiltshire).

Barry Metcalf (Wales MC 1993 NWT 1). Born 30.9.1960, Connahs Quay, Flintshire, Wales. LHB.

Ashley Anthony Metcalfe (Cumberland 1998-03 C&G 4 NWT 6). Born 25.12.1963, Horsforth, Yorkshire. RHB OB. FC for Yorkshire (1983-95), MCC (1987), Orange Free State (1988/89), Nottinghamshire (1996-97). Also ListA for Yorkshire (1983-95), MCC (1987), Orange Free State (1988/89), Nottinghamshire (1996-97). Father-in-law: R.Illingworth (Leicestershire, MCC, Yorkshire).

Colin Peter Metson (Wales MC 2000-04 C&G 6 NWt 3). Born 2.7.1963, Goff's Oak, Hertfordshire. RHB WKT. FC for Middlesex (1981-86), Glamorgan (1987-97), MCC (2001). Also ListA for Middlesex (1981-86), Glamorgan (1987-97), MCC (2001).

James Duncan Meyer (Worcestershire CB 2000 NWT 1). Born 7.3.1966, Wolverhampton, Staffordshire. RHB RM.

David Barrie Middleton (Worcestershire CB 2001 C&G 2). Born 13.10.1965, Bloxwich, Staffordshire. RHB WKT.

Andrew Mildenhall (Wiltshire 1989-90 NWT 2). Born 2.12.1966, Swindon, Wiltshire. RHB RFM.

Andrew John Trevor Miller (Hertfordshire 1988 NWT 1). Born 30.5.1963, Chesham, Buckinghamshire. LHB. FC for OU (1982-85), Middlesex (1983-87). Also ListA for OU (1982-85), Middlesex (1983-87).

Craig Aston Miller (Suffolk 1993-96 NWT 3). Born 24.4.1971, Wanstead, Essex. RHB RFM.

David Richard Miller (Dorset 1999 NWT 1). Born 21.9.1974, Poole, Dorset. RHB Occ WKT.

Geoffrey Miller (Cheshire 1992-94 NWT 3, MC 1993 B&H 1). Born 8.9.1952, Chesterfield, Derbyshire. RHB OB. 34 Tests (1976-84) for England. 25 ODIs (1977-84) for England. FC for Derbyshire (1973-90), MCC (1976/77-82), Natal (1983/84), Essex (1987-89). Also ListA for Derbyshire (1973-90), MCC (1976/77-82), Natal (1983/84), Essex (1987-89).

Geoffrey Vernon Miller (Cambridgeshire 1982-86 NWT 3). Born 18.8.1937, Walsall, Staffordshire. RHB OB.

James Nicholas Miller (Northumberland 2001 C&G 1). Born 18.9.1976, North Shields, Northumberland. RHB.

Martin Graham Miller (Dorset 1999-03 C&G 4 NWT 3). Born 18.3.1972, Poole, Dorset. RHB WKT.

Roger Simon Miller (Dorset 1968 GC 1). Born 16.2.1938, Seaford, Sussex. LHB RFM. FC for MCC (1959). Also ListA for MCC (1959).

Roger Trevor Peter Miller (Hampshire CB 1999-02 C&G 4 NWT 4). Born 23.10.1972, Southampton, Hampshire. RHB RM Occ WKT. Brother: M.C. (Hampshire CB).

Frederick William Millett (Cheshire 1964-68 GC 4, MC North 1972-73 B&H 8). Born 30.3.1928, Macclesfield, Cheshire. Died 30.4.1991, Macclesfield, Cheshire. RHB OB. FC for MC (1960-73). Also ListA for MC (1960-73).

Geoffrey Millman (Bedfordshire 1967-68 GC 3). Born 2.10.1934, Bedford. Died 6.4.2005, Bedford. RHB OB WKT. 6 Tests (1961/62-62) for England. FC for Nottinghamshire (1957-65), MCC (1960-62). Also ListA for Nottinghamshire (1957-65), MCC (1960-62).

Kyle David Mills (Lincolnshire 2001 C&G 1). Born 15.3.1979, Auckland, New Zealand. RHB RM. 18 Tests (2004-08/09) for New Zealand. 92 ODIs (2000/01-08/09) for New Zealand. 9 Int2020s (2004/05-08/09) for New Zealand. FC for Auckland (1998/99-08/09). Also ListA for Auckland (1998/99-08/09).

Robert Alexander Milne (Cambridgeshire 1987-91 NWT 2). Born 13.6.1960, Hackney, London. RHB RM.

Steven Andrew Milner (MC North 1975 B&H 4). Born 22.2.1953, Davyhulme, Manchester, Lancashire. LHB RFM. Brother: S.L. (Cheshire).

Michael Edward Milton (Buckinghamshire 1984-85 NWT 2). Born 28.11.1943, St Pancras, London. RHB SLA.

Malcolm Milward (Staffordshire 1978 GC 1). Born 22.8.1948, Stoke-on-Trent, Staffordshire. RHB RM.

Ryan James Minter (Kent CB 2001-02 C&G 2). Born 24.9.1979, Canterbury, Kent. RHB RMF.

David Alexander Mitchell (Devon 2002 C&G 1). Born 20.2.1980, Carshalton, Surrey. LHB RMF.

Matthew Giles Mixer (Dorset 2003 C&G 1). Born 9.12.1972, North Walsham, Norfolk. LHB LMF.

Timur Mohamed (Suffolk 1979-80 GC 3, MC 1980 B&H 4). Born 7.6.1957, Georgetown, Demerara, Guyana. LHB LB. FC for Guyana (1975/76-86/87), Demerara (1978/79-84/85). Also ListA for Guyana (1975/76-86/87), Demerara (1978/79-84/85). Father: E. (British Guiana, Guyana).

Imraan Mohammad (Gloucestershire CB 2000 NWT 2). Born 31.12.1976, Solihull, Warwickshire. RHB OB. FC for CU (1997-99), Pakistan Customs (1999/00-01/02), Gloucestershire (2000), Hyderabad (2001/02). Also ListA for CU (1997-99), Pakistan Customs (1999/00-01/02), Gloucestershire (2000), Hyderabad (2001/02). Uncle: Hanif Mohammad (Bahawalpur, Karachi, Karachi A, Karachi Whites, Pakistan International Airlines, Pakistan International Airlines A), Wazir Mohammad (Bahawalpur, Karachi, Karachi A, Karachi Blues, Karachi Whites), Mushtaq

Mohammad (Karachi, Karachi A, Karachi Blues, Karachi C, Karachi Whites, MCC, Northamptonshire, Northumberland, Pakistan International Airlines, Pakistan International Airlines A, Peshawar, Shropshire, Staffordshire), father: Sadiq Mohammad (Buckinghamshire, Cornwall, Essex, Gloucestershire, Karachi, Karachi Blues, Karachi Schools, Karachi Whites, MCC, Pakistan International Airlines, Tasmania, United Bank), cousin: Shoaib Mohammad (Karachi, Karachi Blues, Karachi Whites, MCC, Pakistan International Airlines, Pakistan International Airlines B), Asif Mohammad (Faisalabad, Karachi Whites, Pakistan International Airlines, Rawalpindi, Rawalpindi B), uncle: Raees Mohammad (East Pakistan, Karachi, Karachi B, Karachi Blues, Karachi Whites, Peshawar), cousin: Shahid Mohammad (Pakistan International Airlines), Waqar Mohammad (Warwickshire CB).

Mohammad Akhtar (Essex CB 2003 C&G 1). Born 12.12.1977, Gujranwala, Punjab, Pakistan. RHB OB.

Syed Mohammad Ali Bukhari (Wales MC 1999 NWT 1). Born 8.11.1973, Bahawalpur, Punjab, Pakistan. RHB LFM. FC for Lahore City (1993/94), Railways (1993/94), Islamabad (1994/95), United Bank (1994/95), Agriculture Development Bank of Pakistan (1995/96-98/99), Rawalpindi A (1995/96), Bahawalpur (1998/99), Derbyshire (2002-04), Middlesex (2006). Also ListA for Lahore City (1993/94), Railways (1993/94), Islamabad (1994/95), United Bank (1994/95), Agriculture Development Bank of Pakistan (1995/96-98/99), Rawalpindi A (1995/96), Bahawalpur (1998/99), Derbyshire (2002-04), Middlesex (2006). Uncle: Taslim Arif (Karachi, Karachi Blues, Karachi Whites, National Bank of Pakistan, National Bank of Pakistan A, Sind), cousin: Wasim Arif (House Building Finance Corporation, Karachi, Karachi Blues, Karachi Greens, National Bank of Pakistan).

Nadeem Mohammed (Cambridgeshire 1994-01 C&G 1 NWT 4, Middlesex CB 1999 NWT 1). Born 5.9.1968, Peterborough. RHB RM. Twin brother: S. (Cambridgeshire, Huntingdonshire, MCC).

Saleem Mohammed (Cambridgeshire 1994-99 NWT 6). Born 5.9.1968, Peterborough. RHB. Twin brother: N. (Cambridgeshire, Huntingdonshire, Middlesex CB).

Christopher Matti Mole (Sussex CB 1999-02 C&G 4 NWT 1, Devon 2003-05 C&G 4). Born 20.2.1978, Cuckfield, Sussex. LHB WKT.

Dinesh Mongia (Staffordshire 2004 C&G 1). Born 17.4.1977, Chandigarh, India. LHB SLA Occ WKT. 57 ODIs (2000/01-07) for India. 1 Int2020 (2006/07) for India. FC for Punjab (1995/96-06/07), Lancashire (2004), Leicestershire (2005-06). Also ListA for Punjab (1995/96-06/07), Lancashire (2004), Leicestershire (2005-06).

Graham Monkhouse (Cumberland 1987 NWT 1). Born 26.4.1954, Langwathby, Carlisle, Cumberland. RHB RM. FC for Surrey (1981-86). Also ListA for Surrey (1981-86).

Steven Monkhouse (Staffordshire 1989 NWT 1). Born 24.11.1962, Bury, Lancashire. RHB LFM. FC for Warwickshire (1985-86), Glamorgan (1987-88). Also ListA for Warwickshire (1985-86), Glamorgan (1987-88).

Robert David Montgomerie (Oxfordshire 1967-72 GC 3). Born 26.9.1937, Watford, Hertfordshire. RHB LB. Son: R.R. (MCC, Northamptonshire, OU, Sussex).

Harry Ian Moore (Lincolnshire 1971-76 GC 5, MC North 1973-74 B&H 4). Born 28.2.1941, Sleaford, Lincolnshire. RHB RM. FC for Nottinghamshire (1962-69), MC (1973). Also ListA for Nottinghamshire (1962-69), MC (1973).

John David Moore (Staffordshire 1971-78 GC 6, MC North 1975 B&H 4, MC East 1977 B&H 2). Born 19.5.1943, Newcastle-under-Lyme, Staffordshire. RHB RM.

Simon Moore (Essex CB 2000-01 C&G 2 NWT 2). Born 19.6.1973, Harlow, Essex. RHB RFM.

Simon Oliver Moore (Derbyshire CB 1999-02 C&G 1 NWT 1). Born 15.6.1974, Oldham, Lancashire. RHB RM.

Tracey Ian Moore (Norfolk 1965-70 GC 4, MC North 1972-73 B&H 8, MC East 1976 B&H 1). Born 16.12.1941, Ingham, Norfolk. RHB RFM.

David John Mordaunt (Berkshire 1965-76 GC 4). Born 24.8.1937, Chelsea, London. RHB RMF. FC for Sussex (1958-60), MCC (1964). Also ListA for Sussex (1958-60), MCC (1964). Grandfather: G.J. (Kent, MCC, OU), great-grandfather: J.M. (MCC).

Bjorn Haaken David Mordt (Berkshire 2004-05 C&G 2). Born 29.6.1978, Mutare, Zimbabwe. RHB RM.

Gordon Morgan (Suffolk 1984-88 NWT 5). Born 31.8.1959, Kampala, Uganda. RHB RM. Brother: M. (Bedfordshire).

Haydn John Morgan (Devon 1996 NWT 1). Born 5.7.1973, Torquay, Devon. RHB OB. FC for Central Districts (2000/01). Also ListA for Central Districts (2000/01).

John Richard Morgan (Sussex CB 2000-02 C&G 5 NWT 2). Born 16.3.1977, Hastings, Sussex. RHB RMF.

Leon Neil Morgan (Kent CB 2001-03 C&G 3). Born 14.2.1979, Willesborough, Ashford, Kent. RHB.

Michael Morgan (Bedfordshire 1977-85 GC 1 NWT 2). Born 30.9.1952, Edinburgh, Midlothian, Scotland. RHB OB. Brother: G. (Bedfordshire, MCC, Suffolk).

Mark Jonathan Morgan (Buckinghamshire 2000 NWT 1). Born 24.5.1980, Ascot, Berkshire. RHB LB.

Trevor Grahame Anthony Morley (Bedfordshire 1970-73 GC 3). Born 11.8.1933, Hitchin, Hertfordshire. RHB RM.

David Mark Morrell (Norfolk 1992 NWT 1). Born 8.10.1971, Newport, Monmouthshire. RHB WKT.

Graeme Reginald Morris (Northumberland 1986-94 NWT 3). Born 5.2.1963, Newcastle upon Tyne, Northumberland. LHB.

James Calum Morris (Berkshire 2002-03 C&G 2). Born 17.1.1985, Welwyn Garden City, Hertfordshire. RHB LB. FC for Durham UCCE (2005-07), MCC (2007). Also ListA for Durham UCCE (2005-07), MCC (2007). Brother: R.K. (Berkshire, Loughborough UCCE).

Sion Elgan Morris (Wales MC 2002-04 C&G 4). Born 6.9.1977, St Asaph, Flintshire, Wales. LHB.

Ian Stuart Morton (Suffolk 2002-05 C&G 3). Born 14.10.1970, Clacton-on-Sea, Essex. RHB RMF.

Jonathan Moss (Berkshire 2001 C&G 2). Born 4.5.1975, Manly, Sydney, New South Wales, Australia. RHB RM. FC for Victoria (2000/01-06/07), Derbyshire (2004-05). Also ListA for Victoria (2000/01-06/07), Derbyshire (2004-05).

George William Moulds (Derbyshire CB 2001 C&G 2). Born 2.11.1983, Derby. RHB RMF. Brother: B.M. (Derbyshire CB).

John Robert Moyes (Cumberland 1984-89 NWT 6). Born 2.12.1946, Ipswich, Suffolk. RHB OB Occ WKT. Son: J.R. (CU, Cambridge UCCE, Cumberland).

James Robert Moyes (Cumberland 2001 C&G 1). Born 16.12.1974, Workington, Cumberland. RHB WKT. FC for CU (2002), Cambridge UCCE (2002). Also ListA for CU (2002), Cambridge UCCE (2002). Father: J.R. (Cumberland, Suffolk).

Gordon James Muchall (Durham CB 2001 C&G 1). Born 2.11.1982, Newcastle upon Tyne, Northumberland. RHB RM. FC for Durham (2002-08). Also ListA for Durham (2002-08). Brothers: P.B. (Northumberland) and M.J. (Northumberland), grandfather: J.B. (Northumberland).

Mudassar Nazar (Cheshire 1981-88 NWT 5, MC 1985 B&H 2). Born 6.4.1956, Lahore, Punjab, Pakistan. RHB RM. 76 Tests (1976/77-88/89) for Pakistan. 122 ODIs (1977/78-88/89) for Pakistan. FC for Lahore B (1971/72-73/74), Punjab (1973/74), Lahore A (1974/75), Pakistan Universities (1974/75), Habib Bank (1975/76), Pakistan International Airlines (1975/76-77/78), Pakistan International Airlines A (1977/78), United Bank (1978/79-86/87). Also ListA for Lahore B (1971/72-73/74), Punjab (1973/74), Lahore A (1974/75), Pakistan Universities (1974/75), Habib Bank (1975/76), Pakistan International Airlines (1975/76-77/78), Pakistan International Airlines A (1977/78), United Bank (1978/79-86/87). Father: Nazar Mohammad (Muslims, Northern India, Punjab, Punjab University), uncle: Mohammad Sharif (Northern India), cousin: Azmat Hussain (Lahore Greens), brother: Mubashir Nazar (Income Tax Department, Lahore B).

Gareth James Mumford (Shropshire 2001-02 C&G 4). Born 18.6.1982, Bridgnorth, Shropshire. RHB WKT.

Michael Kenneth Munday (Cornwall 2001 C&G 1). Born 22.10.1984, Nottingham. RHB LB. FC for OU (2003-06), Oxford UCCE (2003-06), Somerset (2005-08). Also ListA for OU (2003-06), Oxford UCCE (2003-06), Somerset (2005-08).

James Clifford Thomas Murch (Hertfordshire 2003 C&G 1). Born 8.8.1975, Melbourne, Victoria, Australia. RHB RFM. Father: S.N.C. (Northamptonshire, Victoria).

Anthony John Murphy (Cheshire 1995-99 NWT 4, MC 1997 B&H 3). Born 6.8.1962, Withington, Manchester, Lancashire. RHB RMF. FC for Lancashire (1985-88), Central Districts (1985/86), MC (1986), Surrey (1989-94). Also ListA for Lancashire (1985-88), Central Districts (1985/86), Surrey (1989-94).

Olsen Tzuan Murrain (Leicestershire CB 2001 C&G 2). Born 24.4.1982, Montserrat. RHB RM.

Kevin Stuart Murray (Berkshire 1986-92 NWT 2). Born 3.1.1963, Brisbane, Queensland, Australia. LHB.

Simon Nicholas Murray (Bedfordshire 2000 NWT 1). Born 7.12.1963, Luton, Bedfordshire. RHB OB.

Timothy James Murrills (MC South 1979 B&H 1). Born 22.12.1953, Ecclesall, Sheffield, Yorkshire. RHB RM Occ WKT. FC for CU (1973-76). Also ListA for CU (1973-76). Brothers: S.A. (Cheshire, Oxfordshire) and R.J. (Dorset).

Timothy James Murtagh (Surrey CB 2001 C&G 1). Born 2.8.1981, Lambeth, London. LHB RFM. FC for Surrey (2001-06), Middlesex (2007-08). Also ListA for Surrey (2001-06), Middlesex (2007-08). Uncle: A.J. (Eastern Province, Hampshire), brother: C.P. (Loughborough UCCE, Surrey).

Mushtaq Mohammad (Shropshire 1984-85 NWT 3). Born 22.11.1943, Junagadh, Gujarat, India. RHB LBG. 57 Tests (1958/59-78/79) for Pakistan. 10 ODIs (1972/73-78/79) for Pakistan. FC for Karachi Whites (1956/57-63/64), Karachi C (1957/58), Karachi (1958/59-59/60), Peshawar (1959/60), Pakistan International Airlines (1960/61-81/82), Karachi A (1962/63), MCC (1964), Northamptonshire (1964-77), Karachi Blues (1966/67-67/68), Pakistan International Airlines A (1969/70-70/71). Also ListA for Karachi Whites (1956/57-63/64), Karachi C (1957/58), Karachi (1958/59-59/60), Peshawar (1959/60), Pakistan International Airlines (1960/61-81/82), Karachi A (1962/63), MCC (1964), Northamptonshire (1964-77), Karachi Blues (1966/67-67/68), Pakistan International Airlines A (1969/70-70/71). Brother: Hanif Mohammad (Bahawalpur, Karachi, Karachi A, Karachi Whites, Pakistan International Airlines, Pakistan International Airlines A), Wazir Mohammad (Bahawalpur, Karachi, Karachi A, Karachi Blues, Karachi Whites), Sadiq Mohammad (Buckinghamshire, Cornwall, Essex, Gloucestershire, Karachi, Karachi Blues, Karachi Schools, Karachi Whites, MCC, Pakistan International Airlines, Tasmania, United Bank), nephew: Shoaib Mohammad (Karachi, Karachi Blues, Karachi Whites, MCC, Pakistan International Airlines, Pakistan International Airlines B), I.Mohammad (CU, Cornwall, Gloucestershire, Gloucestershire CB, Hyderabad, Pakistan Customs, Public Works Department), nephew: Asif Mohammad (Faisalabad, Karachi Whites, Pakistan International Airlines, Rawalpindi, Rawalpindi B), brother: Raees Mohammad (East Pakistan, Karachi, Karachi B, Karachi Blues, Karachi Whites, Peshawar), nephew: Shahid Mohammad (Pakistan International Airlines), Waqar Mohammad (Warwickshire CB).

Philip Mustard (Durham CB 2000-03 C&G 3 NWT 3). Born 8.10.1982, Sunderland, Co Durham. LHB WKT. 10 ODIs (2007/08) for England. 2 Int2020s (2007/08) for England. FC for Durham (2002-08). Also ListA for Durham (2002-08). Brother: A. (Durham CB).

Keith Robert Mustow (Oxfordshire 1996-01 C&G 1 NWT 3). Born 26.11.1972, Cirencester, Gloucestershire. LHB.

Alexander James Chandra de Silva Mutucumarana (Huntingdonshire 2001 C&G 1). Born 15.6.1979, Croydon, Surrey. RHB RM.

Simon David Myles (Staffordshire 1992-94 NWT 3, MC 1994-96 B&H 8, Berkshire 1995-02 C&G 1 NWT 5). Born 2.6.1966, Mansfield, Nottinghamshire. RHB RM. FC for Sussex (1987), Warwickshire (1988), MC (1994). Also ListA for Sussex (1987), Warwickshire (1988).

Alan Mynett (Yorkshire CB 1999 NWT 2). Born 5.8.1966, Barnsley, Yorkshire. RHB WKT.

Mohammad Nadeem Khan (Durham CB 2002 C&G 1). Born 10.12.1969, Rawalpindi, Punjab, Pakistan. RHB SLA. 2 Tests (1992/93-98/99) for Pakistan. 2 ODIs (1992/93-94/95) for Pakistan. FC for Karachi (1986/87-88/89), Karachi Blues (1986/87-97/98), Pakistan Universities (1988/89), Karachi Whites (1989/90-98/99), Pakistan Automobiles Corporation (1989/90), National Bank of Pakistan (1991/92-94/95), Pakistan International Airlines (1995/96-02/03). Also ListA for Karachi (1986/87-88/89), Karachi Blues (1986/87-97/98), Pakistan Universities (1988/89), Karachi Whites (1989/90-98/99), Pakistan Automobiles Corporation (1989/90), National Bank of Pakistan (1991/92-94/95), Pakistan International Airlines (1995/96-02/03).

Brother: Moin Khan (Karachi, Karachi Blues, Karachi Dolphins, Karachi Harbour, Karachi Whites, Pakistan International Airlines).

Naeem Akhtar (Cornwall 1999 NWT 1, Derbyshire CB 2002 C&G 1). Born 2.12.1967, Lyallpur (now Faisalabad), Punjab, Pakistan. RHB RFM. FC for Rawalpindi (1990/91-03/04), Rawalpindi A (1994/95), Rawalpindi B (1995/96), Khan Research Laboratories (1997/98-02/03). Also ListA for Rawalpindi (1990/91-03/04), Rawalpindi A (1994/95), Rawalpindi B (1995/96), Khan Research Laboratories (1997/98-02/03).

Ravinder Singh Nagra (Herefordshire 2001-02 C&G 3). Born 29.8.1978, Sandwell, Staffordshire. RHB LFM.

Jigar Kumar Hakumatrai Naik (Leicestershire CB 2002 C&G 2). Born 10.8.1984, Leicester. RHB OB. FC for Leicestershire (2006-08), Loughborough UCCE (2007). Also ListA for Leicestershire (2006-08), Loughborough UCCE (2007).

Aneil Padman Nambiar (Oxfordshire 2003 C&G 1). Born 2.3.1984, Trivandrum (now Thiruvananthapuram), Kerala, India. RHB RM.

Graham Richard Napier (Essex CB 2000 NWT 1). Born 6.1.1980, Colchester, Essex. RHB RM. FC for Essex (1997-08), MCC (2004), Wellington (2008/09). Also ListA for Essex (1997-08), MCC (2004), Wellington (2008/09).

Kevin John Nash (Wiltshire 2000-05 C&G 4 NWT 2). Born 19.10.1975, Derby. RHB RFM.

Malcolm Andrew Nash (Shropshire 1984-85 NWT 3). Born 9.5.1945, Abergavenny, Monmouthshire. LHB LM,SLA. FC for Glamorgan (1966-83). Also ListA for Glamorgan (1966-83).

Mohammad Nasim Khan (Cambridgeshire 2002 C&G 1). Born 1.6.1976, Quetta, Baluchistan, Pakistan. LHB SLA. FC for Pakistan Customs (1999/00-04/05), Quetta (2003/04-08/09), Baluchistan (2007/08-08/09). Also ListA for Pakistan Customs (1999/00-04/05), Quetta (2003/04-08/09), Baluchistan (2007/08-08/09).

Nasim-ul-Ghani (Staffordshire 1971-78 GC 5). Born 14.5.1941, Delhi, India. LHB LM,SLA. 29 Tests (1957/58-72/73) for Pakistan. 1 ODI (1972/73) for Pakistan. FC for Karachi Blues (1956/57), Karachi B (1957/58), Karachi University (1958/59), Pakistan Universities (1958/59), Karachi (1959/60-72/73), Karachi Whites (1961/62-63/64), Karachi A (1962/63), Dacca (1965/66), East Pakistan (1966/67-67/68), Public Works Department (1966/67-71/72), MC (1972), National Bank of Pakistan (1973/74-74/75). Also ListA for Karachi Blues (1956/57), Karachi B (1957/58), Karachi University (1958/59), Pakistan Universities (1958/59), Karachi (1959/60-72/73), Karachi Whites (1961/62-63/64), Karachi A (1962/63), Dacca (1965/66), East Pakistan (1966/67-67/68), Public Works Department (1966/67-71/72), MC (1972), National Bank of Pakistan (1973/74-74/75). Brother: Anis-ul-Ghani (Karachi, Karachi C, Karachi Greens, Karachi Whites, Pakistan Universities, Public Works Department), Atiq-ul-Ghani (Public Works Department), Raees-ul-Ghani (Karachi), Tehzib-ul-Ghani (Commerce Bank).

Rana Naved-ul-Hasan (Herefordshire 2002 C&G 1). Born 28.2.1978, Sheikhupura, Punjab, Pakistan. RHB RFM. 9 Tests (2004/05-06/07) for Pakistan. 62 ODIs (2002/03-06/07) for Pakistan. 2 Int2020s (2006-06/07) for Pakistan. FC for Lahore Division (1999/00), Pakistan Customs (2000/01), Sheikhupura (2000/01-01/02), Allied Bank (2001/02), Water and Power Development Authority (2002/03-06/07), Sialkot (2003/04-05/06), Sussex (2005-07), Punjab (2006/07), Yorkshire (2008). Also ListA for Lahore Division (1999/00), Pakistan Customs (2000/01), Sheikhupura (2000/01-01/02), Allied Bank (2001/02), Water and Power Development Authority (2002/03-06/07), Sialkot (2003/04-05/06), Sussex (2005-07), Punjab (2006/07), Yorkshire (2008).

Steven Paul Naylor (Buckinghamshire 2000-01 C&G 1 NWT 1, Berkshire 2002-05 C&G 4). Born 14.3.1977, Billingham, Co Durham. RHB RFM.

Edward Peter Neal (Hertfordshire 1981-88 NWT 5). Born 2.6.1961, Edinburgh, Midlothian, Scotland. RHB RMF.

Simon Nicholas Neal (Nottinghamshire CB 1999 NWT 1). Born 2.1.1972, Nottingham. RHB RM Occ WKT.

Francis Webb Neate (Berkshire 1965-79 GC 4). Born 13.5.1940, Newbury, Berkshire. RHB. FC for OU (1960-62). Also ListA for OU (1960-62). Brother: P.W. (Berkshire, MCC, OU).

Mark Neave (Northamptonshire CB 2001 C&G 1). Born 11.2.1980, Kettering, Northamptonshire. RHB OB.

Andrew Needham (Hertfordshire 1989-91 NWT 3). Born 23.3.1957, Calow, Derbyshire. RHB OB. FC for Surrey (1977-86), Middlesex (1987-88). Also ListA for Surrey (1977-86), Middlesex (1987-88).

Robert David Nelson (Middlesex CB 2000-02 C&G 1 NWT 2). Born 2.7.1970, Chiswick, Middlesex. LHB OB.

Christopher John Nevin (Hampshire CB 1999 NWT 3). Born 3.8.1975, Dunedin, Otago, New Zealand. RHB WKT. 37 ODIs (1999/00-03/04) for New Zealand. FC for Wellington (1995/96-08/09). Also ListA for Wellington (1995/96-08/09).

Paul Michael New (Berkshire 1983-86 NWT 4). Born 30.9.1953, Wokingham, Berkshire. LHB RMF.

Thomas James New (Leicestershire CB 2001-02 C&G 2). Born 18.1.1985, Sutton-in-Ashfield, Nottinghamshire. LHB WKT. FC for Leicestershire (2004-08), Derbyshire (2008). Also ListA for Leicestershire (2004-08), Derbyshire (2008).

Michael John Newbold (Wales MC 1994-01 C&G 3 NWT 5). Born 6.1.1970, Cardiff, Glamorgan, Wales. RHB LMF.

Oliver James Newby (Lancashire CB 2002 C&G 2). Born 26.8.1984, Blackburn, Lancashire. RHB RFM. FC for Lancashire (2003-08), Nottinghamshire (2005), Gloucestershire (2008). Also ListA for Lancashire (2003-08), Nottinghamshire (2005), Gloucestershire (2008).

Jonathan James Newell (Sussex CB 1999 NWT 1). Born 30.9.1978, Crawley, Sussex. RHB OB. Brothers: M. (Buckinghamshire, Derbyshire, MCC, Sussex, Sussex CB) and K. (Glamorgan, MCC, Matabeleland, Sussex, Wales MC).

Keith Newell (Wales MC 2003-05 C&G 3). Born 25.3.1972, Crawley, Sussex. RHB RM. FC for Sussex (1995-98), Matabeleland (1995/96), Glamorgan (1999-01). Also ListA for Sussex (1995-98), Matabeleland (1995/96), Glamorgan (1999-01). Brothers: M. (Buckinghamshire, Derbyshire, MCC, Sussex, Sussex CB) and J.J. (Buckinghamshire, Sussex CB).

Mark Newell (Sussex CB 1999 NWT 1). Born 19.12.1973, Crawley, Sussex. RHB OB. FC for Sussex (1996-98), Derbyshire (1999). Also ListA for Sussex (1996-98), Derbyshire (1999). Brothers: K. (Glamorgan, MCC, Matabeleland, Sussex, Wales MC) and J.J.(Buckinghamshire, Sussex CB).

Jeremy John Newman (Wiltshire 1983-89 NWT 5). Born 5.6.1962, Malmesbury, Wiltshire. RHB. Brother: N. (Wiltshire).

Paul Geoffrey Newman (Durham 1990 NWT 1, Staffordshire 1991-95 NWT 5, MC 1992-98 B&H 13, Norfolk 1996-03 GC 6 NWT 6). Born 10.1.1959, Evington, Leicester. RHB RFM. FC for Derbyshire (1980-89), MCC (1982), MC (1994). Also ListA for Derbyshire (1980-89), MCC (1982).

Robbie James Newman (Devon 2003 C&G 1). Born 26.2.1981, Birmingham, Warwickshire. RHB OB.

Scott Alexander Newman (Surrey CB 2001 C&G 3). Born 3.11.1979, Epsom, Surrey. LHB RM. FC for Surrey (2002-08). Also ListA for Surrey (2002-08).

Derek George Nicholls (Staffordshire 1976-78 GC 3, MC 1982 B&H 2). Born 18.7.1947, Walsall, Staffordshire. RHB RFM.

Philip James Nicholson (MC 1997-98 B&H 10, Northumberland 1999-05 C&G 4 NWT 4). Born 1.9.1973, Jesmond, Newcastle upon Tyne, Northumberland. RHB WKT.

John Edward MacDonald Nicolson (Cornwall 1995 NWT 1). Born 17.6.1964, Birmingham, Warwickshire. RHB RM.

Benjamin Peter Francis Nolan-Stone (Hampshire CB 2001 C&G 1). Born 13.5.1983, Poole, Dorset. RHB RFM.

David Patrick Norman (Cambridgeshire 1989-00 NWT 7). Born 19.9.1968, Ely, Cambridgeshire. RHB RM.

Jared Simon Gregory Norman (Cambridgeshire 1998-00 NWT 3). Born 28.11.1974, Barnet, Hertfordshire. RHB RM. Brother: A.G. (Cambridgeshire).

Jonathan William Norris (Hampshire CB 2002 C&G 1). Born 28.4.1980, Liss, Hampshire. RHB RM WKT.

Marcus James North (Durham CB 2000-03 C&G 3 NWT 3). Born 28.7.1979, Pakenham, Melbourne, Victoria, Australia. LHB OB. FC for Western Australia (1999/00-08/09), Durham (2004), Lancashire (2005), Derbyshire (2006), Gloucestershire (2007-08). Also ListA for Western Australia (1999/00-08/09), Durham (2004), Lancashire (2005), Derbyshire (2006), Gloucestershire (2007-08).

Philip David North (Wiltshire 1993 NWT 1). Born 16.5.1965, Newport, Monmouthshire. RHB SLA. FC for Glamorgan (1985-89). Also ListA for Glamorgan (1985-89).

Kenneth Norton (Northumberland 1971-77 GC 3). Born 2.11.1932, Gateshead, Co Durham. RHB SLA.

Lee Harvey Nurse (Berkshire 2000-03 C&G 5 NWT 2). Born 24.12.1976, Basingstoke, Hampshire. RHB. Great-uncle: S.M. (Barbados).

Michael Dennis Nurton (Oxfordshire 1970-87 GC 5 NWT 6, MC South 1974-79 B&H 7, MC West 1977-78 B&H 8, MC 1982 B&H 1). Born 11.1.1943, Botley, Hampshire. LHB.

Simon Oakes (Lincolnshire 1996-03 C&G 6 NWT 6, MC 1997-98 B&H 2). Born 9.9.1974, Grantham, Lincolnshire. RHB RFM.

John Francis Martin O'Brien (Cheshire 1987-95 NWT 8). Born 25.5.1961, Birkenhead, Cheshire. RHB SLA.

Neil Terence O'Brien (MC East 1977-78 B&H 8, MC North 1979 B&H 4, Cheshire 1981-89 NWT 9, MC 1981-89 B&H 13). Born 9.3.1945, Heaton Moor, Lancashire. RHB RM. FC for MC (1979-81).

Anthony Philip O'Connor (Shropshire 2001-05 C&G 6). Born 24.6.1980, Bradford, Yorkshire. LHB LM.

Steven Craig Oddy (Lancashire CB 2001 C&G 2). Born 17.5.1979, Rochdale, Lancashire. RHB RM.

Simon Patrick O'Donnell (Northumberland 1989 NWT 1). Born 26.1.1963, Deniliquin, New South Wales, Australia. RHB RFM. 6 Tests (1985-85/86) for Australia. 87 ODIs (1984/85-91/92) for Australia. FC for Victoria (1983/84-92/93). Also ListA for Victoria (1983/84-92/93).

Stephen Ogilby (Cheshire 2001-04 C&G 4). Born 15.4.1976, Strabane, Co Tyrone, Ireland. RHB WKT. FC for Ireland (2004). Also ListA for Ireland (2004).

Steven Ogrizovic (Shropshire 1983-84 NWT 3, MC 1984 B&H 1). Born 12.9.1957, Forest Town, Mansfield, Nottinghamshire. RHB RMF.

Alan Gerald Bernard Old (Durham 1972-73 GC 4, MC North 1973-75 B&H 4). Born 23.9.1945, Middlesbrough, Yorkshire. RHB RFM. FC for Warwickshire (1969). Also ListA for Warwickshire (1969). Brother: C.M. (MCC, MC, Northern Transvaal, Northumberland, Warwickshire, Yorkshire).

Christopher Middleton Old (Northumberland 1986-87 NWT 2). Born 22.12.1948, Middlesbrough, Yorkshire. LHB RFM. 46 Tests (1972/73-81) for England. 32 ODIs (1973-80/81) for England. FC for Yorkshire (1966-82), MCC (1970-79), Northern Transvaal (1981/82-82/83), Warwickshire (1983-85). Also ListA for Yorkshire (1966-82), MCC (1970-79), Northern Transvaal (1981/82-82/83), Warwickshire (1983-85). Brother: A.G.B. (Durham, MC North, Warwickshire).

Martin Olive (Devon 1987 NWT 1). Born 18.4.1958, Watford, Hertfordshire. RHB RM. FC for Somerset (1977-81). Also ListA for Somerset (1977-81).

Philip Robert Oliver (Shropshire 1974 GC 1, MC 1988-89 B&H 6, Staffordshire 1988-90 NWT 3). Born 9.5.1956, West Bromwich, Staffordshire. RHB OB. FC for Warwickshire (1975-82). Also ListA for Warwickshire (1975-82).

Richard Michael Oliver (Devon 1983-85 NWT 3). Born 16.12.1946, Exeter, Devon. RHB WKT.

Martin William Charles Olley (Hertfordshire 1985-89 NWT 5, Cambridgeshire 1991-94 NWT 3). Born 27.11.1963, Romford, Essex. RHB WKT. FC for Northamptonshire (1983), Middlesex (1988). Also ListA for Northamptonshire (1983), Middlesex (1988).

Graham Onions (Durham CB 2003 C&G 1). Born 9.9.1982, Gateshead, Co Durham. RHB RMF. FC for Durham (2004-08), MCC (2007-08). Also ListA for Durham (2004-08), MCC (2007-08).

Luke James O'Reilly (Hertfordshire 1999 NWT 3, Middlesex CB 2001 C&G 1). Born 9.7.1977, Westminster, London. RHB RFM.

Paul John O'Reilly (Hertfordshire 2001-02 C&G 4). Born 4.8.1962, Watford, Hertfordshire. RHB RFM.

Steven Joseph O'Shaughnessy (Cumberland 1994-03 C&G 4 NWT 8). Born 9.9.1961, Bury, Lancashire. RHB RM. FC for Lancashire (1980-87), Worcestershire (1988-89). Also ListA for Lancashire (1980-87), Worcestershire (1988-89).

Michael Peter O'Shea (Wales MC 2005 C&G 1). Born 4.9.1987, Cardiff, Glamorgan, Wales. RHB OB. FC for Glamorgan (2005-07). Also ListA for Glamorgan (2005-07).

Wayne Miles Osman (Hertfordshire 1974-86 GC 5 NWT 5, MC West 1978 B&H 4, MC South 1979 B&H 4, MC 1982-85 B&H 13). Born 19.8.1950, Athens, Greece. LHB LM. FC for Northamptonshire (1970-71). Also ListA for Northamptonshire (1970-71).

David Robert O'Sullivan (Durham 1974-77 GC 3). Born 16.11.1944, Palmerston North, Manawatu, New Zealand. RHB SLA. 11 Tests (1972/73-76/77) for New Zealand. 3 ODIs (1973/74-76/77) for New Zealand. FC for Hampshire (1971-73), Central Districts (1972/73-84/85). Also ListA for Hampshire (1971-73), Central Districts (1972/73-84/85).

Michael Joseph O'Sullivan (Berkshire 1999-01 C&G 1 NWT 1). Born 16.11.1973, Reading, Berkshire. LHB SLA.

Geoffrey Victor Othen (Shropshire 1974-76 GC 2). Born 12.3.1933, Shrewsbury, Shropshire. RHB RM.

David George Ottley (Hertfordshire 1976-86 GC 4 NWT 4, MC West 1976-78 B&H 10, MC South 1979 B&H 2). Born 23.6.1944, Worcester Park, Surrey. RHB. FC for Middlesex (1967), MC (1985). Also ListA for Middlesex (1967), MC (1985).

Denzil Malison Owen (Buckinghamshire 1997 NWT 1). Born 16.10.1955, Manchester, Jamaica. RHB RFM.

John Edward Houghton Owen (Derbyshire CB 2002 C&G 1). Born 7.8.1971, Derby. RHB OB. FC for Derbyshire (1995-97). Also ListA for Derbyshire (1995-97).

Sidney Charles Owen (Staffordshire 1973 GC 2). Born 5.5.1942, Wellington, Shropshire. RHB WKT.

Philip John Oxley (Berkshire 1990-96 NWT 6). Born 7.4.1965, Reading, Berkshire. RHB OB.

Robert John Pack (Northamptonshire CB 1999-00 NWT 2, Bedfordshire 2002 C&G 2). Born 27.8.1970, Kettering, Northamptonshire. LHB SLA.

Derrick Brooks Keith Page (Shropshire 1990 NWT 1, Staffordshire 1992 NWT 1). Born 24.5.1961, Trelawny, Jamaica. RHB RFM.

Jeremy Russell Page (Bedfordshire 2000 NWT 1). Born 6.9.1959, Luton, Bedfordshire. LHB.

Antonio Paul Palladino (Essex CB 2002-03 C&G 2). Born 29.6.1983, Tower Hamlets, London. RHB RMF. FC for Cambridge UCCE (2003-05), Essex (2003-08). Also ListA for Cambridge UCCE (2003-05), Essex (2003-08).

Richard James Pannell (Somerset CB 2001 C&G 1). Born 2.6.1973, Bristol. RHB RM.

Christopher Leslie Park (Dorset 2001-04 C&G 2, Northamptonshire CB 2002 C&G 1). Born 22.7.1983, Poole, Dorset. RHB WKT.

Bradley Parker (Northumberland 2000-05 C&G 4 NWT 3). Born 23.6.1970, Mirfield, Yorkshire. RHB RM. FC for Yorkshire (1992-98). Also ListA for Yorkshire (1992-98).

Ivor John Parker (Cambridgeshire 1982 NWT 1). Born 6.5.1952, Hilton, Cambridgeshire. LHB LFM.

Luke Charles Parker (Warwickshire CB 2001-02 C&G 2). Born 27.9.1983, Coventry, Warwickshire. RHB RM. FC for Oxford UCCE (2004-06), Warwickshire (2005-08), MCC (2006). Also ListA for Oxford UCCE (2004-06), Warwickshire (2005-08), MCC (2006).

Gareth Steven Parkin (Leicestershire CB 2002 C&G 1). Born 5.10.1982, Leicester. RHB RMF.

Ian Charles Parkin (Derbyshire CB 1999-02 C&G 3 NWT 3). Born 12.9.1977, Derby. LHB OB.

Owen Thomas Parkin (Dorset 1992-93 NWT 2). Born 24.9.1972, Coventry, Warwickshire. RHB RM. FC for Glamorgan (1994-03). Also ListA for Glamorgan (1994-03).

Andrew William Parkin-Coates (Lincolnshire 2004 C&G 1). Born 13.5.1985, Doncaster, Yorkshire. RHB RM.

Matthew Edgar Parkinson (Lancashire CB 1999 NWT 1, Cambridgeshire 2000 NWT 1). Born 14.9.1972, Lancaster, Lancashire. RHB RM.

Michael Edward Parlane (Norfolk 2002 C&G 2). Born 22.7.1972, Pukekohe, Auckland, New Zealand. RHB Occ WKT. FC for Northern Districts (1992/93-08/09), Wellington (2003/04-07/08). Also ListA for Northern Districts (1992/93-08/09), Wellington (2003/04-07/08). Brother: N.R. (Northern Districts, Wellington).

Manoj Mansinh Parmar (Oxfordshire 2003 C&G 1). Born 1.3.1967, Botad, Gujarat, India. RHB WKT. FC for Saurashtra (1991/92-01/02). Also ListA for Saurashtra (1991/92-01/02).

David S. Parrott (Oxfordshire 1972 GC 1). RHB.

Christopher Jackson Parry (Buckinghamshire 1970-72 GC 4). Born 31.7.1934, Barnet, Hertfordshire. RHB OB.

David John Parry (Cheshire 1985 NWT 1). Born 9.12.1956, Middlewich, Cheshire. RHB RM.

Derick Recaldo Parry (Cambridgeshire 1982-86 NWT 3). Born 22.12.1954, Cotton Ground, Nevis. RHB OB. 12 Tests (1977/78-79/80) for West Indies. 6 ODIs (1977/78-80/81) for West Indies. FC for Leeward Islands (1975/76-81/82), Combined Leeward and Windward Islands (1976/77-80/81). Also ListA for Leeward Islands (1975/76-81/82), Combined Leeward and Windward Islands (1976/77-80/81).

Dhiraj Devshibhai Parsana (Durham 1978 GC 1). Born 2.12.1947, Rajkot, Gujarat, India. LHB LMF,SLA. 2 Tests (1978/79) for India. FC for Saurashtra (1965/66-82/83), Railways (1967/68-68/69), Gujarat (1969/70-79/80). Also ListA for Saurashtra (1965/66-82/83), Railways (1967/68-68/69), Gujarat (1969/70-79/80).

David Joseph Parsons (Cumberland 1984 NWT 1). Born 28.10.1954, Accrington, Lancashire. RHB LMF. FC for MC (1981). Also ListA for MC (1981).

Gerald Rex Parsons (Cornwall 1970 GC 1). Born 26.1.1934, Portgate, Okehampton, Devon. RHB OB.

Kevin John Parsons (Somerset CB 1999-02 C&G 3 NWT 2). Born 2.5.1973, Taunton, Somerset. RHB Occ WKT. Twin brother: K.A.Parsons (Cornwall, Somerset, Somerset CB).

Michael Parsons (Somerset CB 2002 C&G 1). Born 26.11.1984, Taunton, Somerset. RHB RMF. FC for Somerset (2005). Also ListA for Somerset (2005).

Tony Parton (Shropshire 1988-04 C&G 1 NWT 8). Born 12.1.1967, Wellington, Shropshire. LHB.

David Kent Pashley (Staffordshire 1997 NWT 1). Born 24.5.1972, Stoke-on-Trent, Staffordshire. LHB.

Graeme David Terence Paskins (Buckinghamshire 2000-05 C&G 5 NWT 1). Born 1.6.1972, Southend-on-Sea, Essex. RHB Occ WKT.

Ashok Sitaram Patel (Durham 1981-91 NWT 12, MC 1986 B&H 2). Born 23.9.1956, Nairobi, Kenya. LHB SLA. FC for Middlesex (1978), MC (1986). Also ListA for Middlesex (1978).

Bhavesh Patel (Nottinghamshire CB 2001 C&G 1). Born 15.3.1985, Derby. LHB SLA.

Chetan Morar Patel (Middlesex CB 1999 NWT 1). Born 12.4.1972, Islington, London. LHB RM. FC for Hampshire (1997), OU (1997). Also ListA for Hampshire (1997), OU (1997).

Dipak Patel (Cumberland 1995 NWT 1). Born 28.8.1961, Mombasa, Kenya. RHB SLA.

Depesh Balvant Patel (Worcestershire CB 1999 NWT 1). Born 23.9.1981, Wolverhampton, Staffordshire. RHB RM.

Dipak Narshibhai Patel (Staffordshire 1987 NWT 1). Born 25.10.1958, Nairobi, Kenya. RHB OB. 37 Tests (1986/87-96/97) for New Zealand. 75 ODIs (1986/87-96/97) for New Zealand. FC for Worcestershire (1976-86), Auckland (1985/86-94/95). Also ListA for Worcestershire (1976-86), Auckland (1985/86-94/95). Cousin: H.V. (Herefordshire, Staffordshire, Worcestershire), brother: K.N. (Staffordshire).

Harshad Vallabhbhai Patel (Staffordshire 1989 NWT 1, Herefordshire 1995-03 C&G 6 NWT 6). Born 29.1.1964, Nairobi, Kenya. RHB OB. FC for Worcestershire (1985). Also ListA for Worcestershire (1985). Cousin: D.N. (Auckland, Staffordshire, Worcestershire).

Kishor Patel (Worcestershire CB 2001 C&G 1). Born 16.3.1982. RHB WKT.

Kaushik Narshibhai Patel (Staffordshire 1995-96 NWT 2). Born 8.10.1963, Nairobi, Kenya. LHB. Brother: D.N. (Auckland, Staffordshire, Worcestershire).

Nemesh Girishchandra Patel (Leicestershire CB 1999-02 C&G 5 NWT 2). Born 8.10.1976, Leicester. RHB OB.

Sachin Patel (Middlesex CB 2002 C&G 1). Born 11.12.1983, Wembley, London. RHB.

Sameer Satesh Patel (Berkshire 1999-05 C&G 7 NWT 4). Born 16.6.1976, Reading, Berkshire. RHB OB.

Andrew David Patterson (Bedfordshire 2003 C&G 1). Born 4.9.1975, Belfast, Ireland. RHB WKT. FC for Ireland (1996-00), Sussex (2000). Also ListA for Ireland (1996-00), Sussex (2000). Brother: M.W. (Bedfordshire, Ireland, Surrey, Surrey CB).

Mark William Patterson (Bedfordshire 2002-05 C&G 3). Born 2.2.1974, Belfast, Ireland. RHB RFM. FC for Surrey (1996-99). Also ListA for Surrey (1996-99). Brother: A.D. (Bedfordshire, Ireland, MCC, Surrey CB, Sussex).

Steven Andrew Patterson (Yorkshire CB 2002 C&G 2). Born 3.10.1983, Hull, Yorkshire. RHB RMF. FC for Yorkshire (2005-08). Also ListA for Yorkshire (2005-08).

Ian Pattison (Durham CB 2000-03 C&G 2 NWT 3). Born 5.5.1982, Ryhope, Sunderland, Co Durham. RHB RM. FC for Durham (2002-04). Also ListA for Durham (2002-04).

Duncan Ashley Paveling (Essex CB 2001-02 C&G 2). Born 8.6.1977, Bristol. RHB WKT.

Christopher John Payne (MC South 1975 B&H 2). Born 30.12.1947, Hatfield, Hertfordshire. RHB Occ WKT. FC for Middlesex (1968-70). Also ListA for Middlesex (1968-70).

David Edward Paynter (Northamptonshire CB 2001 C&G 1). Born 25.1.1981, Truro, Cornwall. RHB OB. FC for Northamptonshire (2002-03). Also ListA for Northamptonshire (2002-03). Great-grandfather: E. (Lancashire, MCC).

Daniel James Peacock (Hampshire CB 2002 C&G 1). Born 26.4.1975, Reading, Berkshire. RHB OB. FC for Mashonaland A (1998/99), Mashonaland (1999/00). Also ListA for Mashonaland A (1998/99), Mashonaland (1999/00).

Lee Robert Peacock (Lincolnshire 1999 NWT 1, Huntingdonshire 2001-02 C&G 4). Born 18.1.1974, Cambridge. RHB LFM.

Arthur Martin Pearce (Cornwall 2002-03 C&G 4). Born 14.12.1983, Truro, Cornwall. RHB.

Christopher James Pearce (Worcestershire CB 2003 C&G 1). Born 19.4.1984, Wolverhampton, Staffordshire. RHB LB.

Roger Pearman (Bedfordshire 1973 GC 1, MC South 1973 B&H 4, MC North 1974-75 B&H 5). Born 13.2.1943, Lichfield, Staffordshire. RHB OB. FC for Middlesex (1962-64). Also ListA for Middlesex (1962-64). Brother: H. (CU, Middlesex).

Thomas Joseph Pearman (Hertfordshire 2003 C&G 1). Born 9.1.1979, Welwyn Garden City, Hertfordshire. RHB WKT.

Thomas Pearsall (Staffordshire 1975-78 GC 3, MC North 1979 B&H 2). Born 18.5.1943, West Bromwich, Staffordshire. LHB RAB.

Andrew Stuart Pearson (Bedfordshire 1982-85 NWT 2). Born 25.9.1957, Rustington, Sussex. LHB OB.

David John Pearson (Cumberland 1994-00 NWT 10). Born 16.4.1963, Whalley, Lancashire. LHB WKT.

James Alexander Pearson (Gloucestershire CB 2001 C&G 2). Born 11.9.1983, Bristol. LHB. FC for Gloucestershire (2002-05). Also ListA for Gloucestershire (2002-05).

Kenneth Pearson (MC East 1976-77 B&H 8, Northumberland 1977-89 GC 2 NWT 4, MC North 1979 B&H 2). Born 30.8.1951, Bedlington, Northumberland. RHB. FC for MC (1976). Also ListA for MC (1976).

Karl Pearson (Herefordshire 1999-02 C&G 6 NWT 2). Born 14.8.1974, Stourbridge, Worcestershire. RHB RM.

Simon Pearson (Leicestershire CB 2001 C&G 1). Born 8.5.1982. LHB LB.

Ian George Peck (Bedfordshire 1977-85 GC 1 NWT 1). Born 18.10.1957, Great Staughton, Huntingdonshire. RHB WKT. FC for CU (1978-84), Northamptonshire (1980-81). Also ListA for CU (1978-84), Northamptonshire (1980-81).

Michael James Peck (Suffolk 1990-95 NWT 2). Born 23.1.1967, Creeting St Mary, Stowmarket. RHB.

Giles Simon Peddy (Oxfordshire 2003 C&G 1). Born 16.4.1978, Hemel Hempstead, Hertfordshire. RHB OB.

Nigel David Peel (Cheshire 1992-96 NWT 4). Born 10.11.1967, Wythenshawe, Cheshire. LHB RF.

David Barrington Pennett (Cumberland 1997-02 C&G 4 NWT 4, MC 1998 B&H 5, Cheshire 2003-04 C&G 2). Born 26.10.1969, Leeds, Yorkshire. RHB RFM. FC for Nottinghamshire (1992-96). Also ListA for Nottinghamshire (1992-96).

Christopher Thomas Peploe (Middlesex CB 2001 C&G 1). Born 26.4.1981, Hammersmith, London. LHB SLA. FC for Middlesex (2003-08). Also ListA for Middlesex (2003-08).

Derek James Pepperell (Dorset 1992 NWT 1). Born 28.9.1968, Oxford. LHB WKT.

Bruce Stephen Percy (Buckinghamshire 1990-01 C&G 1 NWT 7). Born 15.6.1966, Horsforth, Yorkshire. RHB RM.

George Cyril Perkins (Suffolk 1966 GC 1). Born 4.6.1911, Wollaston, Northamptonshire. RHB LM,SLA. FC for Northamptonshire (1934-37), MC (1951). Also ListA for Northamptonshire (1934-37), MC (1951).

Jonathan Roy Perkins (Berkshire 2001-05 C&G 4). Born 9.10.1978, Reading, Berkshire. RHB.

Clinton Terrence Perren (Cheshire 2003-04 C&G 2). Born 22.2.1975, Herston, Brisbane, Queensland, Australia. RHB RM. FC for Queensland (1998/99-08/09). Also ListA for Queensland (1998/99-08/09).

Stephen Michael Perrin (Wiltshire 1993-01 C&G 1 NWT 4). Born 27.10.1970, Bradford-on-Avon, Wiltshire. RHB WKT.

Andrew Perry (Sussex CB 2002 C&G 1). Born 20.5.1984, Chichester, Sussex. RHB RM.

Andrew Howard Dawson Perry (Hampshire CB 1999-02 C&G 2 NWT 4). Born 2.7.1976, Portsmouth, Hampshire. RHB OB.

Brian James Perry (Shropshire 1974-84 GC 2 NWT 3, MC North 1975 B&H 1). Born 3.6.1943, Shrewsbury, Shropshire. LHB RFM.

Duncan Christopher Perry (Shropshire 1983 NWT 1). Born 9.12.1962, Manchester, Lancashire. LHB LMF.

Stephen Peter Perryman (Staffordshire 1988 NWT 1). Born 22.10.1955, Yardley, Birmingham, Warwickshire. RHB RM. FC for Warwickshire (1974-81), Worcestershire (1982-83). Also ListA for Warwickshire (1974-81), Worcestershire (1982-83).

Pervez Iqbal (Derbyshire CB 2000 NWT 1). Born 26.12.1975, Rawalpindi, Punjab, Pakistan. Died 2002, Rawalpindi, Punjab, Pakistan. LHB RM. FC for Rawalpindi (1993/94-00/01), Rawalpindi B (1994/95-95/96). Also ListA for Rawalpindi (1993/94-00/01), Rawalpindi B (1994/95-95/96).

Pervez Jamil Mir (Norfolk 1982-85 NWT 4). Born 24.9.1953, Sutrapur, Dacca (now Dhaka, Bangladesh), Pakistan. RHB RMF. 3 ODIs (1975-77/78) for Pakistan. FC for Rawalpindi Blues (1970/71), Lahore A (1971/72-77/78), Punjab (1972/73-77/78), Pakistan Universities (1973/74-74/75), Lahore B (1974/75), Derbyshire (1975), Habib Bank (1975/76-80/81), Punjab A (1975/76), Glamorgan (1979), Lahore City (1982/83-84/85), Lahore City Blues (1984/85). Also ListA for Rawalpindi Blues (1970/71), Lahore A (1971/72-77/78), Punjab (1972/73-7/78), Pakistan Universities (1973/74-74/75), Lahore B (1974/75), Derbyshire (1975), Habib Bank (1975/76-80/81), Punjab A (1975/76), Glamorgan (1979), Lahore City (1982/83-84/85), Lahore City Blues (1984/85). Brother: Shahid Mir (Lahore City, Punjab Greens, Servis Industries).

Vernon Darryl Philander (Devon 2004 C&G 2). Born 24.6.1985, Bellville, Cape Province, South Africa. RHB RMF. 7 ODIs (2007-08) for South Africa. 7 Int2020s (2007/08) for South Africa. FC for Western Province (2003/04-05/06), Western Province Boland (2004/05), Cape Cobras (2005/06-08/09), Middlesex (2008). Also ListA for Western Province (2003/04-05/06), Western Province Boland (2004/05), Cape Cobras (2005/06-2008/09), Middlesex (2008).

Simon Douglas Philbrook (Cumberland 1986 NWT 1). Born 11.10.1965, Luton, Bedfordshire. RHB.

Nevada Phillips (Berkshire 1979 GC 1). Born 15.1.1957, Barbados. RHB OB.

Christopher Arthur Pickett (Buckinghamshire 1965-70 GC 4). Born 26.8.1926, Hedgerley, Buckinghamshire. Died 10.1995, Buckinghamshire. LHB LF,SLA. FC for MC (1953). Also ListA for MC (1953).

James Kenneth Pickup (Cheshire 1981-85 NWT 4). Born 25.9.1952, Stalybridge, Cheshire. RHB WKT. FC for OU (1973-75). Also ListA for OU (1973-75).

Paul John Pickworth (Northumberland 1984 NWT 1). Born 22.9.1958, Corbridge, Northumberland. RHB.

Edwin Philip Picton (Devon 1979-80 GC 3). Born 23.8.1949, Blackpool, Lancashire. LHB.

Adrian Roger Kirshaw Pierson (Cambridgeshire 1992 NWT 1). Born 21.7.1963, Enfield, Middlesex. RHB OB. FC for Warwickshire (1985-91), Leicestershire (1993-97), Somerset (1998-00), Derbyshire (2001). Also ListA for Warwickshire (1985-91), Leicestershire (1993-97), Somerset (1998-00), Derbyshire (2001).

David Robert Pike (Wiltshire 1989 NWT 1). Born 5.9.1963, Swindon, Wiltshire. RHB LM. Brother: C.J.Pike (Wiltshire).

Vyvian John Pike (Dorset 1998-01 C&G 1 NWT 4). Born 13.8.1969, Taunton, Somerset. RHB LB. FC for Gloucestershire (1994-95). Also ListA for Gloucestershire (1994-95).

David George Pilch (Norfolk 1965-83 GC 3 NWT 2, MC North 1974-75 B&H 3). Born 2.2.1943, West Kirby, Cheshire. RHB RM.

Richard Leslie Pilgrim (Nottinghamshire CB 2001 C&G 1). Born 13.6.1982, Sheffield, Yorkshire. RHB OB.

Richard William Pineo (Suffolk 2001-02 C&G 6). Born 11.2.1975, Ipswich, Suffolk. RHB RF.

David James Pipe (Worcestershire CB 2000-01 C&G 1 NWT 1). Born 16.12.1977, Bradford, Yorkshire. RHB WKT. FC for Worcestershire (1998-05), Derbyshire (2006-08). Also ListA for Worcestershire (1998-05), Derbyshire (2006-08).

David John Pipes (Lincolnshire 2000-02 C&G 4 NWT 1). Born 26.4.1977, Lincoln. RHB RM. FC for Nottinghamshire (1994). Also ListA for Nottinghamshire (1994).

Nicholas D. Pishos (Huntingdonshire 2000 NWT 2).

Robert James Pitcher (Berkshire 1995 NWT 1). Born 29.4.1964, Welwyn Garden City, Hertfordshire. RHB SLA.

Geoffrey Plaskitt (Lincolnshire 1967-74 GC 5, MC North 1972 B&H 1). Born 29.4.1940, Grimsby, Lincolnshire. RHB RF.

Benjamin William Whiteley Platt (Shropshire 2002 C&G 1). Born 20.4.1980, St Asaph, Flintshire, Wales. LHB SLA.

Spencer Platt (Warwickshire CB 1999-01 C&G 3 NWT 2). Born 24.8.1974, Coventry, Warwickshire. LHB WKT.

Stephen George Plumb (MC 1980-92 B&H 47, Norfolk 1982-95 NWT 10, Lincolnshire 1997-00 NWT 5). Born 17.1.1954, Wimbish, Essex. RHB RM,OB. FC for Essex (1975-77), MC (1981-86). Also ListA for Essex (1975-77).

Liam Edward Plunkett (Durham CB 2002-03 C&G 2). Born 6.4.1985, Middlesbrough, Yorkshire. RHB RFM. 9 Tests (2005/06-07) for England. 27 ODIs (2005/06-07) for England. 1 Int2020 (2006) for England. FC for Durham (2003-08), Dolphins (2007/08). Also ListA for Durham (2003-08), Dolphins (2007/08).

Brian William Poll (Buckinghamshire 1969-79 GC 8, MC South 1972 B&H 2). Born 5.1.1941, Cheltenham, Gloucestershire. Died 18.6.1999. RHB WKT.

Lee Gordon Pollard (Leicestershire CB 1999-01 C&G 1 NWT 2, Bedfordshire 2003 C&G 2). Born 26.5.1979, Kettering, Northamptonshire. RHB RM.

Martin Lee Pollard (Northumberland 2001-05 C&G 3). Born 2.8.1977, Consett, Co Durham. RHB RM.

Paul Raymond Pollard (Lincolnshire 2003 C&G 2). Born 24.9.1968, Nottingham. LHB RM. FC for Nottinghamshire (1987-98), Worcestershire (1999-01). Also ListA for Nottinghamshire (1987-98), Worcestershire (1999-01).

Stephen Paul Pollard (Cornwall 2001 C&G 1). Born 13.3.1971, Penzance, Cornwall. RHB.

Graeme Anthony Pollock (Leicestershire CB 1999 NWT 1). Born 7.4.1973, Port Elizabeth, Cape Province, South Africa. LHB OB. FC for Transvaal (1991/92-95/96), Transvaal B (1991/92-96/97), Northerns B (1997/98-98/99), Easterns (1999/00). Also ListA for Transvaal (1991/92-95/96), Transvaal B (1991/92-96/97), Northerns B (1997/98-98/99), Easterns (1999/00). Uncle: P.M. (Eastern Province), father: R.G. (Eastern Province, Transvaal), cousin: S.M. (Dolphins, Durham, KwaZulu-Natal, MCC, Natal, Natal B, Warwickshire), brother: A.G. (Easterns, Transvaal, Transvaal B), great-uncle: R.Howden (Natal), grandfather: A.M. (Orange Free State).

Robert Henry Pomphrey (Hertfordshire 1974-81 GC 5 NWT 1, MC South 1979 B&H 1). Born 6.10.1944, Warminster, Wiltshire. RHB.

Alan Mervyn Ponder (Cambridgeshire 1967-83 GC 3 NWT 2). Born 22.8.1947, Cambridge. LHB WKT.

Ian Leslie Pont (MC 1983 B&H 3, Northumberland 1989 NWT 1, Lincolnshire 1990 NWT 1). Born 28.8.1961, Brentwood, Essex. RHB RFM. FC for Nottinghamshire (1982), Essex (1985-88), Natal (1985/86). Also ListA for Nottinghamshire (1982), Essex (1985-88), Natal (1985/86). Brothers: K.R. (Essex) and K. (Essex, MCC).

Andrew Keith Poole (Suffolk 2001 C&G 2). Born 2.7.1967, Middlesbrough, Yorkshire. RHB RFM.

Navdeep Singh Poonia (Warwickshire CB 2002 C&G 1). Born 11.5.1986, Govan, Glasgow, Lanarkshire, Scotland. RHB RMF. 16 ODIs (2006-08) for Scotland. 5 Int2020s (2007/08-08) for Scotland. FC for Warwickshire (2006-08). Also ListA for Warwickshire (2006-08).

Steven Charles Pope (Huntingdonshire 1999 NWT 1, Cornwall 2000-03 C&G 7 NWt 1). Born 15.11.1972, East London, Cape Province, South Africa. RHB LB Occ WKT. FC for Eastern Province (1992/93-94/95), Eastern Province B (1993/94-94/95), Border (1995/96-05/06), Border B (1995/96), Warriors (2004/05-05/06). Also ListA for Eastern Province (1992/93-94/95), Eastern Province B (1993/94-94/95), Border (1995/96-05/06), Border B (1995/96), Warriors (2004/05-05/06). Uncle: K.S.McEwan (Border, Eastern Province, Essex, MCC, Sussex, Western Australia, Western Province), father: C.W.S. (Border).

Stephen Patrick Pope (Gloucestershire CB 1999-01 C&G 2 NWT 3). Born 25.1.1983, Cheltenham, Gloucestershire. RHB WKT. FC for Gloucestershire (2003). Also ListA for Gloucestershire (2003).

Joseph James Porter (Surrey CB 2002 C&G 1). Born 5.5.1980, Hammersmith, London. LHB SLA. FC for Oxford Universities (2000), Oxford UCCE (2001-02). Also ListA for Oxford Universities (2000), Oxford UCCE (2001-02).

Simon Robert Porter (Oxfordshire 1975-87 GC 2 NWT 6). Born 9.8.1950, Cowley, Oxford. RHB OB. FC for OU (1973). Also ListA for OU (1973).

Jonathan Kenneth Potter (Huntingdonshire 1999 NWT 1). Born 14.2.1971, Stamford, Lincolnshire. RHB RFM. Father: C. (Huntingdonshire).

John Ritson Potter (Oxfordshire 1975 GC 2). Born 14.12.1949, Misslesbrough, Yorkshire. RHB.

Laurie Potter (MC 1995-98 B&H 8, Staffordshire 1995-01 C&G 1 NWT 7). Born 7.11.1962, Bexleyheath, Kent. RHB LM,SLA. FC for Kent (1981-85), Griqualand West (1984/85-85/86), Leicestershire (1986-93), Orange Free State (1987/88). Also ListA for Kent (1981-85), Griqualand West (1984/85-85/86), Leicestershire (1986-93), Orange Free State (1987/88). Father-in-law: F.M.Turner (Leicestershire, MCC).

John Potts (Cheshire 1992-93 NWT 2). Born 4.7.1960, Stoke-on-Trent, Staffordshire. RHB RMF.

Harry Pougher (Lincolnshire 1967-88 GC 2 NWT 2). Born 1.2.1941, Scunthorpe, Lincolnshire. RHB OB.

James Christopher Arthur Powell (Cheshire 2001 C&G 1). Born 22.10.1982, Wrexham, Denbighshire, Wales. RHB RMF.

Kirk Howard Antonio Powell (Middlesex CB 2001-02 C&G 4). Born 17.6.1972, Kingston, Jamaica. RHB RFM. FC for Jamaica (1997/98-98/99). Also ListA for Jamaica (1997/98-98/99).

Mark Geoffrey Powell (Norfolk 1995-96 NWT 2, MC 1996 B&H 2). Born 5.8.1972, Romford, Essex. RHB SLA. Brother: J.C. (Essex, Surrey CB).

Robert David Powell (Cambridgeshire 2001 C&G 1). Born 8.5.1979, Scunthorpe, Lincolnshire. RHB WKT.

Neeraj Vijay Prabhu (Herefordshire 2000-01 C&G 1 NWT 1). Born 17.12.1976, Bombay (now Mumbai), Maharashtra, India. RHB RM.

Gary Joseph Pratt (Durham CB 2001 C&G 1). Born 22.12.1981, Bishop Auckland, Co Durham. LHB OB. FC for Durham (2000-06). Also ListA for Durham (2000-06). Brothers: A. (Durham, Durham CB, MCC) and N. (Durham, Durham CB).

Benjamin Peter Price (Cornwall 2001-03 C&G 7). Born 17.8.1981, Truro, Cornwall. RHB.

Colin Leonard Price (Staffordshire 1973 GC 2). Born 24.10.1943, Birmingham, Warwickshire. RHB.

Howard Joseph Price (Lincolnshire 1971 GC 2). Born 20.9.1928, Tredegar, Monmouthshire. Died 30.10.1992, Moulton, Spalding, Lincolnshire. RHB OB.

Stephen James Price (Herefordshire 1998-99 NWT 3, Middlesex CB 2001-02 C&G 4). Born 30.3.1979, Shrewsbury, Shropshire. RHB OB.

Paul John Prichard (Berkshire 2002-05 C&G 5). Born 7.1.1965, Billericay, Essex. RHB RM. FC for Essex (1984-01). Also ListA for Essex (1984-01).

Alan Paul Pridgeon (Shropshire 1991 NWT 1). Born 22.2.1954, Wall Heath, Staffordshire. RHB RM. FC for Worcestershire (1972-89). Also ListA for Worcestershire (1972-89).

Neil Priestley (Lincolnshire 1983-90 NWT 2, MC 1986-89 B&H 6). Born 23.6.1961, Blyborough, Lincolnshire. RHB WKT. FC for Northamptonshire (1981). Also ListA for Northamptonshire (1981).

Neil Prigent (Wiltshire 1993 NWT 1). Born 11.7.1964, Uxbridge, Middlesex. LHB LM.

Thomas Edmund Howard Prime (Cumberland 2001 C&G 2). Born 16.10.1977, Kendal, Westmorland. RHB.

Ian David Prior (Suffolk 1966 GC 1). Born 26.7.1930, Battersea, London. Died 12.11.2007, Ipswich, Suffolk. RHB WKT. FC for MC (1967). Also ListA for MC (1967).

Matthew James Prior (Sussex CB 2000 NWT 1). Born 26.2.1982, Johannesburg, Transvaal, South Africa. RHB WKT. 12 Tests (2007-08/09) for England. 33 ODIs (2004/05-08/09) for England. 5 Int2020s (2007-07/08) for England. FC for Sussex (2001-08), MCC (2005). Also ListA for Sussex (2001-08), MCC (2005).

Stuart Michael Priscott (Gloucestershire CB 2001 C&G 1, Devon 2002 C&G 1). Born 6.7.1971, Bristol. LHB SLA.

Charles Scudamore Pritchard (Devon 1991-94 NWT 4). Born 7.3.1962, Wellington, Shropshire. RHB WKT.

Lawrence Roland Prittipaul (Hampshire CB 1999 NWT 3). Born 19.10.1979, Portsmouth, Hampshire. RHB RM. FC for Hampshire (2000-04). Also ListA for Hampshire (2000-04).

Andrew John Procter (Devon 2000-05 C&G 9 NWT 1). Born 7.9.1968, Preston, Lancashire. RHB OB.

John Proud (Yorkshire CB 2000-01 C&G 1 NWT 2). Born 23.2.1967, Ripon, Yorkshire. LHB.

Christopher John Proudman (Bedfordshire 1985 NWT 1). Born 30.6.1952, Oakham, Rutland. RHB LM.

Giles David Puckle (Surrey CB 2001 C&G 1). Born 24.3.1979, Epsom, Surrey. RHB SLA.

Andrew Charles Puddle (Wales MC 1993-94 NWT 2). Born 10.9.1956, Llanwrst, Denbighshire, Wales. LHB.

Andrew Joseph Pugh (Devon 1990-05 C&G 6 NWT 12). Born 26.5.1969, Torquay, Devon. RHB RM.

Neil Jon Pullen (Leicestershire CB 1999-02 C&G 5 NWT 2). Born 14.9.1977, Leicester. RHB RM Occ WKT.

Barry Francis Simon Purchase (Cornwall 1999 NWT 1). Born 10.7.1965, Rugeley, Staffordshire. RHB.

Iain Colin Purdy (Northumberland 2003 C&G 1). Born 8.4.1986, North Shields, Northumberland. LHB SLA.

James Robert Purvis (Northumberland 1987-89 NWT 2). Born 31.5.1954, Blyth, Northumberland. LHB LMF.

Richard Alexander Pybus (Suffolk 1986 NWT 1). Born 5.7.1964, Newcastle upon Tyne, Northumberland. RHB RFM.

Richard Anthony Pyman (Dorset 1991-99 NWT 5). Born 17.4.1968, Changi, Singapore. RHB RM. FC for CU (1988-91). Also ListA for CU (1988-91).

Richard Michael Pyrah (Yorkshire CB 2001-02 C&G 4). Born 1.11.1982, Dewsbury, Yorkshire. RHB RM. FC for Yorkshire (2004-08). Also ListA for Yorkshire (2004-08).

Qasim Ali Umar (Cumberland 1984-85 NWT 2). Born 9.2.1957, Nairobi, Kenya. RHB RM. 26 Tests (1983/84-86/87) for Pakistan. 31 ODIs (1983/84-86/87) for Pakistan. FC for Karachi Blues (1974/75-75/76), Karachi Whites (1975/76), Sind (1975/76-77/78), Sind B (1975/76), Muslim Commercial Bank (1976/77-82/83), Sind A (1976/77). Also ListA for Karachi Blues (1974/75-75/76), Karachi Whites (1975/76), Sind (1975/76-77/78), Sind B (1975/76), Muslim Commercial Bank (1976/77-82/83), Sind A (1976/77).

Neal Victor Radford (Herefordshire 1997-98 NWT 2, MC 1997 B&H 4). Born 7.6.1957, Luanshya, Zambia. RHB RFM. 3 Tests (1986-87/88) for England. 6 ODIs (1987/88-88) for England. FC for Transvaal B (1978/79-80/81), Transvaal (1979/80-88/89), Lancashire (1980-84), Worcestershire (1985-95). Also ListA for Transvaal B (1978/79-80/81), Transvaal (1979/80-88/89), Lancashire (1980-84), Worcestershire (1985-95). Brothers: G. (Eastern Transvaal, North West, Western Transvaal), W.R. (Boland, Eastern Transvaal, Easterns, Impalas, Orange Free State).

Toby Alexander Radford (Berkshire 1999 NWT 1). Born 3.12.1971, Caerphilly, Glamorgan, Wales. RHB OB. FC for Middlesex (1994-95), Sussex (1996-97). Also ListA for Middlesex (1994-95), Sussex (1996-97).

Dominic Francis Ralfs (Cambridgeshire 1994-99 NWT 6). Born 16.12.1967, Hendon, Middlesex. RHB RM.

James Trevor Ralph (Shropshire 1999-05 C&G 7 NWT 4). Born 9.10.1975, Kidderminster, Worcestershire. RHB LB. FC for Worcestershire (1996). Also ListA for Worcestershire (1996).

Sonny Ramadhin (Lincolnshire 1971 GC 2). Born 1.5.1929, St Charles Village, Trinidad. RHB OB. 43 Tests (1950-60/61) for West Indies. FC for Trinidad (1949/50-52/53), MCC (1961), Lancashire (1964-65). Also ListA for Trinidad (1949/50-52/53), MCC (1961), Lancashire (1964-65). Grandson: K.W.Hogg (Lancashire, Lancashire CB, Nottinghamshire, Otago, Worcestershire), son-in-law: W.Hogg (Lancashire, MCC, Warwickshire).

Alan Ramage (MC 1984 B&H 2). Born 29.11.1957, Guisborough, Yorkshire. LHB RFM. FC for Yorkshire (1979-83). Also ListA for Yorkshire (1979-83).

Gary Ramsden (Yorkshire CB 2002 C&G 1). Born 2.3.1983, Dewsbury, Yorkshire. RHB RMF. FC for Yorkshire (2000). Also ListA for Yorkshire (2000).

Mohammad Irfan Ahmed Rana (Lancashire CB 2001 C&G 1). Born 10.2.1986, Karachi, Pakistan. RHB RFM. FC for Karachi Whites (1989/90-91/92), Pakistan National Shipping Corporation (1990/91). Also ListA for Karachi Whites (1989/90-91/92), Pakistan National Shippping Corporation (1990/91).

Sirimewan Keerthi Ranasinghe (Middlesex CB 2000-02 C&G 4 NWT 2). Born 4.7.1962, Colombo, Sri Lanka. LHB RM. 4 ODIs (1985/86) for Sri Lanka.

Derek William Randall (Suffolk 1996-00 NWT 2). Born 24.2.1951, Retford, Nottinghamshire. RHB RM. 47 Tests (1976/77-84) for England. 49 ODIs (1976-84/85) for England. FC for Nottinghamshire (1972-93), MCC (1974-89). Also ListA for Nottinghamshire (1972-93), MCC (1974-89).

Stephen John Randall (Nottinghamshire CB 1999 NWT 1). Born 9.6.1980, Nottingham. RHB OB. FC for Nottinghamshire (1999-02). Also ListA for Nottinghamshire (1999-02).

Guriqbal Singh Randhawa (Warwickshire CB 2001 C&G 1). Born 27.12.1981, Birmingham, Warwickshire. RHB OB Occ WKT.

Peter Laurence Ranells (Shropshire 1978-85 GC 1 NWT 1). Born 26.12.1954, Bramhall, Cheshire. RHB RFM.

Rajesh Krishnakant Rao (Middlesex CB 2000-02 C&G 2 NWT 2). Born 9.12.1974, Park Royal, Middlesex. RHB LBG. FC for Sussex (1996-99). Also ListA for Sussex (1996-99).

Shaun Rashid (Bedfordshire 2001-05 C&G 7). Born 1.3.1977, Burnley, Lancashire. RHB RMF.

Paul Anthony Rawden (Lincolnshire 1994-97 NWT 3). Born 15.7.1973, Stamford, Lincolnshire. RHB RM.

Matthew James Rawnsley (Herefordshire 2003-04 C&G 2). Born 8.6.1976, Birmingham, Warwickshire. RHB SLA. FC for Worcestershire (1996-02). Also ListA for Worcestershire (1996-02).

Peter Walter Edward Rawson (Suffolk 1984 NWT 1). Born 25.5.1957, Salisbury (now Harare), Zimbabwe. RHB RFM. 10 ODIs (1983-87/88) for Zimbabwe. FC for Natal (1989/90-93/94). Also ListA for Natal (1989/90-93/94).

Brian Read (Cornwall 1970 GC 1). Born 7.3.1939, Camborne, Cornwall. RHB RFM.

Christopher Mark Wells Read (Devon 1995-97 NWT 3). Born 10.8.1978, Paignton, Devon. RHB WKT. 15 Tests (1999-06/07) for England. 36 ODIs (1999/00-06/07) for England. 1 Int2020 (2006) for England. FC for Nottinghamshire (1998-08), MCC (2002). Also ListA for Nottinghamshire (1998-08), MCC (2002).

Michael John Record (Devon 1991 NWT 1). Born 26.2.1966, Exeter, Devon. RHB RM.

Paul Alan Redfarn (Cambridgeshire 1983-89 NWT 3). Born 23.12.1963, Cambridge. RHB WKT.

Vincent Craven Reed (Cambridgeshire 1975 GC 1). Born 21.3.1940, Yelling, Cambridgeshire. RHB RM. Brother: R.A. (Cambridgeshire, Huntingdonshire), cousins: I. (Cambridgeshire, Huntingdonshire), L. (Huntingdonshire), T. (Huntingdonshire), P. (Huntingdonshire) and G. (Huntingdonshire).

Gareth Peter Rees (Wales MC 2003-05 C&G 3). Born 8.4.1985, Swansea, Glamorgan, Wales. LHB LM. FC for Glamorgan (2006-08). Also ListA for Glamorgan (2006-08).

Luke Reeves (Leicestershire CB 2000-01 C&G 2 NWT 1). Born 2.5.1980, Adelaide, South Australia, Australia. RHB WKT.

Bernard Wilfrid Reidy (Cumberland 1984-89 NWT 6). Born 18.9.1953, Bramley Meade, Whalley, Lancashire. LHB LM. FC for Lancashire (1973-82). Also ListA for Lancashire (1973-82).

Carlos Charles Remy (Middlesex CB 2000-01 C&G 1 NWT 2). Born 24.7.1968, Castries, St Lucia. RHB RM. FC for Sussex (1989-95), Leicestershire (1996). Also ListA for Sussex (1989-95), Leicestershire (1996).

James Phillip Rendell (Gloucestershire CB 1999-02 C&G 3 NWT 1). Born 24.1.1980, Bristol. RHB OB.

Adam Paul Rennocks (Leicestershire CB 2001-02 C&G 3). Born 29.1.1982, Leicester. RHB LM.

Simon John Renshaw (Cheshire 1994-04 C&G 3 NWT 2, Staffordshire 2005 C&G 1). Born 6.3.1974, Bebington, Cheshire. RHB RMF. FC for Hampshire (1996-00). Also ListA for Hampshire (1996-00).

Alan Chambers Revill (Berkshire 1965 GC 1). Born 27.3.1923, Sheffield, Yorkshire. Died 6.7.1998, Brent, London. RHB OB. FC for Derbyshire (1946-57), Leicestershire (1958-60). Also ListA for Derbyshire (1946-57), Leicestershire (1958-60). Father: T.F. (Derbyshire).

Gavin Reynolds (Lancashire CB 2001 C&G 1). Born 15.4.1979, Liverpool, Lancashire. RHB RM.

Giles Denys Reynolds (Dorset 1990-00 NWT 7). Born 13.7.1967, Monchengladbach, Germany. RHB WKT. FC for OU (1988-89). Also ListA for OU (1988-89).

John Rhodes (Devon 1995-01 C&G 1 NWT 2). Born 4.9.1962, Lancaster, Lancashire. RHB RM.

Gary Sedgwick Rice (Cambridgeshire 1982-88 NWT 3). Born 24.8.1960, Leicester. RHB RM. Father: A.S. (Leicestershire).

John Michael Rice (Wiltshire 1983-84 NWT 2). Born 23.10.1949, Chandlers Ford, Hampshire. RHB RM. FC for Hampshire (1971-82). Also ListA for Hampshire (1971-82).

Kevin Geoffrey Rice (Devon 1985-91 NWT 6). Born 13.1.1965, Morchard Bishop, Devon. RHB OB.

Paul Christopher Rice (Suffolk 1979-81 GC 3 NWT 1). Born 22.2.1948, Exeter, Devon. LHB.

Alexander Charles Richards (Essex CB 1999-03 C&G 3 NWT 3). Born 13.9.1971, Ilford, Essex. RHB OB.

David Michael Richards (Wiltshire 1964-65 GC 2). Born 6.11.1931, Bath, Somerset. RHB RFM.

Ian Michael Richards (Durham 1982 NWT 1). Born 9.12.1957, Stockton-on-Tees, Co Durham. LHB RM. FC for Northamptonshire (1976-79). Also ListA for Northamptonshire (1976-79).

Mark Allan Elliott Richards (Devon 2002-05 C&G 3). Born 9.4.1974, Bridport, Dorset. RHB RM.

Alan Richardson (Staffordshire 1996-98 NWT 3, MC 1998 B&H 3). Born 6.5.1975, Newcastle-under-Lyme, Staffordshire. RHB RMF. FC for Derbyshire (1995), Warwickshire (1999-04), Middlesex (2005-08). Also ListA for Derbyshire (1995), Warwickshire (1999-04), Middlesex (2005-08).

Andrew Robert Richardson (Dorset 1987 NWT 1). Born 2.6.1965, Weymouth, Dorset. RHB WKT.

Charles Adrian Richardson (Lincolnshire 1966-74 GC 4). Born 5.6.1946, Stamford, Lincolnshire. RHB.

Mark Hunter Richardson (Buckinghamshire 2001 C&G 1). Born 11.6.1971, Hastings, Hawke's Bay, New Zealand. LHB SLA. 38 Tests (2000/01-04/05) for New Zealand. 4 ODIs (2001/02) for New Zealand. FC for Auckland (1989/90-04/05), Otago (1992/93-00/01), MCC (2001). Also ListA for Auckland (1989/90-04/05), Otago (1992/93-00/01), MCC (2001).

Ronald Alfred Richardson (Cheshire 1968 GC 2). Born 10.11.1927, North Duffield, Yorkshire. Died 17.11.1998, Willaston, Wirral, Cheshire. LHB. FC for North Eastern Transvaal (1954/55-58/59). Also ListA for North Eastern Transvaal (1954/55-58/59).

21 Tests (1972/73-78) for England. 8 ODIs (1973-78) for England. FC for Surrey (1964-82), MCC (1969/70-76), Griqualand West (1973/74), MC (1985-86). Also ListA for Surrey (1964-82), MCC (1969/70-76), Griqualand West (1973/74).

Colin Roper (Dorset 1968 GC 1). Born 25.7.1936, Litton Cheney, Bridport, Dorset. RHB WKT. FC for Hampshire (1957). Also ListA for Hampshire (1957).

Franklyn Albert Rose (Herefordshire 2003-04 C&G 2). Born 1.2.1972, Chalky Hill, St Ann, Jamaica. RHB RF. 19 Tests (1996/97-00) for West Indies. 27 ODIs (1996/97-00) for West Indies. FC for Jamaica (1992/93-02/03), Northamptonshire (1998), Gauteng (2001/02), Surrey (2003). Also ListA for Jamaica (1992/93-02/03), Northamptonshire (1998), Gauteng (2001/02), Surrey (2003).

William Rose (Norfolk 1965-70 GC 2). Born 8.12.1934, Great Yarmouth, Norfolk. LHB SLA.

Paul Gregory Roshier (Buckinghamshire 1991-93 NWT 3). Born 10.10.1963, Mount Beauty, Victoria, Australia. RHB RMF.

Trevor Kenneth Rosier (Bedfordshire 1968-73 GC 3, MC South 1973 B&H 2). Born 14.1.1943, Stockwell, London. RHB RM.

Nathan William Round (Worcestershire CB 1999-03 C&G 2 NWT 1, Herefordshire 2000-01 C&G 4 NWT 1). Born 21.8.1980, Stourbridge, Worcestershire. RHB RM.

James George Castell Rowe (Kent CB 2002 C&G 1). Born 4.7.1979, Farnborough, Kent. LHB SLA. FC for Durham UCCE (2001). Also ListA for Durham UCCE (2001). Father: C.J.C. (Glamorgan, Kent, MCC).

Russell John Rowe (Wiltshire 1999-05 C&G 5 NWT 3). Born 14.5.1975, Salisbury, Wiltshire. RHB OB.

Mark Rowell (Oxfordshire 2002 C&G 1). Born 9.9.1973, Carlisle, Cumberland. RHB RM.

Christopher Neil Rowlands (Huntingdonshire 1999-01 C&G 3 NWt 3). Born 2.9.1970, Cambridge. RHB OB.

Christopher Francis Baines Paul Rudd (Devon 1984-85 NWT 2). Born 9.12.1963, Sutton Coldfield, Warwickshire. RHB OB. FC for Derbyshire (1986-87). Also ListA for Derbyshire (1986-87).

Raymond Keith Rudd (MC North 1973 B&H 1). Born 8.5.1946, Terrington St Clement, Norfolk. LHB LFM.

William Douglas Rudge (Gloucestershire CB 2001-02 C&G 2). Born 15.7.1983, Bristol. RHB RMF. FC for Gloucestershire (2005-08). Also ListA for Gloucestershire (2005-08).

Lee Joseph Rushworth (Durham CB 2001 C&G 1). Born 18.6.1982, Sunderland, Co Durham. RHB.

Scott Nicholas Ruskin (Hertfordshire 2001 C&G 2). Born 12.1.1975, Hertford. RHB RMF.

Edwin Peter Russell (Wiltshire 1964 GC 1). Born 12.8.1939, Salisbury, Wiltshire. RHB.

Timothy Peter Russell (Buckinghamshire 1985-93 NWT 3). Born 27.2.1958, High Wycombe, Buckinghamshire. RHB WKT.

William Eric Russell (Berkshire 1976 GC 1). Born 3.7.1936, Dumbarton, Dunbartonshire, Scotland. RHB RM. 10 Tests (1961/62-67) for England. FC for Middlesex (1956-72), MCC (1958-67). Also ListA for Middlesex (1956-72), MCC (1958-67).

David John Rutherford (Northumberland 1999-03 C&G 3 NWT 4). Born 6.4.1976, Ashington, Northumberland. LHB RFM.

Allan Edward Henry Rutter (Norfolk 1965 GC 1). Born 24.12.1928, Bickley, Kent. RHB. FC for CU (1953). Also ListA for CU (1953).

Colin Rutterford (Suffolk 1966-84 GC 5 NWT 3, MC East 1978 B&H 3). Born 1.8.1943, Lakenham, Norfolk. RHB RFM. Son: M.J. (Suffolk).

Saad Khan Janjua (Essex CB 2002-03 C&G 2). Born 7.11.1973, Lahore, Punjab, Pakistan. RHB RM. FC for Railways (1995/96), Lahore City (1998/99), Pakistan Customs (1999/00), Lahore Whites (2000/01), Islamabad (2001/02), Zarai Taraqiati Bank (2002/03), Khan Research Laboratories (2004/05). Also ListA for Railways (1995/96), Lahore City (1998/99), Pakistan Customs (1999/00), Lahore Whites (2000/01), Islamabad (2001/02), Zarai Taraqiati Bank (2002/03), Khan Research Laboratories (2004/05).

John Leonard Sadler (Yorkshire CB 1999 NWT 1). Born 19.11.1981, Dewsbury, Yorkshire. LHB LBG. FC for Leicestershire (2003-07), Derbyshire (2008). Also ListA for Leicestershire (2003-07), Derbyshire (2008).

Arif Saeed (Essex CB 1999-01 C&G 1 NWT 2). Born 30.8.1967, Sialkot, Punjab, Pakistan. RHB RFM.

Martin John Saggers (MC 1996 B&H 5, Norfolk 1996 NWT 1). Born 23.5.1972, King's Lynn, Norfolk. RHB RFM. 3 Tests (2003/04-04) for England. FC for Durham (1996-98), Kent (1999-08), MCC (2004), Essex (2007). Also ListA for Durham (1996-98), Kent (1999-08), MCC (2004), Essex (2007).

Mark Leonard Saggers (Cambridgeshire 1982-83 NWT 2). Born 28.5.1959, Cambridge. RHB WKT.

Christopher Frederick Sains (Essex CB 2000 NWT 1). Born 3.8.1978, Romford, Essex. RHB RFM.

Naheem Sajjad (Warwickshire CB 1999-02 C&G 2 NWT 2). Born 26.9.1966, Mirpur, Sind, Pakistan. RHB LFM.

Ross David Salmon (Staffordshire 1992 NWT 1). Born 6.11.1964, Leek, Staffordshire. RHB RM.

Edward Kevin Sample (Cumberland 1985-92 NWT 3). Born 19.2.1961, Barrow-in-Furness, Lancashire. RHB RFM.

Philip James Sampson (Surrey CB 2000 NWT 1). Born 6.9.1980, Manchester, Lancashire. RHB RFM. FC for Surrey (2002-04). Also ListA for Surrey (2002-04).

Ian Edward Wakefield Sanders (Dorset 1986 NWT 1). Born 26.2.1961, Edinburgh, Midlothian, Scotland. RHB RFM. FC for CU (1984). Also ListA for CU (1984).

Gary Don Sandford (Bedfordshire 1991-00 NWT 8, Huntingdonshire 2001-02 C&G 4). Born 7.7.1964, Stevenage, Hertfordshire. RHB WKT.

Neil Fredrick Sargeant (Middlesex CB 2000 NWT 2). Born 8.11.1965, Hammersmith, London. RHB WKT. FC for Surrey (1989-95). Also ListA for Surrey (1989-95).

Darren Graham Savage (Norfolk 1991 NWT 1). Born 24.9.1968, King's Lynn, Norfolk. RHB RMF.

Robert Rodney Savage (Wiltshire 1988-93 NWT 2). Born 20.12.1960, Southampton, Hampshire. RHB.

Lee Savident (Dorset 2003 C&G 1). Born 22.10.1976, St Martin's, Guernsey. RHB RM. FC for Hampshire (1997-00). Also ListA for Hampshire (1997-00).

Thomas Edward Savill (Nottinghamshire CB 2001 C&G 2). Born 16.5.1983, Sheffield, Yorkshire. RHB RMF. FC for Cambridge UCCE (2002-06), Nottinghamshire (2002), CU (2003-06). Also ListA for Cambridge UCCE (2002-06), Nottinghamshire (2002), CU (2003-06).

Graham John Saville (Norfolk 1968-69 GC 2). Born 5.2.1944, Leytonstone, Essex. RHB LBG. FC for Essex (1963-74), MC (1969). Also ListA for Essex (1963-74), MC (1969). Cousin: G.A.Gooch (Essex, MCC, Western Province).

Graham Paul Savin (Oxfordshire 1989-02 C&G 3 NWT 8). Born 22.9.1964, Oxford. LHB LM.

John Richard Savin (Wiltshire 1964-73 GC 3). Born 23.11.1942, Malmesbury, Wiltshire. RHB RFM.

Sunil Sawney (Dorset 1989-91 NWT 2). Born 30.12.1962, Newport Pagnell, Buckinghamshire. RHB OB.

Paul Richard Sawyer (Buckinghamshire 1997-05 C&G 7 NWT 3). Born 26.12.1979, High Wycombe, Buckinghamshire. LHB LB.

Mark Saxelby (Cheshire 1996 NWT 1, Nottinghamshire CB 2000 NWT 1). Born 4.1.1969, Worksop, Nottinghamshire. Died 12.10.2000, Beeston, Nottinghamshire. LHB RM. FC for Nottinghamshire (1989-93), Durham (1994-95), Derbyshire (2000). Also ListA for Nottinghamshire (1989-93), Durham (1994-95), Derbyshire (2000). Brother: K. (Nottinghamshire), nephew: I.D. (Gloucestershire, Nottinghamshire).

Graeme Scarratt (Durham 1972 GC 1). Born 14.9.1945, Hartlepool, Co Durham. LHB LB.

Michael Graeme Scothern (Cumberland 1988-97 NWT 6, MC 1995 B&H 1). Born 9.3.1961, Skipton, Yorkshire. RHB RFM. FC for Worcestershire (1985). Also ListA for Worcestershire (1985).

Andrew William Scott (Durham 1985 NWT 2). Born 13.2.1960, Geelong, Victoria, Australia. Died 3.9.2006, Corio, Victoria, Australia. RHB RFM.

Ben James Matthew Scott (Middlesex CB 1999 NWT 1). Born 4.8.1981, Isleworth, Middlesex. RHB WKT. FC for Surrey (2003), Middlesex (2004-08). Also ListA for Surrey (2003), Middlesex (2004-08).

Darren Anthony Scott (Kent CB 2002 C&G 1). Born 26.8.1972, Canterbury, Kent. LHB OB. FC for Kent (1998-00). Also ListA for Kent (1998-00).

Gary Michael Scott (Durham CB 2001-02 C&G 3). Born 21.7.1984, Sunderland, Co Durham. RHB RM,OB. FC for Durham (2001-06). Also ListA for Durham (2001-06).

Matthew Alexander Scott (Hampshire CB 1999 NWT 3). Born 15.9.1979, Portsmouth, Hampshire. RHB RM.

Martin Paul Scott (Wiltshire 1972 GC 1). Born 6.11.1943, Corsham, Wiltshire. RHB WKT.

Mark Stephen Scott (Worcestershire CB 1999 NWT 1). Born 10.3.1959, Muswell Hill, Middlesex. RHB OB. FC for Worcestershire (1981-83). Also ListA for Worcestershire (1981-83).

Peter James Scott (Nottinghamshire CB 2001 C&G 1). Born 20.11.1982, Nottingham. RHB OB.

Richard John Scott (Dorset 1983-98 NWT 3). Born 2.11.1963, Bournemouth, Hampshire. LHB RM. FC for Hampshire (1988-90), Gloucestershire (1991-93). Also ListA for Hampshire (1988-90), Gloucestershire (1991-93).

Stephen Paul Scott (Northumberland 1986-87 NWT 2). Born 18.2.1962, Newcastle upon Tyne, Northumberland. RHB RMF.

Timothy John Adam Scriven (Buckinghamshire 1988-99 NWT 9). Born 15.12.1965, High Wycombe, Buckinghamshire. RHB SLA. FC for Somerset (1988-89), MC (1994). Also ListA for Somerset (1988-89), MC (1994).

Michael E. Scrutton (Suffolk 1966 GC 1). RMF.

Christopher Peter Seal (Suffolk 1999-01 C&G 5 NWT 2). Born 25.7.1973, Minster, Margate, Kent. LHB LM.

Jason Paul Searle (Wiltshire 2000-01 C&G 1 NWT 2). Born 16.5.1976, Bath, Somerset. RHB OB. FC for Durham (1994-98). Also ListA for Durham (1994-98).

Luke Alexander Sears (Hampshire CB 1999 NWT 3). Born 3.4.1980, Portsmouth, Hampshire. RHB RM.

Kevin Graham Sedgbeer (Somerset CB 1999-02 C&G 3 NWT 1, Huntingdonshire 2000 NWT 2). Born 20.9.1972, Taunton, Somerset. RHB SLA.

Richard John Sellers (Northumberland 2001 C&G 1). Born 8.3.1980, Bolton, Lancashire. RHB OB.

Andrew John Sexton (Dorset 2000 NWT 2). Born 23.7.1979, Southampton, Hampshire. LHB OB. FC for Hampshire (2000). Also ListA for Hampshire (2000).

Russell John Sexton (Derbyshire CB 2002 C&G 1). Born 9.10.1978, Derby. RHB WKT.

Adam Charles Hilton Seymour (Cornwall 1995 NWT 1, Suffolk 1999-00 NWT 2). Born 7.12.1967, Royston, Hertfordshire. LHB RM. FC for Essex (1988-91), Worcestershire (1992-94). Also ListA for Essex (1988-91), Worcestershire (1992-94).

Stewart Anthony Seymour (Berkshire 1997-01 C&G 2 NWT 4). Born 3.3.1974, Ascot, Berkshire. RHB OB.

Derek Shackleton (Dorset 1973 GC 1). Born 12.8.1924, Todmorden, Yorkshire. Died 27.9.2007, Canford Magna, Dorset. RHB RM. 7 Tests (1950-63) for England. FC for Hampshire (1948-69), MCC (1950-57). Also ListA for Hampshire (1948-69), MCC (1950-57). Son: J.H. (Dorset, Gloucestershire).

Julian Howard Shackleton (Dorset 1990-98 NWT 6). Born 29.1.1952, Todmorden, Yorkshire. RHB RM. FC for Gloucestershire (1971-78). Also ListA for Gloucestershire (1971-78). Father: D. (Dorset, Hampshire, MCC).

Bilal Mustapha Shafayat (Nottinghamshire CB 2000-01 C&G 1 NWT 1). Born 10.7.1984, Nottingham. RHB RMF. FC for Nottinghamshire (2001-08), National Bank of Pakistan (2004/05), Northamptonshire (2005-06), Pakistan Customs (2007/08-08/09). Also ListA for Nottinghamshire (2001-08), National Bank of Pakistan (2004/05), Northamptonshire (2005-06), Pakistan Customs (2007/08-08/09). Brother: R.M. (Nottinghamshire CB).

Rashid Menhas Shafayat (Nottinghamshire CB 1999 NWT 1). Born 18.6.1980, Nottingham. RHB RM WKT. Brother: B.M. (MCC, National Bank of Pakistan, Northamptonshire, Nottinghamshire, Nottinghamshire CB, Pakistan Customs).

Imran Hussain Shah (Northumberland 1999-03 C&G 1 NWT 1). Born 8.9.1978, Newcastle upon Tyne, Northumberland. RHB SLA.

Shahid Nazir Bajwa (Northumberland 2002-03 C&G 3). Born 4.12.1977, Faisalabad, Punjab, Pakistan. RHB RFM. 15 Tests (1996/97-06/07) for Pakistan. 17 ODIs (1996-99/00) for Pakistan. FC for Faisalabad (1995/96-05/06), Habib Bank (1997/98-07/08), Gujranwala (1998/99). Also ListA for Faisalabad (1995/96-05/06), Habib Bank (1997/98-07/08), Gujranwala (1998/99). Brother: Shehzad Nazir (Faisalabad).

Adrian Shankar (Bedfordshire 2005 C&G 1). Born 7.5.1982, Ascot, Berkshire. RHB OB. FC for CU (2002-05), Cambridge UCCE (2002-05). Also ListA for CU (2002-05), Cambridge UCCE (2002-05).

Adam John Shantry (Northamptonshire CB 2002 C&G 1). Born 13.11.1982, Bristol. LHB LFM. FC for Northamptonshire (2003-04), Warwickshire (2006-07), Glamorgan (2008). Also ListA for Northamptonshire (2003-04), Warwickshire (2006-07), Glamorgan (2008). Father: B.K. (Dorset, Gloucestershire, Shropshire), brother: J.D. (MC, Shropshire).

Brian Keith Shantry (Dorset 1983-86 NWT 2, Shropshire 1990-93 NWT 2). Born 26.5.1955, Southmead, Bristol. LHB LFM. FC for Gloucestershire (1978-79). Also ListA for Gloucestershire (1978-79). Sons: A.J. (Glamorgan, Northamptonshire, Northamptonshire CB, Shropshire, Wales MC, Warwickshire) and J.D. (MC, Shropshire).

Tristan Neil Shardlow (Wiltshire 1990-05 C&G 4 NWT 2). Born 1.6.1970, Bristol. LHB WKT.

Suneal Sharma (Nottinghamshire CB 2002 C&G 1). Born 2.4.1986, Nottingham. LHB LM.

Christopher James Sharp (Essex CB 1999 NWT 1). Born 23.5.1964, Orsett, Essex. RHB OB.

Kevin Sharp (Shropshire 1993-97 NWT 2, MC 1994-96 B&H 6). Born 6.4.1959, Leeds, Yorkshire. LHB OB Occ WKT. FC for Yorkshire (1976-90), MCC (1979), Griqualand West (1981/82-83/84). Also ListA for Yorkshire (1976-90), MCC (1979), Griqualand West (1981/82-83/84).

Marcus Anthony Sharp (Cumberland 1994-03 C&G 6 NWT 10, MC 1995-98 B&H 18). Born 1.6.1970, Oxford. LHB RM. FC for Lancashire (1991). Also ListA for Lancashire (1991).

Steven Sharp (Cumberland 1986-94 NWT 6, MC 1990 B&H 2). Born 22.9.1962, Barrow-in-Furness, Lancashire. RHB.

Thomas Granville Sharp (Cornwall 1999-03 C&G 8 NWT 1). Born 7.11.1977, Truro, Cornwall. RHB OB.

Philip John Sharpe (Norfolk 1982 NWT 1). Born 27.12.1936, Shipley, Yorkshire. RHB OB. 12 Tests (1963-69) for England. FC for Yorkshire (1958-74), MC (1959-60), MCC (1963-69), Derbyshire (1975-76). Also ListA for Yorkshire (1958-74), MC (1959-60), MCC (1963-69), Derbyshire (1975-76).

Peter Samuel Sharpe (Norfolk 1965 GC 1). Born 21.11.1944, Sussex. Died 1.12.2000, Witney, Oxfordshire.

Toby John Sharpe (Dorset 2000 NWT 1). Born 5.7.1981, Camden, London. RHB RFM. FC for Oxford UCCE (2001-03). Also ListA for Oxford UCCE (2001-03).

David Andrew Shaw (Berkshire 1990-95 NWT 4). Born 10.2.1967, Maidenhead, Berkshire. RHB RM.

Graham Shaw (Durham CB 1999-00 NWT 4). Born 14.3.1962, Saltburn, Yorkshire. RHB OB.

Jonathan William Shaw (Nottinghamshire CB 1999 NWT 1, Herefordshire 2001 C&G 1). Born 4.5.1980, Nottingham. RHB RM,OB.

Kevin George Shaw (Suffolk 2001-02 C&G 3). Born 30.4.1971, Bury St Edmunds, Suffolk. RHB RM.

Paul Frank Shaw (Staffordshire 1993-04 C&G 6 NWT 6). Born 28.7.1967, Burton-on-Trent, Staffordshire. LHB RM.

Simon Max Shearman (Buckinghamshire 1992-93 NWT 2). Born 13.11.1964, Aylesbury, Buckinghamshire. RHB.

Grant John James Sheen (Kent CB 1999-01 C&G 2 NWT 3). Born 21.6.1974, Bromley, Kent. RHB OB.

Kamran Pasha Sheeraz (Shropshire 1999 NWT 1). Born 28.12.1973, Wellington, Shropshire. RHB RMF. FC for Gloucestershire (1994-97). Also ListA for Gloucestershire (1994-97).

Richard John Shenton (Cheshire 2001 C&G 2). Born 27.5.1972, Macclesfield, Cheshire. RHB RFM.

Gavin Francis Shephard (Warwickshire CB 2001 C&G 2). Born 20.8.1971, Birmingham, Warwickshire. RHB LM. Twin brother: S.F. (Warwickshire CB).

Grant Sheppard (Wiltshire 1993 NWT 1). Born 6.12.1972, Bradford-on-Avon, Wiltshire. LHB RFM.

John Shepperd (Norfolk 1965-68 GC 2). Born 8.5.1937, Willesden, Middlesex. RHB RFM. FC for Middlesex (1959-60). Also ListA for Middlesex (1959-60).

Zaheer Abbas Sher (MC 1996 B&H 1, Bedfordshire 1997-99 NWT 5, Buckinghamshire 2001-05 C&G 8). Born 13.1.1975, Slough, Berkshire. RHB RM.

David Sherrington (Durham CB 1999 NWT 3). Born 1.9.1961, Easington, Co Durham. RHB WKT.

Anthony Laird Shillinglaw (Cheshire 1964-68 GC 4). Born 25.5.1937, Birkenhead, Cheshire. RHB RM.

Adam Mark Shimmons (Shropshire 1997-04 C&G 7 NWT 4). Born 16.10.1972, Hillingdon, Middlesex. LHB RFM.

Jonathan Andrew Ship (Warwickshire CB 2001 C&G 1). Born 23.4.1981, West Bromwich, Staffordshire. LHB.

Simon Shipp (Nottinghamshire CB 2000 NWT 1). Born 27.4.1983, Cambridge. RHB RFM.

Peter Anthony Shippey (Cambridgeshire 1964-72 GC 5, MC North 1972 B&H 4). Born 31.8.1939, Newton, Wisbech, Cambridgeshire. LHB OB. FC for MCC (1967), MC (1969-71). Also ListA for MCC (1967), MC (1969-71). Brother: S.W. (Cambridgeshire).

Samuel Ward Shippey (Cambridgeshire 1964-67 GC 2). Born 13.6.1937, Wisbech, Cambridgeshire. RHB LB. Brother: P.A. (Cambridgeshire, MCC, MC, MC North).

Damian Cyrus Shirazi (Hampshire CB 2000-02 C&G 3 NWT 1). Born 23.3.1983, Neath, Glamorgan, Wales. LHB RM. FC for Loughborough UCCE (2006). Also ListA for Loughborough UCCE (2006).

Charles Edward Shreck (Cornwall 1999-02 C&G 5 NWT 2). Born 6.1.1978, Truro, Cornwall. RHB RFM. FC for Nottinghamshire (2003-08), Wellington (2005/06-07/08), MCC (2008). Also ListA for Nottinghamshire (2003-08), Wellington (2005/06-07/08), MCC (2008).

Daniel Graeme Shurben (Northumberland 2005 C&G 1). Born 10.11.1983, Sunderland, Co Durham. LHB.

Christopher James Siddall (Yorkshire CB 2000 NWT 1). Born 11.12.1979, Sheffield, Yorkshire. LHB OB.

Roger John Sillence (Wiltshire 1999-00 NWT 4). Born 29.6.1977, Salisbury, Wiltshire. RHB RMF. FC for Gloucestershire (2001-05), Worcestershire (2006-07). Also ListA for Gloucestershire (2001-05), Worcestershire (2006-07).

Stuart Simmonds (Sussex CB 1999 NWT 1). Born 23.1.1976, Birmingham, Warwickshire. RHB RMF.

Paul Clifford Patrick Simmonite (Cheshire 1994 NWT 1). Born 17.3.1971, Burnley, Lancashire. RHB RM.

Mark Lawrence Simmons (Berkshire 1979-95 GC 1 NWT 11). Born 2.6.1955, Windsor, Berkshire. LHB SLA.

Philip Verant Simmons (Durham 1989-90 NWT 2, Wales MC 2000-02 C&G 6 NWT 3). Born 18.4.1963, Arima, Trinidad. RHB RM. 26 Tests (1987/88-97/98) for West Indies. 143 ODIs (1987/88-99) for West Indies. FC for Trinidad and Tobago (1982/83-00/01), Leicestershire (1994-98), Easterns (1996/97-99/00). Also ListA for Trinidad and Tobago (1982/83-00/01), Leicestershire (1994-98), Easterns (1996/97-99/00).

Robert George Simons (Hertfordshire 1964-66 GC 2). Born 23.3.1922, Watford, Hertfordshire. RHB WKT. FC for MC (1959). Also ListA for MC (1959).

David Paul Simpkins (Wiltshire 1984-93 NWT 5). Born 28.3.1962, Chippenham, Wiltshire. RHB OB. FC for Gloucestershire (1982). Also ListA for Gloucestershire (1982). Father: D.W. (Wiltshire).

David William Simpkins (Wiltshire 1969-73 GC 2). Born 29.5.1934, Derry Hill, Wiltshire. LHB WKT. Son: D.P. (Gloucestershire, Wiltshire).

Peter Anthony Simpkins (Berkshire 1966 GC 2). Born 27.11.1928, Dover, Kent. RHB SLA.

Robert Reed Simpson (Cheshire 1983 NWT 1). Born 8.7.1962, Altrincham, Cheshire. RHB.

Thomas Andrew Simpson (Middlesex CB 2000 NWT 1). Born 7.11.1974, Hampstead, London. LHB.

Anthony Erin Skeggs (Hertfordshire 2003 C&G 1). Born 16.3.1972, Croydon, Surrey. RHB RM. Brother: R.J. (Hertfordshire).

Richard John Skone (Wales MC 2002 C&G 1). Born 17.6.1974, Penarth, Glamorgan, Wales. LHB OB.

Richard Philip Skyrme (Herefordshire 1995-97 NWT 2). Born 23.12.1960, Hereford. RHB OB.

John Kenneth Edward Slack (Buckinghamshire 1969 GC 1). Born 23.12.1930, Marylebone, London. RHB. FC for CU (1954). Also ListA for CU (1954).

Douglas Norman Frank Slade (MC North 1974 B&H 1, Shropshire 1974-78 GC 3, MC East 1976 B&H 3). Born 24.8.1940, Feckenham, Worcestershire. RHB SLA. FC for Worcestershire (1958-71), MCC (1959-66). Also ListA for Worcestershire (1958-71), MCC (1959-66). Son: N.D. (Shropshire).

Oliver Michael Slipper (Surrey CB 2000 NWT 1). Born 10.3.1976, Slough, Berkshire. RHB RFM.

Lloyd Peter Sluman (Berkshire 1985 NWT 1). Born 13.2.1952, Helston, Cornwall. RHB RMF.

Adrian Mark Small (Devon 1999 NWT 2). Born 12.1.1973, Portsmouth, Hampshire. RHB LB.

David Smit (Derbyshire CB 1999-02 C&G 2 NWT 3). Born 23.7.1976, Nottingham. RHB. Sister: J. (East Midlands Women, Emeralds, Nottinghamshire Women).

Anthony Christopher Smith (MC 1993-94 B&H 2, Wales MC 1993-04 C&G 2 NWT 2). Born 15.8.1961, Burnley, Lancashire. RHB SLA.

Anthony Mervyn Smith (Wiltshire 1964-69 GC 3). Born 26.2.1930, Castle Combe, Wiltshire. LHB SLA. FC for MC (1965). Also ListA for MC (1965).

Bradley Smith (Sussex CB 1999 NWT 1). Born 28.9.1969, Margate, Kent. RHB RM.

Colin W. Smith (Buckinghamshire 1965 GC 1).

David Embleton Smith (Buckinghamshire 1974-87 GC 2 NWT 4). Born 18.11.1945, Harpenden, Hertfordshire. RHB RM.

Donald Joseph Smith (Cheshire 1968 GC 2). Born 19.10.1933, Stockport, Cheshire. LHB RFM. FC for CU (1955-57). Also ListA for CU (1955-57).

David Martin Smith (Hertfordshire 1989-91 NWT 3). Born 21.1.1962, Keresley, Coventry, Warwickshire. LHB SLA. FC for Warwickshire (1981-83). Also ListA for Warwickshire (1981-83).

David Thomas Smith (Cumberland 1994 NWT 1). Born 13.6.1970, Salford, Lancashire. LHB RM.

Gareth Smith (Durham CB 1999-01 C&G 1 NWT 6). Born 20.7.1966, Jarrow, Co Durham. RHB LFM. FC for Northamptonshire (1986-89), Warwickshire (1990). Also ListA for Northamptonshire (1986-89), Warwickshire (1990).

Graeme Craig Smith (Hampshire CB 2000 NWT 1). Born 1.2.1981, Johannesburg, Transvaal, South Africa. LHB OB. 1 Test (2005/06) for ICC World XI, 74 Tests (2001/02-08/09) for South Africa. 1 ODI (2005/06) for African XI, 135 ODIs (2001/02-08/09) for South Africa. 12 Int2020s (2005/06-07/08) for South Africa. FC for Western Province (2000/01-03/04), Western Province Boland (2004/05), Somerset (2005). Also ListA for Western Province (2000/01-03/04), Western Province Boland (2004/05), Somerset (2005).

Geoffrey John Smith (Hertfordshire 1969 FC 2). Born 2.4.1935, Braintree, Essex. RHB OB. FC for Essex (1955-66), MCC (1963). Also ListA for Essex (1955-66), MCC (1963).

Jack Smith (Bedfordshire 1967-73 GC 6, MC South 1973 B&H 4). Born 7.3.1936, Stotfold, Bedfordshire. RHB OB. FC for MC (1965). Also ListA for MC (1965).

Joseph Abraham Smith (Shropshire 1976-85 GC 2 NWT 1, MC 1982 B&H 2). Born 23.3.1946, Kingston, Jamaica. LHB LFM.

James Douglas Smith (Leicestershire CB 1999-00 NWT 2). Born 21.4.1977, Leicester. RHB WKT.

John Graham David Smith (Durham 1982 NWT 1). Born 21.8.1950, Stockton-on-Tees, Co Durham. RHB LM.

Karl Brian Smith (Leicestershire CB 2001 C&G 1). Born 23.9.1978, Leicester. RHB RM.

Lawrence Kilner Smith (Wiltshire 1993 NWT 1). Born 6.1.1964, Mirfield, Yorkshire. RHB Occ WKT. FC for Worcestershire (1985-87). Also ListA for Worcestershire (1985-87). Father: D.H.K. (Derbyshire, Gloucestershire, MCC, Orange Free State).

Matthew Eric Smith (Hertfordshire 2001 C&G 2). Born 29.4.1977, Harrow, Middlesex. RHB OB.
Michael W. Smith (Oxfordshire 1967 GC 1). RHB WKT.
Neil Smith (Cheshire 1988-89 NWT 3). Born 1.4.1949, Ossett, Yorkshire. Died 3.3.2003, Dewsbury, Yorkshire. RHB WKT. FC for Yorkshire (1970-71), MC (1972), Essex (1973-81). Also ListA for Yorkshire (1970-71), MC (1972), Essex (1973-81).
Neil Michael Knight Smith (Shropshire 2004 C&G 1). Born 27.7.1967, Solihull, Warwickshire. RHB OB. 7 ODIs (1995/96-96) for England. FC for Warwickshire (1987-03). Also ListA for Warwickshire (1987-03). Father: M.J.K. (Leicestershire, MCC, OU, Warwickshire), great-grandfather: R.C.Leach (Lancashire).
Peter Bruce Smith (Oxfordshire 1967-75 GC 5). Born 18.3.1944, Headington, Oxfordshire. RHB RM. FC for OU (1967). Also ListA for OU (1967).
Paul Christopher Smith (Middlesex CB 2002 C&G 1). Born 29.4.1975, Hillingdon, London. RHB WKT.
Robert Smith (Cumberland 2001 C&G 1). Born 1.2.1982, St Bees, Cumbria. LHB.
Royston Anthony Smith (Essex CB 2000-02 C&G 2 NWT 1). Born 14.3.1974, Romford, Essex. RHB RM.
Timothy David Smith (Oxfordshire 2001 C&G 2). Born 21.1.1983, Sheffield, Yorkshire. RHB.
Trevor Mark Smith (Suffolk 2002-05 C&G 4). Born 18.1.1977, Derby. LHB RM. FC for Derbyshire (1997-01). Also ListA for Derbyshire (1997-01).
Timothy Stewart Smith (Hertfordshire 1983-90 NWT 8, MC 1984 B&H 4, Cambridgeshire 1994-04 C&G 6 NWT 5). Born 29.12.1953, Henham, Essex. RHB SLA. FC for MC (1985).
William Albert Smith (MC South 1972 B&H 4, Wiltshire 1972-73 GC 2). Born 15.9.1937, Salisbury, Wiltshire. LHB RM. FC for Surrey (1961-70). Also ListA for Surrey (1961-70). Son: A.W. (Surrey).
Adam Charles Smyth (Warwickshire CB 2000 NWT 1). Born 16.5.1981, Walsgrave, Coventry, Warwickshire. RHB RM.
John Stephen Snashall (Sussex CB 2001 C&G 2). Born 12.10.1982, Eastbourne, Sussex. RHB RM.
William Edward Sneath (Bedfordshire 1999-03 C&G 7 NWT 3). Born 26.4.1977, Bedford. RHB RFM.
Andrew Mark Snell (Cornwall 1995-96 NWT 2). Born 19.9.1975, Truro, Cornwall. RHB WKT.
Stephen David Snell (Hampshire CB 2001 C&G 1). Born 27.2.1983, Winchester, Hampshire. RHB WKT. FC for Gloucestershire (2005-08). Also ListA for Gloucestershire (2005-08).
David Roy Snellgrove (Lancashire CB 1999-02 C&G 4 NWT 1). Born 22.8.1967, Liverpool, Lancashire. RHB OB. Father: K.L. (Cheshire, Lancashire, MC).
Jeffrey James Snowden (Kent CB 2001 C&G 1). Born 15.9.1973, Dartford, Kent. RHB WKT.
Andrew Edward Snowdon (Cornwall 1986 NWT 1). Born 26.9.1965, Plymouth, Devon. LHB RM. Brother: M.T. (Cornwall).
Michael Thomas Snowdon (Cornwall 1975 GC 1). Born 3.4.1947, Callington, Cornwall. RHB RM. Brother: A.E. (Cornwall).
Derek William Soakell (Durham 1973 GC 2). Born 7.12.1939, Haswell, Co Durham. RHB RM.
John William Solanky (Devon 1969 GC 1). Born 30.6.1942, Dar-es-Salaam, Tanzania. Died 7.10.2003, Carrickfergus, Co Antrim, Ireland. RHB RM,OB. FC for Glamorgan (1972-76). Also ListA for Glamorgan (1972-76).
Hugo Finlay Grant Southwell (Sussex CB 2000-01 C&G 2 NWT 1). Born 14.5.1980, Hammersmith, London. RHB RM.
Christopher Rukshan Soza (Berkshire 1996 NWT 1). Born 24.12.1966, Colombo, Sri Lanka. RHB.
Jamie Sparrow (Essex CB 1999 NWT 1). Born 22.1.1971, Bishop's Stortford, Hertfordshire. RHB RFM. Brother: R. (Cambridgeshire, MCC).
Martin Peter Speight (Northumberland 2002-03 C&G 2). Born 24.10.1967, Walsall, Staffordshire. RHB WKT. FC for Sussex (1986-96), Wellington (1989/90-92/93), Durham (1997-01). Also ListA for Sussex (1986-96), Wellington (1989/90-92/93), Durham (1997-01).
Arthur John Spencer (Wiltshire 1984 NWT 1). Born 18.8.1954, Wigan, Lancashire. RHB RFM.
Ian Stuart Spencer (Cheshire 2003 C&G 1). Born 26.8.1984, Whiston, Lancashire. RHB WKT.
Benjamin Lee Spendlove (Derbyshire CB 2001 C&G 2). Born 4.11.1978, Belper, Derbyshire. RHB OB. FC for Derbyshire (1997-00). Also ListA for Derbyshire (1997-00).

Russell Anthony Spiers (Staffordshire 1991-94 NWT 3). Born 10.7.1962, Leicester. RHB SLA.

James Ashley Stuart Spires (Warwickshire CB 2001 C&G 1). Born 12.11.1979, Solihull, Warwickshire. RHB SLA. FC for Warwickshire (2001-02). Also ListA for Warwickshire (2001-02).

Wayne Spooner (Nottinghamshire CB 1999 NWT 1). Born 25.10.1979, Worksop, Nottinghamshire. LHB LFM.

Andrew John Squire (Suffolk 1993-01 C&G 1 NWT 3). Born 9.3.1964, Mildenhall, Suffolk. RHB RM.

Robert Charles Staddon (Devon 1969 GC 1). Born 11.12.1944, Exeter, Devon. LHB.

Daniel Martin Stamp (Norfolk 1990-91 NWT 2). Born 23.11.1966, Paddington, London. RHB OB.

James Alfred Standen (MC South 1972 B&H 2). Born 30.5.1935, Edmonton, Middlesex. RHB RM. FC for Worcestershire (1959-70). Also ListA for Worcestershire (1959-70).

Timothy Paul Andrew Standing (Cheshire 1992-93 NWT 2). Born 6.8.1964, Hyde, Cheshire. RHB WKT.

Keith Standring (Bedfordshire 1994 NWT 1). Born 17.5.1965, Luton, Bedfordshire. LHB LMF.

Edward John Stanford (Kent CB 1999-01 C&G 2 NWT 5). Born 21.1.1971, Dartford, Kent. LHB SLA. FC for Kent (1995-97). Also ListA for Kent (1995-97).

Craig Stanley (Northumberland 1994-00 NWT 3). Born 17.12.1971, North Shields, Northumberland. RHB RFM.

Neil Alan Stanley (Bedfordshire 1994-03 C&G 8 NWT 5). Born 16.5.1968, Bedford. RHB RM. FC for Northamptonshire (1988-92). Also ListA for Northamptonshire (1988-92).

Simon Francis Stanway (Buckinghamshire 1997-05 C&G 8 NWT 4). Born 22.4.1966, Aylesbury, Buckinghamshire. RHB RM.

Ben Richard Frank Staunton (Gloucestershire CB 2001-02 C&G 4). Born 9.1.1977, Bath, Somerset. RHB OB.

James Malcolm Steadman (Bedfordshire 2002-03 C&G 4). Born 15.2.1983, Bedford. RHB RMF.

Mark Gregory Stear (Berkshire 1988-92 NWT 5). Born 8.12.1958, Kensington, London. RHB RMF.

Malcolm Geoffrey Stedman (Bedfordshire 1982 NWT 1). Born 28.4.1948, West Ham, Essex. RHB.

Marcus Harvey Steed (Northamptonshire CB 2001-02 C&G 4, Bedfordshire 2003-05 C&G 3). Born 8.5.1975, Market Harborough, Leicestershire. RHB RMF.

Simon Andrew Steel (Suffolk 1996 NWT 1). Born 2.10.1969, Ipswich, Suffolk. RHB RFM.

Arran Spencer Steele (Northamptonshire CB 1999 NWT 1). Born 14.1.1975, Corby, Northamptonshire. RHB LB. Father: D.S. (Bedfordshire, Derbyshire, Leicestershire, MCC, Northamptonshire, Staffordshire), uncle: J.F. (Glamorgan, Leicestershire, Natal, Natal B, Staffordshire), brother: M.V. (Staffordshire).

David Stanley Steele (Bedfordshire 1985 NWT 1). Born 29.9.1941, Bradeley, Staffordshire. RHB SLA. 8 Tests (1975-76) for England. 1 ODI (1976) for England. FC for Northamptonshire (1963-84), MCC (1967-76), Derbyshire (1979-81), Leicestershire (1980/81). Also ListA for Northamptonshire (1963-84), MCC (1967-76), Derbyshire (1979-81), Leicestershire (1980/81). Brother: J.F. (Glamorgan, Leicestershire, Natal, Natal B, Staffordshire), sons: M.V. (Staffordshire) and A.S. (Northamptonshire CB), cousin: B.S.Crump (MCC, Northamptonshire, Staffordshire), uncle: S.Crump (MC, Staffordshire).

Howard Keith Chillingworth Steele (Cambridgeshire 1972 GC 1). Born 6.4.1951, Epsom, Auckland, New Zealand. RHB RM. FC for CU (1970-72), Auckland (1974/75). Also ListA for CU (1970-72), Auckland (1974/75).

Mark Vincent Steele (Staffordshire 1998 NWT 1). Born 13.11.1976, Corby, Northamptonshire. LHB RFM. Father: D.S. (Bedfordshire, Derbyshire, Leicestershire, MCC, Northamptonshire, Staffordshire), uncle: J.F. (Glamorgan, Leicestershire, Natal, Natal B, Staffordshire), brother: A.S. (Northamptonshire CB).

William Frederick Stelling (Berkshire 1999 NWT 2). Born 30.6.1969, Johannesburg, Transvaal, South Africa. RHB RFM. 15 ODIs (2006-07) for Netherlands. FC for Western Province (1991/92), Western Province B (1991/92-93/94), Boland (1994/95-96/97), Boland B (1994/95), Leicestershire (2000), Netherlands (2006). Also ListA for Western Province (1991/92), Western

Province B (1991/92-93/94), Boland (1994/95-96/97), Boland B (1994/95), Leicestershire (2000), Netherlands (2006).

Justin Christopher John Stephens (Cornwall 1999-03 C&G 7 NWT 2). Born 12.8.1979, Penzance, Cornwall. RHB RM.

Philip John Stephens (Cornwall 1986 NWT 1). Born 7.5.1960, Hertford. RHB.

Harold William Stephenson (Dorset 1968 GC 1). Born 18.7.1920, Haverton Hill, Co Durham. Died 23.4.2008, Taunton, Somerset. RHB WKT. FC for Somerset (1948-64), MCC (1950-55/56). Also ListA for Somerset (1948-64), MCC (1950-55/56).

Martin Graham Stephenson (Cambridgeshire 1972-92 GC 1 NWT 6). Born 25.3.1949, Huntingdon. RHB OB.

Mark Edward Stevens (Berkshire 1986-91 NWT 5). Born 16.3.1959, Taunton, Somerset. RHB WKT.

Paul James Stevens (Sussex CB 1999-02 C&G 5 NWT 3). Born 31.7.1973, Eastbourne, Sussex. RHB WKT.

Barry Stewart (Northumberland 2000 NWT 1). Born 3.12.1980, North Shields, Northumberland. RHB RM.

Kirk David Edward Stewart (Hampshire CB 1999 NWT 3). Born 1.1.1974, Marondellas, Zimbabwe. RHB RFM.

David Alexander Stiff (Yorkshire CB 2001 C&G 1). Born 20.10.1984, Dewsbury, Yorkshire. RHB RF. FC for Kent (2004-06). Also ListA for Kent (2004-06).

Christopher James Stockdale (Cumberland 1986-92 NWT 5, MC 1988-89 B&H 5). Born 15.5.1965, Carlisle, Cumberland. RHB RM.

David Charles Stockings (Norfolk 1968 GC 1). Born 22.7.1946, Cambridge. RHB.

Peter Laurence Bowring Stoddart (Buckinghamshire 1965 GC 1). Born 24.6.1934, Regent's Park, London. RHB. FC for MCC (1958). Also ListA for MCC (1958).

John Stanley Stoker (Durham 1974 GC 2). Born 29.5.1944, Bearpark, Co Durham. RHB RMF.

Ian William Edward Stokes (Staffordshire 1997-98 NWT 2). Born 22.2.1964, Solihull, Warwickshire. LHB.

Christopher Stone (Dorset 1983-90 NWT 5). Born 11.5.1951, St Neots, Huntingdonshire. RHB OB.

Stuart Andrew Stoneman (Cheshire 1998-01 C&G 1 NWT 3, Devon 2002 C&G 1). Born 12.8.1971, Hammersmith, London. RHB RFM.

Timothy Christopher Stonock (Northumberland 2003 C&G 1). Born 29.3.1985, Sunderland, Co Durham. RHB OB.

David Benjamin Storer (Lincolnshire 1990-94 NWT 3). Born 31.3.1968, Grantham, Lincolnshire. RHB RM.

Luke Robert Francis Stoughton (Middlesex CB 2001 C&G 1). Born 6.9.1977, Hammersmith, London. RHB.

Neil Andrew Stovold (Gloucestershire CB 2001-02 C&G 3). Born 24.2.1983, Bristol. RHB OB. Brother: N.C. (Gloucestershire, Gloucestershire CB, Loughborough UCCE, Shropshire), father: A.W. (Gloucestershire, MCC, Northumberland, Orange Free State), uncle: M.W. (Gloucestershire).

Nicholas Craig Stovold (Gloucestershire CB 2000-01 C&G 3 NWT 2). Born 18.6.1981, Bristol. RHB. Father: A.W. (Gloucestershire, MCC, Northumberland, Orange Free State), uncle: M.W. (Gloucestershire), brother: N.A. (Gloucestershire CB, Loughborough UCCE).

Terence V. Strange (Oxfordshire 1970 GC 1). RHB RF.

Keith Harvey Stride (MC North 1975 B&H 1, Staffordshire 1975-78 GC 4). Born 10.1.1944, Dunstall, Staffordshire. RHB LFM.

Paul Francis John Strong (Buckinghamshire 1993 NWT 1). Born 3.12.1964, Ruislip, Middlesex. RHB.

Pieter Coenraad Strydom (Huntingdonshire 2002 C&G 1). Born 10.6.1969, Somerset East, Cape Province, South Africa. RHB SLA. 2 Tests (1999/00) for South Africa. 10 ODIs (1999/00) for South Africa. FC for Eastern Province B (1987/88-91/92), Border (1992/93-03/04), Warriors (2004/05). Also ListA for Eastern Province B (1987/88-91/92), Border (1992/93-03/04), Warriors (2004/05).

Ian Charles Derby Stuart (Dorset 1987-99 NWT 2). Born 13.10.1964, Port Elizabeth, Cape Province, South Africa. RHB RM.

Leonard George Stubbs (Hertfordshire 1969-71 GC 3). Born 24.10.1938, Calcutta (now Kolkata), Bengal, India. RHB.

John Peter Stuck (Suffolk 1978 GC 1). Born 19.11.1943, Ipswich, Suffolk. LHB WKT.

Peter David Stuckey (Dorset 1968 GC 1). Born 18.3.1940, Bournemouth, Hampshire. RHB RFM.

Michael John Sturgeon (Suffolk 1986 NWT 1). Born 1.12.1958, Bury St Edmunds, Suffolk. RHB WKT.

Peter Mark Such (Cambridgeshire 2002 C&G 1). Born 12.6.1964, Helensburgh, Dunbartonshire, Scotland. RHB OB. 11 Tests (1993-99) for England. FC for Nottinghamshire (1982-86), Leicestershire (1987-89), Essex (1990-01). Also ListA for Nottinghamshire (1982-86), Leicestershire (1987-89), Essex (1990-01).

Mark Edward Sullivan (Buckinghamshire 1998 NWT 1). Born 20.10.1964, Sasolburg, Orange Free State, South Africa. RHB OB.

John Sunley (Lincolnshire 1966-76 GC 4, MC East 1976-77 B&H 4). Born 10.10.1946, Grimsby, Lincolnshire. RHB RM.

Arul Vivasvan Suppiah (Somerset CB 2002 C&G 1, Devon 2003-05 C&G 4). Born 30.8.1983, Kuala Lumpur, Malaysia. RHB SLA. FC for Somerset (2002-08). Also ListA for Somerset (2002-08). Brother: R.V. (Malaysia).

David Surridge (Hertfordshire 1983-93 NWT 8, MC 1983-86 B&H 13). Born 6.1.1956, Bishop's Stortford, Hertfordshire. RHB RFM. FC for CU (1979), Gloucestershire (1980-82), MC (1986). Also ListA for CU (1979), Gloucestershire (1980-82).

Michael David Richard Sutliff (Leicestershire CB 1999-02 C&G 2 NWT 2, Gloucestershire CB 2001 C&G 1). Born 8.11.1975, Melton Mowbray, Leicestershire. LHB Occ WKT.

James Arthur Sutton (Cheshire 1964-86 GC 4 NWT 4, MC North 1975 B&H 1). Born 26.6.1939, Longsight, Manchester, Lancashire. LHB OB. FC for MC (1969-72). Also ListA for MC (1969-72).

Christopher Andrew Swallow (Suffolk 2001-05 C&G 6). Born 27.12.1981, Ipswich, Suffolk. RHB OB.

Pieter Johannes Swanepoel (Yorkshire CB 2001-02 C&G 4, Cambridgeshire 2004 C&G 1). Born 30.3.1977, Paarl, Cape Province, South Africa. RHB RMF. FC for Yorkshire (2003). Also ListA for Yorkshire (2003).

Alec James Swann (Northamptonshire CB 2000 NWT 1). Born 26.10.1976, Northampton. RHB OB Occ WKT. FC for Northamptonshire (1996-01), Lancashire (2002-04). Also ListA for Northamptonshire (1996-01), Lancashire (2002-04). Brother: G.P. (Bedfordshire, MCC, Northamptonshire, Nottinghamshire), father: R. (Bedfordshire, Northamptonshire CB, Northumberland).

Raymond Swann (Northumberland 1971 GC 1, Bedfordshire 1991 NWT 1, Northamptonshire CB 1999 NWT 1). Born 2.10.1950, Stannington, Morpeth, Northumberland. RHB RM. Sons: A.J. (Bedfordshire, Lancashire, Northamptonshire, Northamptonshire CB) and G.P. (Bedfordshire, MCC, Northamptonshire, Nottinghamshire).

Paul Aaron Swannell (Huntingdonshire 1999-02 C&G 1 NWT 1, Cambridgeshire 2004 C&G 1). Born 6.7.1980, Cambridge. RHB OB.

Peter Michael Swanwick (Staffordshire 1971 GC 1). Born 10.12.1945, Rocester, Staffordshire. RHB WKT.

Matthew Swarbrick (Dorset 1998-03 C&G 2 NWT 3). Born 8.8.1977, Stockport, Cheshire. RHB.

Peter Douglas Swart (Cambridgeshire 1975 GC 1, MC North 1975 B&H 1). Born 27.4.1946, Bulawayo, Zimbabwe. Died 13.3.2000, Newlands, Cape Town, Cape Province, South Africa. RHB RM. FC for Rhodesia (1965/66), Western Province (1967/68-80/81), Glamorgan (1978-79), Boland (1981/82-82/83), Western Province B (1983/84-84/85). Also ListA for Rhodesia (1965/66), Western Province (1967/68-80/81), Glamorgan (1978-79), Boland (1981/82-82/83), Western Province B (1983/84-84/85).

Nicholas Taylor Swetman (Wales MC 2004 C&G 1). Born 27.9.1984, Penarth, Glamorgan, Wales. RHB RFM.

Malcolm Swift (Wiltshire 1999 NWT 1). Born 21.4.1974, Southport, Lancashire. RHB RM.

John Warwick Swinburne (Shropshire 1976 GC 1). Born 4.12.1939, Wath-on-Dearne, Yorkshire. RHB OB. FC for Northamptonshire (1970-74). Also ListA for Northamptonshire (1970-74).

Gordon Robert Swinney (Somerset CB 1999 NWT 1). Born 4.1.1974, Bath, Somerset. RHB OB.

James Frederick Sykes (Durham 1990 NWT 1). Born 30.12.1965, Shoreditch, London. RHB OB. FC for Middlesex (1983-89). Also ListA for Middlesex (1983-89).

Jamie Peter John Sylvester (MC 1996-97 B&H 6, Berkshire 1997 NWT 1, Herefordshire 1998-00 NWT 2, Wales MC 1999-02 C&G 6 NWT 3). Born 31.7.1971, Cardiff, Glamorgan, Wales. RHB OB.

Ryan William Sylvester (Wales MC 1999-02 C&G 6 NWT 6). Born 20.4.1975, Cardiff, Glamorgan, Wales. RHB LB.

Steven Antony Sylvester (Hertfordshire 1999-00 NWT 4). Born 26.9.1968, Chalfont St Giles, Buckinghamshire. RHB LFM Occ WKT. FC for Middlesex (1991-92), Nottinghamshire (1994). Also ListA for Middlesex (1991-92), Nottinghamshire (1994).

Marc Joseph Symington (Northumberland 2003-05 C&G 2). Born 10.1.1980, Newcastle upon Tyne, Northumberland. RHB RM. FC for Durham (1998-02). Also ListA for Durham (1998-02). Grandfather: J.R. (Northumberland).

Keith Thomas Talboys (Oxfordshire 1967 GC 1). Born 19.12.1931, Oxford. RHB.

David Allan Tall (Devon 1992 NWT 1). Born 20.12.1963, Plympton, Devon. RHB RM.

James Martin Tandy (Worcestershire CB 2000-01 C&G 1 NWT 1). Born 16.1.1981, Wolverhampton, Staffordshire. RHB.

Ian Joseph Tansley (Cheshire 1985-88 NWT 3). Born 22.1.1962, Stepping Hill, Stockport, Cheshire. RHB.

Alistair Gordon Tapp (Cambridgeshire 2000 NWT 2). Born 9.3.1964, St Peter Port, Guernsey. RHB SLA.

Tauseef Ali Kazmi (Essex CB 2002-03 C&G 2). Born 26.11.1973, Chakwal, Punjab, Pakistan. RHB RM. FC for Rawalpindi (1999/00). Also ListA for Rawalpindi (1999/00).

Billy Victor Taylor (Wiltshire 1999 NWT 1). Born 11.1.1977, Southampton, Hampshire. LHB RMF. FC for Sussex (1999-03), Hampshire (2004-06). Also ListA for Sussex (1999-03), Hampshire (2004-08). Brother: J.L. (Wiltshire).

Christopher Glyn Taylor (Gloucestershire CB 1999 NWT 1). Born 27.9.1976, Bristol. RHB OB Occ WKT. FC for Gloucestershire (2000-08). Also ListA for Gloucestershire (2000-08).

David Kenneth Taylor (Oxfordshire 2001 C&G 1, Buckinghamshire 2002 C&G 2, Berkshire 2004 C&G 1). Born 17.12.1974, Oxford. LHB LMF. Also ListA for Worcestershire (2003), Derbyshire (2004).

George Michael Taylor (Cheshire 1981 NWT 1). Born 15.8.1944, Stockport, Cheshire. LHB LM. Son: A.J.Bond (Suffolk).

James Lee Taylor (Wiltshire 1999-02 C&G 2 NWT 3). Born 2.11.1974, Southampton, Hampshire. RHB RM. Brother: B.V. (Hampshire, Sussex, Wiltshire).

Jonathan Paul Taylor (Staffordshire 1989-90 NWT 2, Norfolk 2002 C&G 2). Born 8.8.1964, Ashby-de-la-Zouch, Leicestershire. LHB LFM. 2 Tests (1992/93-94) for England. 1 ODI (1992/93) for England. FC for Derbyshire (1984-86), Northamptonshire (1991-01). Also ListA for Derbyshire (1984-86), Northamptonshire (1991-01).

Martin Taylor (Devon 1984-87 NWT 2). Born 10.4.1957, Liverpool, Lancashire. LHB LFM.

Matthew Taylor (Lancashire CB 2000 NWT 2). Born 13.11.1973, Bolton, Lancashire. RHB SLA. FC for Derbyshire (1994). Also ListA for Derbyshire (1994).

Neil Raymond Taylor (Dorset 1989-91 NWT 3, MC 1989-92 B&H 14). Born 9.2.1964, Boscombe, Bournemouth, Hampshire. RHB RMF. FC for Middlesex (1990), MC (1990). Also ListA for Middlesex (1990).

Nicholas Simon Taylor (Norfolk 1990 NWT 1). Born 2.6.1963, Holmfirth, Yorkshire. RHB RFM. FC for Yorkshire (1982-83), Surrey (1984-85), Somerset (1986). Also ListA for Yorkshire (1982-83), Surrey (1984-85), Somerset (1986). Father: K. (Auckland, MCC, MC, Norfolk, Yorkshire).

Peter Michael Taylor (Bedfordshire 1967 GC 1). Born 11.12.1942, Cranfield, Bedfordshire. LHB.

Steven Kirby Taylor (Norfolk 1992 NWT 1). Born 28.11.1963, York. RHB.

Timothy John Taylor (Cheshire 1981 NWT 1). Born 28.3.1961, Romiley, Cheshire. RHB SLA. FC for Lancashire (1981-82), MC (1981), OU (1981-82). Also ListA for Lancashire (1981-82), MC (1981), OU (1981-82).

Keith Teasdale (Cheshire 1985-87 NWT 3). Born 26.3.1954, Castle Eden, Co Durham. LHB RM.

Christopher Mark Bagshaw Tetley (Middlesex CB 2001 C&G 1). Born 13.9.1974, Worcester. LHB LB.

Matthew Charles Theedom (Devon 1999-02 C&G 1 NWT 3). Born 1.10.1977, Exeter, Devon. RHB RFM.

James Edward Theunissen (Berkshire 2003 C&G 1). Born 7.12.1981, Camden, London. RHB RFM.

Joseph Thewlis (Northumberland 1971-77 GC 2). Born 14.4.1939, Percy Main, Northumberland. RHB. Nephew: M.J. (MCC, Northumberland), brother: J. (Northumberland).

Michael James Thewlis (Northumberland 1994 NWT 1). Born 19.1.1970, Ashington, Northumberland. RHB RM. Uncle: J. (Northumberland), father: J. (Northumberland).

Alfonso Clive Thomas (Staffordshire 2005 C&G 1). Born 9.2.1977, Cape Town, Cape Province, South Africa. RHB RFM. 1 Int2020 (2006/07) for South Africa. FC for Western Province B (1998/99), North West (2000/01-02/03), Northerns (2003/04-05/06), Titans (2004/05-07/08), Warwickshire (2007), Somerset (2008). Also ListA for Western Province B (1998/99), North West (2000/01-02/03), Northerns (2003/04-05/06), Titans (2004/05-07/08), Warwickshire (2007), Somerset (2008).

Aaron Courteney Thomas (Nottinghamshire CB 2001 C&G 2). Born 6.5.1985, Edmonton, Middlesex. RHB WKT. FC for Nottinghamshire (2003). Also ListA for Nottinghamshire (2003).

Anatole Winston Thomas (Buckinghamshire 1998-05 C&G 3 NWT 1). Born 26.3.1970, Hammersmith, London. RHB RF.

Christopher Thomas (Hertfordshire 1983 NWT 1). Born 26.5.1959, Billingham, Co Durham. RHB SLA.

David Robert Thomas (Norfolk 1984-99 NWT 12, MC 1990-95 B&H 8). Born 26.1.1963, Swardeston, Norfolk. LHB RFM. FC for MC (1990). Brother: P.W. (Norfolk), nephew: M.W. (Cambridgeshire, Norfolk).

Gary Malcolm Thomas (Cornwall 1995-03 C&G 8 NWT 4). Born 31.10.1973, Penzance, Cornwall. RHB RM.

Kevin Oliver Thomas (Cambridgeshire 1991 NWT 1). Born 20.6.1963, Mile End, London. RHB RFM. FC for Essex (1990). Also ListA for Essex (1990).

Karl Perry Terence Thomas (Nottinghamshire CB 1999 NWT 1). Born 2.6.1973, Nottingham. RHB RM.

Martin David Thomas (Oxfordshire 1980-81 GC 1 NWT 1). Born 8.6.1952, Altrincham, Cheshire. RHB OB.

Mark Wynne Thomas (Norfolk 1996-99 NWT 4). Born 30.1.1977, Norwich, Norfolk. RHB RFM. Uncle: D.R. (MCC, MC, Norfolk), father: P.W. (Norfolk).

Paul Anthony Thomas (Shropshire 1992 NWT 1, Herefordshire 1999-01 C&G 3 NWT 2). Born 3.6.1971, Perry Barr, Birmingham, Warwickshire. RHB RM. FC for Worcestershire (1995-97), Derbyshire (1999). Also ListA for Worcestershire (1995-97), Derbyshire (1999).

Philip Anthony Thomas (Cheshire 2001 C&G 1). Born 17.8.1978, Liverpool, Lancashire. RHB SLA.

Peter Dylan Thomas (Bedfordshire 1991-94 NWT 2). Born 22.8.1964, Willesden, Middlesex. RHB OB.

Peter Wynne Thomas (Norfolk 1983 NWT 1). Born 11.4.1952, Swardeston, Norfolk. RHB RFM. Son: M.W.Thomas (Cambridgeshire, Norfolk), brother: D.R.Thomas (MCC, MC, Norfolk).

Benjamin John Thompson (Oxfordshire 1999-01 C&G 2 NWT 2). Born 3.12.1980, Oxford. RHB OB.

G. Thompson (Northamptonshire CB 1999 NWT 1).

Jeremy Thompson (Wiltshire 1989-90 NWT 2). Born 23.9.1963, Bath, Somerset. RHB RFM.

Jackson Gladwin Thompson (Gloucestershire CB 2002 C&G 1). Born 7.2.1986, Nasik, Maharashtra, India. LHB OB. FC for Gloucestershire (2007). Also ListA for Gloucestershire (2007).

Matthew James Thompson (Northumberland 1999 NWT 1). Born 16.7.1974, Newcastle upon Tyne, Northumberland. RHB RM. Father: A.S. (Northumberland).

Philip Leslie Thorn (Wiltshire 1983-84 NWT 2). Born 17.11.1951, St George, Bristol. RHB SLA. FC for Gloucestershire (1974). Also ListA for Gloucestershire (1974).

Charles William Alexander Thornely (Cambridgeshire 1988 NWT 1). Born 5.10.1958, Lancaster, Lancashire. RHB.

Nicholas David Thornicroft (Yorkshire CB 2001 C&G 1). Born 23.1.1985, York. LHB RFM. FC for Yorkshire (2002-07), Essex (2005). Also ListA for Yorkshire (2002-07), Essex (2005).

Neil Jonathan Thurgood (Dorset 1999-04 C&G 3 NWT 2). Born 18.2.1977, Bournemouth, Hampshire. RHB RFM.

Colin John Tibbett (MC South 1979 B&H 1). Born 18.3.1951, Luton, Bedfordshire. RHB.

John Kevin Tierney (Devon 1985-91 NWT 5). Born 17.6.1964, Ashford, Kent. RHB RFM.

Michael Stuart Tiffin (Northumberland 1989-92 NWT 2). Born 7.6.1958, Haltwhistle, Northumberland. RHB WKT. Son: S.F. (Northumberland).

Henry William Tilly (Hertfordshire 1964-71 GC 5). Born 25.5.1932, Edmonton, Middlesex. RHB RFM. FC for Middlesex (1954-61), MCC (1955-60), MC (1967). Also ListA for Middlesex (1954-61), MCC (1955-60), MC (1967).

Matthew Arthur Tilt (Shropshire 2000-05 C&G 4 NWT 3). Born 25.7.1981, Shrewsbury, Shropshire. RHB WKT.

Peter John Timmis (Staffordshire 1971-73 GC 3). Born 30.7.1942, Stoke-on-Trent, Staffordshire. Died 10.5.1988, Northampton. RHB RFM. FC for MC (1971). Also ListA for MC (1971).

Richard Thomas Timms (Somerset CB 2002 C&G 1). Born 9.9.1984, Bristol. RHB RFM. FC for CU (2005-08), Cambridge UCCE (2005-08). Also ListA for CU (2005-08), Cambridge UCCE (2005-08).

John Tindale (Durham 1988 NWT 1). Born 9.10.1967, Durham. RHB RMF.

Mark Robert Tipping (Norfolk 1998 NWT 1). Born 27.10.1963, Norwich, Norfolk. LHB.

Paul Anthony Tipton (Cheshire 1982-83 NWT 2). Born 26.5.1954, Manchester, Lancashire. RHB OB.

James George Tizzard (Dorset 2001 GC 1). Born 12.11.1982, Isleworth, Middlesex. RHB RMF.

Paul Adrian Todd (MC 1986-87 B&H 8). Born 12.3.1953, Morton, Southwell, Nottinghamshire. RHB RM. FC for Nottinghamshire (1972-82), MC (1986), Glamorgan (1987). Also ListA for Nottinghamshire (1972-82), Glamorgan (1987).

Jeffrey Graham Tolchard (Devon 1969-83 GC 4 NWT 1, MC 1980-83 B&H 12). Born 17.3.1944, Torquay, Devon. RHB RM Occ WKT. FC for Leicestershire (1970-77), MC (1981). Also ListA for Leicestershire (1970-77). Brothers: R.W. (Devon, Leicestershire, MCC) and R.C. (Devon, MC South), nephews: R.G.Twose (Central Districts, Devon, Northern Districts, Warwickshire, Wellington) and R.P.Twose (Devon).

Raymond Charles Tolchard (Devon 1978-84 GC 4 NWT 2, MC South 1979 B&H 4). Born 13.10.1953, Torquay, Devon. Died 31.7.2004, Marldon, Devon. RHB. Brothers: R.W. (Devon, Leicestershire, MCC) and J.G. (Devon, Leicestershire, MC), nephews: R.G.Twose (Central Districts, Devon, Northern Districts, Warwickshire, Wellington) and R.P.Twose (Devon).

Christopher Mark Tolley (Nottinghamshire CB 2001 C&G 2). Born 30.12.1967, Kidderminster, Worcestershire. RHB LMF. FC for Worcestershire (1989-95), Nottinghamshire (1996-01). Also ListA for Worcestershire (1989-95), Nottinghamshire (1996-01).

John Richard Tolliday (Devon 1978-79 GC 2). Born 14.12.1947, Exeter, Devon. RHB.

Keith Patrick Tomlins (Wiltshire 1993 NWT 1). Born 23.10.1957, Kingston-upon-Thames, Surrey. RHB RM. FC for Middlesex (1977-85), Gloucestershire (1986-87). Also ListA for Middlesex (1977-85), Gloucestershire (1986-87).

James Andrew Tomlinson (Hampshire CB 2000 NWT 1, Wiltshire 2001 C&G 1). Born 12.6.1982, Winchester, Hampshire. LHB LM. FC for Hampshire (2002-08). Also ListA for Hampshire (2002-08).

Steven Charles Benjamin Tomlinson (Devon 2001 C&G 1). Born 21.12.1978, Bridgetown, St Michael, Barbados. RHB RMF.

Giles John Toogood (Shropshire 1992 NWT 1, Cambridgeshire 1995 NWT 1). Born 19.11.1961, West Bromwich, Staffordshire. RHB OB,RM. FC for OU (1982-89). Also ListA for OU (1982-89).

Christopher Donald Michael Tooley (Kent CB 1999 NWT 1). Born 19.4.1964, Bromley, Kent. RHB RM. FC for OU (1985-87). Also ListA for OU (1985-87).

Thomas Donald Topley (Norfolk 1984-85 NWT 2). Born 25.2.1964, Canterbury, Kent. RHB RMF. FC for Essex (1985-94), Surrey (1985), Griqualand West (1987/88). Also ListA for Essex (1985-94), Surrey (1985), Griqualand West (1987/88). Brother: P.A. (Kent, MCC).

David Anthony Toseland (Cornwall 1975-00 GC 3 NWT 2). Born 22.12.1952, Redruth, Cornwall. RHB OB.

Mark Andrew Tournier (Nottinghamshire CB 2002 C&G 1). Born 3.5.1971, Melbourne, Victoria, Australia. RHB RFM.

David Edward John Townsend (Devon 1993 NWT 1). Born 26.10.1965, Tiverton, Devon. RHB RM.

Gareth Terence John Townsend (Devon 1994-01 C&G 2 NWT 9, MC 1996 B&H 2). Born 28.6.1968, Tiverton, Devon. RHB. FC for Somerset (1990-92). Also ListA for Somerset (1990-92).

Anthony David Towse (Lincolnshire 1996 NWT 1, Wales MC 1998-04 C&G 7 NWT 4). Born 22.4.1968, Bridlington, Yorkshire. LHB RMF. FC for Yorkshire (1988). Also ListA for Yorkshire (1988).

Stanley John Trafford (Staffordshire 1976 GC 1). Born 21.12.1945, Leek, Staffordshire. RHB.

Robert Christopher Travers (Somerset CB 2001 C&G 1). Born 18.3.1982, Taunton, Somerset. RHB OB.

David John Traylor (Devon 1969 GC 1). Born 29.3.1943, Torquay, Devon. RHB.

Glyn Robert Treagus (Dorset 2000-04 C&G 5 NWT 2). Born 10.12.1974, Rustington, Sussex. RHB RM.

James Cullum Tredwell (Kent CB 2000-01 C&G 3 NWT 1). Born 27.2.1982, Ashford, Kent. LHB OB Occ WKT. FC for Kent (2001-08), MCC (2004-08). Also ListA for Kent (2001-08), MCC (2004-08).

Peter David Trego (Somerset CB 1999-01 C&G 1 NWT 1). Born 12.6.1981, Weston-super-Mare, Somerset. RHB RM. FC for Somerset (2000-08), Kent (2003), Middlesex (2005). Also ListA for Somerset (2000-08), Kent (2003), Middlesex (2005).

Christopher Richard Trembath (Wiltshire 1987 NWT 1). Born 27.9.1961, Willesden, Middlesex. RHB RM. FC for Gloucestershire (1982-84). Also ListA for Gloucestershire (1982-84).

Christopher Timothy Tremlett (Hampshire CB 2000 NWT 1). Born 2.9.1981, Southampton, Hampshire. RHB RFM. 3 Tests (2007) for England. 9 ODIs (2005-08) for England. 1 Int2020 (2007/08) for England. FC for Hampshire (2000-08). Also ListA for Hampshire (2000-08). Grandfather: M.F. (Central Districts, Hawke's Bay, MCC, Somerset), father: T.M. (Hampshire, MCC).

Peter Charles Trend (Lincolnshire 1997-00 NWT 5). Born 26.8.1974, Wolverhampton, Staffordshire. RHB WKT.

Michael Oswald Trenwith (Cornwall 1975-80 GC 2). Born 12.2.1945, Penzance, Cornwall. RHB RM.

Matthew Robin Trevor (Leicestershire CB 2002 C&G 2). Born 1.9.1982, Leicester. RHB RFM.

Damon James Trigger (Kent CB 1999-03 C&G 4 NWT 6). Born 22.4.1972, Lower Hutt, Wellington, New Zealand. RHB RMF.

Richard Ian Trotman (Somerset CB 1999 NWT 1). Born 8.1.1972, Keynsham, Somerset. RHB RM.

Andrew John Trott (Bedfordshire 1997-05 C&G 7 NWT 4). Born 26.9.1968, Wellingborough, Northamptonshire. RHB LB.

Keith Trotter (Durham 1989 NWT 1). Born 18.1.1962, Silksworth, Sunderland, Co Durham. RHB RFM.

Jamie Oliver Troughton (Warwickshire CB 1999-01 C&G 2 NWT 2). Born 2.3.1979, Camden, London. LHB SLA. 6 ODIs (2003) for England. FC for Warwickshire (2001-08). Also ListA for Warwickshire (2001-08). Great-grandfather: H.T.Crichton (Berkshire, Warwickshire).

Richard Parkinson Waite (Durham CB 2001-03 C&G 2). Born 6.6.1980, Stockton-on-Tees, Co Durham. RHB OB.

John Robert Wake (Bedfordshire 1985-91 NWT 2). Born 13.2.1953, Hexham, Northumberland. RHB OB. Son: C.J.Wake (Bedfordshire, Cambridgeshire, Durham UCCE, Northamptonshire CB).

Paul George Wakefield (Cheshire 1983 NWT 1). Born 6.3.1957, Crewe, Cheshire. LHB LB.

John Alan Wakeling (Nottinghamshire CB 1999 NWT 1). Born 8.1.1979, Nottingham. LHB WKT.

Alexander George Wakely (Bedfordshire 2005 C&G 1). Born 3.11.1988, Hammersmith, London. RHB OB. FC for Northamptonshire (2007-08). Also ListA for Northamptonshire (2007-08).

Sean Richard Walbridge (Dorset 1992-03 C&G 4 NWT 3). Born 17.6.1969, Weymouth, Dorset. RHB SLA.

Jonathan Edwin Peter Walford (Bedfordshire 2005 C&G 1). Born 24.1.1982, Hornchurch, Essex. LHB RM.

Andrew John Walker (Yorkshire CB 1999-00 NWT 3). Born 29.10.1971, Bradford, Yorkshire. RHB OB.

James Ross Walker (Norfolk 1999-03 C&G 5 NWT 1). Born 4.3.1981, Norwich, Norfolk. RHB WKT.

Nicholas Guy Eades Walker (Hertfordshire 2001-03 C&G 2). Born 7.8.1984, Enfield, Middlesex. RHB RFM. FC for Derbyshire (2004-05), Leicestershire (2006-07). Also ListA for Derbyshire (2004-05), Leicestershire (2006-07).

Peter David Walker (Devon 1978 GC 1). Born 20.8.1952, Stretford, Manchester, Lancashire. LHB RFM.

Stephen Wall (Cumberland 1987-89 NWT 3). Born 10.12.1959, Ulverston, Lancashire. RHB RMF. FC for Warwickshire (1984-85). Also ListA for Warwickshire (1984-85).

Gary Wallen (MC West 1977-78 B&H 8, Devon 1978-88 GC 4 NWT 3). Born 9.4.1955, Exeter, Devon. RHB LB. Brother: C. (Devon).

Christopher David Walsh (Cambridgeshire 2000 NWT 1). Born 6.11.1975, Pembury, Kent. RHB LB. FC for Kent (1996-98). Also ListA for Kent (1996-98). Father: D.R. (MCC, OU).

Matthew James Walshe (Hertfordshire 1993 NWT 1). Born 1.4.1970, Welwyn Garden City, Hertfordshire. RHB RFM.

Andrew Peter Walton (Kent CB 2000 NWT 3). Born 28.2.1965, Zimbabwe. RHB RM.

Richard Timothy Walton (Cornwall 1995 NWT 1). Born 1.6.1967, Newquay, Cornwall. LHB.

Timothy Charles Walton (Cambridgeshire 2001 C&G 1). Born 8.11.1972, Low Lead, York. RHB RM Occ WKT. FC for Northamptonshire (1994-97), Essex (1999). Also ListA for Northamptonshire (1994-97), Essex (1999).

Waqar Mohammad (Warwickshire CB 2001 C&G 1). Born 3.10.1968, Karachi, Sind, Pakistan. RHB LB. Uncle: Hanif Mohammad (Bahawalpur, Karachi, Karachi A, Karachi Whites, Pakistan International Airlines, Pakistan International Airlines A), father: Wazir Mohammad (Bahawalpur, Karachi, Karachi A, Karachi Blues, Karachi Whites), uncle: Mushtaq Mohammad (Karachi, Karachi A, Karachi Blues, Karachi C, Karachi Whites, MCC, Northamptonshire, Northumberland, Pakistan International Airlines, Pakistan International Airlines A, Peshawar, Shropshire, Staffordshire), uncle: Sadiq Mohammad (Buckinghamshire, Cornwall, Essex, Gloucestershire, Karachi, Karachi Blues, Karachi Schools, Karachi Whites, MCC, Pakistan International Airlines, Tasmania, United Bank), cousin: Shoaib Mohammad (Karachi, Karachi Blues, Karachi Whites, MCC, Pakistan International Airlines, Pakistan International Airlines B), I.Mohammad (CU, Cornwall, Gloucestershire, Gloucestershire CB, Hyderabad, Pakistan Customs, Public Works Department), Asif Mohammad (Faisalabad, Karachi Whites, Pakistan International Airlines, Rawalpindi, Rawalpindi B), uncle: Raees Mohammad (East Pakistan, Karachi, Karachi B, Karachi Blues, Karachi Whites, Peshawar), cousin: Shahid Mohammad (Pakistan International Airlines).

Andrew James Ward (Buckinghamshire 2003 C&G 1). Born 23.6.1981, Dartford, Kent. RHB WKT.

David Christopher Ward (Derbyshire CB 1999-00 NWT 2). Born 20.7.1981, Brisbane, Queensland, Australia. RHB RM. Father: A. (Border, Derbyshire, Leicestershire, MCC).

David Mark Ward (MC 1998 B&H 2, Hertfordshire 1999-03 C&G 3 NWT 4). Born 10.2.1961, Croydon, Surrey. RHB OB Occ WKT. FC for Surrey (1985-96), MCC (2001). Also ListA for Surrey (1985-96), MCC (2001).

Michael John Paul Ward (Norfolk 1996 NWT 1). Born 12.9.1971, Oldham, Lancashire. RHB OB. FC for Lancashire (1991). Also ListA for Lancashire (1991).

Steven Ward (Durham 1987 NWT 1). Born 30.10.1958, Horden, Co Durham. LHB RMF.

Timothy William Ward (Devon 1987-93 NWT 4). Born 28.10.1963, Paignton, Devon. RHB RM.

John Henry Wardle (Cambridgeshire 1964-67 GC 4). Born 8.1.1923, Ardsley, Yorkshire. Died 23.7.1985, Hatfield, Doncaster, Yorkshire. LHB SLA,SLC. 28 Tests (1947/48-57) for England. FC for Yorkshire (1946-58), MCC (1947/48-56/57). Also ListA for Yorkshire (1946-58), MCC (1947/48-56/57).

Stephen Nicholas Warman (Lincolnshire 1990-01 C&G 2 NWT 7). Born 24.8.1967, Lincoln. RHB.

Christopher James Warn (Suffolk 2001-05 C&G 7). Born 22.5.1979, Little Waltham, Chelmsford, Essex. RHB WKT. FC for Derbyshire (2002). Also ListA for Derbyshire (2002).

Alan Esmond Warner (Worcestershire CB 2000 NWT 1). Born 12.5.1957, Winson Green, Birmingham, Warwickshire. RHB RFM. FC for Worcestershire (1982-84), Derbyshire (1985-96). Also ListA for Worcestershire (1982-84), Derbyshire (1985-96).

Graham Sydney Warner (Staffordshire 1976-86 GC 1 NWT 3). Born 27.11.1945, Darlaston, Staffordshire. RHB OB Occ WKT. FC for Warwickshire (1966-71). Also ListA for Warwickshire (1966-71).

Nicholas Alexander Warren (Warwickshire CB 2001 C&G 1). Born 26.6.1982, Moseley, Birmingham, Warwickshire. RHB RFM. FC for Warwickshire (2002-05). Also ListA for Warwickshire (2002-05).

Paul Michael Warren (Devon 1997-01 C&G 2 NWT 2, Wales MC 1999 NWT 1). Born 18.1.1978, Plymouth, Devon. RHB RM. FC for Glamorgan (1997). Also ListA for Glamorgan (1997).

Anthony George Warrington (MC South 1973-75 B&H 7, Suffolk 1978-81 GC 4 NWT 1). Born 28.3.1947, Ipswich, Suffolk. RHB. FC for MC (1973-74). Also ListA for MC (1973-74). Son: G. (MCC).

Wasim Hasan Raja (Durham 1979-87 GC 3 NWT 3). Born 3.7.1952, Multan, Punjab, Pakistan. Died 23.8.2006, Marlow, Buckinghamshire. LHB LBG. 57 Tests (1972/73-84/85) for Pakistan. 54 ODIs (1972/73-84/85) for Pakistan. FC for Lahore Greens (1967/68-73/74), Lahore (1968/69), Lahore A (1969/70), Punjab University (1969/70-71/72), Sargodha (1969/70), Punjab (1971/72-78/79), Pakistan Universities (1972/73), Pakistan International Airlines A (1973/74), National Bank of Pakistan (1974/75-87/88), National Bank of Pakistan A (1975/76), Lahore City Blues (1984/85), Lahore City Whites (1985/86). Also ListA for Lahore Greens (1967/68-73/74), Lahore (1968/69), Lahore A (1969/70), Punjab University (1969/70-71/72), Sargodha (1969/70), Punjab (1971/72-78/79), Pakistan Universities (1972/73), Pakistan International Airlines A (1973/74), National Bank of Pakistan (1974/75-87/88), National Bank of Pakistan A (1975/76), Lahore City Blues (1984/85), Lahore City Whites (1985/86). Brother: Rameez Raja (Allied Bank, Islamabad, Lahore City, Lahore City A, Lahore City Whites, Pakistan National Shipping Corporation, Punjab, Servis Industries), cousin: Atif Rauf (Agriculture Development Bank of Pakistan, Islamabad, Lahore City), father: Saleem Akhtar (Multan, Sargodha), brother: Zaeem Raja (Bahawalpur, Lahore A, Lahore B, Multan, Punjab, Servis Industries).

Jonathan Arthur Waterhouse (Staffordshire 1988-96 NWT 3). Born 11.4.1965, Leek, Staffordshire. RHB.

Huw Thomas Waters (Wales MC 2005 C&G 1). Born 26.9.1986, Cardiff, Glamorgan, Wales. RHB RM. FC for Glamorgan (2005-08). Also ListA for Glamorgan (2005-08).

Stuart Nicholas Varney Waterton (Oxfordshire 1989-94 NWT 4, MC 1990-92 B&H 5). Born 6.12.1960, Dartford, Kent. RHB WKT. FC for Kent (1980-85), Northamptonshire (1986-87), Lancashire (1990). Also ListA for Kent (1980-85), Northamptonshire (1986-87), Lancashire (1990).

Michael Watkinson (Cheshire 1982 NWT 1). Born 1.8.1961, Westhoughton, Lancashire. RHB RM,OB. 4 Tests (1995-95/96) for England. 1 ODI (1995/96) for England. FC for Lancashire (1982-99). Also ListA for Lancashire (1982-99).

Alexander Garth MacLaren Watson (Dorset 1973 GC 1). Born 27.2.1945, Lucknow, Uttar Pradesh, India. LHB RFM. FC for OU (1965-68). Also ListA for OU (1965-68).

Douglas James Watson (Derbyshire CB 1999 NWT 1, Suffolk 2005 C&G 1). Born 15.5.1973, Pietermaritzburg, Natal, South Africa. RHB RM. FC for Natal (1993/94-97/98), Natal B (1993/94-95/96), KwaZulu-Natal (1998/99-03/04), Dolphins (2004/05-07/08), KwaZulu-Natal Inland (2008/09). Also ListA for Natal (1993/94-97/98), Natal B (1993/94-95/96), KwaZulu-Natal (1998/99-03/04), Dolphins (2004/05-07/08), KwaZulu-Natal Inland (2008/09).

John Martin Watson (Durham 1964 GC 2). Born 17.4.1921, High Spen, Co Durham. LHB RMF,OB.

Mark Andrew Watts (Wiltshire 1987-88 NWT 2). Born 20.8.1963, Wroughton, Wiltshire. RHB RFM.

Peter Willett Watts (Berkshire 1966 GC 2). Born 17.7.1947, Penang, Malaysia. SLA.

Stephen John Watts (Bedfordshire 2003-05 C&G 2). Born 1.5.1979, Luton, Bedfordshire. RHB OB.

Simon David Weale (Middlesex CB 1999 NWT 1). Born 16.9.1967, Knightsbridge, London. RHB SLA. FC for OU (1986-90). Also ListA for OU (1986-90).

Jason Richard Weaver (Shropshire 1990-91 NWT 2). Born 11.8.1968, Wellington, Shropshire. RHB WKT.

Simon Webb (Lincolnshire 2002 C&G 2). Born 24.9.1981, Grimsby, Lincolnshire. RHB.

Peter John Webley (Bedfordshire 1971 GC 1). Born 18.7.1942, Luton, Bedfordshire. LHB LBG.

Thomas Webley (Somerset CB 2001-02 C&G 2). Born 2.3.1983, Bristol. LHB SLA. FC for Cambridge UCCE (2003-05), Somerset (2003). Also ListA for Cambridge UCCE (2003-05), Somerset (2003).

Andrew John Webster (Staffordshire 1985-88 NWT 4, MC 1986-88 B&H 6). Born 5.3.1959, Rolleston-on-Dove, Staffordshire. LHB RM. FC for Worcestershire (1981-82). Also ListA for Worcestershire (1981-82).

Lesroy Charlesworth Weekes (Lincolnshire 1997 NWT 1, Yorkshire CB 1999 NWT 1). Born 19.7.1971, Montserrat. RHB RFM. FC for Leeward Islands (1993/94-96/97), Yorkshire (1994-00), Northamptonshire (2001). Also ListA for Leeward Islands (1993/94-96/97), Yorkshire (1994-00), Northamptonshire (2001).

Nicholas Paul Weekes (Sussex CB 2001 C&G 1). Born 20.10.1981, Crawley, Sussex. RHB RF.

Peter Edward Wellings (Staffordshire 1998-00 NWT 4, Middlesex CB 2001-02 C&G 4). Born 5.3.1970, Wolverhampton, Staffordshire. RHB RM. FC for Middlesex (1996-97). Also ListA for Middlesex (1996-97).

Benjamin Mark Wellington (Somerset CB 1999 NWT 1). Born 30.4.1974, Taunton, Somerset. RHB RM.

Guy Edward Welton (Lincolnshire 2004 C&G 1). Born 4.5.1978, Grimsby, Lincolnshire. RHB OB. FC for Nottinghamshire (1997-03). Also ListA for Nottinghamshire (1997-03).

David Alan Wenlock (Staffordshire 1985 NWT 1). Born 16.4.1959, Leicester. RHB RM. FC for Leicestershire (1980-82). Also ListA for Leicestershire (1980-82).

James Colin Went (Essex CB 2003 C&G 1). Born 7.1.1982, Reading, Berkshire. LHB RM.

Bryn West (Bedfordshire 2000 NWT 1). Born 6.3.1975, Westoning, Flitwick, Bedfordshire. RHB RM.

Frederick Michael Westcott (Durham 1967-68 GC 2). Born 20.11.1941, Corbridge, Northumberland. RHB.

Stuart Alker Westley (Suffolk 1978-83 GC 4 NWT 2). Born 21.3.1947, Fishergate, Preston, Lancashire. RHB WKT. FC for OU (1968-69), Gloucestershire (1969-71), MC (1976). Also ListA for OU (1968-69), Gloucestershire (1969-71), MC (1976). Twin brother: R.B. (OU).

Martin John Weston (Herefordshire 1995 NWT 1). Born 8.4.1959, Worcester. RHB RM. FC for Worcestershire (1979-93). Also ListA for Worcestershire (1979-93).

Michael Philip Weston (Durham 1972 GC 2). Born 21.8.1938, Durham. RHB LBG. Sons: R.M.S. (Derbyshire, Derbyshire CB, Durham, MCC, Middlesex), W.P.C. (Derbyshire, Gloucestershire, Worcestershire).

Ian James Westwood (Warwickshire CB 2001-02 C&G 4). Born 13.7.1982, Birmingham, Warwickshire. LHB OB. FC for Warwickshire (2003-08). Also ListA for Warwickshire (2003-08).

Robert Duncan Whalley (Lancashire CB 2001 C&G 1). Born 17.10.1979, Blackburn, Lancashire. RHB WKT.

David Mark Wheatman (Cumberland 2000-01 C&G 3 NWT 1). Born 31.1.1966, Kendal, Westmorland. Died 24.10.2004, St John's Wood, London. RHB LFM.

Mark Robin Whitaker (Norfolk 1969 GC 1). Born 20.9.1946, Walton-on-Thames, Surrey. RHB RFM. FC for CU (1965-67). Also ListA for CU (1965-67).

Gary George Whitbread (Huntingdonshire 1999 NWT 1). Born 1.7.1957, Huntingdon. RHB WKT.

Andrew Paul White (Oxfordshire 1994 NWT 1). Born 29.11.1967, Reading, Berkshire. RHB RFM.

Brian Humphrey White (Wiltshire 1965-90 GC 3 NWT 6, MC South 1972-74 B&H 6). Born 3.10.1944, Salisbury, Wiltshire. LHB.

Christopher Charles E. White (Essex CB 2002 C&G 1). Born 15.2.1980, Epping, Essex. RHB RM.

David Geoffrey White (Lancashire CB 1999 NWT 1). Born 5.8.1967, Horwich, Lancashire. RHB RMF.

Gareth Andrew White (Cumberland 2002 C&G 1). Born 28.1.1979, Whitehaven, Cumberland. RHB OB.

Giles William White (Devon 1992-93 NWT 2). Born 23.3.1972, Barnstaple, Devon. RHB LB Occ WKT. FC for Somerset (1991), Hampshire (1994-02). Also ListA for Somerset (1991), Hampshire (1994-02).

Jonathan William White (Gloucestershire CB 1999-02 C&G 4 NWT 3). Born 21.8.1979, Bristol. RHB LM.

Matthew Richard White (Bedfordshire 1994-98 NWT 3). Born 26.9.1969, Bedford. RHB RF. Father: R.H. (Bedfordshire).

Richard Howard White (Bedfordshire 1967 GC 1). Born 27.4.1934, Carlton, Bedfordshire. RHB RFM. Son: M.R. (Bedfordshire).

Simon Paul White (Hertfordshire 2001-03 C&G 5). Born 4.12.1975, St Albans, Hertfordshire. RHB RM.

Jonathan David Whitney (Shropshire 2005 C&G 1). Born 7.4.1985, Bridgnorth, Shropshire. RHB RFM.

Jason Peter Whittaker (Cheshire 2001-04 C&G 4). Born 24.7.1971, Farnworth, Bolton, Lancashire. RHB RFM.

Paul Kevin Whittaker (Norfolk 1984-85 NWT 2). Born 7.8.1956, Oxford. RHB RFM.

Christopher Mark Whyborn (Cambridgeshire 1997 NWT 1). Born 19.8.1966, Winchester, Hampshire. RHB RFM.

Clive Wicks (Lincolnshire 1988 NWT 1). Born 18.5.1949, Boston, Lincolnshire. LHB.

Paul Stuart Widdowson (Leicestershire CB 2000 NWT 1). Born 27.3.1974, Leicester. RHB RM.

Simon Widdup (Yorkshire CB 2002 C&G 3). Born 10.11.1977, Doncaster, Yorkshire. RHB OB Occ WKT. FC for Yorkshire (2000-01). Also ListA for Yorkshire (2000-01).

Kumarjit Mahinda Wijesuriya (Suffolk 1996-99 NWT 2). Born 25.7.1957, Colombo, Sri Lanka. RHB OB.

Jonathan Ritchie Wileman (Lincolnshire 1994-97 NWT 2, Surrey CB 1999-01 C&G 1 NWT 1). Born 19.8.1970, Sheffield, Yorkshire. RHB RM. FC for Nottinghamshire (1992-96), MC (1994). Also ListA for Nottinghamshire (1992-96), MC (1994).

John Stuart Wilkinson (Durham 1973-85 GC 9 NWT 3, MC East 1977-78 B&H 7, MC North 1979 B&H 4). Born 18.10.1942, Ebchester, Co Durham. RHB RFM.

Matthew Owen Wilkinson (Norfolk 2003 C&G 1). Born 17.12.1980, Norwich, Norfolk. RHB.

Richard Wilkinson (Yorkshire CB 2001-02 C&G 4). Born 11.11.1977, Barnsley, Yorkshire. RHB OB. FC for Yorkshire (1998). Also ListA for Yorkshire (1998).

Eric George Willcock (Cornwall 1970-86 GC 4 NWT 1). Born 28.9.1947, St Ives, Cornwall. LHB OB.

Kevin James Willcock (Cornwall 1995-96 NWT 2). Born 8.3.1973, Tavistock, Devon. RHB RM.

Duncan Richard Willetts (Herefordshire 2004 C&G 1). Born 26.10.1983, Stourbridge, Worcestershire. RHB.

Frank Terence Willetts (Cornwall 1980 GC 1). Born 20.11.1939, Birmingham, Warwickshire. LHB. FC for Somerset (1964-67). Also ListA for Somerset (1964-67).

Peter Willey (Northumberland 1992 NWT 1). Born 6.12.1949, Sedgefield, Co Durham. RHB OB. 26 Tests (1976-86) for England. 26 ODIs (1977-85/86) for England. FC for Northamptonshire (1966-83), MCC (1975-85), Eastern Province (1982/83-84/85), Leicestershire (1984-91). Also ListA for Northamptonshire (1966-83), MCC (1975-85), Eastern Province (1982/83-84/85), Leicestershire (1984-91). Son: D.J. (Bedfordshire).

Andrew Royd Williams (Shropshire 1992 NWT 1). Born 13.9.1965, Wrexham, Denbighshire, Wales. RHB OB.

A. S. Williams (Cumberland 2001 C&G 1).

Christopher Williams (Essex CB 2002 C&G 1). Born 17.3.1983, Rochford, Essex. LHB RMF.

Christopher David Williams (Bedfordshire 1982 NWT 1). Born 15.11.1954, Gosford, New South Wales, Australia. LHB RFM.

Dean Ross Williams (Cumberland 2001-03 C&G 2). Born 8.12.1980, Barrow-in-Furness, Lancashire. RHB WKT.

Gary Douglas Williams (Staffordshire 1991 NWT 1, Worcestershire CB 2000 NWT 1). Born 1.9.1965, Wolverhampton, Staffordshire. RHB RM.

Graham Geoffrey Williams (Gloucestershire CB 2002 C&G 1). Born 16.12.1985, Bristol. RHB RM.

Gareth John Williams (Worcestershire CB 2001-03 C&G 5). Born 12.12.1973, Birmingham, Warwickshire. LHB RFM.

John Charles Williams (Somerset CB 2000 NWT 1). Born 8.11.1980, Weston-super-Mare, Somerset. RHB RM.

Jeremy James Williams (Devon 2001-02 C&G 2). Born 19.1.1979, Plymouth, Devon. RHB WKT.

John Michael Williams (Buckinghamshire 1972 GC 1). Born 11.6.1941, Stourport-on-Severn, Worcestershire. RHB RFM.

Kelvin Claudius Williams (Northumberland 1984-92 NWT 3). Born 29.5.1959, Carapichaima, Trinidad. RHB RFM. FC for Trinidad and Tobago (1981/82-89/90), MCC (1999). Also ListA for Trinidad and Tobago (1981/82-89/90), MCC (1999).

Neil FetzGerald Williams (Cornwall 2000 NWT 1). Born 2.7.1962, Hopewell, St Vincent. Died 27.3.2006, Kingston, St Vincent. RHB RFM. 1 Test (1990) for England. FC for Middlesex (1982-94), Windward Islands (1982/83-91/92), Tasmania (1983/84), MCC (1984-85), Essex (1995-98). Also ListA for Middlesex (1982-94), Windward Islands (1982/83-91/92), Tasmania (1983/84), MCC (1984-85), Essex (1995-98).

Oliver Charles W. Williams (Leicestershire CB 2002 C&G 2). Born 28.4.1983, Northampton. RHB.

Robert James Williams (Oxfordshire 1996-03 C&G 2 NWT 3). Born 12.12.1970, Newnham, Cambridge. RHB OB Occ WKT.

Stephen Williams (Wiltshire 1989-90 NWT 2). Born 11.3.1954, Rodbourne Cheney, Wiltshire. RHB LB. FC for Gloucestershire (1978). Also ListA for Gloucestershire (1978).

Simon Lee Williams (Cambridgeshire 1995-96 NWT 2, Kent CB 1999-00 NWT 6). Born 3.9.1970, Lambeth, London. RHB WKT. Twin brother: T.C. (Cambridgeshire, Kent CB).

Stephen Mark Williams (Cornwall 1995-00 NWT 4). Born 23.10.1967, Redruth, Cornwall. RHB RM.

Dominic Williamson (Shropshire 2001-02 C&G 2). Born 15.11.1975, Durham. RHB RM. FC for Leicestershire (1996-00). Also ListA for Leicestershire (1996-00).

John Gordon Williamson (Durham 1964-68 GC 4). Born 4.4.1936, Norton-on-Tees, Co Durham. RHB RFM. FC for Northamptonshire (1959-62). Also ListA for Northamptonshire (1959-62).

Steven Martin Willis (Devon 1992-94 NWT 3). Born 19.9.1969, Dawlish, Devon. RHB.

William Paul Willis (Lincolnshire 1974-76 GC 3). Born 15.6.1952, Durham. RHB RFM.

Greg Richard Willott (Staffordshire 2001-03 C&G 2). Born 13.6.1980, Stoke-on-Trent, Staffordshire. LHB LFM.

Charl Myles Willoughby (Berkshire 2000 NWT 2). Born 3.12.1974, Cape Town, Cape Province, South Africa. LHB LFM. 2 Tests (2003) for South Africa. 3 ODIs (1999/00-03) for South Africa. FC for Boland (1994/95-99/00), Boland B (1994/95-95/96), Western Province (2000/01-03/04),

MCC (2001-04), Western Province Boland (2004/05), Leicestershire (2005), Cape Cobras (2005/06-06/07), Somerset (2006-08). Also ListA for Boland (1994/95-99/00), Boland B (1994/95-95/96), Western Province (2000/01-03/04), MCC (2001-04), Western Province Boland (2004/05), Leicestershire (2005), Cape Cobras (2005/06-06/07), Somerset (2006-08).

Alan Willows (Dorset 1991-95 NWT 4). Born 24.4.1961, Portslade, Brighton, Sussex. RHB SLA. FC for Sussex (1980-83). Also ListA for Sussex (1980-83).

Peter James Wilshaw (Nottinghamshire CB 2002 C&G 1, Staffordshire 2005 C&G 1). Born 15.7.1987, Newcastle-under-Lyme, Staffordshire. RHB RM. FC for Oxford UCCE (2006-08). Also ListA for Oxford UCCE (2006-08).

Alan Geoffrey Wilson (Cumberland 1984 NWT 1). Born 1.6.1942, Kendal, Westmorland. RHB RM.

Alan Robert Wilson (Cambridgeshire 1964-67 GC 4). Born 19.11.1936, Littleport, Cambridgeshire. RHB RM.

Andrew Robert Wilson (Cumberland 1996 NWT 1). Born 1.3.1970, Kendal, Westmorland. RHB OB.

David Wilson (Durham CB 2002-03 C&G 2). Born 14.11.1966, Durham. RHB WKT.

Daniel Graeme Wilson (Cambridgeshire 2000-01 C&G 3 NWT 2, Huntingdonshire 2002 C&G 1). Born 18.2.1977, Paddington, London. RHB RM. FC for Essex (1997-98). Also ListA for Essex (1997-98).

Elliott James Wilson (Cambridgeshire 2003 C&G 1). Born 3.11.1976, St Pancras, London. RHB RM. FC for Worcestershire (1998-00). Also ListA for Worcestershire (1998-00).

Elliot James Wilson (Warwickshire CB 2002 C&G 1, Lincolnshire 2003-04 C&G 2). Born 10.11.1979, Hertford. RHB RM.

Graham Bradley Wilson (Lincolnshire 1996 NWT 1). Born 17.11.1970, Scunthorpe, Lincolnshire. RHB WKT.

Joseph Robert Wilson (Dorset 2002-03 C&G 2). Born 16.1.1965, Birkenhead, Cheshire. RHB RM.

Kristian John Wilson (Dorset 2001 C&G 2). Born 11.9.1982, Poole, Dorset. RHB RMF.

Russell Wilson (Wiltshire 1983 NWT 1). Born 17.3.1959, Blackpool, Lancashire. RHB RFM.

Nicholas James Wilton (Berkshire 2002 C&G 2). Born 23.9.1978, Pembury, Kent. RHB WKT. FC for Sussex (1998-01). Also ListA for Sussex (1998-01).

John Bowen Windows (Northumberland 1999-05 C&G 5 NWT 4). Born 6.5.1976, Newcastle upon Tyne, Northumberland. RHB RM.

Hugh Mervyn Winfield (Lincolnshire 1971 GC 2). Born 13.6.1933, Gainsborough, Lincolnshire. RHB. FC for Nottinghamshire (1954-66). Also ListA for Nottinghamshire (1954-66).

Derek Charles Wing (Cambridgeshire 1964-86 GC 6 NWT 3, MC North 1972-75 B&H 12, MC East 1976-77 B&H 6, MC 1980 B&H 1). Born 11.2.1943, Wisbech, Cambridgeshire. RHB RFM. FC for MCC (1967-68), MC (1969-76). Also ListA for MCC (1967-68).

Andrew Richard Wingfield Digby (Dorset 1986-92 NWT 5, MC 1989 B&H 1). Born 25.7.1950, Sherborne, Dorset. LHB RM. FC for OU (1971-77). Also ListA for OU (1971-77).

Vincent Paul Winn (Huntingdonshire 1999-00 NWT 3). Born 26.7.1966, Cambridge. RHB.

Andrew Charles Winstone (Sussex CB 2001 C&G 1). Born 16.3.1975, Wells, Somerset. RHB OB.

Dwain Alan Winter (Wiltshire 1999-01 C&G 1 NWT 4). Born 28.3.1964, Devizes, Wiltshire. LHB RM Occ WKT.

David Arthur James Wise (Oxfordshire 1985-93 NWT 7). Born 21.3.1963, Tiddington, Oxfordshire. RHB RM.

Ian Alexander Wishart (MC North 1979 B&H 1). Born 25.12.1948, Greenside. RHB RMF.

John Paul Wolstenholme (Northamptonshire CB 2000 NWT 1). Born 7.5.1982, Northampton. RHB RFM. FC for Northamptonshire (2005). Also ListA for Northamptonshire (2005). Brother: M.A. (Northamptonshire CB).

Mark Andrew Wolstenholme (Northamptonshire CB 1999-01 C&G 3 NWT 2). Born 20.10.1979, Northampton. RHB RM. Brother: J.P. (Northamptonshire, Northamptonshire CB).

David Robert Womble (Staffordshire 1997-05 C&G 6 NWT 5). Born 23.2.1977, Stoke-on-Trent, Staffordshire. RHB RM.

Barry Wood (Cheshire 1986-89 NWT 4). Born 26.12.1942, Ossett, Yorkshire. RHB RM. 12 Tests (1972-78) for England. 13 ODIs (1972-82) for England. FC for Yorkshire (1964), Lancashire

(1966-79), Eastern Province (1971/72-73/74), MCC (1972-72/73), Derbyshire (1980-83). Also ListA for Yorkshire (1964), Lancashire (1966-79), Eastern Province (1971/72-73/74), MCC (1972-72/73), Derbyshire (1980-83). Son: N.T. (Cheshire, Lancashire), brother: R. (Worcestershire, Yorkshire).

John Wood (Durham 1991 NWT 1). Born 22.7.1970, Crofton, Wakefield, Yorkshire. RHB RFM. FC for Durham (1992-00), Lancashire (2001-04). Also ListA for Lancashire (2001-04).

Julian Ross Wood (Berkshire 1994-05 C&G 8 NWT 5). Born 21.11.1968, Winchester, Hampshire. LHB RM. FC for Hampshire (1989-93). Also ListA for Hampshire (1989-93).

Matthew James Wood (Devon 2000-03 C&G 1 NWT 1). Born 30.9.1980, Exeter, Devon. RHB OB. FC for Somerset (2001-07), MCC (2007), Nottinghamshire (2008). Also ListA for Somerset (2001-07), MCC (2007), Nottinghamshire (2008).

Nathan Theodore Wood (Cheshire 2001 C&G 1). Born 4.10.1974, Thornhill Edge, Yorkshire. LHB OB. FC for Lancashire (1996-00). Also ListA for Lancashire (1996-00). Father: B. (Cheshire, Derbyshire, Eastern Province, Lancashire, MCC, Yorkshire), uncle: R. (Worcestershire, Yorkshire).

Stuart Leslie Wood (Cheshire 1966-68 GC 3, MC North 1975 B&H 2). Born 27.11.1939, Crewe, Cheshire. LHB.

John Douglas Woodford (MC North 1975 B&H 1, Northumberland 1977 GC 1). Born 9.9.1943, Little Horton, Bradford, Yorkshire. RHB RM. FC for Yorkshire (1968-72). Also ListA for Yorkshire (1968-72).

Mark Christopher Woodman (Devon 1988-95 NWT 6). Born 12.2.1967, Orpington, Kent. RHB RM.

Paul Joseph Woodroffe (Buckinghamshire 1999-03 C&G 2 NWT 3). Born 12.6.1964, Hillingdon, Middlesex. RHB RM.

Darryl Craig Woods (Oxfordshire 1991-94 NWT 3). Born 5.1.1964, Oxford. RHB.

Malcolm David Woods (Cumberland 1984-92 NWT 7). Born 22.7.1955, Carlisle, Cumberland. RHB OB. Son: D.A. (Cheshire).

James Ralph Woodward (Huntingdonshire 2000-01 C&G 2 NWT 2). Born 19.11.1963, Peterborough. RHB.

Philip Bryan Wormald (Shropshire 1988-91 NWT 4). Born 4.5.1963, Sutton-in-Ashfield, Nottinghamshire. RHB RMF.

Damian Jo Lomax Worrad (Dorset 2002-04 C&G 2). Born 6.11.1974, Crewe, Cheshire. RHB RFM.

Allan Worthy (Durham CB 2000-03 C&G 3 NWT 1, Northumberland 2005 C&G 1). Born 1.1.1974, South Hetton, Co Durham. RHB RM.

Andrew James Wright (Huntingdonshire 2002 C&G 1). Born 20.6.1980, Peterborough. LHB.

Ashley Spencer Wright (Leicestershire CB 1999-01 C&G 1 NWT 2, Lincolnshire 2004 C&G 1). Born 21.10.1980, Grantham, Lincolnshire. RHB RM. FC for Leicestershire (2001-02). Also ListA for Leicestershire (2001-02). Brother: L.J. (Leicestershire, Leicestershire CB, Sussex).

Edward Wright (Norfolk 1982 NWT 1). Born 3.4.1945, Reymerston, Norfolk. RHB LFM.

Greg Daniel Wright (Staffordshire 2001 C&G 1). Born 30.8.1979, Wolverhampton, Staffordshire. LHB SLA.

Hedley James Wootton Wright (Suffolk 1985-89 NWT 4). Born 20.6.1953, Spilsby, Lincolnshire. LHB RMF.

James Douglas Weatherley Wright (Hertfordshire 1974-81 GC 1 NWT 1). Born 24.1.1948, Hampstead, London. RHB RMF.

Jonathan Patrick Wright (Herefordshire 1995 NWT 1, Worcestershire CB 1999-01 C&G 3 NWT 2). Born 4.6.1965, Sheffield, Yorkshire. RHB RM.

Luke James Wright (Leicestershire CB 2001 C&G 1). Born 7.3.1985, Grantham, Lincolnshire. RHB RM. 16 ODIs (2007-08) for England. 8 Int2020s (2007/08-08) for England. FC for Leicestershire (2003), Sussex (2004-08). Also ListA for Leicestershire (2003), Sussex (2004-08). Brother: A.S. (Leicestershire, Leicestershire CB, Lincolnshire, Staffordshire).

Lawrence William Wright (Hertfordshire 1964 GC 1). Born 11.5.1940, Hertford. RHB.

Martin Charles Gerrard Wright (Hertfordshire 1986-89 NWT 4). Born 13.7.1963, Hemel Hempstead, Hertfordshire. RHB. Brother: N.P.G. (Hertfordshire, MCC).

Mark James William Wright (Middlesex CB 2001 C&G 1). Born 1.2.1981, Edmonton, Middlesex. RHB OB.

Nicholas Peter Gerrard Wright (Hertfordshire 1983-91 NWT 7). Born 9.1.1960, Mill Hill, London. LHB. Brother: M.C.G. (Hertfordshire).

Thomas Anthony Wright (Devon 2002-03 C&G 2). Born 1.5.1983, Barnstaple, Devon. LHB RFM.

T. Martin Wright (Norfolk 1965 GC 1). Born 16.10.1934, Wombwell, Yorkshire. RHB RF.

Stephen Christopher Wundke (Cheshire 1982-98 NWT 2). Born 2.7.1961, North Adelaide, South Australia, Australia. LHB LFM,SLA. FC for South Australia (1985/86-86/87). Also ListA for South Australia (1985/86-86/87).

Julian George Wyatt (Devon 1993-95 NWT 3). Born 19.6.1963, Paulton, Somerset. RHB RM. FC for Somerset (1983-89). Also ListA for Somerset (1983-89).

Stephen John Wyatt (Berkshire 2001 C&G 1). Born 10.3.1971, Newbury, Berkshire. LHB.

Adrian Paul Acheson Wykes (Cambridgeshire 1987-89 NWT 3). Born 7.2.1958, Westminster, London. RHB RM.

Richard Melvyn Wyld (Nottinghamshire CB 2000-02 C&G 2 NWT 1). Born 7.11.1982, Nottingham. LHB RM.

Malcolm Ernest Wynn (Bedfordshire 1970 GC 1). Born 10.12.1948, Flintwick, Bedfordshire. RHB RM.

Michael Howard Yardy (Sussex CB 1999-00 NWT 3). Born 27.11.1980, Pembury, Kent. LHB LM. 6 ODIs (2006-07) for England. 3 Int2020s (2006-07) for England. FC for Sussex (2000-08). Also ListA for Sussex (2000-08).

Christopher Joseph Yates (Hampshire CB 2000-01 C&G 1 NWT 1). Born 10.8.1981, Aldershot, Hampshire. LHB RFM.

Kenneth Clement Yates (Cambridgeshire 1964 GC 1). Born 4.8.1938, Keetmanshoop, Namibia. RHB Occ WKT. FC for CU (1961). Also ListA for CU (1961).

Stephen Colin Yates (Cheshire 1985-86 NWT 2). Born 30.8.1951, Manchester, Lancashire. RHB.

Douglas Ian Yeabsley (Devon 1969-87 GC 5 NWT 4, MC South 1972-79 B&H 16, MC West 1976-78 B&H 12, MC 1980 B&H 4). Born 3.1.1942, Exeter, Devon. LHB LMF. FC for MC (1974-81). Sons: R.S. (Devon, Middlesex, OU) and M.I. (CU).

Richard Stuart Yeabsley (Devon 1990 NWT 1). Born 2.11.1973, St Albans, Hertfordshire. RHB RMF. FC for OU (1993-95). Also ListA for OU (1993-95). Brother: M.I. (CU), father: D.I. (Devon, MC, MC South, MC West).

David Leslie York (Shropshire 1974 GC 1). Born 13.4.1941, Quatt, Bridgnorth, Shropshire. RHB RFM.

Stuart Ernest York (Buckinghamshire 1975 GC 1). Born 21.9.1938, Harpole, Northamptonshire. RHB LB.

Michael Youll (Northumberland 1971-77 GC 3). Born 26.4.1939, Jesmond, Newcastle upon Tyne, Northumberland. LHB SLA. FC for Warwickshire (1956-57). Also ListA for Warwickshire (1956-57). Son: O.S. (Northumberland).

Oliver Seymour Youll (Northumberland 1994-99 NWT 2). Born 11.12.1970, Jesmond, Newcastle upon Tyne, Northumberland. LHB LB. Father: M. (MC, Northumberland, Warwickshire).

Barry James Young (Bedfordshire 1997 NWT 1). Born 12.10.1975, Luton, Bedfordshire. RHB.

David John Young (Middlesex CB 2002 C&G 2). Born 11.12.1977, Coventry, Warwickshire. RHB.

Iain Young (Durham 1990 NWT 1). Born 24.9.1965, Sunderland, Co Durham. RHB RFM. Brother: C. (Durham).

Shaun Young (Bedfordshire 2001-03 C&G 7). Born 13.6.1970, Burnie, Tasmania, Australia. LHB RFM. 1 Test (1997) for Australia. FC for Tasmania (1991/92-01/02), Gloucestershire (1997). Also ListA for Tasmania (1991/92-01/02), Gloucestershire (1997). Brother: C.M. (Tasmania).

Stuart Harrison Young (Durham 1964-72 GC 5). Born 6.7.1938, Blackhall, Co Durham. LHB RF. FC for MC (1959-69). Also ListA for MC (1959-69).

William Young (Huntingdonshire 2000 NWT 2). Born 14.12.1970, Peterborough. LHB LMF.

Michael Edward Younger (Northumberland 1984-94 NWT 5). Born 29.11.1951, Corbridge, Northumberland. LHB SLA.

CAREER RECORDS 1963-2005

				M	I	NO	Runs	HS	Avg	100	50	Balls	Runs	Wkts	BB	Avg	RpO	4I	Ct	St
J.Abbas	Ches	1999	GC	1	1	0	6	6	6.00	-	-								-	
R.G.Abeynaike	Bed	1982	GC	1	1	0	26	26	26.00	-	-	30	8	0	-	-	1.60	-	1	
J.Abrahams	Shr	1989-1991	GC	3	3	0	179	79	59.66	-	2	138	100	0	-	-	4.34	-	2	
A.R.Adams	Here	2001	GC	2	2	0	55	46	27.50	-	-	120	98	4	2-29	24.50	4.90	-	2	
J.C.Adams	Berk	2003	GC	1	1	0	8	8	8.00	-	-	36	23	0	-	-	3.83	-	-	
	Wilt	1004	GC	1	1	0	43	43	43.00	-	-								1	
K.Adams	Lin	2002	GC	1	1	1	1	1*	-	-	-	36	25	1	1-25	25.00	4.16	-	-	
N.J.Adams	Cambsh	1987-2001	GC	10	9	1	264	104*	33.00	1	1	161	123	3	1-10	41.00	4.58	-	2	
	MC	1993	BH	1	1	0	11	11	11.00	-	-								-	
	Norf	1997	GC	1	1	0	0	0	0.00	-	-	18	13	0	-	-	4.33	-	-	
	Hunt	2002	GC	1	1	0	31	31	31.00	-	-	60	54	1	1-54	54.00	5.40	-	-	
T.W.Adcock	Nmb	1994	GC	1	1	0	28	28	28.00	-	-								-	
J.P.Addison	Sta	1987-1991	GC	3	3	0	24	11	8.00	-	-	12	19	0	-	-	9.50	-	-	
	MC	1988	BH	1	1	0	2	2	2.00	-	-								-	
S.R.Ades	SusCB	2000-2001	GC	5	3	0	5	3	1.66	-	-	264	206	5	2-37	41.20	4.68	-	1	
S.K.Adlard	Lin	1976	GC	1	1	0	6	6	6.00	-	-	36	33	1	1-33	33.00	5.50	-	-	
Adnan Akram	EssCB	2002-2003	GC	2	2	0	88	61	44.00	-	1	12	18	0	-	-	9.00	-	-	
Adnan Saleem	Buck	2002-2005	GC	5	3	1	2	2	1.00	-	-	179	161	5	3-24	32.20	5.39	-	1	
S.J.Adshead	Here	1999	GC	2	2	0	41	22	20.50	-	-								2	2
	LeiCB	2001	GC	1	1	0	29	29	29.00	-	-								1	
	Shr	2003	GC	1	1	1	77	77*	-	-	1								2	
A.S.Afzaal	NottCB	2001	GC	1															-	
K.Afzaal	DerbCB	1999	GC	1	1	0	14	14	14.00	-	-								-	
A.C.Agar	Norf	1983-1984	GC	2	2	0	3	3	1.50	-	-	126	66	2	2-44	33.00	3.14	-	1	
Agha Zahid	Dev	1983-1985	GC	3	3	0	70	31	23.33	-	-	198	100	4	2-34	25.00	3.03	-	-	
J.R.Airey	Lin	1990	GC	1	1	0	0	0	0.00	-	-	60	60	1	1-60	60.00	6.00	-	-	
S.J.Airey	Lin	2003	GC	1	1	1	2	2*	-	-	-	42	22	2	2-22	11.00	3.14	-	-	
Ajaz Akhtar	Cambsh	1991-2004	GC	16	13	1	278	78	23.16	-	1	874	570	23	4-28	24.78	3.91	2	6	
D.A.Alderman	SusCB	1999-2001	GC	6	4	1	38	14*	12.66	-	-	338	168	3	1-15	56.00	2.98	-	-	
M.S.Alexander	KntCB	1999-2001	GC	9	8	1	182	107*	26.00	1	-								4	1
J.Alford	Wilt	1972-1973	GC	2	2	0	13	8	6.50	-	-	90	36	2	2-29	18.00	2.40	-	-	
Kabir Ali	WorCB	2000-2001	GC	2	1	0	7	7	7.00	-	-	60	52	2	2-52	26.00	5.20	-	-	
Kadeer Ali	WorCB	1999-2002	GC	2	2	0	90	66	45.00	-	1	21	21	0	-	-	6.00	-	-	
S.J.Ali	Oxfsh	2001	GC	1	1	0	7	7	7.00	-	-	30	33	1	1-33	33.00	6.60	-	1	
T.Allcock	Norf	1965-1968	GC	2	2	0	28	24	14.00	-	-								1	
A.P.W.Allen	WarCB	2002	GC	1	1	0	10	10	10.00	-	-								1	
	Dev	2005	GC	1	1	0	5	5	5.00	-	-								-	
C.W.Allen	Dor	1983	GC	1	1	0	7	7	7.00	-	-	36	14	0	-	-	2.33	-	1	
F.E.Allen	Dur	1968	GC	1	1	0	2	2	2.00	-	-								-	
J.Allenby	DurCB	2002	GC	1	1	0	4	4	4.00	-	-								-	
H.L.Alleyne	Buck	1984-1985	GC	2	2	0	3	3	1.50	-	-	120	75	3	2-49	25.00	3.75	-	-	
A.W.Allin	Dev	1979-1995	GC	11	7	1	30	17	5.00	-	-	744	482	9	2-43	53.55	3.88	-	-	
	MC	1980-1981	BH	5	3	1	12	6	6.00	-	-	300	191	3	3-37	63.66	3.82	-	1	

				M	I	NO	Runs	HS	Avg	100	50	Balls	Runs	Wkts	BB	Avg	RpO	4I	Ct	St
M.L.Allin	Dev	2002-2003	GC	2	2	1	23	19	23.00	-	-								3	1
P.J.W.Allott	Sta	1993	GC	1	1	0	3	3	3.00	-	-	72	45	1	1-45	45.00	3.75	-	-	
K.Altaf	DerbCB	2001	GC	1	1	0	1	1	1.00	-	-	60	69	0	-	-	6.90	-	-	
D.A.Altree	WarCB	1999	GC	1	1	0	6	6	6.00	-	-	30	13	0	-	-	2.60	-	-	
M.Amarnath	Dur	1977-1978	GC	2	2	0	2	2	1.00	-	-	144	87	3	2-65	29.00	3.62	-	-	
	Wilt	1984	GC	1	1	0	3	3	3.00	-	-	72	39	1	1-39	39.00	3.25	-	-	
S.R.Ambrose	Hert	1974-1976	GC	4	4	0	66	27	16.50	-	-								2	
C.Amos	Norf	1994-2003	GC	13	13	0	233	76	17.92	-	1								5	
J.V.Anders	Shr	1997-2002	GC	6	6	0	107	51	17.83	-	1	24	7	0	-	-	1.75	-	-	
J.M.Anderson	LanCB	2000	GC	2	1	1	5	5*	-	-	-	120	98	3	2-64	32.66	4.90	-	-	
M.B.Anderson	Nmb	1984	GC	1	1	0	11	11	11.00	-	-								1	
G.M.Andrew	SomCB	2000-2001	GC	2	1	0	1	1	1.00	-	-	53	35	0	-	-	3.96	-	1	
S.J.W.Andrew	Hert	1999-2000	GC	4	2	1	3	2*	3.00	-	-	204	122	6	3-34	20.33	3.58	-	-	
S.J.Andrews	SurCB	2001	GC	1	1	0	0	0	0.00	-	-	36	27	0	-	-	4.50	-	-	
D.J.Angove	Corn	1996	GC	1	1	0	6	6	6.00	-	-	72	65	4	4-65	16.25	5.41	1	-	
T.J.Angove	Corn	1986	GC	1	1	0	13	13	13.00	-	-								-	
G.Angus	Nmb	1994-2002	GC	7	5	1	21	10	5.25	-	-	414	297	10	2-25	29.70	4.30	-	6	
T.S.Anning	Dev	2002-2005	GC	2	1	0	5	5	5.00	-	-	83	60	3	3-40	20.00	4.33	-	-	
J.E.Anyon	Cumb	2003	GC	1	1	0	0	0	0.00	-	-	42	46	1	1-46	46.00	6.57	-	1	
J.D.Appleyard	Hert	1966-1974	GC	5	5	3	13	6*	6.50	-	-	274	129	5	2-11	25.80	2.82	-	1	
Aqeel Ahmed	Dev	2003-2004	GC	2	1	1	1	1*	-	-	-	92	85	1	1-27	85.00	5.54	-	-	
G.F.Archer	Sta	2000-2004	GC	9	9	2	371	89*	53.00	-	4								4	
N.J.Archer	Sta	1984-1995	GC	12	12	0	198	45	16.50	-	-								4	
N.B.Archibald	Shr	2001	GC	1	1	0	3	3	3.00	-	-								-	
Arfan Akram	EssCB	2002-2003	GC	2	2	1	10	10*	10.00	-	-								-	
A.Armstrong	Hert	2002	GC	1	1	0	3	3	3.00	-	-								-	
J.M.Armstrong	LanCB	2002	GC	2	2	0	1	1	0.50	-	-								-	
N.J.Armstrong	Lin	1996-2000	GC	3	3	3	27	15*	-	-	-	138	75	5	2-18	15.00	3.26	-	1	
K.A.Arnold	Oxfsh	1981-2003	GC	16	11	3	48	20	6.00	-	-	1026	776	14	2-46	55.42	4.53	-	2	
	MC	1985-1995	BH	14	8	3	12	4*	2.40	-	-	734	476	12	3-25	39.66	3.89	-	4	
K.L.T.Arthurton	Buck	1997-2000	GC	2	2	0	66	48	33.00	-	-	132	99	7	4-53	14.14	4.50	1	1	
A.C.Ashford	Corn	1977	GC	1	1	0	5	5	5.00	-	-	42	34	0	-	-	4.85	-	-	
D.J.Ashley	Shr	1983-1989	GC	6	5	1	36	13	9.00	-	-								6	1
R.L.Ashton	Bed	1991	GC	1	1	0	1	1	1.00	-	-	12	25	0	-	-	12.50	-	-	
	NhCB	1999-2000	GC	2	2	1	7	5*	7.00	-	-	88	73	1	1-30	73.00	4.97	-	2	
Asif Din	Shr	1997-2001	GC	7	7	1	128	60	21.33	-	1	426	239	4	2-25	59.75	3.36	-	-	
Asim Munir	Cumb	2002	GC	1	1	0	8	8	8.00	-	-	60	72	2	2-72	36.00	7.20	-	-	
C.W.J.Athey	Suf	2001-2002	GC	5	4	0	122	71	30.50	-	1								1	
G.Atkins	Buck	1965-1970	GC	3	2	0	16	16	8.00	-	-								-	
P.D.Atkins	Buck	1999-2003	GC	10	10	2	276	110	34.50	1	1								9	
P.Atkinson	Nmb	1971	GC	1	1	0	0	0	0.00	-	-								-	
S.R.Atkinson	Dur	1973-1985	GC	12	12	0	263	80	21.91	-	1								7	
	MCN	1974	BH	1	1	0	4	4	4.00	-	-								-	
	MCE	1978	BH	3	3	0	104	84	34.66	-	1								-	
	MC	1986-1989	BH	7	7	0	82	25	11.71	-	-								-	
V.Atri	NottCB	2001	GC	1	1	0	0	0	0.00	-	-								-	

				M	I	NO	Runs	HS	Avg	100	50	Balls	Runs	Wkts	BB	Avg	RpO	4I	Ct	St
P.G.M.August	Bed	1982-1985	GC	2	1	0	16	16	16.00	-	-								2	
D.Austen	NhCB	2000	GC	1								56	36	0	-	-	3.85	-	-	
I.D.Austin	Cumb	2002	GC	1	1	0	16	16	16.00	-	-	60	25	4	4-25	6.25	2.50	1	-	
R.J.Austin	Norf	2001	GC	1	1	0	1	1	1.00	-	-	60	13	1	1-13	13.00	1.30	-	1	
R.J.Baggs	Dev	1997-1999	GC	2	2	0	23	18	11.50	-	-								-	
W.J.L.Bagshawe	DerbCB	2001	GC	1	1	0	44	44	44.00	-	-								-	
S.V.Bahutule	SurCB	2002	GC	1	1	0	105	105	105.00	1	-	60	47	1	1-47	47.00	4.70	-	-	
R.R.Baigent	Buck	1992	GC	1	1	0	44	44	44.00	-	-								-	
P.A.C.Bail	Wilt	1989-1990	GC	2	2	0	70	66	35.00	-	1								-	
D.Bailey	Dur	1967	GC	1	1	0	2	2	2.00	-	-								-	
	MCN	1973-1979	BH	16	16	1	367	83	24.46	-	3	182	90	4	3-31	22.50	2.96	-	3	
	MCE	1976-1978	BH	6	6	0	61	22	10.16	-	-	150	55	4	3-20	13.75	2.20	-	1	
	MC	1980-1984	BH	18	18	1	273	66	16.05	-	2	200	164	2	1-10	82.00	4.92	-	3	
	Ches	1981-1983	GC	3	3	0	30	30	10.00	-	-	66	48	1	1-36	48.00	4.36	-	-	
D.B.Bailey	Cambsh	1965	GC	1	1	0	2	2	2.00	-	-								-	
G.L.Bailey	Norf	1998	GC	1	1	1	2	2*	-	-	-	30	25	0	-	-	5.00	-	-	
H.J.Bailey	Dur	1964-1968	GC	4	4	1	57	30	19.00	-	-	156	82	6	3-37	13.66	3.15	-	-	
M.D.Bailey	Suf	1986-1990	GC	5	4	1	6	4	2.00	-	-	253	148	4	3-42	37.00	3.50	-	-	
M.J.Bailey	Wilt	1983-1984	GC	2	2	0	54	31	27.00	-	-	114	81	1	1-50	81.00	4.26	-	-	
	Here	1995	GC	1	1	0	0	0	0.00	-	-	42	35	0	-	-	5.00	-	-	
O.J.Bailey	SomCB	2001	GC	1															1	
R.J.Bailey	Sta	2002	GC	1	1	0	19	19	19.00	-	-	24	16	3	3-16	5.33	4.00	-	-	
R.R.Bailey	Buck	1975-1979	GC	2	1	0	13	13	13.00	-	-	120	75	1	1-39	75.00	3.75	-	-	
	MCW	1978	BH	2	2	0	9	9	4.50	-	-	90	41	1	1-27	41.00	2.73	-	1	
M.R.Bainbridge	SurCB	1999-2001	GC	5	5	0	151	38	30.20	-	-	192	136	6	3-27	22.66	4.25	-	2	
P.Bainbridge	Dur	1991	GC	1	1	0	27	27	27.00	-	-	72	42	0	-	-	3.50	-	-	
F.C.Baines	Berk	1965-1966	GC	3	3	3	8	4*	-	-	-	221	116	2	2-43	58.00	3.14	-	1	
A.F.Baker	Suf	1999	GC	1	1	1	1	1*	-	-	-	37	42	0	-	-	6.81	-	-	
	SurCB	2002	GC	1	1	0	0	0	0.00	-	-	60	67	2	2-67	33.50	6.70	-	-	
D.J.H.Baker	Cambsh	1972-1982	GC	3	3	0	30	23	10.00	-	-								1	
J.Baker	Dor	1968	GC	1	1	0	20	20	20.00	-	-	36	19	0	-	-	3.16	-	-	
P.A.Baker	Berk	1966	GC	2	2	0	14	9	7.00	-	-								-	
T.M.Baker	NhCB	2002	GC	1	1	0	63	63	63.00	-	1	60	49	1	1-49	49.00	4.90	-	-	
S.Ball	DurCB	1999-2000	GC	6	6	0	80	23	13.33	-	-	246	211	7	3-45	30.14	5.14	-	-	
M.Bamford	Shr	2001	GC	1	1	0	6	6	6.00	-	-								-	
M.J.Banes	KntCB	2001-2003	GC	3	3	0	110	82	36.66	-	1	12	11	1	1-11	11.00	5.50	-	2	
B.C.Banks	Bed	1991	GC	1	1	1	12	12*	-	-	-	12	8	0	-	-	4.00	-	-	
D.Banks	HamCB	1999-2002	GC	5	3	0	16	7	5.33	-	-								6	1
D.A.Banks	Sta	1986-1994	GC	5	5	1	125	62*	31.25	-	1	48	49	2	2-49	24.50	6.12	-	2	
	WorCB	2000-2001	GC	4	2	0	17	12	8.50	-	-	60	46	2	2-46	23.00	4.60	-	1	
N.D.R.Bannister	LanCB	2000	GC	2	2	0	66	62	33.00	-	1								-	
D.Banton	Oxfsh	1967-1972	GC	3	3	0	25	13	8.33	-	-	180	60	0	-	-	2.00	-	-	
E.A.E.Baptiste	Cumb	1994	GC	1	1	0	2	2	2.00	-	-	72	35	0	-	-	2.91	-	-	
Baqar Rizvi	Wilt	2002-2005	GC	3	3	0	86	47	28.66	-	-	42	31	0	-	-	4.42	-	-	
M.R.Barfoot	WorCB	1999	GC	1								18	10	0	-	-	3.33	-	-	

				M	I	NO	Runs	HS	Avg	100	50	Balls	Runs	Wkts	BB	Avg	RpO	4I	Ct	St
A.H.Barker	Wilt	1969-1973	GC	3	3	0	40	19	13.33	-	-	24	37	0	-	-	9.25	-	-	
	MCS	1972-1973	BH	3	3	0	32	26	10.66	-	-	110	49	3	2-24	16.33	2.67	-	-	
P.D.Barker	Suf	1981-1988	GC	5	5	0	35	14	7.00	-	-								1	
R.G.R.Barlow	Here	1997	GC	1	1	0	15	15	15.00	-	-								-	
	MidCB	2001	GC	1	1	0	2	2	2.00	-	-								1	
A.S.Barnard	Shr	1978-1992	GC	10	6	3	54	28	18.00	-	-	641	379	12	4-47	31.58	3.54	1	4	
	MC	1985	BH	3	3	1	15	10	7.50	-	-	144	60	1	1-38	60.00	2.50	-	1	
A.C.Barnes	Here	2003	GC	1	1	0	19	19	19.00	-	-	30	21	0	-	-	4.20	-	-	
D.E.Barnes	Cumb	2003	GC	1	1	0	17	17	17.00	-	-								-	
S.N.Barnes	Wilt	1993	GC	1								72	93	0	-	-	7.75	-	-	
	GloCB	2000-2001	GC	5	3	1	16	8	8.00	-	-	234	106	7	2-15	15.14	2.71	-	-	
T.H.Barnes	Lin	1971-1976	GC	5	2	1	0	0*	0.00	-	-	348	168	3	1-25	56.00	2.89	-	-	
	MCN	1974	BH	1	1	0	1	1	1.00	-	-	66	41	1	1-41	41.00	3.72	-	-	
	Norf	1982	GC	1								72	34	1	1-34	34.00	2.83	-	-	
	Wilt	1983-1984	GC	2	1	0	13	13	13.00	-	-	138	157	3	2-95	52.33	6.82	-	-	
A.A.Barnett	Berk	1996	GC	1	1	0	22	22	22.00	-	-	72	54	0	-	-	4.50	-	-	
K.J.Barnett	Sta	2003-2005	GC	3	3	0	44	21	14.66	-	-	78	62	1	1-41	62.00	4.76	-	1	
W.C.P.Barnicoat	Corn	1970	GC	1	1	0	2	2	2.00	-	-	72	24	1	1-24	24.00	2.00	-	-	
C.J.Barnsley	WalMC	2002	GC	1								18	34	0	-	-	11.33	-	-	
A.J.L.Barr	WalMC	1998-2001	GC	4	4	0	46	30	11.50	-	-	240	191	7	3-47	27.28	4.77	-	-	
D.J.Barr	WarCB	2001-2002	GC	4	4	0	38	21	9.50	-	-								1	
	Buck	2003-2005	GC	2	2	0	51	51	25.50	-	1								1	
T.Barratt	NhCB	2001	GC	1								30	40	0	-	-	8.00	-	-	
J.Barrett	Norf	1982	GC	1	1	0	1	1	1.00	-	-								-	
K.A.O.Barrett	Dev	1998-2002	GC	2	2	0	9	6	4.50	-	-								-	
C.M.Barrow	LanCB	2001	GC	1	1	0	1	1	1.00	-	-	22	21	0	-	-	5.72	-	-	
J.K.Barrow	Berk	1994-2001	GC	9	3	0	21	16	7.00	-	-	492	343	11	4-31	31.18	4.18	1	1	
T.J.Barry	Buck	1990-1993	GC	4	4	1	83	39	27.66	-	-	198	165	6	3-49	27.50	5.00	-	-	
T.I.Barwell	Wilt	1972-1973	GC	2	2	0	16	9	8.00	-	-								1	
	MCS	1972	BH	3	3	1	99	64*	49.50	-	1								1	
S.R.Barwick	WalMC	1998-2001	GC	8	5	3	11	5*	5.50	-	-	476	241	13	3-44	18.53	3.03	-	-	
P.R.Bates	Wilt	2001	GC	2	2	0	18	18	9.00	-	-								-	
R.J.Bates	Wilt	1999-2005	GC	9	8	0	101	24	12.62	-	-	416	378	11	3-16	34.36	5.45	-	6	
R.T.Bates	Lin	1990-1990	GC	1	1	0	5	5	5.00	-	-								-	
	NottCB	2002	GC	1	1	0	1	1	1.00	-	-	60	30	0	-	-	3.00	-	-	
C.J.Batt	Berk	2001	GC	2	1	0	7	7	7.00	-	-	102	68	4	2-31	17.00	4.00	-	-	
I.N.Battelley	Norf	1970-1970	GC	1	1	0	29	29	29.00	-	-								-	
A.J.Batterley	Ches	2002	GC	1	1	0	43	43	43.00	-	-								1	
G.J.Batty	SurCB	2000	GC	1	1	0	7	7	7.00	-	-	56	42	2	2-42	21.00	4.50	-	2	
J.D.Batty	YorCB	1999	GC	1	1	1	24	24*	-	-	-								-	
	Buck	2000-2003	GC	8	8	2	150	36*	25.00	-	-	450	299	7	3-51	42.71	3.98	-	2	
J.N.Batty	Oxfsh	1996	GC	1	1	0	1	1	1.00	-	-								-	
	MC	1996	BH	5	5	1	61	26*	15.25	-	-								4	
M.E.Beale	Dor	1968-1973	GC	2	2	0	3	3	1.50	-	-								-	1
J.D.Bean	Ches	1992-1999	GC	8	8	0	77	22	9.62	-	-								7	
M.Beaty	MCE	1978	BH	4	4	1	2	2	0.66	-	-								2	

				M	I	NO	Runs	HS	Avg	100	50	Balls	Runs	Wkts	BB	Avg	RpO	4I	Ct	St
T.Beck	Bed	1970	GC	1	1	1	0	0*	-	-	-	36	23	0	-	-	3.83	-	-	
D.Beckett	Oxfsh	1980	GC	1								60	57	0	-	-	5.70	-	-	
D.K.Beckett	MCN	1979	BH	1	1	0	1	1	1.00	-	-								-	
R.D.Bedbrook	Wilt	2001-2005	GC	4	4	3	53	24*	53.00	-	-	216	164	5	2-49	32.80	4.55	-	3	
P.Beech	Cumb	1996-1999	GC	4	4	0	92	42	23.00	-	-	150	139	2	1-21	69.50	5.56	-	-	
R.N.Beeson	Lin	1966-1967	GC	2	2	0	0	0	0.00	-	-								2	
A.J.Bell	Dor	2001	GC	1	1	1	22	22*	-	-	-								-	
I.R.Bell	WarCB	1999	GC	1	1	0	10	10	10.00	-	-	3	2	0	-	-	4.00	-	-	
K.M.Bell	WalMC	1993-2001	GC	8	8	0	123	39	15.37	-	-	12	17	0	-	-	8.50	-	1	
T.A.Bell	Hert	1966	GC	1	1	0	105	105	105.00	1	-								-	
M.R.Bellhouse	Oxfsh	2000-2001	GC	2	2	0	33	24	16.50	-	-	108	64	0	-	-	3.55	-	-	
R.J.Belmont	Norf	1991	GC	1	1	0	9	9	9.00	-	-	72	53	1	1-53	53.00	4.41	-	-	
C.C.Benham	HamCB	2001	GC	1	1	0	0	0	0.00	-	-								-	
J.E.Benjamin	Sta	1986-1987	GC	2	2	0	24	19	12.00	-	-	138	102	3	2-37	34.00	4.43	-	-	
J.A.Benn	Nmb	1992	GC	1	1	0	1	1	1.00	-	-								-	
G.M.Bennett	SomCB	1999-2000	GC	2	2	0	6	5	3.00	-	-	30	34	0	-	-	6.80	-	-	
M.R.M.Bennett	KntCB	2002-2003	GC	2	2	1	41	31	41.00	-	-								-	2
J.G.E.Benning	Buck	2001	GC	2	2	0	43	23	21.50	-	-	18	26	1	1-26	26.00	8.66	-	1	
J.D.P.Benson	Cambsh	1986	GC	1	1	0	85	85	85.00	-	1	13	13	0	-	-	6.00	-	-	
J.R.Benstead	DerbCB	2000-2002	GC	6	6	0	165	65	27.50	-	2	19	10	0	-	-	3.15	-	2	
	Sta	2005	GC	1	1	0	5	5	5.00	-	-								1	
P.F.Berrill	Hunt	2000	GC	2	2	0	10	10	5.00	-	-								-	
P.J.Berry	Cumb	1995	GC	1	1	0	81	81	81.00	-	1								1	
K.P.Berryman	Corn	1995-2002	GC	3	2	0	6	6	3.00	-	-	156	165	3	2-67	55.00	6.34	-	-	
A.J.Bethel	YorCB	1999-2002	GC	10	10	0	143	38	14.30	-	-								2	
I.R.Beven	Hert	1981	GC	1	1	0	10	10	10.00	-	-	18	25	1	1-25	25.00	8.33	-	-	
S.R.Bevins	Here	1995-1997	GC	2	2	0	34	26	17.00	-	-								-	
P.W.Bichener	Bed	1971	GC	1	1	0	1	1	1.00	-	-	72	80	2	2-80	40.00	6.66	-	2	
D.A.Bick	Hert	1971	GC	1	1	0	3	3	3.00	-	-	24	30	0	-	-	7.50	-	-	
K.D.Biddulph	Dur	1964-1972	GC	5	4	1	1	1*	0.33	-	-	366	169	5	3-20	33.80	2.77	-	-	
K.R.J.Bingham	KntCB	2002	GC	2	1	0	0	0	0.00	-	-								-	
T.Binnion	NottCB	2002	GC	1	1	0	20	20	20.00	-	-								1	
S.D.Birbeck	DurCB	1999-2000	GC	6	6	0	163	88	27.16	-	1	132	78	3	2-38	26.00	3.54	-	1	
P.C.Birtwisle	Dur	1968-1983	GC	11	11	2	223	59	24.77	-	1								4	
	MCE	1977	BH	1	1	0	8	8	8.00	-	-								-	
S.J.Birtwisle	DurCB	2002-2003	GC	2	2	0	35	32	17.50	-	-								1	
I.E.Bishop	Dev	1998-2004	GC	5	4	2	9	7	4.50	-	-	270	222	4	2-90	55.50	4.93	-	-	
	SurCB	1999	GC	1	1	1	0	0*	-	-	-	30	33	0	-	-	6.60	-	-	
J.E.Bishop	Suf	2000	GC	1	1	0	0	0	0.00	-	-	42	17	1	1-17	17.00	2.42	-	-	
K.C.Bishop	Suf	1979-1980	GC	2	2	2	3	3*	-	-	-	72	27	1	1-27	27.00	2.25	-	-	
G.R.Black	Buck	1985-1993	GC	8	8	1	36	14	5.14	-	-	423	328	10	3-83	32.80	4.65	-	4	
M.I.Black	Ches	2003	GC	1	1	0	6	6	6.00	-	-	60	36	1	1-36	36.00	3.60	-	-	
G.J.Blackburn	Ches	1987-1988	GC	3	3	0	23	19	7.66	-	-	152	107	5	2-21	21.40	4.22	-	1	
K.R.Blackburn	SomCB	1999-2001	GC	3	3	0	26	20	8.66	-	-								-	
T.G.Blades	Lin	1974	GC	2	2	1	52	50*	52.00	-	1								2	1
R.G.Blair	Bed	1994	GC	1	1	0	21	21	21.00	-	-								-	

				M	I	NO	Runs	HS	Avg	100	50	Balls	Runs	Wkts	BB	Avg	RpO	4I	Ct	St
P.M.Blakeley	Shr	1993	GC	1	1	0	23	23	23.00	-	-	48	69	0	-	-	8.62	-	-	
I.P.C.Blakemore	Here	1997	GC	1	1	0	7	7	7.00	-	-	12	19	0	-	-	9.50	-	-	
I.N.Blanchett	Cambsh	2001	GC	2	1	0	20	20	20.00	-	-	120	63	5	3-24	12.60	3.15	-	1	
T.G.Bland	Norf	1968	GC	1	1	0	7	7	7.00	-	-	72	29	1	1-29	29.00	2.41	-	-	
D.C.Blank	Sta	1984-1990	GC	7	7	4	60	23*	20.00	-	-	468	347	9	3-75	38.55	4.44	-	-	
D.A.Blenkiron	Dur	1991	GC	1	1	0	56	56	56.00	-	1								-	
H.C.Blofeld	Norf	1965	GC	1	1	0	60	60	60.00	-	1								-	
S.M.Bloyce	Berk	2004	GC	1	1	0	0	0	0.00	-	-	36	66	1	1-66	66.00	11.00	-	-	
D.J.P.Boden	Sta	1998-2000	GC	4	3	0	25	12	8.33	-	-	197	172	1	1-43	172.00	5.23	-	-	
	Shr	2001	GC	1	1	0	8	8	8.00	-	-	48	25	2	2-25	12.50	3.12	-	-	
I.A.Bond	Dev	1999	GC	2								102	77	3	2-38	25.66	4.52	-	1	
R.E.Bond	Buck	1969-1979	GC	5	3	1	20	9	10.00	-	-	330	146	10	5-17	14.60	2.65	1	2	
	MCS	1973-1974	BH	4	4	4	15	8*	-	-	-	228	131	5	2-25	26.20	3.44	-	-	
R.J.Bond	Suf	1983-1983	GC	1	1	0	27	27	27.00	-	-								-	
C.D.Booden	Buck	1987-1993	GC	5	3	1	3	3	1.50	-	-	256	145	2	2-12	72.50	3.39	-	2	
S.B.Boon	Hert	1964	GC	1	1	0	1	1	1.00	-	-								-	
T.J.Boon	Norf	1996-1997	GC	2	2	0	20	12	10.00	-	-	66	63	1	1-63	63.00	5.72	-	1	
P.A.Booth	YorCB	2000-2001	GC	3	2	1	21	12	21.00	-	-	180	80	4	2-22	20.00	2.66	-	1	
R.Boothroyd	Sta	1975-1976	GC	2	1	0	0	0	0.00	-	-	144	82	1	1-50	82.00	3.41	-	-	
R.S.Bopara	EssCB	2001	GC	1	1	0	1	1	1.00	-	-								-	
C.W.Boroughs	Here	1998-2004	GC	12	11	1	322	72	32.20	-	3	216	155	4	2-41	38.75	4.30	-	4	
C.R.Borrett	Norf	2001-2003	GC	5	4	0	15	10	3.75	-	-	18	30	0	-	-	10.00	-	-	
P.C.Borrett	Norf	1970	GC	1	1	0	1	1	1.00	-	-								-	
D.Borthwick	Nmb	1994	GC	1	1	0	0	0	0.00	-	-								-	
T.J.Bostock	Ches	1992-1996	GC	4	4	0	57	42	14.25	-	-	66	55	0	-	-	5.00	-	-	
W.N.Boustead	Cumb	1984-1986	GC	3	2	2	22	17*	-	-	-								2	
J.N.B.Bovill	Buck	1998-1999	GC	3	2	0	4	4	2.00	-	-	174	106	7	3-64	15.14	3.65	-	-	
J.D.P.Bowden	KntCB	1999-2003	GC	12	11	0	342	98	31.09	-	2								4	
D.M.Bowen	MidCB	1999-2000	GC	3	3	0	63	29	21.00	-	-								-	
R.B.Bowers	SurCB	2001-2002	GC	4	3	2	4	2*	4.00	-	-	168	149	6	3-50	24.83	5.32	-	-	
D.J.Bowett	Shr	1997-2005	GC	3	3	2	32	11*	32.00	-	-	42	15	0	-	-	2.14	-	-	
M.Bowyer	Buck	1997-2003	GC	5	5	0	114	43	22.80	-	-								2	
M.K.L.Boyden	Norf	1997-1999	GC	3	1	1	8	8*	-	-	-								3	
C.N.Boyns	Shr	1983	GC	1	1	0	12	12	12.00	-	-								-	
I.J.Boyton	MidCB	2001	GC	1	1	0	31	31	31.00	-	-	24	21	1	1-21	21.00	5.25	-	-	
P.L.Bradbury	Oxfsh	1980	GC	1	1	0	22	22	22.00	-	-	60	55	1	1-55	55.00	5.50	-	1	
C.C.Bradfield	Hunt	2001	GC	3	3	0	32	21	10.66	-	-	66	84	4	2-17	21.00	7.63	-	3	
R.L.Bradford	Norf	1984	GC	1	1	0	1	1	1.00	-	-								-	
S.A.Bradford	Lin	1996-1999	GC	3	3	1	29	15*	14.50	-	-	150	104	4	2-52	26.00	4.16	-	-	
P.Bradley	MCN	1973-1975	BH	11	9	5	32	12*	8.00	-	-	708	353	11	4-45	32.09	2.99	1	1	
	Shr	1974	GC	1	1	0	1	1	1.00	-	-	72	45	1	1-45	45.00	3.75	-	-	
	MCE	1976	BH	4	2	1	18	15*	18.00	-	-	251	170	1	1-44	170.00	4.06	-	1	
P.J.Bradshaw	Norf	1997-2003	GC	11	8	3	37	20*	7.40	-	-	591	393	19	4-30	20.68	3.98	1	2	
W.D.Bragg	WalMC	2005	GC	1	1	1	41	41*	-	-	-								1	
B.M.Brain	MC	1982	BH	1								48	18	2	2-18	9.00	2.25	-	-	
S.Bramhall	Ches	1994-2001	GC	8	7	1	54	23	9.00	-	-								8	2

				M	I	NO	Runs	HS	Avg	100	50	Balls	Runs	Wkts	BB	Avg	RpO	4I	Ct	St
A.R.Bray	KntCB	2000-2001	GC	5	2	0	5	5	2.50	-	-	170	150	4	2-18	37.50	5.29	-	-	
K.G.Bray	WarCB	1999-2001	GC	4	4	0	54	36	13.50	-	-	197	105	4	2-15	26.25	3.19	-	-	
D.H.Breakwell	Shr	1974-1976	GC	2	2	2	0	0*	-	-	-	139	62	5	3-28	12.40	2.67	-	-	
A.N.Bressington	GloCB	1999-2000	GC	3	2	0	98	54	49.00	-	1	150	86	5	3-21	17.20	3.44	-	1	
N.S.Bressington	GloCB	2000	GC	2	1	0	6	6	6.00	-	-	12	10	0	-	-	5.00	-	1	
N.A.Brett	SurCB	2002	GC	2	1	0	2	2	2.00	-	-	114	129	1	1-48	129.00	6.78	-	-	
C.T.Bruce	YorCB	2001-2002	GC	3	2	0	27	17	13.50	-	-	174	154	2	1-29	77.00	5.31	-	1	
G.D.Bridge	DurCB	1999-2002	GC	4	3	1	43	19	21.50	-	-	212	159	3	2-36	53.00	4.50	-	1	
M.P.Briers	Here	1998	GC	1	1	0	0	0	0.00	-	-								-	
P.D.Briggs	Ches	1968	GC	2	2	0	76	60	38.00	-	1								-	
	Bed	1970-1971	GC	2	2	0	90	69	45.00	-	1								1	
D.S.Brignull	LeiCB	1999-2001	GC	2	2	1	15	9*	15.00	-	-	112	85	4	2-35	21.25	4.55	-	1	
T.R.Bristow	Bed	2001-2002	GC	3															1	
D.P.Britton	Dor	2001	GC	1	1	1	0	0*	-	-	-	42	30	2	2-30	15.00	4.28	-	-	
D.L.Broadbent	YorCB	2002	GC	1	1	1	17	17*	-	-	-	36	31	0	-	-	5.16	-	-	
R.G.Broadbent	Hert	1964	GC	1	1	0	2	2	2.00	-	-								-	
D.J.Brock	Sta	1996-1999	GC	3	3	1	25	19	12.50	-	-	124	85	2	1-21	42.50	4.11	-	-	
	Ches	2000	GC	1	1	1	0	0*	-	-	-	60	33	1	1-33	33.00	3.30	-	1	
S.M.Brogan	Here	1995	GC	1	1	0	10	10	10.00	-	-								-	
	NottCB	1999-2000	GC	2	2	0	94	61	47.00	-	1								-	
B.Brook	YorCB	2000-2001	GC	4	2	1	3	3	3.00	-	-								5	
M.E.W.Brooker	Sta	1984	GC	1	1	1	14	14*	-	-	-	72	19	0	-	-	1.58	-	-	
A.P.Brookes	WarCB	1999	GC	1	1	1	6	6*	-	-	-	60	21	1	1-21	21.00	2.10	-	-	
C.E.W.Brooks	Berk	1965-1966	GC	3	3	1	43	37*	21.50	-	-	12	12	0	-	-	6.00	-	2	
K.G.Brooks	Lin	1983	GC	1	1	0	51	51	51.00	-	1	18	23	0	-	-	7.66	-	-	
	Suf	1986-1987	GC	2	2	1	35	26*	35.00	-	-								-	
R.D.Brooks	Oxfsh	2000-2001	GC	2	2	0	37	23	18.50	-	-								1	
A.Brown	Nmb	1971-1977	GC	3	1	0	5	5	5.00	-	-	142	83	2	2-26	41.50	3.50	-	-	
	MCN	1974	BH	4	4	0	19	9	4.75	-	-	208	65	3	3-21	21.66	1.87	-	2	
A.D.Brown	Suf	1984-2001	GC	8	7	0	67	51	9.57	-	1								5	2
A.G.Brown	Nmb	2003	GC	1	1	0	4	4	4.00	-	-	25	24	0	-	-	5.76	-	-	
A.M.Brown	Suf	2001-2002	GC	7	7	1	95	44*	15.83	-	-								2	
C.Brown	Norf	2001-2003	GC	6	5	1	68	33	17.00	-	-	276	199	5	2-39	39.80	4.32	-	2	
G.Brown	SomCB	1999	GC	1	1	0	3	3	3.00	-	-								1	
G.K.Brown	Dur	1989-1990	GC	2	2	0	66	42	33.00	-	-								-	
	MC	1989-1991	BH	12	12	0	298	82	24.83	-	1	6	8	0	-	-	8.00	-	4	
	DurCB	1999-2001	GC	6	6	0	38	15	6.33	-	-								1	
J.F.Brown	Sta	1995	GC	1								72	72	1	1-72	72.00	6.00	-	-	
M.Brown	Cambsh	1982-1983	GC	2	2	0	0	0	0.00	-	-	144	93	3	2-44	31.00	3.87	-	1	
P.A.Brown	Dev	1986-1990	GC	3	3	2	93	67*	93.00	-	1	144	132	2	2-49	66.00	5.50	-	-	
S.J.E.Brown	Dur	1991	GC	1	1	1	7	7*	-	-	-	72	73	1	1-73	73.00	6.08	-	-	
B.S.Browne	Ches	2004	GC	1	1	1	13	13*	-	-	-	16	13	0	-	-	4.87	-	-	
J.T.A.Bruce	Cumb	2001	GC	1	1	0	0	0	0.00	-	-								-	
I.Brunnschweiler	HamCB	2002	GC	1	1	0	37	37	37.00	-	-								2	
A.P.Bryan	WorCB	2001	GC	3	1	1	3	3*	-	-	-	52	32	0	-	-	3.69	-	-	
R.B.Bryan	Dev	1999-2003	GC	2	1	0	0	0	0.00	-	-	54	72	0	-	-	8.00	-	-	

				M	I	NO	Runs	HS	Avg	100	50	Balls	Runs	Wkts	BB	Avg	RpO	4I	Ct	St
P.R.J.Bryson	Ches	1995-2002	GC	9	9	1	138	59	17.25	-	1								3	
A.C.Buck	Oxfsh	1967	GC	1	1	1	3	3*	-	-	-	24	14	0	-	-	3.50	-	1	
C.R.J.Budd	GloCB	1999-2001	GC	5	5	1	158	65	39.50	-	2								3	
	Wilt	2002-2005	GC	3	3	0	41	27	13.66	-	-								2	
M.P.L.Bulbeck	SomCB	2001	GC	1								55	18	5	5-18	3.60	1.96	1	-	
D.A.Bulfield	Dor	1973	GC	1	1	0	5	5	5.00	-	-								-	
J.J.Bull	LeiCB	2001	GC	1	1	0	10	10	10.00	-	-	24	12	1	1-12	12.00	3.00	-	1	
C.K.Bullen	Bed	1994-1997	GC	2	2	0	19	17	9.50	-	-	72	67	3	3-58	22.33	5.58	-	-	
	SurCB	1999-2001	GC	6	6	2	103	36	25.75	-	-	343	221	7	2-16	31.57	3.86	-	3	
G.Bulpitt	Sta	2001-2004	GC	7	3	1	4	2*	2.00	-	-	328	184	8	3-39	23.00	3.36	-	2	
R.A.Bunting	Norf	1985-1995	GC	5	5	1	48	18*	12.00	-	-	282	230	6	3-40	38.33	4.89	-	1	
	MC	1987	BH	4	1	1	0	0*	-	-	-	204	167	4	2-43	41.75	4.91	-	2	
A.J.Burch	Suf	2001	GC	1															2	
O.E.Burford	Lin	2001-2004	GC	8	7	1	123	55	20.50	-	1								5	1
G.I.Burgess	MC	1981-1982	BH	3	3	0	8	7	2.66	-	-	174	92	4	3-25	23.00	3.17	-	2	
J.Burgoyne	WorCB	1999	GC	1	1	1	0	0*	-	-	-	54	46	1	1-46	46.00	5.11	-	-	
W.A.Burgoyne	Berk	1976	GC	1	1	1	0	0*	-	-	-	66	25	0	-	-	2.27	-	2	
M.K.Burley	Corn	2001	GC	1	1	1	0	0*	-	-	-								2	1
P.Burn	Dur	1985-1991	GC	6	5	0	81	43	16.20	-	-	18	17	0	-	-	5.66	-	1	
	Nmb	1992	GC	1	1	0	0	0	0.00	-	-								-	
	DurCB	1999	GC	2	2	0	36	25	18.00	-	-								-	
M.I.Burns	Cumb	2002	GC	2	1	0	1	1	1.00	-	-								4	2
N.D.Burns	Buck	1997-1999	GC	4	4	0	90	51	22.50	-	1								5	1
A.J.Burridge	Dur	1964-1972	GC	6	6	0	181	95	30.16	-	1								4	
	MCN	1972-1974	BH	10	10	1	181	76	20.11	-	1	24	25	0	-	-	6.25	-	4	
	MCS	1975	BH	4	4	0	63	34	15.75	-	-	86	71	4	3-40	17.75	4.95	-	1	
	MCW	1976-1978	BH	12	12	1	170	46	15.45	-	-	60	45	1	1-9	45.00	4.50	-	4	
	Hert	1976-1977	GC	4	4	0	44	34	11.00	-	-								2	
S.Burrow	Berk	1983	GC	1	1	0	14	14	14.00	-	-	72	18	0	-	-	1.50	-	1	
	Buck	1985-1993	GC	7	7	1	121	57*	20.16	-	1	398	273	8	3-32	34.12	4.11	-	2	
	MC	1988	BH	2	2	0	48	28	24.00	-	-	54	43	1	1-43	43.00	4.77	-	-	
	Hert	1999-2000	GC	4	2	0	28	16	14.00	-	-	180	140	6	2-27	23.33	4.66	-	1	
T.G.Burrows	Berk	2003	GC	1	1	0	1	1	1.00	-	-								1	
M.T.Burt	SomCB	2001	GC	1	1	0	2	2	2.00	-	-								2	1
A.W.Burton	YorCB	1999	GC	1	1	1	2	2*	-	-	-	54	30	3	3-30	10.00	3.33	-	-	
M.A.E.Burton	Cambsh	1995	GC	1	1	0	0	0	0.00	-	-	60	51	0	-	-	5.10	-	-	
	Hunt	1999-2002	GC	7	7	0	134	34	19.14	-	-	360	208	7	2-22	29.71	3.46	-	1	
R.L.Burton	Shr	1974-1978	GC	3	3	0	53	47	17.66	-	-								2	
	MCN	1974	BH	1	1	0	5	5	5.00	-	-								-	
	Lin	1983-1988	GC	2	2	1	13	9*	13.00	-	-	126	128	0	-	-	6.09	-	-	
R.P.L.Burton	Shr	2001	GC	1	1	0	28	28	28.00	-	-								-	
R.N.Busby	Oxfsh	1975-1987	GC	9	7	2	46	22	9.20	-	-	576	317	5	1-15	63.40	3.30	-	4	
	MC	1987-1988	BH	3	1	0	9	9	9.00	-	-	156	97	2	1-35	48.50	3.73	-	1	
J.E.Bush	Oxfsh	1967	GC	1	1	0	14	14	14.00	-	-								-	
W.J.Bushby	Bed	1967-1973	GC	6	5	1	110	80*	27.50	-	1	366	224	4	2-10	56.00	3.67	-	2	
D.N.Butcher	Dev	1992	GC	1	1	1	1	1*	-	-	-	72	48	2	2-48	24.00	4.00	-	1	

				M	*I*	*NO*	*Runs*	*HS*	*Avg*	*100*	*50*	*Balls*	*Runs*	*Wkts*	*BB*	*Avg*	*RpO*	*4I*	*Ct*	*St*
G.P.Butcher	Hert	2003	GC	1	1	0	126	126	126.00	1	-	60	70	0	-	-	7.00	-	-	
K.A.Butler	Suf	1993	GC	1	1	0	17	17	17.00	-	-								1	
N.V.Butler	Buck	1965	GC	1	1	0	5	5	5.00	-	-								-	
R.P.Butler	Lin	1983-1988	GC	2	2	0	37	33	18.50	-	-	17	20	3	3-20	6.66	7.05	-	1	
T.Butler	Buck	1987-1990	GC	4	4	0	79	44	19.75	-	-								-	
A.B.Byram	Shr	1990-2002	GC	13	11	2	127	32*	14.11	-	-	726	465	14	4-24	33.21	3.84	1	5	
G.J.Byram	Shr	1997-2001	GC	8	6	0	77	56	12.83	-	1	357	254	10	3-33	25.40	4.26	-	-	
A.M.Cade	Cambsh	1991-1992	GC	2	2	1	18	18*	18.00	-	-								-	
	Hunt	1999	GC	1	1	0	5	5	5.00	-	-								-	
J.R.Cade	Hunt	1999-2001	GC	1	1	0	6	6	6.00	-	-	36	25	1	1-25	25.00	4.16	-	-	
J.F.Cadman	Suf	1966	GC	1	1	0	7	7	7.00	-	-	24	24	0	-	-	6.00	-	-	
B.L.Cairns	Dur	1979-1988	GC	5	5	0	121	54	24.20	-	1	348	181	5	2-35	36.20	3.12	-	3	
	MC	1980-1981	BH	4	4	0	107	54	26.75	-	1	210	132	5	2-35	26.40	3.77	-	2	
L.B.Caldicott	Here	1999	GC	1	1	1	35	35*	-	-	-	47	37	3	3-37	12.33	4.72	-	-	
P.J.Caley	Suf	1983-2005	GC	22	21	5	514	88*	32.12	-	2	558	508	6	2-24	84.66	5.46	-	7	
D.J.Callaghan	Suf	1999-2001	GC	7	7	0	197	59	28.14	-	1	376	247	7	3-28	35.28	3.94	-	2	
I.W.Callen	Nmb	1977	GC	2	1	1	1	1*	-	-	-	132	72	5	3-50	14.40	3.27	-	-	
G.S.Calway	Dor	1987-1993	GC	6	6	0	176	105	29.33	1	-	202	174	2	1-34	87.00	5.16	-	2	
	MC	1992	BH	3	3	0	5	3	1.66	-	-	126	105	1	1-10	105.00	5.00	-	1	
J.Cameron	NottCB	2000	GC	1	1	0	6	6	6.00	-	-	24	17	0	-	-	4.25	-	-	
P.Camm	DerbCB	1999-2001	GC	3	2	0	20	20	10.00	-	-	143	145	4	4-52	36.25	6.08	1	-	
G.R.A.Campbell	SusCB	2000-2002	GC	7	7	0	346	141	49.42	1	3								1	
H.J.Campbell-Ferguson	Cambsh	1965-1967	GC	2	2	2	16	12*	-	-	-								1	
G.B.Camplin	Lin	1966-1967	GC	2	2	0	0	0	0.00	-	-	144	90	4	3-38	22.50	3.75	-	-	
M.C.Cannons	Oxfsh	1994	GC	1	1	0	2	2	2.00	-	-								-	
D.J.Capel	NhCB	2001-2002	GC	3	3	0	95	57	31.66	-	1	120	77	4	3-35	19.25	3.85	-	2	
S.P.Caple	GloCB	2002	GC	1	1	0	0	0	0.00	-	-								-	
I.J.Capon	WalMC	2003	GC	1								24	25	1	1-25	25.00	6.25	-	-	
M.A.Carberry	SurCB	1999	GC	2	2	0	23	19	11.50	-	-								-	
C.S.Carey	Norf	2001	GC	2	2	0	43	23	21.50	-	-	30	15	1	1-15	15.00	3.00	-	1	
N.Carlier	EssCB	1999-2000	GC	3	3	0	92	56	30.66	-	1								1	
I.D.Carr	Sta	2000	GC	2	1	0	1	1	1.00	-	-	107	85	5	3-34	17.00	4.76	-	2	
J.D.Carr	Hert	1991	GC	1	1	0	14	14	14.00	-	-	36	13	0	-	-	2.16	-	-	
J.R.Carruthers	YorCB	1999-2001	GC	6	4	1	9	9	3.00	-	-	306	182	8	2-16	22.75	3.56	-	1	
G.J.Carsberg	Lin	1988	GC	1	1	0	1	1	1.00	-	-								-	
D.M.Carter	Suf	1995	GC	1	1	1	3	3*	-	-	-	72	31	3	3-31	10.33	2.58	-	1	
J.R.Carter	Norf	1985	GC	1	1	0	8	8	8.00	-	-								1	
N.A.Carter	Corn	2002	GC	2	1	1	10	10*	-	-	-	104	66	3	2-21	22.00	3.80	-	-	
T.J.Carter	SurCB	1999-2001	GC	4	4	0	47	29	11.75	-	-								2	
D.Cartledge	Sta	1984-1995	GC	9	9	0	124	26	13.77	-	-	114	87	3	2-21	29.00	4.57	-	2	
N.D.J.Cartmel	Berk	1992-1994	GC	2	1	0	27	27	27.00	-	-								2	
C.Casemore	Berk	1976	GC	1	1	0	6	6	6.00	-	-								-	
G.R.Cass	Shr	1976-1978	GC	2	2	0	22	21	11.00	-	-								3	1
J.Cassell	Dor	1995-1999	GC	2	2	0	29	24	14.50	-	-								-	
M.D.Catley	Suf	2001-2002	GC	3	2	0	15	9	7.50	-	-								1	

				M	I	NO	Runs	HS	Avg	100	50	Balls	Runs	Wkts	BB	Avg	RpO	4I	Ct	St
R.J.Catley	Suf	1996-2003	GC	9	9	0	152	65	16.88	-	1								2	
T.M.Catley	Suf	2005	GC	1	1	0	6	6	6.00	-	-								-	
D.N.Catterall	Shr	2003-2005	GC	3	2	0	45	28	22.50	-	-	114	82	3	2-24	27.33	4.31	-	-	
S.C.Catterall	LanCB	2000-2002	GC	4	4	2	64	37*	32.00	-	-	108	73	1	1-34	73.00	4.05	-	-	
C.N.Cavener	Hert	1993-2001	GC	2	2	0	3	2	1.50	-	-	72	56	1	1-56	56.00	4.66	-	-	
B.A.Chambers	SusCB	1999	GC	1	1	0	4	4	4.00	-	-	54	30	1	1-30	30.00	3.33	-	1	
J.E.Chambers	EssCB	2001	GC	1	1	0	0	0	0.00	-	-	24	25	0	-	-	6.25	-	-	
L.J.Champniss	Buck	1972-1974	GC	2	1	0	0	0	0.00	-	-	144	85	2	1-32	42.50	3.54	-	-	
C.R.M.Chaplin	Corn	1970-1977	GC	3	3	0	45	22	15.00	-	-	30	14	0	-	-	2.80	-	-	
N.J.Chapman	Oxfsh	1975	GC	1	1	0	9	9	9.00	-	-								-	
R.J.Chapman	Lin	2000-2003	GC	8	8	3	149	53*	29.80	-	1	338	285	11	4-18	25.90	5.05	1	1	
S.Chapman	DurCB	2000	GC	3	3	0	129	64	43.00	-	2	96	76	4	3-39	19.00	4.75	-	-	
	Nmb	2001-2003	GC	4	4	0	120	44	30.00	-	-	169	149	4	3-40	37.25	5.28	-	2	
D.M.Chard	GloCB	2001	GC	1								60	28	1	1-28	28.00	2.80	-	-	
	Wilt	2002	GC	1	1	1	7	7*	-	-	-	60	36	2	2-36	18.00	3.60	-	-	
B.E.F.Cheesman	Berk	1965-1966	GC	3	3	0	60	31	20.00	-	-	96	71	1	1-37	71.00	4.43	-	1	
G.E.J.Child	Berk	1976-1985	GC	5	5	1	33	12*	8.25	-	-								6	1
A.B.Chivers	Wilt	1964	GC	1	1	0	0	0	0.00	-	-								-	
D.A.Christmas	Lin	1991-2004	GC	14	13	3	153	29	15.30	-	-	710	571	10	2-48	57.10	4.82	-	6	
A.J.Churchill	EssCB	1999-2001	GC	4	4	0	19	10	4.75	-	-	210	145	5	2-32	29.00	4.14	-	1	
D.A.Clapp	SusCB	2000	GC	2	2	0	14	10	7.00	-	-	36	46	3	3-46	15.33	7.66	-	-	
S.G.Clark	YorCB	2002	GC	2	2	0	53	52	26.50	-	1	18	31	1	1-31	31.00	10.33	-	-	
A.J.Clarke	EssCB	2001	GC	1	1	0	0	0	0.00	-	-	54	19	0	-	-	2.11	-	-	
A.R.Clarke	Buck	1997-2003	GC	9	5	0	5	5	1.00	-	-	503	370	17	5-36	21.76	4.41	2	2	
	Norf	2000	GC	2	1	1	0	0*	-	-	-	120	57	2	2-32	28.50	2.85	-	-	
D.P.Clarke	Bed	1977	GC	1	1	0	1	1	1.00	-	-	72	19	0	-	-	1.58	-	-	
D.R.Clarke	Bed	1994-2003	GC	14	13	3	514	176*	51.40	1	2								5	
G.J.Clarke	Cumb	1985-1997	GC	7	7	0	132	61	18.85	-	1								1	
J.Clarke	Lin	1999-2003	GC	8	8	0	173	53	21.62	-	1								1	
R.Clarke	SurCB	2001	GC	1	1	0	2	2	2.00	-	-	24	14	1	1-14	14.00	3.50	-	-	
J.A.Claughton	Berk	1983-1985	GC	3	3	0	29	19	9.66	-	-								-	
	MC	1983	BH	1	1	0	40	40	40.00	-	-								-	
	Dor	1989-1991	GC	2	2	0	64	35	32.00	-	-								1	
O.J.Clayson	Bed	2000-2001	GC	5	5	2	99	56*	33.00	-	1								-	
C.J.Clements	Oxfsh	1980-1987	GC	3	3	0	9	5	3.00	-	-								-	
S.M.Clements	Suf	1978-1996	GC	13	13	0	169	59	13.00	-	1	228	145	5	3-30	29.00	3.81	-	1	
	MC	1983	BH	1								30	23	0	-	-	4.60	-	-	
J.I.Clifford	WarCB	2001-2002	GC	2	2	1	8	5*	8.00	-	-								2	1
P.R.Clifford	Wilt	1999	GC	2	2	1	49	34*	49.00	-	-	120	85	4	3-46	21.25	4.25	-	-	
J.L.Clinch	Suf	1995	GC	1	1	0	18	18	18.00	-	-								1	
R.I.Clitheroe	WalMC	1998-2001	GC	3	3	0	37	23	12.33	-	-								1	1
T.L.Clough	Hert	1964-1971	GC	5	5	0	112	47	22.40	-	-								1	
J.Clutterbuck	SurCB	1999	GC	1	1	0	11	11	11.00	-	-								-	
N.G.Cock	Corn	1975-1980	GC	2	2	0	12	7	6.00	-	-								1	
I.Cockbain	Ches	1985-2001	GC	17	17	0	296	65	17.41	-	2								10	
	MC	1993-1997	BH	14	13	2	278	65*	25.27	-	2								4	

				M	I	NO	Runs	HS	Avg	100	50	Balls	Runs	Wkts	BB	Avg	RpO	4I	Ct	St
C.P.Crowe	LeiCB	2000-2002	GC	4	4	0	79	35	19.75	-	-	12	19	0	-	-	9.50	-	1	
S.C.Crowley	Norf	1993-1996	GC	4	4	1	5	2*	1.66	-	-								4	2
L.J.Crozier	Nmb	1999-2005	GC	8	6	3	14	6*	4.66	-	-	438	369	12	3-30	30.75	5.05	-	2	
R.Cruttenden	Berk	1979	GC	1	1	1	26	26*	-	-	-	72	52	1	1-52	52.00	4.33	-	-	
E.P.Cruz	SurCB	2001-2002	GC	5	3	0	24	11	8.00	-	-								1	2
J.Cullip	Wilt	1987-1988	GC	2	2	0	12	9	6.00	-	-								2	
S.Cummings	Ches	1986-1987	GC	2	2	1	1	1*	1.00	-	-								-	2
J.W.J.Cundle	Hert	1964	GC	1	1	0	2	2	2.00	-	-								-	
C.J.Cunnell	Suf	1966	GC	1	1	0	3	3	3.00	-	-								1	
R.E.Cunnell	Suf	1966-1979	GC	4	4	1	55	40	18.33	-	-	18	28	1	1-28	28.00	9.33	-	1	
N.S.Curnow	Corn	2001-2002	GC	3	3	0	37	25	12.33	-	-								1	
M.R.Currie	Ches	2001-2002	GC	3	3	0	118	94	39.33	-	1								1	
I.J.Curtis	Oxfsh	1986-1996	GC	10	4	4	3	2*	-	-	-	458	356	5	2-53	71.20	4.66	-	2	
B.J.Cutbill	Ches	2002	GC	2								114	99	2	1-49	49.50	5.21	-	1	
A.D.Cuthall	Cambsh	1987	GC	1	1	0	0	0	0.00	-	-								-	
C.E.Dagnall	Cumb	1998	GC	1	1	0	4	4	4.00	-	-	54	37	1	1-37	37.00	4.11	-	-	
A.Dalby	Nmb	1989	GC	1	1	0	6	6	6.00	-	-	60	87	3	3-87	29.00	8.70	-	-	
J.R.Dale	Lin	1974-1976	GC	3	1	0	1	1	1.00	-	-	204	124	6	3-33	20.66	3.64	-	-	
	MCN	1974	BH	1	1	1	2	2*	-	-	-	66	43	1	1-43	43.00	3.90	-	-	
M.A.P.Dale	WorCB	2001-2002	GC	2	1	0	0	0	0.00	-	-								-	
D.A.T.Dalton	WarCB	1999-2002	GC	8	8	0	126	46	15.75	-	-	306	210	10	3-16	21.00	4.11	-	1	
R.N.Dalton	Bed	1994-1999	GC	4	4	0	76	56	19.00	-	1	138	124	6	2-32	20.66	5.39	-	-	
	MC	1997-1998	BH	7	7	0	173	76	24.71	-	2	262	255	6	3-28	42.50	5.83	-	2	
P.A.J.Dancy	MidCB	2001	GC	1	1	0	1	1	1.00	-	-	30	39	1	1-39	39.00	7.80	-	-	
R.Dandy	WarCB	2001	GC	1	1	0	0	0	0.00	-	-								-	
A.Daniels	NhCB	2002	GC	1	1	0	2	2	2.00	-	-								-	
D.M.Daniels	Dor	1968	GC	1	1	0	10	10	10.00	-	-								-	
	MCS	1972	BH	4	4	0	34	16	8.50	-	-								3	
	MCW	1977	BH	4	4	0	55	26	13.75	-	-								1	
	Bed	1977-1982	GC	2	2	0	27	20	13.50	-	-	3	1	0	-	-	2.00	-	-	
S.A.B.Daniels	Dur	1980-1983	GC	2	2	1	3	2*	3.00	-	-	144	96	0	-	-	4.00	-	-	
T.O.Dann	NhCB	2000-2001	GC	4	3	1	52	27	26.00	-	-								2	
I.J.Darlington	DerbCB	1999-2002	GC	6	6	1	163	58	32.60	-	1	229	202	4	3-19	50.50	5.29	-	-	
D.A.Dass	Bed	2001	GC	1															2	2
J.Davey	Dev	1983-1985	GC	2	1	0	1	1	1.00	-	-	120	88	3	2-45	29.33	4.40	-	-	
M.J.Davidson	Shr	1992-1993	GC	2	2	0	42	42	21.00	-	-								1	
A.J.Davies	WalMC	2005	GC	1	1	0	17	17	17.00	-	-	36	24	2	2-24	12.00	4.00	-	-	
G.R.Davies	WalMC	2001	GC	2	2	0	15	8	7.50	-	-								2	
J.Davies	WalMC	1998-2002	GC	4	3	2	4	4*	4.00	-	-	228	155	4	1-30	38.75	4.07	-	1	
J.R.Davies	Lin	2002-2004	GC	4	1	1	2	28	-	-	-	216	177	7	3-40	25.28	4.91	-	2	
M.Davies	WalMC	1998-2001	GC	7	5	2	70	30*	23.33	-	-	330	209	6	2-34	34.83	3.80	-	2	
M.Davies	DurCB	2000-2001	GC	4	2	0	6	6	3.00	-	-	168	95	3	1-11	31.66	3.39	-	-	
M.R.Davies	Shr	1985-2000	GC	10	10	0	199	89	19.90	-	1								1	
N.M.Davies	Here	2001-2004	GC	8	7	2	77	39*	15.40	-	-	349	249	8	4-72	31.12	4.28	1	4	
P.G.T.Davies	DerbCB	2000	GC	1	1	0	0	0	0.00	-	-								-	
R.J.Davies	Berk	1979	GC	1	1	0	7	7	7.00	-	-	12	11	0	-	-	5.50	-	1	

				M	I	NO	Runs	HS	Avg	100	50	Balls	Runs	Wkts	BB	Avg	RpO	4I	Ct	St
S.M.Davies	WorCB	2002-2003	GC	2	1	0	13	13	13.00	-	-								-	
W.O.Davies	Shr	1999	GC	1	1	0	18	18	18.00	-	-								-	2
A.T.Davis	Berk	1965-1966	GC	3	3	0	68	47	22.66	-	-								-	
E.Davis	Cambsh	1967	GC	1	1	0	6	6	6.00	-	-								-	
K.Davis	Corn	1970	GC	1	1	0	4	4	4.00	-	-	72	30	2	2-30	15.00	2.50	-	-	
M.R.Davis	Wilt	1989	GC	1	1	0	1	1	1.00	-	-	66	53	1	1-53	53.00	4.81	-	-	
R.P.Davis	Berk	2001	GC	3	2	0	57	56	28.50	-	1	162	99	4	2-27	24.75	3.66	-	2	
S.D.L.Davis	Bed	1991	GC	1	1	0	14	14	14.00	-	-								-	
S.P.Davis	Dur	1982-1983	GC	2	1	0	10	10	10.00	-	-	144	83	12	7-32	6.91	3.45	2	-	
	MC	1982-1983	BH	3	2	2	8	7*	-	-	-	180	72	5	4-11	14.40	2.40	1	-	
I.J.Davison	Bed	1967-1968	GC	3	1	0	22	22	22.00	-	-	208	124	3	2-17	41.33	3.57	-	-	
O.A.Dawkins	WalMC	2001-2004	GC	5	3	0	29	18	9.66	-	-	66	81	1	1-21	81.00	7.36	-	2	
I.Dawood	Here	2000-2004	GC	9	9	0	294	60	32.66	-	2								13	2
G.Dawson	Bed	1967	GC	1	1	0	14	14	14.00	-	-								-	
J.P.Dawson	Shr	1974-1984	GC	6	6	1	40	16	8.00	-	-	180	151	4	2-53	37.75	5.03	-	3	
R.I.Dawson	Dev	1990-2005	GC	13	13	0	492	138	37.84	1	4	66	64	2	1-15	32.00	5.81	-	2	
R.K.J.Dawson	Dev	1999-2000	GC	3	3	0	14	7	4.66	-	-	131	88	4	2-32	22.00	4.03	-	1	
A.C.Day	DurCB	2001-2002	GC	2	1	0	1	1	1.00	-	-	114	68	4	2-32	17.00	3.57	-	-	
A.P.Day	Hert	1966-1974	GC	5	5	0	107	53	21.40	-	1								1	
P.J.Deakin	Dor	1999-2004	GC	6	6	0	52	23	8.66	-	-	80	62	4	2-6	15.50	4.65	-	4	
A.Dean	Bed	1991	GC	1	1	0	0	0	0.00	-	-	29	20	2	2-20	10.00	4.13	-	-	
M.M.Dean	WarCB	2002	GC	1	1	1	8	8*	-	-	-	54	63	0	-	-	7.00	-	-	
S.A.Dean	Hert	1983-1987	GC	3	3	0	54	42	18.00	-	-								-	
S.J.Dean	Sta	1986-2002	GC	21	21	0	302	72	14.38	-	1								12	
	MC	1992-1998	BH	27	26	0	583	56	22.42	-	1								7	
S.E.Dearden	LanCB	1999-2002	GC	7	7	1	211	67*	35.16	-	1	312	220	10	4-31	22.00	4.23	1	2	
C.J.Debenham	Hert	1977	GC	1	1	0	3	3	3.00	-	-								-	
P.de Bruyn	Norf	2003	GC	1	1	0	9	9	9.00	-	-								1	
Z.de Bruyn	SurCB	2000-2001	GC	3	3	1	158	113*	79.00	1	-	18	22	2	2-22	11.00	7.33	-	-	
S.A.Deitz	Lin	2002-2004	GC	4	4	0	89	56	22.25	-	1	24	28	0	-	-	7.00	-	2	
R.O.Demming	Bed	1973-1977	GC	2	2	0	34	17	17.00	-	-	66	64	0	-	-	5.81	-	1	
A.C.Denness	Berk	1965-1966	GC	3	3	1	35	18	17.50	-	-	216	107	7	4-56	15.28	2.97	1	1	
N.A.Denning	Berk	2001-2005	GC	5	3	2	3	2	3.00	-	-	237	182	7	3-22	26.00	4.60	-	-	
M.J.Dennington	KntCB	2003	GC	1	1	0	1	1	1.00	-	-	48	51	1	1-51	51.00	6.37	-	-	
P.J.Densham	Oxfsh	1980-1983	GC	3	3	1	17	10	8.50	-	-	24	16	0	-	-	4.00	-	-	
P.H.de Prez	Ches	1987	GC	1	1	0	11	11	11.00	-	-	54	33	0	-	-	3.66	-	-	
J.Derrick	WalMC	1993-2000	GC	3	2	0	21	17	10.50	-	-	180	90	4	2-21	22.50	3.00	-	2	
	MC	1993	BH	1	1	0	13	13	13.00	-	-	66	30	0	-	-	2.72	-	-	
D.S.de Silva	Shr	1983	GC	1	1	0	24	24	24.00	-	-	72	30	2	2-30	15.00	2.50	-	-	
F.R.Dethridge	Bed	1982	GC	1	1	0	31	31	31.00	-	-	42	21	1	1-21	21.00	3.00	-	-	
R.T.de Ville	Sta	1971-1973	GC	2	2	0	2	1	1.00	-	-	42	42	1	1-18	42.00	6.00	-	-	
I.M.Dews	YorCB	1999	GC	1	1	0	37	37	37.00	-	-	36	24	0	-	-	4.00	-	-	
R.R.Dibden	HamCB	2001-2002	GC	3	2	0	18	13	9.00	-	-	162	128	4	2-40	32.00	4.74	-	2	
P.J.Dicks	Cambsh	1988-1989	GC	2	2	0	35	22	17.50	-	-								-	
R.J.Digman	Ches	1964-1966	GC	2	2	0	0	0	0.00	-	-	138	34	3	2-10	11.33	1.47	-	-	
M.Dimond	SomCB	1999-2002	GC	5	4	1	35	13*	11.66	-	-	272	176	6	2-41	29.33	3.88	-	1	

				M	I	NO	Runs	HS	Avg	100	50	Balls	Runs	Wkts	BB	Avg	RpO	4I	Ct	St
N.A.Din	Ches	2002-2004	GC	4	4	0	118	75	29.50	-	1								-	
A.Dindar	Berk	1983	GC	1	1	0	0	0	0.00	-	-	6	2	0	-	-	2.00	-	-	
J.H.Dixon	Wilt	1988	GC	1	1	0	12	12	12.00	-	-	72	59	1	1-59	59.00	4.91	-	1	
S.B.Dixon	Norf	1990-1993	GC	3	3	0	7	6	2.33	-	-								-	
C.M.Doar	DerbCB	2001	GC	2	2	1	0	08	0.00	-	-	60	59	1	1-44	59.00	5.90	-	1	
N.P.Dobbs	Lin	1988-1994	GC	3	3	2	3	2	3.00	-	-	0	0	0	-	-			1	
M.C.Dobson	NhCB	2001	GC	1	1	0	1	1	1.00	-	-	48	58	1	1-58	58.00	7.25	-	-	
	Lin	2002-2004	GC	3	3	0	158	90	52.66	-	2	96	99	1	1-50	99.00	6.18	-	1	
T.P.J.Dodd	Berk	1988-1989	GC	2	2	1	19	15	19.00	-	-	90	46	2	2-37	23.00	3.06	-	-	
D.H.Dodds	DerbCB	2000-2001	GC	3	2	2	0	0*	-	-	-	114	116	0	-	-	6.10	-	-	
C.W.Dodsley	DurCB	2001	GC	1	1	1	1	1*	-		-	18	18	0	-	-	6.00	-	-	
M.E.Doggrell	Dor	1968	GC	1	1	0	0	0	0.00	-	-	42	15	0	-	-	2.14	-	-	
M.J.Doidge	YorCB	1999-2001	GC	6	6	1	98	54*	19.60	-	1								1	
J.A.Donaldson	Norf	1968-1969	GC	2	2	0	37	21	18.50	-	-								1	
R.P.Done	Suf	1979-1980	GC	3	3	0	57	53	19.00	-	1	210	95	6	3-9	15.83	2.71	-	-	
B.T.P.Donelan	Cambsh	1995-1999	GC	5	5	0	97	32	19.40	-	-	264	242	2	1-52	121.00	5.50	-	1	
K.Donohue	Dev	1986-2000	GC	11	10	3	110	31	15.71	-	-	686	544	13	3-41	41.84	4.75	-	2	
D.R.Doshi	Hert	1976	GC	2	2	0	4	4	2.00	-	-	102	42	4	4-23	10.50	2.47	1	-	
N.D.Doshi	Buck	2001	GC	1	1	0	0	0	0.00	-	-	18	12	1	1-12	12.00	4.00	-	-	
P.J.Douglas	Suf	1993	GC	1	1	0	2	2	2.00	-	-	72	54	0	-	-	4.50	-	-	
M.P.Dowman	Lin	2003-2004	GC	3	3	0	59	29	19.66	-	-	168	134	8	4-30	16.75	4.78	1	-	
R.H.Downend	Sta	1971-1975	GC	4	4	0	76	24	19.00	-	-	180	126	6	3-35	21.00	4.20	-	1	
	MCN	1972-1975	BH	5	5	0	8	3	1.60	-	-	228	134	7	3-31	19.14	3.52	-	-	
M.A.Downes	Shr	2001-2005	GC	5	4	0	42	16	10.50	-	-	102	115	3	2-39	38.33	6.76	-	2	
P.R.Draper	Wilt	1999-2001	GC	2	2	0	12	10	6.00	-	-	60	61	0	-	-	6.10	-	1	
D.R.Drepaul	Buck	2001-2002	GC	5	4	1	87	47*	29.00	-	-								1	4
J.S.Drewett	Berk	1965	GC	1	1	0	1	1	1.00	-	-								-	
J.N.Dreyer	WarCB	2000	GC	1	1	0	19	19	19.00	-	-	60	28	0	-	-	2.80	-	-	
R.Dreyer	Nmb	1986-1987	GC	2	2	0	31	26	15.50	-	-								1	
R.C.Driver	Corn	1996-2003	GC	3	3	0	38	19	12.66	-	-	90	96	1	1-58	96.00	6.40	-	-	
D.B.Drury	Cumb	1985	GC	1	1	0	4	4	4.00	-	-								1	
N.R.C.Dumelow	DerbCB	1999-2000	GC	2	2	0	56	32	28.00	-	-	90	63	2	2-21	31.50	4.20	-	-	
J-P.Duminy	Dev	2003	GC	1	1	0	25	25	25.00	-	-	18	17	0	-	-	5.66	-	-	
A.A.Duncan	Buck	2005	GC	1								30	42	0	-	-	8.40	-	-	
P.J.Dunkley	Ches	1981	GC	1	1	1	16	16*	-	-	-								-	
M.T.Dunn	Hert	1971-1981	GC	7	7	1	44	13	7.33	-	-	396	255	9	3-27	28.33	3.86	-	-	
	MCS	1973	BH	1	1	0	1	1	1.00	-	-	66	31	0	-	-	2.81	-	2	
	MCW	1976-1977	BH	8	8	2	142	41	23.66	-	-	468	278	3	1-29	92.66	3.56	-	1	
M.S.T.Dunstan	Corn	1970-1986	GC	5	5	0	73	28	14.60	-	-								1	
	MCW	1977-1978	BH	6	6	0	108	33	18.00	-	-								1	
	MCS	1979	BH	1	1	0	6	6	6.00	-	-								-	
C.D.Durant	Cambsh	1997-2001	GC	7	4	2	19	12*	9.50	-	-								5	2
A.W.Durley	Bed	1967-1973	GC	6	6	0	140	75	23.33	-	1								3	
W.J.Durston	SomCB	2000-2002	GC	2	2	0	75	50	37.50	-	1	84	75	2	1-32	37.50	5.35	-	-	
A.J.Dutton	Sta	1988-1996	GC	6	6	0	126	34	21.00	-	-	316	213	2	1-31	106.50	4.04	-	-	
P.N.S.Dutton	Nmb	1987-1994	GC	4	4	1	49	26*	16.33	-	-	36	26	0	-	-	4.33	-	1	

				M	I	NO	Runs	HS	Avg	100	50	Balls	Runs	Wkts	BB	Avg	RpO	4I	Ct	St
S.M.Dutton	Cumb	1987-2001	GC	15	14	4	309	68*	30.90	-	2								21	1
R.J.Dyer	Sta	1990-1992	GC	2	1	0	0	0	0.00	-	-	90	78	0			5.20	-	-	
S.Dyson	Ches	1989	GC	1	1	0	0	0	0.00	-	-	48	52	0			6.50	-	-	
R.E.East	Suf	1993	GC	1	1	0	13	13	13.00	-	-	72	48	0			4.00	-	3	
S.M.Eaton	Ches	2001-2002	GC	3	2	0	28	28	14.00	-	-	162	117	3	2-52	39.00	4.33	-	1	
G.W.Ecclestone	Cambsh	1992-2002	GC	6	6	0	118	92	19.66	-	1	36	20	0			3.33	-	2	
	MC	1997	BH	1	1	0	0	0	0.00	-	-								1	
	EssCB	1999-2001	GC	5	5	0	143	66	28.60	-	1	90	94	0			6.26	-	4	
S.C.Ecclestone	Cambsh	1992	GC	1	1	0	1	1	1.00	-	-	18	22	0			7.33	-	-	
J.L.Ede	DerbCB	2002	GC	1	1	0	10	10	10.00	-	-	30	20	1	1-20	20.00	4.00	-	-	
R.S.Edmonds	LanCB	2000	GC	2	2	1	15	15*	15.00	-	-								1	1
P.W.Edmondson	Oxfsh	1970	GC	1	1	0	0	0	0.00	-	-								-	
G.Edmunds	Shr	1988-1993	GC	5	3	2	27	24*	27.00	-	-	312	209	2	1-41	104.50	4.01	-	-	
B.R.Edrich	Oxfsh	1967-1970	GC	2	2	0	34	30	17.00	-	-								-	
J.W.Edrich	Suf	1983-1990	GC	5	5	0	101	52	20.20	-	1	2	2	0			6.00	-	1	
W.J.Edrich	Norf	1965-1970	GC	4	4	0	48	36	12.00	-	-	70	76	2	2-76	38.00	6.51	-	1	
A.N.Edwards	GloCB	1999-2000	GC	3	3	1	41	38	20.50	-	-	144	77	3	3-38	25.66	3.20	-	2	
	Here	2001	GC	3	3	1	55	34*	27.50	-	-	72	52	2	2-34	26.00	4.33	-	-	
C.J.Edwards	Dev	1985	GC	1	1	0	5	5	5.00	-	-								-	
D.J.Edwards	Sta	2001-2002	GC	2	1	0	5	5	5.00	-	-	120	73	1	1-28	73.00	3.65	-	1	
G.D.Edwards	Corn	2000-2003	GC	7	7	4	134	31*	44.66	-	-								5	2
G.I.Edwards	Berk	1999	GC	1	1	0	5	5	5.00	-	-	36	30	0			5.00	-	-	
J.H.Edwards	Dev	1985-1991	GC	6	6	1	52	22*	10.40	-	-	6	9	0			9.00	-	2	
J.K.S.Edwards	Buck	1972-1979	GC	5	5	1	81	39*	20.25	-	-								1	
	MCS	1973-1974	BH	8	8	0	143	41	17.87	-	-								2	
	MCW	1976	BH	4	4	0	34	12	8.50	-	-								1	
S.J.Edwards	Buck	1987-1992	GC	3	3	2	27	25*	27.00	-	-	216	101	3	2-14	33.66	2.80	-	1	
	MC	1988	BH	1	1	1	2	2*	-	-	-	24	23	0			5.75	-	-	
T.Edwards	Corn	2001	GC	2	2	1	67	53*	67.00	-	1								3	
W.G.Edwards	WalMC	1993-1994	GC	2	2	1	33	28*	33.00	-	-	72	36	1	1-36	36.00	3.00	-	1	
W.J.Edwards	Corn	1975	GC	1	1	0	6	6	6.00	-	-								-	
P.J.Eele	Dev	1969	GC	1	1	0	2	2	2.00	-	-								2	
J.B.Elleray	Cumb	1985-1986	GC	2	1	0	8	8	8.00	-	-	102	63	0			3.70	-	1	
E.T.Elliot-Square	Dor	1999	GC	1	1	1	20	20*	-	-	-	60	61	0			6.10	-	1	
J.A.Elliot-Square	Dor	2001	GC	1	1	0	1	1	1.00	-	-	18	21	0			7.00	-	-	
D.J.Ellis	Dur	1964	GC	2	2	0	3	2	1.50	-	-								-	
M.T.Ellis	Norf	1990-1991	GC	2	2	1	0	0*	0.00	-	-	86	45	2	2-33	22.50	3.13	-	1	
R.G.P.Ellis	Hert	1993	GC	1	1	0	6	6	6.00	-	-								-	
S.W.K.Ellis	Shr	1999	GC	1	1	1	10	10*	-	-	-	48	39	2	2-39	19.50	4.87	-	-	
	WorCB	2001	GC	2	1	0	13	13	13.00	-	-	60	46	1	1-14	46.00	4.60	-	-	
B.C.A.Ellison	Oxfsh	1996	GC	1	1	0	42	42	42.00	-	-	72	53	3	3-53	17.66	4.41	-	-	
C.J.Ellison	Corn	1999	GC	1	1	0	5	5	5.00	-	-	60	64	3	3-64	21.33	6.40	-	1	
D.R.Ellison	EssCB	2001	GC	1	1	0	0	0	0.00	-	-	54	48	1	1-48	48.00	5.33	-	-	
R.Ellwood	Cumb	1989-1995	GC	4	3	2	29	24*	29.00	-	-	186	120	3	2-49	40.00	3.87	-	-	
J.E.Emburey	Berk	2000	GC	2	1	0	2	2	2.00	-	-	116	58	6	4-13	9.66	3.00	1	-	
J.M.Engelke	Hert	2000	GC	1	1	1	0	0*	-	-	-	60	8	3	3-8	2.66	0.80	-	-	

				M	I	NO	Runs	HS	Avg	100	50	Balls	Runs	Wkts	BB	Avg	RpO	4I	Ct	St
R.J.English	Suf	1966	GC	1	1	0	0	0	0.00	-	-	42	59	1	1-59	59.00	8.42	-	1	
R.Entwistle	Cumb	1984	GC	1	1	0	0	0	0.00	-	-								-	
D.E.Essenhigh	Wilt	1965-1969	GC	2	2	0	20	19	10.00	-	-	1	1	0	-	-	6.00	-	-	
R.O.Estwick	Lin	1983	GC	1	1	0	5	5	5.00	-	-	72	76	2	2-76	38.00	6.33	-	1	
S.P.Eva	Corn	1986	GC	1	1	1	0	0*	-	-	-							-	-	
A.W.Evans	WalMC	2003-2005	GC	3	3	0	76	60	25.33	-	1	30	23	1	1-23	23.00	4.60	-	-	
B.G.Evans	Hert	1983-1991	GC	4	4	0	83	46	20.75	-	-								1	
C.Evans	WalMC	1994	GC	1	1	0	12	12	12.00	-	-								-	
D.J.Evans	Hert	1969	GC	2	2	0	10	10	5.00	-	-								-	
G.R.Evans	Dev	1978	GC	1	1	1	2	2*	-	-	-								-	
I.J.Evans	Oxfsh	2001	GC	3	3	0	21	18	7.00	-	-	36	36	1	1-36	36.00	6.00	-	1	
J.B.Evans	Lin	1966-1971	GC	4	3	1	18	13*	9.00	-	-	288	175	2	1-26	87.50	3.64	-	-	
K.P.Evans	Shr	2000-2001	GC	4	3	1	23	9*	11.50	-	-	234	169	6	3-37	28.16	4.33	-	1	
M.R.Evans	Hert	1999-2002	GC	4	4	0	103	37	25.75	-	-	25	24	2	2-9	12.00	5.76	-	2	
P.J.Evans	Oxfsh	2001	GC	1	1	1	1	1*	-	-	-	42	47	1	1-47	47.00	6.71	-	-	
R.A.Evans	Oxfsh	1983-1996	GC	10	5	0	41	24	8.20	-	-	594	394	9	3-46	43.77	3.97	-	4	
	MC	1988-1995	BH	18	12	6	68	28*	11.33	-	-	942	549	4	1-26	137.25	3.49	-	2	
R.J.Evans	Lin	1994-1997	GC	3	3	0	21	15	7.00	-	-								-	
	MC	1995-1996	BH	7	6	0	135	56	22.50	-	1								1	
W.V.Evans	Dur	1964	GC	1	1	0	0	0	0.00	-	-								-	
M.A.Everett	Hert	1999-2002	GC	4	4	0	26	14	6.50	-	-								-	
C.D.Eyden	DerbCB	2001	GC	3	3	0	5	3	1.66	-	-	38	60	1	1-60	60.00	9.47	-	-	
M.J.Eyles	Buck	2001-2003	GC	2	2	0	5	5	2.50	-	-								-	
D.R.Eyre	LanCB	1999-2001	GC	4	3	1	4	2*	2.00	-	-	228	107	3	2-9	35.66	2.81	-	1	
D.H.R.Fairey	Cambsh	1964-1975	GC	6	6	1	72	22	14.40	-	-	168	61	3	2-8	20.33	2.17	-	5	
R.J.Falconer	SurCB	1999	GC	1	1	0	6	6	6.00	-	-								-	
R.E.Falkner	NhCB	1999-2001	GC	4	4	1	122	46	40.66	-	-								1	2
W.Falla	Nmb	1992-2000	GC	5	5	0	184	80	36.80	-	2	3	4	0	-	-	8.00	-	-	
I.J.Fantham	Bed	1998-2000	GC	3	2	0	32	32	16.00	-	-	162	158	0	-	-	5.85	-	-	
H.J.Farnsworth	SurCB	2000	GC	1	1	0	10	10	10.00	-	-								-	
A.Farooque	WarCB	1999	GC	1	1	0	5	5	5.00	-	-	18	17	0	-	-	5.66	-	-	
	Here	2000-2002	GC	6	6	2	47	21*	11.75	-	-	240	170	4	1-16	42.50	4.25	-	4	
J.C.Farrow	Ches	2002-2002	GC	2								90	109	2	2-81	54.50	7.26	-	-	
N.W.Farrow	Buck	1992	GC	1	1	0	1	1	1.00	-	-								-	
R.D.E.Farrow	Norf	1992-1993	GC	2	2	0	21	16	10.50	-	-								-	
R.A.Fay	MidCB	2000	GC	2	2	1	21	16	21.00	-	-	90	63	2	2-31	31.50	4.20	-	-	
C.D.Fearnley	Lin	1971	GC	2	2	1	100	55*	100.00	-	1								1	
M.R.Featherstone	KntCB	1999-2000	GC	6	6	1	205	104*	41.00	1	1								6	
M.A.Fell	MC	1986-1998	BH	10	9	1	125	67	15.62	-	1	78	74	3	2-55	24.66	5.69	-	-	
	Lin	1988-2003	GC	15	15	1	428	77	30.57	-	2	468	356	11	4-20	32.36	4.56	1	10	
G.M.Fellows	Shr	2005	GC	1	1	0	8	8	8.00	-	-	18	16	1	1-16	16.00	5.33	-	1	
J.P.Fellows-Smith	Hert	1966	GC	1	1	0	7	7	7.00	-	-	62	30	2	2-30	15.00	2.90	-	-	
C.G.Feltham	Sta	1996-1997	GC	2	2	1	24	18	24.00	-	-	11	8	0	-	-	4.36	-	-	
S.A.R.Ferguson	Suf	1984	GC	1	1	0	12	12	12.00	-	-								-	
R.S.Ferley	KntCB	2001-2002	GC	2	1	0	6	6	6.00	-	-	82	43	3	2-30	14.33	3.14	-	-	
N.J.Ferraby	LeiCB	2002	GC	2	2	0	1	1	0.50	-	-	42	31	0	-	-	4.42	-	-	

				M	I	NO	Runs	HS	Avg	100	50	Balls	Runs	Wkts	BB	Avg	RpO	4I	Ct	St
L.D.Ferreira	Dor	1998	GC	1	1	0	7	7	7.00	-	-	18	26	0	-	-	8.66	-	-	
Q.Ferreira	SurCB	1999	GC	2	2	0	5	3	2.50	-	-	120	97	1	1-45	97.00	4.85	-	2	
J.M.Fielding	Cumb	1996-2001	GC	11	10	0	67	23	6.70	-	-	524	358	10	3-47	35.80	4.09	-	2	
	MC	1997-1998	BH	6	6	0	43	26	7.16	-	-	234	237	6	2-47	39.50	6.07	-	3	
J.M.Finch	SusCB	2001-2002	GC	3	3	1	60	26	30.00	-	-	60	22	1	1-22	22.00	2.20	-	-	
C.C.Finegan	Ches	1999-2002	GC	5	4	1	15	11	5.00	-	-	294	175	11	3-31	15.90	3.57	-	-	
R.J.Finney	Norf	1990-1994	GC	5	5	0	109	34	21.80	-	-								-	
P.G.B.Fisher	LeiCB	1999-2001	GC	3	3	3	1	1*	-	-	-	174	120	1	1-18	120.00	4.13	-	2	
R.W.Fisher	Ches	2001-2004	GC	3	2	1	23	22	23.00	-	-	180	98	2	1-28	49.00	3.26	-	1	
J.D.Fitton	Cumb	1994	GC	1	1	0	1	1	1.00	-	-								2	
S.D.Fitzgerald	EssCB	1999-2001	GC	4	4	0	40	19	10.00	-	-								2	1
S.M.Fitzgerald	Dor	1990	GC	1	1	1	2	2*	-	-	-								-	2
R.L.Flack	Suf	1966	GC	1	1	0	46	46	46.00	-	-								-	
I.N.Flanagan	EssCB	2001	GC	1	1	0	3	3	3.00	-	-								-	
	Cambsh	2002-2004	GC	2	2	0	83	45	41.50	-	-	48	49	0	-	-	6.12	-	-	
I.Fletcher	Hert	1990-2003	GC	4	4	0	91	60	22.75	-	1	38	46	1	1-20	46.00	7.26	-		
S.D.Fletcher	Lin	1994	GC	1	1	0	12	12	12.00	-	-	54	61	0	-	-	6.77	-	-	
G.W.Flower	Ches	1998	GC	1	1	0	8	8	8.00	-	-	6	0	0	-	-	0.00	-	-	
J.E.Flower	Berk	1965	GC	1	1	0	1	1	1.00	-	-								-	
R.W.Flower	MC	1982	BH	2								84	43	0	-	-	3.07	-	1	
	Sta	1984-1988	GC	4	3	1	20	9*	10.00	-	-	198	143	2	2-34	71.50	4.33	-	-	
G.I.Foley	Ches	2000	GC	1	1	0	38	38	38.00	-	-	42	37	1	1-37	37.00	5.28	-	-	
N.A.Folland	Dev	1984-2001	GC	16	16	0	410	104	25.62	1	2	20	55	1	1-52	55.00	16.50	-	12	
	MC	1989-1992	BH	17	17	3	660	100*	47.14	1	6								10	
N.G.Folland	Dev	1986	GC	1	1	0	30	30	30.00	-	-								-	
	Bed	1991	GC	1	1	0	10	10	10.00	-	-								-	
D.Follett	Sta	2000-2005	GC	7	3	3	12	9*	-	-	-	372	224	16	4-17	14.00	3.61	1	3	
A.J.Foot	Dor	1989	GC	1	1	0	0	0	0.00	-	-								-	
M.H.A.Footitt	NottCB	2001	GC	1								18	18	0	-	-	6.00	-	-	
G.C.Ford	Oxfsh	1984-1991	GC	8	7	0	187	62	26.71	-	2								-	
M.D.Ford	Dor	2004	GC	1	1	0	1	1	1.00	-	-	30	28	0	-	-	5.60	-	-	
D.J.Forder	GloCB	1999-2001	GC	3	3	3	6	3*	-	-	-	156	117	1	1-25	117.00	4.50	-	1	
S.M.Forshaw	Dor	1998-2002	GC	5	4	1	12	7*	4.00	-	-	234	216	7	2-22	30.85	5.53	-	1	
R.C.G.Fortin	Berk	1966	GC	2	2	0	19	18	9.50	-	-								1	
C.H.Forward	HamCB	2002	GC	1	1	0	20	20	20.00	-	-								-	
D.J.Foster	Berk	1995	GC	1	1	0	21	21	21.00	-	-	24	31	0	-	-	7.75	-	-	
J.Foster	Shr	1983-1991	GC	8	8	0	181	63	22.62	-	2								5	
M.J.Foster	WarCB	2000	GC	1	1	0	1	1	1.00	-	-								-	
N.A.Foster	Norf	1995	GC	1	1	0	36	36	36.00	-	-	36	37	0	-	-	6.16	-	-	
S.J.Foster	YorCB	1999-2002	GC	6	6	0	82	44	13.66	-	-	324	160	13	5-26	12.30	2.96	2	4	
	Nmb	2000	GC	3	3	1	51	38*	25.50	-	-	174	96	12	6-52	8.00	3.31	1	1	
A.R.Fothergill	Dur	1983-1991	GC	7	6	2	65	24	16.25	-	-								6	3
	MC	1989-1991	BH	9	8	2	89	45*	14.83	-	-								9	
R.J.Fouhy	Wilt	1999	GC	1	1	1	1	1*	-	-	-	60	34	1	1-34	34.00	3.40	-	-	
B.C.Fourie	NhCB	2001-2002	GC	4	4	1	33	19	11.00	-	-	189	152	2	1-21	76.00	4.82	-	2	
P.A.Fowler	Oxfsh	1981-1987	GC	4	4	0	137	119	34.25	1	-								-	

				M	I	NO	Runs	HS	Avg	100	50	Balls	Runs	Wkts	BB	Avg	RpO	4I	Ct	St
M.G.Fowles	Here	1995-1997	GC	2	2	1	2	2*	2.00	-	-	132	146	3	2-73	48.66	6.63	-	1	
A.Fox	Ches	1987-1989	GC	4	4	1	24	11	8.00	-	-	238	133	8	4-24	16.62	3.35	1	-	
N.Fox	Norf	1993-2000	GC	8	8	0	135	68	16.87	-	1	54	45	1	1-23	45.00	5.00	-	2	
D.T.Foy	LanCB	1999-2000	GC	2	2	0	23	19	11.50	-	-	106	63	1	1-36	63.00	3.56	-	-	
K.N.Foyle	Wilt	1988-1993	GC	3	3	0	22	16	7.33	-	-								2	
B.J.France	Suf	2003	GC	1	1	0	8	8	8.00	-	-								-	
G.D.Franklin	Sta	2002-2003	GC	2	2	0	102	63	51.00	-	1								2	
J.G.Franks	Lin	1983-1988	GC	2	2	0	52	42	26.00	-	-								-	
A.G.J.Fraser	MidCB	1999-2002	GC	5	5	1	155	57*	38.75	-	1	84	79	2	2-36	39.50	5.64	-	-	
T.D.Fray	Berk	1999-2005	GC	6	6	1	128	87*	25.60	-	1								4	
B.J.Frazer	Hert	2001-2003	GC	5	5	0	74	24	14.80	-	-	222	215	7	3-56	30.71	5.81	-	3	
P.J.Free	Norf	2000-2001	GC	4	3	1	18	12*	9.00	-	-								-	
G.D.Freear	Cambsh	2001-2004	GC	4	4	1	36	21	12.00	-	-								-	
A.N.French	WalMC	2001-2002	GC	2	2	0	16	15	8.00	-	-	78	59	3	3-35	19.66	4.53	-	-	
N.French	Lin	1988-1994	GC	3	3	0	26	18	8.66	-	-	210	161	2	1-56	80.50	4.60	-	1	
M.Frost	WalMC	1994	GC	1	1	0	0	0	0.00	-	-	30	28	0	-	-	5.60	-	-	
J.A.W.Fry	SurCB	1999-2002	GC	5	4	0	161	90	40.25	-	2								3	
D.W.Furnival	LeiCB	2001	GC	1	1	0	9	9	9.00	-	-								-	
G.R.Furse	Corn	1986-1996	GC	3	3	0	4	2	1.33	-	-	120	86	1	1-17	86.00	4.29	-	-	
N.A.Fusedale	Berk	1992-2000	GC	4	3	1	33	32*	16.50	-	-	264	198	3	2-19	66.00	4.50	-	3	
C.B.Gadsby	Cambsh	1964-1972	GC	5	4	2	14	8	7.00	-	-	210	96	3	2-34	32.00	2.74	-	2	
N.T.Gadsby	Cambsh	1982-2004	GC	22	21	1	344	63	17.20	-	2	235	228	7	3-44	32.57	5.82	-	5	
N.A.Gage	WalMC	2001-2002	GC	6	4	3	24	12*	24.00	-	-	324	272	5	2-42	54.40	5.03	-	1	
A.W.Gale	YorCB	2001-2002	GC	3	3	0	35	17	11.66	-	-								1	
S.C.Gale	Shr	1976-1985	GC	5	5	0	156	68	31.20	-	1								-	
D.A.Gallop	Oxfsh	1980-1984	GC	3	2	1	19	19*	19.00	-	-	216	207	6	2-39	34.50	5.75	-	-	
D.J.Gandhi	EssCB	2001	GC	2	2	0	28	23	14.00	-	-	84	46	3	3-19	15.33	3.28	-	-	
N.J.C.Gandon	Lin	1990-1991	GC	2	2	0	31	31	15.50	-	-								-	
D.D.Gardner	Wilt	1965-1969	GC	2	2	0	31	20	15.50	-	-								1	
L.R.Gardner	Hert	1964-1966	GC	2	2	0	16	14	8.00	-	-								1	
P.L.Garlick	Dor	1993-1995	GC	2	1	0	0	0	0.00	-	-	71	61	0	-	-	5.15	-	-	
J.P.Garner	Norf	2000-2002	GC	6	5	0	54	27	10.80	-	-								3	
P.J.Garner	Oxfsh	1975-1994	GC	16	15	2	168	53	12.92	-	1	120	130	2	1-37	65.00	6.50	-	4	
	MC	1985	BH	2	2	0	22	17	11.00	-	-								-	
E.S.Garnett	Ches	1996	GC	1	1	1	0	0*	-	-	-	18	25	0	-	-	8.33	-	-	
M.A.Garnham	Cambsh	1986-1988	GC	3	3	0	149	110	49.66	1	-								-	
	MC	1987-1988	BH	7	6	2	86	38*	21.50	-	-								1	3
A.G.Garnsworth	SomCB	2002	GC	1	1	0	1	1	1.00	-	-								2	
A.R.Garofall	Hert	1971-1989	GC	12	12	2	67	26	6.70	-	-	547	325	12	3-28	27.08	3.56	-	6	
	MCS	1972-1974	BH	9	9	0	91	38	10.11	-	-	282	179	6	3-71	29.83	3.80	-	1	
R.A.Gautrey	Cambsh	1964-1967	GC	4	4	0	74	26	18.50	-	-								2	
N.R.Gaywood	Dev	1985-1998	GC	8	8	0	162	69	20.25	-	1	2	5	0	-	-	15.00	-	1	
	MC	1993-1998	BH	4	4	0	66	30	16.50	-	-								2	
C.M.Gazzard	Corn	1999	GC	1	1	0	16	16	16.00	-	-								2	

				M	I	NO	Runs	HS	Avg	100	50	Balls	Runs	Wkts	BB	Avg	RpO	4I	Ct	St
M.E.Gear	Bed	1970-1982	GC	5	5	0	39	19	7.80	-	-								1	
	MCS	1973	BH	3	3	0	50	22	16.66	-	-								-	
	Buck	1984	GC	1	1	0	1	1	1.00	-	-								-	
S.Gear	WarCB	2000	GC	1	1	0	27	27	27.00	-	-								1	
K.L.Geary	LeiCB	2001	GC	2	1	0	0	0	0.00	-	-								1	
I.J.Gemmell	MCN	1979	BH	2	2	0	6	6	3.00	-	-	47	28	0	-	-	3.57	-	-	
	Ches	1981-1983	GC	3	3	1	41	20*	20.50	-	-	162	104	3	2-58	34.66	3.85	-	-	
	MC	1981-1982	BH	5	5	1	12	7	3.00	-	-	246	188	4	1-27	47.00	4.58	-	2	
K.Gentle	Bed	1985	GC	1	1	0	13	13	13.00	-	-								-	
M.T.George	KntCB	2003	GC	1	1	0	7	7	7.00	-	-	54	61	1	1-61	61.00	6.77	-	-	
N.T.P.George	Corn	2001	GC	2	1	0	0	0	0.00	-	-	30	49	1	1-49	49.00	9.80	-	-	
P.S.George	WalMC	1999-2001	GC	8	5	2	53	23*	17.66	-	-	357	267	5	3-51	53.40	4.48	-	4	
W.M.George	Corn	2000	GC	1	1	0	4	4	4.00	-	-								-	
B.D.Gessner	Sta	1978	GC	1	1	1	9	9*	-	-	-	72	51	1	1-51	51.00	4.25	-	-	
C.R.Gibbens	Wilt	2000-2001	GC	4	3	2	4	3*	4.00	-	-	240	107	4	2-27	26.75	2.67	-	-	
P.J.K.Gibbs	Sta	1973	GC	2	2	0	16	13	8.00	-	-								1	
	MCN	1973	BH	4	4	0	93	43	23.25	-	-	30	13	1	1-13	13.00	2.60	-	1	
O.D.Gibson	Sta	2001	GC	3	3	1	143	102*	71.50	1	-	150	97	3	2-49	32.33	3.88	-	-	
A.P.R.Gidman	GloCB	2001	GC	3	3	0	50	23	16.66	-	-	129	106	1	1-43	106.00	4.93	-	1	
W.R.S.Gidman	GloCB	2002	GC	1	1	0	12	12	12.00	-	-								-	
C.R.Gilbert	YorCB	2002	GC	1	1	0	13	13	13.00	-	-	42	33	0	-	-	4.71	-	1	
N.Gilbert	Hert	1984-1999	GC	7	6	1	79	33	15.80	-	-								1	
N.S.Gill	Lin	1996	GC	1	1	0	0	0	0.00	-	-	71	44	4	4-44	11.00	3.71	1	1	
	YorCB	2000-2002	GC	6	5	2	102	37*	34.00	-	-	322	210	11	3-24	19.09	3.91	-	3	
P.N.Gill	Sta	1971-1984	GC	7	7	0	178	52	25.42	-	2								3	
	MCE	1976-1978	BH	12	12	0	146	41	12.16	-	-								4	
I.Gillespie	Shr	2002	GC	1	1	1	26	26*	-	-	-	24	28	0	-	-	7.00	-	-	
S.R.Gillespie	Nmb	1987	GC	1	1	0	3	3	3.00	-	-	72	44	1	1-44	44.00	3.66	-	-	
D.E.Gillett	Lin	1996-2000	GC	2	2	0	17	16	8.50	-	-								2	
M.A.Gilliver	YorCB	1999-2001	GC	4	4	0	98	48	24.50	-	-								1	
M.T.Gitsham	SomCB	2001	GC	2	1	0	15	15	15.00	-	-								-	
C.Gladwin	Suf	1988-1990	GC	2	2	0	19	14	9.50	-	-	78	70	3	3-64	23.33	5.38	-	1	
N.Gladwin	Hert	2001	GC	1	1	0	8	8	8.00	-	-								-	1
M.J.Glasson	Wilt	1999-2004	GC	5	5	0	54	23	10.80	-	-								1	
J.D.Glendenen	Dur	1989-1991	GC	3	3	0	129	109	43.00	1	-								-	
	Cumb	1999-2000	GC	5	4	0	57	43	14.25	-	-	3	4	0	-	-	8.00	-	1	
L.J.Goddard	YorCB	2002	GC	2	2	1	19	19*	19.00	-	-								5	
A.F.Gofton	DerbCB	2000	GC	1	1	0	17	17	17.00	-	-	60	76	2	2-76	38.00	7.60	-	-	
R.P.Gofton	Suf	1995	GC	1	1	0	6	6	6.00	-	-	42	60	0			8.57	-	-	
C.F.E.Goldie	MidCB	2001	GC	1	1	1	1	1*	-	-	-								-	
A.K.Golding	Suf	1990-1996	GC	4	3	0	22	15	7.33	-	-	288	125	5	2-15	25.00	2.60	-	1	
J.M.Golding	KntCB	1999	GC	3	2	0	52	47	26.00	-	-	150	141	0			5.64	-	2	
	Wilt	2005	GC	1	1	0	10	10	10.00	-	-	60	46	2	2-46	23.00	4.60	-	-	
D.J.Goldsmith	Buck	1987-1991	GC	5	5	2	7	4	2.33	-	-								1	
S.C.Goldsmith	Norf	1993-2003	GC	15	15	0	309	47	20.60	-	-	826	597	16	4-64	37.31	4.33	1	7	
	MC	1995-1998	BH	6	5	0	47	17	9.40	-	-	162	152	3	2-22	50.66	5.62	-	2	

				M	I	NO	Runs	HS	Avg	100	50	Balls	Runs	Wkts	BB	Avg	RpO	4I	Ct	St
D.B.Goldstraw	HamCB	2002	GC	1	1	0	0	0	0.00	-	-	60	30	1	1-30	30.00	3.00	-	-	
I.Gompertz	Dev	1999-2000	GC	3	3	0	41	18	13.66	-	-	48	39	1	1-5	39.00	4.87	-	-	
P.A.Gooch	MCW	1978	BH	4	3	1	13	7	6.50	-	-	199	127	2	1-28	63.50	3.82	-	2	
	Buck	1979	GC	1	1	1	2	2*	-	-	-	72	51	3	3-51	17.00	4.25	-	-	
	MCS	1979	BH	4	3	0	9	8	3.00	-	-	156	100	0	-	-	3.84	-	-	
A.J.Good	MCE	1978	BH	1	1	0	0	0	0.00	-	-	66	21	3	3-21	7.00	1.90	-	-	
	MCN	1979	BH	4	3	1	16	8	8.00	-	-	150	56	0	-	-	2.24	-	-	
J.R.Goode	NhCB	1999	GC	1	1	0	1	1	1.00	-	-								-	
	Wilt	2001	GC	1	1	0	29	29	29.00	-	-								-	
P.A.Goodman	Cambsh	1967	GC	1	1	0	9	9	9.00	-	-								-	
A.J.Goodwin	DerbCB	2001	GC	2	2	0	38	38	19.00	-	-								1	
P.S.J.Goodwin	Sta	2004-2005	GC	2	2	0	34	31	17.00	-	-								4	2
R.Goodyer	Oxfsh	1975	GC	1															1	
D.B.Gorman	Berk	1984-1988	GC	4	4	0	44	28	11.00	-	-								-	
D.E.Gorrod	SurCB	2001-2002	GC	4	3	0	66	49	22.00	-	-	162	120	4	3-37	30.00	4.44	-	-	
C.S.Gott	YorCB	1999	GC	1															-	
A.J.Gough	WorCB	2001	GC	1	1	0	14	14	14.00	-	-	54	30	1	1-30	30.00	3.33	-	-	
M.J.Goulding	Dev	1978-1985	GC	7	3	1	0	08	0.00	-	-	403	239	11	5-21	21.72	3.55	1	-	
M.R.Gouldstone	Bed	1991	GC	1	1	0	2	2	2.00	-	-								-	
	Hert	1993	GC	1	1	1	68	68*	-	-	1								1	
	Lin	1996-1997	GC	2	2	0	49	37	24.50	-	-								2	
P.N.Gover	HamCB	2001-2002	GC	3	3	0	44	34	14.66	-	-								2	
J.P.Govett	Berk	1996	GC	1								72	103	3	3-103	34.33	8.58	-	-	
C.C.Graham	Suf	1983-1985	GC	3	1	0	1	1	1.00	-	-	187	126	3	2-36	42.00	4.04	-	1	
D.A.Graham	Here	1997-1999	GC	4	4	0	28	14	7.00	-	-								1	
I.D.Graham	Suf	1990-2001	GC	11	11	0	122	48	11.09	-	-	536	397	18	4-17	22.05	4.44	2	2	
J.A.Graham	Nmb	2001-2005	GC	4	4	0	78	55	19.50	-	1	18	26	0	-	-	8.66	-	3	
J.N.Graham	Nmb	1984	GC	1	1	0	0	0	0.00	-	-	72	30	3	3-30	10.00	2.50	-	-	
P.C.Graham	MC	1985-1994	BH	2								108	62	1	1-35	62.00	3.44	-	-	
	Nmb	1986-1994	GC	5	3	1	4	4*	2.00	-	-	360	205	5	2-28	41.00	3.41	-	2	
	YorCB	1999	GC	1	1	0	4	4	4.00	-	-	24	12	0	-	-	3.00	-	-	
J.M.H.Graham-Brown																				
	Dor	1990-1991	GC	2	2	0	76	58	38.00	-	1	6	3	0	-	-	3.00	-	-	
J.B.Grant	Cambsh	2004	GC	1	1	0	0	0	0.00	-	-	42	48	2	2-48	24.00	6.85	-	-	
M.A.Grant	Suf	1978	GC	1	1	0	15	15	15.00	-	-	72	41	1	1-41	41.00	3.41	-	-	
R.J.Grant	Sta	1989-1990	GC	2	1	1	0	0*	-	-	-	144	109	0	-	-	4.54	-	-	
J.D.Gray	Ches	1993-1995	GC	3	3	1	80	51*	40.00	-	1								3	
	Sta	1999	GC	1	1	0	1	1	1.00	-	-								1	
A.D.Greasley	Ches	1995-1996	GC	2	2	0	2	2	1.00	-	-	114	50	1	1-31	50.00	2.63	-	-	
E.J.Greatrex	Norf	1970	GC	1	1	0	12	12	12.00	-	0								1	
B.C.Green	Dev	1980	GC	2	2	0	113	59	56.50	-	2	96	42	1	1-34	42.00	2.62	-	2	
C.R.F.Green	Cambsh	1989	GC	1								60	35	0	-	-	3.50	-	-	
D.J.Green	Wilt	1964	GC	1	1	0	0	0	0.00	-	-	0	0	0	-	-			-	
J.A.Green	Bed	2002	GC	2								66	47	4	2-18	11.75	4.27	-	2	
J.E.Green	Suf	1966	GC	1	1	1	13	13*	-	-	-								-	
M.R.Green	Sta	1975-1978	GC	4	3	1	49	27*	24.50	-	-								3	

				M	I	NO	Runs	HS	Avg	100	50	Balls	Runs	Wkts	BB	Avg	RpO	4I	Ct	St
P.Green	LanCB	1999-2002	GC	6	6	1	107	63	21.40	-	1	50	47	1	1-32	47.00	5.64	-	3	
R.C.Green	Suf	1983-1990	GC	7	6	2	29	8*	7.25	-	-	426	235	6	3-44	39.16	3.30	-	1	
	MC	1987-1991	BH	11	5	4	36	14	36.00	-	-	600	471	10	3-67	47.10	4.71	-	-	
J.A.Greenhalgh	DerbCB	2001	GC	1	1	0	1	1	1.00	-	-	42	49	1	1-49	49.00	7.00	-	-	
T.F.Greenshield	Dur	1974-1978	GC	4	4	0	42	20	10.50	-	-								-	
S.Greensword	Dur	1972-1990	GC	20	20	2	392	73	21.77	-	2	1152	548	19	4-28	28.84	2.85	1	4	
	MCN	1973	BH	1	1	0	20	20	20.00	-	-	42	27	0			3.85	-	-	
	Nmb	1977-1992	GC	3	2	0	43	26	21.50	-	-	168	49	3	2-22	16.33	1.75	-	2	
	MC	1980-1992	BH	35	30	7	513	46	22.30	-	-	1590	955	28	3-38	34.10	3.60	-	2	
C.H.M.Greetham	Dev	1969-1969	GC	1	1	0	32	32	32.00	-	-								1	
D.J.Greetham	HamCB	2001-2002	GC	3	3	1	8	6*	4.00	-	-	120	104	2	2-52	52.00	5.20	-	3	
M.R.Gribble	Dev	2002	GC	1	1	1	6	6*	-	-	-								1	
A.D.Griffin	Hert	1999-2000	GC	4	4	2	227	121	113.50	1	1								7	3
F.A.Griffith	Cambsh	2000	GC	1	1	0	1	1	1.00	-	-	60	26	0	-	-	2.60	-	-	
A.Griffiths	MC	1981-1985	BH	7	7	2	73	17	14.60	-	-								4	1
	Sta	1984-1988	GC	5	5	0	46	33	9.20	-	-								5	2
A.D.Griffiths	WalMC	1993-1994	GC	2	1	0	6	6	6.00	-	-	102	87	4	3-57	21.75	5.11	-	1	
C.J.Griffiths	LeiCB	1999-2001	GC	3	2	0	38	25	19.00	-	-	168	90	4	2-19	22.50	3.21	-	-	
P.J.Griffiths	WarCB	2002	GC	1	1	0	3	3	3.00	-	-	18	26	0			8.66	-	-	
M.P.Guest	GloCB	2002	GC	1	1	1	29	29*	-	-	-								1	1
R.J.Gulliver	Wilt	1969-1983	GC	4	4	0	34	15	8.50	-	-	196	131	3	1-24	43.66	4.01	-	-	
	MCW	1976	BH	3	3	0	41	21	13.66	-	-	173	109	1	1-43	109.00	3.78	-	-	
	MCS	1979	BH	1	1	0	8	8	8.00	-	-	38	33	0	-	-	5.21	-	-	
N.E.L.Gunter	Berk	2001-2005	GC	2	2	0	6	5	3.00	-	-	66	76	1	1-51	76.00	6.90	-	-	
A.Habib	Berk	1995	GC	1	1	0	3	3	3.00	-	-								-	
P.J.Hacker	Lin	1983-1994	GC	2	2	1	31	26*	31.00	-	-	144	107	4	2-42	26.75	4.45	-	-	
	Ches	1985	GC	1								48	32	0	-	-	4.00	-	-	
N.P.Hackett	Sta	1991-1994	GC	4	3	2	2	2*	2.00	-	-	222	156	4	3-45	39.00	4.21	-	1	
	MC	1992	BH	2	1	1	3	3*	-	-	-	132	95	4	3-55	23.75	4.31	-	3	
A.Hafeez	Shr	2000	GC	1	1	0	4	4	4.00	-	-	36	25	0	-	-	4.16	-	1	
	WorCB	2001-2003	GC	4	4	0	71	28	17.75	-	-	108	120	1	1-63	120.00	6.66	-	3	
S.T.Hahn	Oxfsh	1970-1972	GC	2	2	0	28	25	14.00	-	-								-	
R.J.Hailey	MC	1982	BH	1	1	1	1	1*	-	-	-	66	45	0	-	-	4.09	-	-	
	Hert	1983-1988	GC	6	3	2	10	7*	10.00	-	-	318	212	6	4-32	35.33	4.00	1	2	
D.A.Hale	Oxfsh	1987-1991	GC	4	3	0	41	33	13.66	-	-	192	133	2	2-35	66.50	4.15	-	1	
	MC	1989	BH	2	2	0	17	11	8.50	-	-	74	73	3	2-36	24.33	5.91	-	-	
T.S.Hale	Cambsh	1964-1967	GC	4	4	0	68	51	17.00	-	1								1	
A.J.Halford	Norf	1969-1970	GC	2	2	0	5	5	2.50	-	-	144	107	2	1-34	53.50	4.45	-	2	
D.J.Halfyard	Dur	1972	GC	2	1	0	2	2	2.00	-	-	144	46	5	3-35	9.20	1.91	-	-	
	MCN	1972-1973	BH	2	2	0	23	17	11.50	-	-	108	28	1	1-13	28.00	1.55	-	1	
	Corn	1975-1977	GC	2	2	0	14	14	7.00	-	-	144	67	3	3-30	22.33	2.79	-	1	
A.J.Hall	Ches	1994-2004	GC	6	6	0	116	66	19.33	-	1								3	
A.J.Hall	DurCB	1999	GC	3	3	0	156	78	52.00	-	2	144	105	2	1-19	52.50	4.37	-	1	
	Suf	2002	GC	1	1	0	16	16	16.00	-	-	60	33	4	4-33	8.25	3.30	1	1	
C.J.Hall	Ches	1999-2000	GC	3	3	1	22	98	11.00	-	-	120	97	5	3-38	19.40	4.85	-	2	
D.C.R.Hall	Berk	1976	GC	1	1	0	0	0	0.00	-	-								-	

				M	I	NO	Runs	HS	Avg	100	50	Balls	Runs	Wkts	BB	Avg	RpO	4I	Ct	St
H.M.Hall	Berk	1996-2000	GC	6	6	0	189	108	31.50	1	-	42	53	0	-	-	7.57	-	4	
J.R.Hall	Dor	1989-1991	GC	3	3	0	43	17	14.33	-	-	72	81	1	1-16	81.00	6.75	-	1	
M.J.Hall	DerbCB	2000-2001	GC	2	2	0	15	8	7.50	-	-	90	104	0	-	-	6.93	-	-	
M.P.Hall	SurCB	2001-2002	GC	3	3	1	18	14*	9.00	-	-								3	
R.H.F.Hall	Here	1997-1998	GC	2	2	0	82	53	41.00	-	1								-	
R.J.Hall	Here	2004	GC	1	1	1	54	54*	-	-	1								1	
T.J.Hall	Dor	1973	GC	1	1	0	23	23	23.00	-	-								1	
T.L.Hall	Berk	1996-2002	GC	2	2	0	8	8	4.00	-	-								1	
D.Hallack	DerbCB	2002	GC	1	1	0	9	9	9.00	-	-								-	
G.Hallam	Nmb	1999-2003	GC	6	6	2	68	36	17.00	-	-								1	
G.D.Halliday	Nmb	1984-1986	GC	2	2	0	60	57	30.00	-	1	90	88	2	2-75	44.00	5.86	-	-	
S.J.Halliday	Dor	1983-1987	GC	3	3	0	19	9	6.33	-	-								1	
S.J.Halliday	Suf	1987-1995	GC	5	5	0	18	13	3.60	-	-								1	1
D.Halliwell	Cumb	1984-1989	GC	6	3	1	28	25*	14.00	-	-	387	229	9	4-57	25.44	3.55	1	-	
N.R.Halsall	Ches	1964-1968	GC	4	4	0	27	16	6.75	-	-	90	43	2	2-37	21.50	2.86	-	1	
R.G.Halsall	SusCB	2000-2001	GC	5	3	1	36	17	18.00	-	-	126	103	5	4-34	20.60	4.90	1	-	
G.E.Hames	Buck	1999	GC	1	1	0	16	16	16.00	-	-								-	
N.G.Hames	Buck	1984-1991	GC	7	7	0	44	12	6.28	-	-								1	
S.W.Hampson	Ches	1998	GC	1	1	0	0	0	0.00	-	-	42	32	0	-	-	4.57	-	-	
D.A.Hancock	Sta	1971-1978	GC	6	6	0	129	68	21.50	-	1								1	
	MCN	1972-1975	BH	13	13	0	174	35	13.38	-	-								2	
	MCE	1977-1978	BH	5	5	0	27	11	5.40	-	-								1	
N.D.Hancock	Dev	1999-2005	GC	10	10	3	324	113*	46.28	1	1	531	407	15	3-18	27.13	4.59	-	5	
F.L.Q.Handley	Norf	1970-1990	GC	6	6	0	76	40	12.66	-	-								3	
	MCN	1979	BH	2	2	0	3	2	1.50	-	-								-	
	MC	1985	BH	2	2	0	5	5	2.50	-	-								-	
J.M.Hands	Corn	1996-2003	GC	8	8	0	187	61	23.37	-	1	378	245	10	3-25	24.50	3.88	-	4	
M.D.Hands	Corn	1977	GC	1	1	0	5	5	5.00	-	-								1	
M.Hanna	Wilt	1964-1965	GC	2	2	0	5	4	2.50	-	-								-	
R.J.Harding	Here	1995-1998	GC	3	3	1	29	17	14.50	-	-	156	136	0	-	-	5.23	-	1	
G.C.Hardstaff	Ches	1964-1968	GC	4	4	0	45	45	11.25	-	-	214	122	5	4-31	24.40	3.42	1	2	
	MCN	1972	BH	2	2	0	19	15	9.50	-	-	90	53	4	3-39	13.25	3.53	-	-	
M.Hardwicke	Dor	1968	GC	1	1	0	4	4	4.00	-	-	1	4	0	-	-	24.00	-	-	
D.W.Hardy	Dur	1964-1967	GC	3	2	0	15	15	7.50	-	-	6	6	0	-	-	6.00	-	1	
J.J.E.Hardy	Dor	1992-1998	GC	4	4	1	217	90*	72.33	-	2								-	
J.M.Hargreaves	Suf	1966	GC	1	1	0	2	2	2.00	-	-	66	44	2	2-44	22.00	4.00	-	-	
D.S.Harland	YorCB	2001-2002	GC	4	4	0	38	16	9.50	-	-								2	
T.Harland	Dur	1974-1978	GC	4	4	1	26	16	8.66	-	-								5	
N.W.Harper	Oxfsh	1975-1975	GC	2	2	0	10	6	5.00	-	-								-	
R.F.Harriott	Dev	1978-1980	GC	4	4	1	58	27*	19.33	-	-								-	
A.W.Harris	WalMC	1993-1994	GC	2	2	0	6	5	3.00	-	-								-	
F.W.Harris	Buck	1965-1975	GC	7	5	0	30	13	6.00	-	-	456	214	11	4-21	19.45	2.81	2	-	
G.A.R.Harris	Hert	1990-1993	GC	3	2	0	10	10	5.00	-	-	168	116	2	2-32	58.00	4.14	-	-	
K.R.Harris	Ches	1982	GC	1	1	0	17	17	17.00	-	-								-	
P.R.Harris	Bed	1977	GC	1	1	0	9	9	9.00	-	-								-	

				M	I	NO	Runs	HS	Avg	100	50	Balls	Runs	Wkts	BB	Avg	RpO	4I	Ct	St
J.C.Harrison	Buck	1998-2005	GC	2	2	1	34	34	34.00	-	-	132	124	1	1-80	124.00	5.63	-	1	
	Lin	1999-2002	GC	8	8	0	164	71	20.50	-	1	120	76	1	1-35	76.00	3.80	-	5	
M.T.Harrison	SusCB	2002	GC	1	1	1	7	7*	-	-	-	35	41	1	1-41	41.00	7.02	-	-	
T.W.Harrison	MidCB	1999-2000	GC	2	2	0	13	12	6.50	-	-	24	14	1	1-14	14.00	3.50	-	-	
J.P.Hart	LeiCB	2001	GC	2	2	0	3	3	1.50	-	-	96	90	1	1-68	90.00	5.62	-	-	
	NottCB	2001	GC	2	2	0	10	10	5.00	-	-	96	78	4	3-36	19.50	4.87	-	-	
D.J.B.Hartley	Berk	1988-1997	GC	7	3	0	8	8	2.66	-	-	368	301	4	2-35	75.25	4.90	-	-	
J.S.Hartley	Oxfsh	1989-1993	GC	6	5	0	99	46	19.80	-	-	264	202	6	2-48	33.66	4.59	-	1	
J.D.Harvey	Hert	1993	GC	1	1	0	20	20	20.00	-	-								2	
	LanCB	1999-2001	GC	2	2	0	19	15	9.50	-	-								1	
J.F.Harvey	Cambsh	1975	GC	1	1	0	14	14	14.00	-	-	54	27	1	1-27	27.00	3.00	-	-	
	MCN	1975	BH	1	1	0	56	56	56.00	-	1								1	
	MCE	1976	BH	3	3	1	45	34*	22.50	-	-	6	20	0			20.00	-	-	
	Berk	1979-1986	GC	5	5	0	17	8	3.40	-	-								3	
N.P.Harvey	Berk	2001	GC	1	1	0	7	7	7.00	-	-								2	1
R.P.Harvey	Sta	1998-2005	GC	11	9	1	201	66	25.12	-	1	18	23	0			7.66	-	2	
S.R.Harvey	Norf	1995	GC	1	1	0	39	39	39.00	-	-								-	
A.R.Harwood	Buck	1984-1992	GC	7	7	0	143	57	20.42	-	1								2	
P.J.Harwood	Norf	1998	GC	1	1	0	1	1	1.00	-	-								-	
S.J.Hassan	NottCB	1999	GC	1	1	0	14	14	14.00	-	-								-	
	LeiCB	2001	GC	1	1	1	1	1*	-	-	-								2	
	WorCB	2002	GC	2	1	1	5	5*	-	-	-								-	
S.A.Hatteea	Oxfsh	1972	GC	1	1	1	5	5*	-	-	-	56	32	4	4-32	8.00	3.42	1	-	
C.A.Haupt	Oxfsh	1999-2001	GC	4	4	1	182	126*	60.66	1	-	74	56	1	1-33	56.00	4.54	-	2	
A.C.Hawkins	Sta	1987	GC	1	1	0	7	7	7.00	-	-	66	38	1	1-38	38.00	3.45	-	1	
R.W.Hawkins	Oxfsh	2002	GC	1	1	0	3	3	3.00	-	-								-	
I.A.Hawtin	Oxfsh	1999-2003	GC	6	5	2	46	20*	15.33	-	-								7	
G.W.Hayes	Shr	1974	GC	1	1	0	0	0	0.00	-	-								1	
K.A.Hayes	Cumb	1988-1989	GC	2	2	0	29	29	14.50	-	-								-	
P.J.Hayes	Suf	1981-1989	GC	6	6	2	40	26*	10.00	-	-	300	110	5	2-14	22.00	2.20	-	2	
D.R.Hayward	Dor	1968-1983	GC	3	3	0	11	7	3.66	-	-	216	62	6	3-15	10.33	1.72	-	-	
R.E.Hayward	Buck	1979-1984	GC	2	2	0	41	40	20.50	-	-								1	
	MCS	1979	BH	4	3	0	33	15	11.00	-	-	102	65	2	2-37	32.50	3.82	-	1	
	MC	1984	BH	4	4	1	199	78*	66.33	-	2								1	
M.A.Hazleton	SusCB	2001	GC	1								18	27	0			9.00	-	-	
G.T.Headley	Berk	1990-1994	GC	3	3	0	35	13	11.66	-	-	168	124	1	1-35	124.00	4.42	-	-	
R.D.Healey	Dev	1969	GC	1	1	0	3	3	3.00	-	-	67	14	6	6-14	2.33	1.25	1	-	
T.M.Heap	Sta	1994-1995	GC	2	1	0	7	7	7.00	-	-	108	81	2	2-58	40.50	4.50	-	-	
A.T.Heather	Nmb	1999-2005	GC	5	5	0	138	79	27.60	-	1								1	
A.J.Hedley	DurCB	1999	GC	3	3	0	54	46	18.00	-	-								1	
A.K.Hele	Dev	1998-2001	GC	6	6	3	40	19	13.33	-	-								8	2
T.J.Hemp	WalMC	1999	GC	1	1	0	1	1	1.00	-	-								-	
C.R.Hemsley	Shr	1976	GC	1	1	0	4	4	4.00	-	-	18	13	0			4.33	-	-	
C.W.Henderson	WorCB	2000-2001	GC	3	1	0	32	32	32.00	-	-	180	83	5	2-8	16.60	2.76	-	1	
H.B.Henderson	Nmb	1971	GC	1															1	

				M	I	NO	Runs	HS	Avg	100	50	Balls	Runs	Wkts	BB	Avg	RpO	4I	Ct	St
S.P.Henderson	Hert	1987-1989	GC	3	3	0	43	17	14.33	-	-								1	
	MC	1987-1988	BH	5	5	1	105	51	26.25	-	1								1	
T.Henderson	Berk	2002-2003	GC	2	2	0	15	12	7.50	-	-	84	53	3	3-30	17.66	3.78	-	-	
D.H.Henson	Sta	1971-1973	GC	3	3	1	49	28	24.50	-	-	177	67	4	3-16	16.75	2.27	-	1	
R.Herbert	Suf	1984-1986	GC	3	3	0	26	17	8.66	-	-	156	82	1	1-37	82.00	3.15	-	-	
	MC	1986-1987	BH	8	8	1	106	26*	15.14		-	392	279	6	3-26	46.50	4.27	-	3	
	Hert	1987	GC	1	1	0	37	37	37.00	-	-	66	36	1	1-36	36.00	3.27	-	-	
R.S.Herman	MCS	1979	BH	2	2	0	2	2	1.00	-	-	78	49	1	1-32	49.00	3.76	-	2	
P.W.A.Heseltine	Dur	1991	GC	1	1	1	5	5*	-	-	-	72	37	1	1-37	37.00	3.08	-	-	
P.J.Heseltine	Berk	1989	GC	1	1	0	30	30	30.00	-	-								1	
	Lin	1991	GC	1	1	0	2	2	2.00	-	-								-	
C.J.Hewison	DurCB	1999	GC	2	2	0	19	19	9.50	-	-								1	
	Nmb	2002-2003	GC	2	2	0	70	69	35.00	-	1	12	20	0	-	-	10.00	-	1	
D.J.Heyes	LanCB	1999-2000	GC	3	3	0	41	27	13.66	-	-								1	
J.Hibberd	HamCB	2001	GC	1															-	
	Wilt	2002-2005	GC	3	3	0	27	26	9.00	-	-	150	80	7	4-48	11.42	3.20	1	1	
A.J.E.Hibbert	EssCB	1999-2001	GC	4	4	0	94	59	23.50	-	1								2	
T.L.Hickling	Buck	1970	GC	2	2	0	2	2	1.00	-	-								1	
T.C.Hicks	Dor	2000	GC	1	1	0	0	0	0.00	-	-	60	61	0	-	-	6.10	-	-	
M.A.Higgs	Lin	2003	GC	1	1	0	50	50	50.00	-	1	12	16	0	-	-	8.00	-	3	
R.G.Hignett	Ches	1993-2003	GC	14	14	1	473	84	36.38	-	6	180	170	8	3-21	21.25	5.66	-	2	
	MC	1995-1998	BH	5	4	0	34	23	8.50	-	-	79	88	5	3-25	17.60	6.68	-	2	
J.C.Hildreth	SomCB	2002	GC	1	1	0	4	4	4.00	-	-	36	44	1	1-44	44.00	7.33	-	1	
E.V.Hill	MidCB	2001	GC	1	1	1	3	3*	-	-	-								-	1
G.R.Hill	Dev	1992	GC	1	1	0	14	14	14.00	-	-								-	
	WorCB	2000-2003	GC	5	5	2	153	56*	51.00	-	1								4	
M.R.Hill	Sta	1978	GC	2	2	0	20	14	10.00	-	-								-	
I.J.Hilsum	HamCB	2000	GC	1	1	1	13	13*	-	-	-	24	10	0	-	-	2.50	-	-	
R.J.E.Hindley	HamCB	2001-2002	GC	4	4	2	50	38	25.00	-	-	124	92	3	2-27	30.66	4.45	-	2	
J.E.Hindson	NottCB	2000-2002	GC	4	4	0	56	15	14.00	-	-	84	87	1	1-61	87.00	6.21	-	3	
S.G.Hinks	GloCB	1999	GC	1	1	0	0	0	0.00	-	-	12	10	2	2-10	5.00	5.00	-	1	
L.E.Hitchings	Buck	1965	GC	1	1	0	3	3	3.00	-	-								1	
J.J.Hitchmough	Ches	1985-1992	GC	7	7	0	66	22	9.42	-	-								2	
J.S.Hitchmough	Ches	1982-1989	GC	4	4	0	65	34	16.25	-	-	186	117	4	2-37	29.25	3.77	-	3	
	MC	1985-1986	BH	5	4	0	19	9	4.75	-	-	186	128	3	2-41	42.66	4.12	-	-	
D.J.F.Hoare	Bed	1967-1970	GC	4	3	0	43	34	14.33	-	-								1	
P.D.B.Hoare	Bed	1985-1999	GC	7	5	0	52	17	10.40	-	-	72	64	2	2-64	32.00	5.33	-	5	
G.R.Hobbins	Oxfsh	1975-1986	GC	4	4	1	36	15*	12.00	-	-	216	149	3	2-57	49.66	4.13	-	1	
A.D.Hobbs	Cambsh	1965	GC	1	1	0	4	4	4.00	-	-								-	
R.N.S.Hobbs	MCE	1976	BH	3	3	1	20	20	10.00	-	-	108	107	0	-	-	5.94	-	-	
	Suf	1978	GC	1	1	0	4	4	4.00	-	-	54	18	1	1-18	18.00	2.00	-	-	
A.D.Hobson	Sta	1992	GC	1	1	0	0	0	0.00	-	-								-	
M.R.Hobson	HamCB	2002	GC	2	1	1	6	6*	-	-	-	102	102	5	3-54	20.40	6.00	-	-	
A.J.Hodd	SusCB	2002	GC	1	1	0	1	1	1.00	-	-								1	
R.Hodgkinson	NottCB	2001	GC	1								48	36	2	2-36	18.00	4.50	-	-	
M.Hodgkiss	WorCB	2001	GC	2	1	1	48	48*	-	-	-	81	28	3	3-16	9.33	2.07	-	-	

				M	I	NO	Runs	HS	Avg	100	50	Balls	Runs	Wkts	BB	Avg	RpO	4I	Ct	St
A.S.Hodgson	Dor	1973	GC	1	1	0	2	2	2.00	-	-	72	37	1	1-37	37.00	3.08	-	-	
G.D.Hodgson	Cumb	1986-1987	GC	2	2	0	59	35	29.50	-	-								-	
J.Hodgson	Berk	1997	GC	1	1	1	53	53*	-	-	1								1	
	KntCB	2001-2002	GC	2	2	1	51	29*	51.00	-	-								-	
K.I.Hodgson	Buck	1984-1988	GC	5	5	0	51	24	10.20	-	-	144	110	0	-	-	4.58	-	2	
T.P.Hodgson	SurCB	2000-2001	GC	3	3	0	76	33	25.33	-	-								-	
E.R.Hodson	Norf	1984	GC	1	1	0	12	12	12.00	-	-								-	
M.D.Hodson	Lin	1976	GC	1	1	1	16	16*	-	-	-								-	
	MCN	1979	BH	2	2	0	4	4	2.00	-	-								-	
D.S.Hoffman	Cambsh	1989	GC	1	1	1	17	17*	-	-	-	66	61	0	-	-	5.54	-	-	
C.A.Holcomb	Dor	1999	GC	1	1	0	1	1	1.00	-	-								-	
V.A.Holder	MC	1981	BH	2	2	1	28	22*	28.00	-	-	72	78	2	1-32	39.00	6.50	-	1	
K.F.Holding	Ches	1964-1968	GC	4	4	3	12	5*	12.00	-	-								2	
M.Holland	Wilt	1989-1990	GC	2	2	1	0	0*	0.00	-	-	102	53	0	-	-	3.11	-	-	
D.C.Holliday	Cambsh	1983	GC	1	1	0	27	27	27.00	-	-								-	
A.P.Hollingsworth	SurCB	2001-2002	GC	2	2	0	56	29	28.00	-	-	120	83	3	3-36	27.66	4.15	-	2	
H.B.Hollington	Hert	1971-1974	GC	2	2	0	50	50	25.00	-	1								-	
	MCS	1972-1974	BH	5	5	0	143	78	28.60	-	1	1	4	0	-	-	24.00	-	2	
K.J.Hollis	DerbCB	2000-2001	GC	4	3	1	18	7*	9.00	-	-								1	2
P.W.Holman	Cambsh	1975	GC	1	1	0	4	4	4.00	-	-								-	
G.L.Home	Shr	2001-2005	GC	6	5	0	39	16	7.80	-	-								-	
R.W.Hooker	Buck	1970-1975	GC	6	6	2	152	65	38.00	-	1	271	185	4	2-30	46.25	4.09	-	2	
O.C.Hopkins	WalMC	2001-2002	GC	2	2	0	10	9	5.00	-	-	30	29	2	2-29	14.50	5.80	-	1	
C.D.Hopkinson	SusCB	2001	GC	2	2	0	58	43	29.00	-	-	90	88	0	-	-	5.86	-	1	
S.W.Horne	Cumb	2001	GC	1	1	1	2	2*	-	-	-								-	
R.W.Horner	Berk	1995	GC	1	1	0	32	32	32.00	-	-								-	
R.Horrell	Dev	1996-2000	GC	3	2	1	25	25*	25.00	-	-	96	70	2	1-33	35.00	4.37	-	-	
R.E.W.G.Horridge	LanCB	1999-2001	GC	5	5	2	69	27*	23.00	-	-								1	
M.Horrocks	Here	2003-2004	GC	2	1	1	3	3*	-	-	-	66	78	1	1-46	78.00	7.09	-	-	
S.D.Horsfall	Sta	1997-1998	GC	2	2	0	2	2	1.00	-	-	72	43	1	1-28	43.00	3.58	-	-	
P.J.Horton	LanCB	2002	GC	2	2	0	49	26	24.50	-	-								-	
P.Hough	Wilt	1965	GC	1	1	0	25	25	25.00	-	-								-	
K.H.House	Dor	1973	GC	1	1	0	15	15	15.00	-	-								2	
J.S.Howarth	MCE	1977	BH	2	2	1	4	4*	4.00	-	-	126	39	2	1-19	19.50	1.85	-	-	
C.R.Howell	WarCB	1999-2002	GC	5	5	0	33	16	6.60	-	-	12	17	0	-	-	8.50	-	1	
	Sta	2005	GC	1	1	0	16	16	16.00	-	-								-	
R.T.J.Howell	GloCB	2000-2001	GC	3	2	1	35	20*	35.00	-	-	42	35	1	1-35	35.00	5.00	-	-	
R.W.J.Howitt	Lin	1999-2002	GC	7	7	0	146	52	20.85	-	1	72	83	1	1-33	83.00	6.91	-	2	
	Berk	2003-2004	GC	2	2	0	9	7	4.50	-	-								-	
R.F.Howlett	Suf	1978-1984	GC	5	5	1	71	35*	17.75	-	-	18	7	0	-	-	2.33	-	1	
	MCE	1978	BH	1	1	1	31	31*	-	-	-								-	
T.Howorth	Cambsh	1975	GC	1	1	0	19	19	19.00	-	-	24	20	0	-	-	5.00	-	-	
B.J.Hoyle	SomCB	2001	GC	1	1	0	11	11	11.00	-	-								1	
R.D.Hudson	Hunt	1999	GC	1	1	0	12	12	12.00	-	-								1	
R.D.P.Huggins	Norf	1982-1985	GC	4	4	0	91	29	22.75	-	-								1	
T.B.Huggins	Cambsh	2001	GC	1	1	0	2	2	2.00	-	-								-	

				M	I	NO	Runs	HS	Avg	100	50	Balls	Runs	Wkts	BB	Avg	RpO	4I	Ct	St
J.G.Hughes	Bed	1998-2001	GC	10	6	0	77	30	12.83	-	-	426	315	8	3-17	39.37	4.43	-	1	
K.J.Hughes	Oxfsh	1991-1992	GC	3	1	0	4	4	4.00	-	-								4	
N.D.Hughes	Hert	1999-2000	GC	2	2	0	25	25	12.50	-	-	96	107	1	1-73	107.00	6.68	-	1	
Q.J.Hughes	DurCB	2000-2002	GC	4	4	0	135	51	33.75	-	1	24	22	0	-	-	5.50	-	2	
	Cumb	2003	GC	1	1	0	0	0	0.00	-	-	60	53	1	1-53	53.00	5.30	-	-	
R.D.Hughes	Here	1999-2004	GC	7	6	0	78	39	13.00	-	-								1	
T.J.Hughes	Dur	1974	GC	2	2	0	63	35	31.50	-	-	3	0	1	1-0	0.00	0.00	-	-	
J.A.Hulme	Shr	1983	GC	1	1	0	10	10	10.00	-	-								-	
S.Humble	DurCB	2001-2002	GC	2	2	0	5	5	2.50	-	-	84	62	5	3-33	12.40	4.42	-	1	
	Nmb	2005	GC	1	1	1	88	88*	-	-	1	42	40	0	-	-	5.71	-	-	
N.V.Humphrey	WarCB	2001-2002	GC	5	5	0	128	58	25.60	-	1								-	
R.G.Humphrey	Buck	1984-1985	GC	2	2	1	42	39*	42.00	-	-								3	
E.Humphreys	Hunt	2000	GC	1	1	0	0	0	0.00	-	-								-	
M.I.Humphries	Sta	1990-2003	GC	18	15	5	183	41*	18.30	-	-								18	1
	MC	1992-1995	BH	8	7	1	124	27	20.66	-	-								6	1
P.J.Humphries	Here	1998-2001	GC	5	2	2	6	5*	-	-	-	270	185	6	2-25	30.83	4.11	-	-	
C.A.Hunkin	SomCB	2000-2001	GC	2	2	1	10	10*	10.00	-	-	96	69	1	1-25	69.00	4.31	-	-	
M.P.Hunt	Dev	2002-2004	GC	5	5	0	206	74	41.20	-	2								-	
S.A.Hunt	Corn	1986	GC	1	1	0	2	2	2.00	-	-	72	87	0	-	-	7.25	-	-	
T.A.Hunte	Cumb	1992-2001	GC	4	4	1	97	82	32.33	-	1	1	6	0	-	-	36.00	-	-	
C.M.G.Hunter	Dor	1968-1973	GC	2	2	0	26	18	13.00	-	-	60	26	0	-	-	2.60	-	1	
	MCS	1972	BH	3	3	0	12	6	4.00	-	-	144	123	3	1-21	41.00	5.12	-	-	
I.D.Hunter	DurCB	2001-2003	GC	2	2	0	15	13	7.50	-	-	114	74	3	2-45	24.66	3.89	-	1	
R.L.A.Hunter	HamCB	2000	GC	1	1	0	33	33	33.00	-	-								-	1
R.B.Hurd	Buck	1997-1998	GC	2	2	0	33	18	16.50	-	-								1	
J.Hurn	Wilt	1964	GC	1	1	0	8	8	8.00	-	-								-	
J.Hurrell	Corn	1970	GC	1	1	0	10	10	10.00	-	-	72	30	1	1-30	30.00	2.50	-	-	
G.Hurst	Dur	1982-1986	GC	4	3	0	14	7	4.66	-	-								1	
M.Hussain	EssCB	2001	GC	1	1	0	12	12	12.00	-	-	18	22	0	-	-	7.33	-	-	
D.J.Hussey	SusCB	2001	GC	3	3	1	164	118*	82.00	1	-	161	161	6	3-48	26.83	6.00	-	4	
R.M.Hutchings	LeiCB	1999-2001	GC	4	4	0	28	15	7.00	-	-								2	
I.J.F.Hutchinson	Shr	1985	GC	1	1	0	8	8	8.00	-	-								-	
R.W.Hutchison	Buck	1974-1975	GC	2	2	1	33	26*	33.00	-	-	36	46	1	1-46	46.00	7.66	-	-	
	MCS	1974-1975	BH	8	8	0	73	27	9.12	-	-	246	169	6	4-68	28.16	4.12	1	3	
J.Iberson	Hert	1964-1966	GC	2	2	1	0	0*	0.00	-	-	93	57	4	3-37	14.25	3.67	-	-	
Ijaz Ahmed	Dur	1991	GC	1	1	0	10	10	10.00	-	-	66	79	0	-	-	7.18	-	-	
M.J.Ikin	Sta	1971-1978	GC	7	7	0	89	47	12.71	-	-	288	177	6	3-13	29.50	3.68	-	2	
	MCE	1977	BH	2	2	0	60	59	30.00	-	1	132	91	1	1-38	91.00	4.13	-	1	
A.Ikram	WalMC	1993	GC	1								36	33	0	-	-	5.50	-	-	
R.K.Illingworth	WorCB	2002	GC	2	2	2	65	53*	-	-	1	120	64	2	1-26	32.00	3.20	-	-	
N.J.Ilott	Hert	1993	GC	1	1	0	14	14	14.00	-	-								-	
Imran Tahir	Sta	2004-2005	GC	2	2	1	42	41*	42.00	-	-	114	54	4	3-31	13.50	2.84	-	-	
J.D.Inchmore	Wilt	1987	GC	1	1	0	3	3	3.00	-	-	72	62	2	2-62	31.00	5.16	-	-	
M.J.Ingham	Cumb	1996	GC	1	1	0	13	13	13.00	-	-								1	
P.G.Ingham	Nmb	1984	GC	1	1	0	9	9	9.00	-	-								-	
R.Inglis	Dur	1964-1973	GC	8	8	0	152	47	19.00	-	-	192	83	2	1-23	41.50	2.59	-	3	

				M	I	NO	Runs	HS	Avg	100	50	Balls	Runs	Wkts	BB	Avg	RpO	4I	Ct	St
L.R.Ingram	Hunt	1999-2000	GC	3	3	1	18	13	9.00	-	-	156	99	3	1-26	33.00	3.80	-	1	
D.L.Iniff	NhCB	1999	GC	1								48	37	1	1-37	37.00	4.62	-	1	
K.J.Innes	Bed	2005	GC	1	1	0	6	6	6.00	-	-	24	39	0	-	-	9.75	-	-	
R.F.Innes	Norf	1983	GC	1	1	1	0	0*	-	-	-	66	34	0	-	-	3.09	-	1	
H.Iqbal	KntCB	1999-2003	GC	8	6	1	105	33	21.00	-	-								2	
Z.Iqbal	NottCB	1999-2002	GC	2	2	1	57	56*	57.00	-	1	84	80	1	1-29	80.00	5.71	-	-	
Irfan Rana	LanCB	2001	GC	1	1	0	18	18	18.00	-	-	12	29	0	-	-	14.50	-	-	
J.Jacklin	Cambsh	1975	GC	1	1	1	0	0*	-	-	-	72	40	3	3-40	13.33	3.33	-	-	
A.F.D.Jackman	NottCB	1999-2002	GC	4	4	0	148	73	37.00	-	2								-	
B.S.Jackson	Berk	1986-1994	GC	4	4	1	29	14	9.66	-	-	276	172	5	3-38	34.40	3.73	-	2	
D.C.Jackson	Dur	1983-1985	GC	4	4	0	64	40	16.00	-	-								4	
R.N.Jackson	SusCB	2001	GC	4	4	0	56	22	14.00	-	-								-	
C.M.Jaggard	Buck	1997	GC	1	1	0	28	28	28.00	-	-								-	
K.Jahangir	Hert	1993-2000	GC	5	5	0	168	92	33.60	-	1	186	202	5	4-57	40.40	6.51	1	2	
	MC	1995	BH	1	1	0	0	0	0.00	-	-								1	
B.G.James	Sta	1973	GC	2	2	0	19	19	9.50	-	-	110	50	3	3-35	16.66	2.72	-	-	
G.D.James	EssCB	2002-2003	GC	2	2	1	52	51*	52.00	-	1								-	
M.H.James	Hert	1993-2002	GC	9	9	0	89	26	9.88	-	-								1	
P.M.James	SurCB	1999-2000	GC	3	2	1	32	23*	32.00	-	-								2	
I.Jamshed	WorCB	2002-2003	GC	3	1	0	4	4	4.00	-	-	166	124	10	5-36	12.40	4.48	1	-	
D.A.Janes	Buck	1965-1972	GC	4	4	0	135	95	33.75	-	1								3	
G.M.Jarrett	Bed	1967-1977	GC	7	5	2	26	14*	8.66	-	-	486	298	6	3-21	49.66	3.67	-	2	
K.B.S.Jarvis	Here	1995	GC	1	1	0	4	4	4.00	-	-	66	45	2	2-45	22.50	4.09	-	2	
P.A.Jeacock	Oxfsh	1999-2001	GC	4	2	2	13	9*	-	-	-	216	123	3	2-23	41.00	3.41	-	1	
M.Jean-Jacques	Buck	1984-1985	GC	2	2	2	1	1*	-	-	-	102	58	1	1-47	58.00	3.41	-	-	
R.I.Jefferson	Norf	1968-1970	GC	3	3	0	70	55	23.33	-	1	198	98	4	2-15	24.50	2.96	-	3	
	MCN	1972	BH	3	3	0	0	0	0.00	-	-	186	110	1	1-33	110.00	3.54	-	-	
B.R.Jeffries	Oxfsh	1972-1975	GC	3	3	1	46	46	23.00	-	-	128	80	3	3-31	26.66	3.75	-	1	
	MCS	1974-1975	BH	6	6	0	46	17	7.66	-	-	264	199	4	2-29	49.75	4.52	-	1	
	MCW	1978	BH	2	1	0	15	15	15.00	-	-	132	69	3	2-36	23.00	3.13	-	-	
A.C.Jelfs	Lin	1991	GC	1	1	0	25	25	25.00	-	-	54	51	0	-	-	5.66	-	-	
M.P.Jenkin	Corn	2002	GC	1	1	0	6	6	6.00	-	-	42	44	2	2-44	22.00	6.28	-	1	
L.J.P.Jenkins	KntCB	2001	GC	4	2	1	91	50*	91.00	-	1								-	
P.E.Jenkins	WalMC	1999	GC	1	1	1	1	1*	-	-	-	60	32	2	2-32	16.00	3.20	-	-	
S.H.G.Jenkins	WalMC	1998-1999	GC	3	3	0	73	44	24.33	-	-								3	
S.P.Jenkins	SomCB	1999-2000	GC	2	2	0	58	42	29.00	-	-								-	
T.J.Jenner	Cambsh	1972	GC	1	1	0	5	5	5.00	-	-	66	32	0	-	-	2.90	-	-	
C.J.R.Jennings	NhCB	2001	GC	1	1	1	2	2*	-	-	-	30	29	1	1-29	29.00	5.80	-	-	
R.A.Jennings	GloCB	2001	GC	1	1	1	12	12*	-	-	-								1	
R.S.Jerome	Hert	2000	GC	1	1	0	1	1	1.00	-	-	60	12	1	1-12	12.00	1.20	-	-	
J.F.Jervis	Sta	2001	GC	1	1	0	19	19	19.00	-	-								-	
R.M.Jervis	Sta	1999	GC	1								36	36	2	2-36	18.00	6.00	-	1	
P.M.Jobson	Oxfsh	1989-1994	GC	6	5	0	50	30	10.00	-	-								2	
D.F.V.Johns	Buck	1965	GC	1	1	0	19	19	19.00	-	-								-	
P.I.Johns	Corn	1977-1980	GC	2	2	0	2	2	1.00	-	-	144	67	3	2-26	22.33	2.79	-	-	

				M	I	NO	Runs	HS	Avg	100	50	Balls	Runs	Wkts	BB	Avg	RpO	4I	Ct	St
R.L.Johns	Hert	1976-1983	GC	5	4	1	18	18*	6.00	-	-	288	200	8	4-31	25.00	4.16	1	1	
	MCW	1977	BH	1	1	1	1	1*	-	-	-	54	45	0	-	-	5.00	-	-	
	MCS	1979	BH	3	2	0	2	2	1.00	-	-	116	84	4	2-33	21.00	4.34	-	-	
	MC	1980	BH	1	1	0	2	2	2.00	-	-	12	26	0	-	-	13.00	-	-	
A.A.Johnson	Nmb	1971-1977	GC	3	2	0	8	8	4.00	-	-	190	81	4	2-35	20.25	2.55	-	-	
	Dur	1973	GC	1	1	0	1	1	1.00	-	-	54	21	0	-	-	2.33	-	-	
A.N.Johnson	Shr	1989-2001	GC	8	8	1	121	62	17.28	-	1	36	36	0	-	-	6.00	-	3	
D.Johnson	Lin	1966-1967	GC	2	2	0	42	35	21.00	-	-								2	
G.Johnson	Dur	1984-1987	GC	5	4	2	34	20*	17.00	-	-	312	186	4	2-35	46.50	3.57	-	2	
J.S.Johnson	Shr	1974-1989	GC	7	7	0	55	27	7.85	-	-								3	
	MCE	1978	BH	3	3	0	30	25	10.00	-	-								4	
	MCN	1979	BH	4	4	0	132	51	33.00	-	1								1	
	MC	1980	BH	2	2	0	22	22	11.00	-	-								-	
P.D.Johnson	MCE	1978	BH	1	1	0	21	21	21.00	-	-								1	
	MC	1980-1982	BH	8	8	0	69	28	8.62	-	-								6	
R.K.Johnson	SurCB	2001-2002	GC	3	3	1	24	12*	12.00	-	-	60	63	0	-	-	6.30	-	1	
T.Johnson	Lin	1971-1976	GC	5	5	0	33	14	6.60	-	-								1	
W.Johnson	Dur	1988	GC	1	1	0	16	16	16.00	-	-								-	
W.R.Johnson	Wilt	1989	GC	1	1	1	14	14*	-	-	-								-	
D.Johnston	MCS	1975	BH	1	1	0	8	8	8.00	-	-								-	
	Berk	1976-1979	GC	2	2	0	105	68	52.50	-	1								-	
	MCW	1976	BH	3	3	0	26	18	8.66	-	-								-	
J.Johnston	Dur	1977-1989	GC	8	5	4	8	8*	8.00	-	-	559	277	7	2-31	39.57	2.97	-	-	
A.Jones	Oxfsh	1996	GC	1	1	1	5	5*	-	-	-	24	34	0	-	-	8.50	-	-	
A.J.Jones	WalMC	1993-2005	GC	13	13	1	306	93	25.50	-	2								6	
	MC	1998	BH	3	3	0	31	30	10.33	-	-								-	
	Sta	2000	GC	1	1	1	0	0*	-	-	-	60	52	2	2-52	26.00	5.20	-	-	
C.Jones	Cambsh	2001-2004	GC	3	3	0	49	26	16.33	-	-								-	
C.I.M.Jones	Hert	1969	GC	2	2	0	19	19	9.50	-	-								-	
C.M.P.Jones	MidCB	2002	GC	2	2	1	0	0*	0.00	-	-	78	65	1	1-47	65.00	5.00	-	3	
G.A.Jones	Buck	1972-1979	GC	4	4	0	59	47	14.75	-	-	138	87	3	1-3	29.00	3.78	-	1	
	MCS	1975	BH	1	1	0	17	17	17.00	-	-	66	30	2	2-30	15.00	2.72	-	-	
	MCW	1976	BH	2	2	0	20	10	10.00	-	-	30	27	0	-	-	5.40	-	-	
H.R.Jones	WarCB	2001-2002	GC	2	2	0	82	72	41.00	-	1								-	
I.Jones	SomCB	2001	GC	1	1	0	6	6	6.00	-	-	60	33	2	2-33	16.50	3.30	-	1	
J.B.R.Jones	Shr	1983-2002	GC	20	20	0	502	83	25.10	-	3	52	51	3	3-20	17.00	5.88	-	5	
J.H.Jones	Berk	1976-1992	GC	11	6	3	20	12*	6.66	-	-	678	534	15	4-35	35.60	4.72	2	1	
K.V.Jones	MCS	1975	BH	4	4	0	33	14	8.25	-	-	240	122	2	1-15	61.00	3.05	-	1	
	MCW	1976-1977	BH	7	6	0	29	17	4.83	-	-	414	121	7	2-17	17.28	1.75	-	2	
	Bed	1977-1982	GC	2	2	0	5	3	2.50	-	-	140	32	2	2-22	16.00	1.37	-	-	
L.O.Jones	WalMC	2000-2002	GC	5	4	0	51	38	12.75	-	-	210	165	7	2-11	23.57	4.71	-	3	
P.H.Jones	Suf	1978-1981	GC	4	4	0	39	16	9.75	-	-	192	91	1	1-22	91.00	2.84	-	2	
P.S.Jones	WalMC	1994	GC	1	1	1	26	26*	-	-	-	18	30	0	-	-	10.00	-	-	
R.Jones	Dev	2001	GC	1								60	38	2	2-38	19.00	3.80	-	-	
R.A.Jones	Buck	2002	GC	1	1	0	11	11	11.00	-	-								-	
R.O.Jones	MidCB	1999-2002	GC	3	3	0	10	5	3.33	-	-	36	38	4	3-24	9.50	6.33	-	-	

				M	I	NO	Runs	HS	Avg	100	50	Balls	Runs	Wkts	BB	Avg	RpO	4I	Ct	St
T.D.Jones	EssCB	1999-2000	GC	3	3	1	46	29*	23.00	-	-	144	107	4	2-36	26.75	4.45	-	-	
A.M.Jorden	Bed	1977	GC	1	1	0	1	1	1.00	-	-	30	9	0	-	-	1.80	-	-	
J.R.Jordison	DerbCB	2001	GC	2	1	0	0	0	0.00	-	-	94	63	2	2-27	31.50	4.02	-	-	
B.Joshi	WarCB	2001	GC	2	2	1	12	9*	12.00	-	-	54	41	4	3-9	10.25	4.55	-	-	
P.Joubert	Suf	2003	GC	1	1	0	46	46	46.00	-	-	60	82	4	4-82	20.50	8.20	1	-	
G.S.Joyce	KntCB	1999	GC	3	2	0	10	6	5.00	-	-								4	
S.G.Joyner	Oxfsh	1992-1996	GC	4	3	0	11	11	3.66	-	-	228	221	1	1-48	221.00	5.81	-	1	
S.J.Jurgensen	SusCB	1999	GC	1	1	0	4	4	4.00	-	-	60	48	0	-	-	4.80	-	-	
G.S.Kandola	WorCB	2001-2003	GC	5	4	0	122	53	30.50	-	1								-	
R.Karim	NottCB	2000	GC	1	1	0	0	0	0.00	-	-	35	22	1	1-22	22.00	3.77	-	-	
Kashif Ibrahim	SusCB	2000	GC	2	2	0	120	63	60.00	-	2	56	43	2	2-35	21.50	4.60	-	-	
R.I.Kaufman	NhCB	2000-2001	GC	2	2	1	9	7	9.00	-	-	60	49	1	1-49	49.00	4.90	-	-	
	Oxfsh	2003	GC	1	1	0	0	0	0.00	-	-	60	48	2	2-48	24.00	4.80	-	1	
M.J.Kay	Hunt	2001-2002	GC	3	2	1	38	28*	38.00	-	-	96	56	0	-	-	3.50	-	1	
R.L.Keates	Dor	2002-2004	GC	3	2	0	3	2	1.50	-	-	120	82	3	2-48	27.33	4.10	-	-	
M.Keech	Dor	2001	GC	1	1	0	73	73	73.00	-	1								1	
S.D.Kelk	Lin	1988	GC	1	1	1	2	2*	-	-	-	54	54	1	1-54	54.00	6.00	-	1	
M.J.Kellaway	YorCB	2001-2002	GC	2	2	2	50	26*	-	-	-								1	
S.A.Kellett	Cambsh	1996-2003	GC	11	11	0	287	79	26.09	-	2	54	78	0	-	-	8.66	-	2	
P.A.C.Kelly	Ches	1964-1968	GC	4	4	0	35	16	8.75	-	-								1	
J.M.Kemp	WorCB	2003	GC	1	1	0	13	13	13.00	-	-	60	54	0	-	-	5.40	-	-	
C.P.C.Kendall	Corn	1970-1975	GC	2	2	0	10	10	5.00	-	-	126	83	1	1-42	83.00	3.95	-	-	
N.M.Kendrick	Berk	1997	GC	1								72	46	1	1-46	46.00	3.83	-	-	
	SurCB	1999	GC	1	1	0	13	13	13.00	-	-	42	36	0	-	-	5.14	-	-	
S.G.Kenlock	SurCB	1999-2000	GC	3	2	1	5	3	5.00	-	-	180	104	3	2-21	34.66	3.46	-	-	
A.Kennedy	Dor	1983-1987	GC	3	3	0	55	39	18.33	-	-	108	70	1	1-6	70.00	3.88	-	1	
	MC	1983	BH	3	3	0	52	43	17.33	-	-	61	39	0	-	-	3.83	-	-	
A.Kennedy	EssCB	2001-2003	GC	3	3	0	72	27	24.00	-	-	36	37	1	1-37	37.00	6.16	-	2	
J.Kennedy	Dur	1967-1968	GC	2	2	0	28	23	14.00	-	-								-	
J.P.Kent	Corn	1995-2003	GC	11	11	1	201	80	20.10	-	1	256	157	6	3-21	26.16	3.67	-	1	
R.K.Kenway	HamCB	2001	GC	2	1	0	47	47	47.00	-	-								-	
D.H.Kerry	Dor	2002	GC	1	1	0	2	2	2.00	-	-	24	20	0	-	-	5.00	-	1	
R.A.Kettleborough	YorCB	2000	GC	2	2	0	56	31	28.00	-	-	120	78	2	1-37	39.00	3.90	-	-	
A.A.Khan	Cambsh	2001	GC	2	1	0	3	3	3.00	-	-	120	101	1	1-33	101.00	5.05	-	-	
R.M.Khan	DerbCB	2000	GC	1	1	0	29	29	29.00	-	-								-	
W.G.Khan	WarCB	2002	GC	1	1	0	27	27	27.00	-	-	60	47	1	1-47	47.00	4.70	-	1	
D.A.Kidner	Dor	2000-2004	GC	3	3	2	28	23*	28.00	-	-	78	65	1	1-21	65.00	5.00	-	-	
P.D.King	Suf	2000-2005	GC	4	4	2	31	15*	15.50	-	-	120	136	2	1-40	68.00	6.80	-	2	
R.D.King	Sta	2004	GC	1	1	0	6	6	6.00	-	-								-	
R.E.King	NhCB	2001-2002	GC	2	2	0	2	2	1.00	-	-	90	66	2	2-39	33.00	4.40	-	1	
R.Kingshott	Norf	1990-1992	GC	3	3	2	18	9	18.00	-	-	180	99	1	1-29	99.00	3.30	-	2	
J.H.Kingstone	Berk	2004	GC	1	1	1	17	17*	-	-	-								-	
C.R.G.Kippax	Cumb	2002	GC	1	1	0	5	5	5.00	-	-	30	41	0	-	-	8.20	-	-	

				M	I	NO	Runs	HS	Avg	100	50	Balls	Runs	Wkts	BB	Avg	RpO	4I	Ct	St
P.J.Kippax	Nmb	1977	GC	2	1	0	5	5	5.00	-	-	18	7	0	-	-	2.33	-	-	
	MCE	1977	BH	2	2	0	54	42	27.00	-	-	66	20	0	-	-	1.81	-	-	
	Dur	1978-1987	GC	9	9	1	128	39	16.00	-	-	642	360	20	3-24	18.00	3.36	-	1	
S.A.J.Kippax	Cumb	1995-2000	GC	5	4	1	32	14*	10.66	-	-	234	165	5	2-31	33.00	4.23	-	3	
W.A.Kirby	NottCB	2000	GC	1	1	0	3	3	3.00	-	-								-	
G.M.Kirk	Suf	1999-2002	GC	9	4	3	4	3*	4.00	-	-	528	300	14	3-16	21.42	3.40	-	-	
C.G.Knight	HamCB	2001	GC	2	1	1	11	11*	-	-	-	48	57	0	-	-	7.12	-	-	
C.R.Knight	Cumb	1992	GC	1	1	0	21	21	21.00	-	-								-	
M.J.Knight	Ches	2002	GC	1															1	
R.D.V.Knight	MC	1988	BH	2	2	0	56	38	28.00	-	-	102	74	2	1-36	37.00	4.35	-	-	
C.S.Knightley	Oxfsh	1996-2003	GC	5	5	1	109	61*	27.25	-	1								4	
J.A.Knott	Bed	2001-2005	GC	9	7	1	193	66*	32.16	-	1								11	4
G.A.Knowles	LanCB	2000-2002	GC	6	6	0	126	33	21.00	-	-								3	
S.T.Knox	Cumb	1996-2002	GC	13	13	2	320	108*	29.09	1	-								5	
S.H.Kotak	WarCB	2002	GC	1	1	0	11	11	11.00	-	-	60	56	2	2-56	28.00	5.60	-	1	
R.Kotkamp	Hert	2002	GC	1	1	0	5	5	5.00	-	-	42	39	1	1-39	39.00	5.57	-	-	
P.Kumar	Cumb	2003	GC	1	1	0	0	0	0.00	-	-	60	33	2	2-33	16.50	3.30	-	-	
A.Kuruvilla	Ches	2001	GC	1	1	0	0	0	0.00	-	-	54	21	4	4-21	5.25	2.33	1	-	
S.J.Lacey	DerbCB	2001	GC	1	1	0	15	15	15.00	-	-	60	26	1	1-26	26.00	2.60	-	1	
D.J.Laitt	Oxfsh	1967-1972	GC	3	3	0	36	24	12.00	-	-	198	86	6	3-29	14.33	2.60	-	1	
	MCS	1972-1973	BH	6	5	3	48	31*	24.00	-	-	361	177	8	3-28	22.12	2.94	-	1	
B.Laity	Corn	1970-1977	GC	3	3	0	81	66	27.00	-	1								-	
C.S.Lamb	Ches	1994-2001	GC	4	2	0	6	5	3.00	-	-	222	119	2	2-16	59.50	3.21	-	-	
T.C.Z.Lamb	Dor	1998-2004	GC	3	2	1	15	15*	15.00	-	-								2	
G.A.Lambert	YorCB	1999	GC	1	1	0	0	0	0.00	-	-	18	22	2	2-22	11.00	7.33	-	-	
T.L.Lambert	Berk	2001-2005	GC	7	4	2	24	18*	12.00	-	-	336	207	9	2-19	23.00	3.69	-	-	
S.R.Lampitt	WorCB	2003	GC	1	1	1	26	26*	-	-	-	60	67	0	-	-	6.70	-	-	
P.M.Lamsdale	Berk	1999	GC	2	1	0	10	10	10.00	-	-	90	86	2	1-35	43.00	5.73	-	-	
R.Lancaster	Sta	1976	GC	1	1	1	4	4*	-	-	-	72	61	1	1-61	61.00	5.08	-	-	
R.J.Lanchbury	Wilt	1984-1987	GC	2	2	0	54	40	27.00	-	-								1	
	MC	1985	BH	2	2	0	10	10	5.00	-	-								-	
B.R.Lander	Dur	1972-1982	GC	11	7	1	73	28	12.16	-	-	621	388	14	5-15	27.71	3.74	1	1	
	MCN	1973-1974	BH	3	3	0	7	4	2.33	-	-	115	42	1	1-16	42.00	2.19	-	-	
	MCE	1976-1978	BH	12	11	2	42	8	4.66	-	-	666	429	10	3-39	42.90	3.86	-	1	
D.M.Lane	Hert	1999	GC	2	1	0	2	2	2.00	-	-	60	53	1	1-38	53.00	5.30	-	-	
	Bed	2003	GC	1	1	0	10	10	10.00	-	-	60	37	1	1-37	37.00	3.70	-	0	
M.G.Lane	Berk	1996-2001	GC	8	6	4	73	24*	36.50	-	-								1	3
R.P.Lane	Buck	1998-2005	GC	10	10	0	237	95	23.70	-	2	167	206	4	2-48	51.50	7.40	-	4	
J.H.Langworth	WalMC	1999-2000	GC	6	6	1	124	67*	24.80	-	1								3	
R.D.Large	NhCB	2001	GC	1	1	0	27	27	27.00	-	-								-	
W.Larkins	Bed	1997-2000	GC	6	6	0	75	59	12.50	-	1								5	
	MC	1997	BH	5	5	0	58	26	11.60	-	-								3	
	Hunt	2001	GC	3	3	0	142	73	47.33	-	2								1	
J.P.T.Latham	Cambsh	1998	GC	1	1	0	12	12	12.00	-	-	24	16	0	-	-	4.00	-	-	
M.E.Latham	Nmb	1971	GC	1	1	1	26	26*	-	-	-	36	32	0	-	-	5.33	-	-	

				M	I	NO	Runs	HS	Avg	100	50	Balls	Runs	Wkts	BB	Avg	RpO	4I	Ct	St
S.V.Laudat	Oxfsh	1991-2002	GC	10	10	2	229	58	28.62	-	2	400	336	6	2-15	56.00	5.04	-	3	
	MC	1996-1997	BH	7	7	1	95	43*	15.83	-	-	340	308	5	2-40	61.60	5.43	-	-	
S.A.Launder	Oxfsh	2002-2003	GC	2	2	0	2	2	1.00	-	-	120	103	4	2-50	25.75	5.15	-	1	
B.J.Lawes	Dor	2001-2004	GC	3	3	0	31	20	10.33	-	-								-	
A.Lawrence	Corn	1977	GC	1	1	0	0	0	0.00	-	-	72	26	0	-	-	2.16	-	-	
I.S.Lawrence	Cambsh	1986-1989	GC	4	4	0	78	74	19.50	-	1								-	
J.Lawrence	Lin	1966	GC	1	1	1	2	2*	-	-	-	42	37	0	-	-	5.28	-	-	
W.J.Lawry	Corn	1970-1980	GC	3	2	1	1	1	1.00	-	-								2	
P.J.Lawson	Cumb	2001-2002	GC	3	1	0	9	9	9.00	-	-	90	107	1	1-51	107.00	7.13	-	1	
S.J.Layton	Cambsh	2004	GC	1	1	1	0	0*	-	-	-								-	
P.S.Lazenbury	GloCB	1999	GC	1	1	0	3	3	3.00	-	-								-	
	KntCB	2001	GC	3	2	1	112	88*	112.00	-	1	30	28	1	1-28	28.00	5.60	-	1	
	Here	2002	GC	2	2	0	71	71	35.50	-	1	42	49	3	3-49	16.33	7.00	-	-	
C.W.Leach	Dur	1964	GC	2	2	1	28	27*	28.00	-	-	48	48	1	1-48	48.00	6.00	-	1	
	Buck	1969-1970	GC	3	3	1	48	39*	24.00	-	-								1	
D.Leather	Ches	1999	GC	1	1	0	19	19	19.00	-	-	30	46	0	-	-	9.20	-	-	
D.N.Leech	Ches	2004	GC	1	1	0	8	8	8.00	-	-								1	
A.O.F.le Fleming	Dev	1994-1996	GC	2	1	0	0	0	0.00	-	-	114	100	2	2-42	50.00	5.26	-	-	
S.J.Legg	Dor	1989	GC	1	1	0	66	66	66.00	-	1								-	
C.P.Lello	Corn	1996-2000	GC	3	3	0	37	20	12.33	-	-	48	55	1	1-43	55.00	6.87	-	2	
T.A.Lester	Oxfsh	1989-1993	GC	4	4	0	57	25	14.25	-	-								-	
	MC	1990	BH	3	2	0	18	14	9.00	-	-								-	
C.Lethbridge	Cambsh	1986-1987	GC	2	2	0	1	1	0.50	-	-	108	38	2	2-18	19.00	2.11	-	-	
C.Lever	Buck	1965-1975	GC	8	6	0	69	20	11.50	-	-	468	301	7	3-19	43.00	3.85	-	2	
P.J.Lewington	MCW	1978	BH	1	1	0	0	0	0.00	-	-	36	25	1	1-25	25.00	4.16	-	-	
	Berk	1979-1991	GC	6	4	3	12	9*	12.00	-	-	342	172	5	3-23	34.40	3.01	-	-	
A.S.Lewis	Hert	2003	GC	1	1	0	4	4	4.00	-	-								-	
J.C.M.Lewis	Norf	1990-1992	GC	2	2	0	10	9	5.00	-	-	120	103	2	2-66	51.50	5.15	-	1	
J.M.Lewis	Cumb	1999-2002	GC	9	8	0	140	65	17.50	-	1	272	182	8	3-10	22.75	4.01	-	2	
R.V.Lewis	MCW	1978	BH	3	3	0	16	16	5.33	-	-								1	
	MCS	1979	BH	3	2	0	86	76	43.00	-	1								1	
	MC	1980-1983	BH	7	7	0	62	31	8.85	-	-								1	
	Dor	1983-1986	GC	2	2	0	28	28	14.00	-	-								-	
V.B.Lewis	Dor	1983-1992	GC	6	5	0	25	11	5.00	-	-								1	
M.G.Lickley	Berk	1983-1992	GC	9	9	0	165	44	18.33	-	-	54	41	1	1-15	41.00	4.55	-	1	
D.G.C.Ligertwood																				
	Hert	1991	GC	1	1	1	37	37*	-	-	-								-	
D.G.Light	MCS	1974	BH	1	1	0	6	6	6.00	-	-								-	
J.E.G.Lincoln	KntCB	2001-2003	GC	5	3	0	11	10	3.66	-	-	89	87	1	1-15	87.00	5.86	-	-	
S.J.Lines	Bed	1982-1985	GC	2	2	0	3	2	1.50	-	-	66	41	4	3-28	10.25	3.72	-	2	
S.G.Lishman	Nmb	1984	GC	1	1	0	0	0	0.00	-	-	66	53	2	2-53	26.50	4.81	-	-	
L.R.J.List	Oxfsh	1999-2001	GC	4	3	0	20	10	6.66	-	-	147	104	2	1-24	52.00	4.24	-	1	
J.W.Lister	Dur	1983-1988	GC	7	7	0	142	46	20.28	-	-	36	35	1	1-35	35.00	5.83	-	2	
J.B.Livermore	Wilt	1969	GC	1	1	0	2	2	2.00	-	-	66	56	0	-	-	5.09	-	-	
S.J.B.Livermore	Norf	1992-2002	GC	7	7	2	83	23*	16.60	-	-								-	
N.J.Llong	Norf	2000	GC	2	2	0	21	16	10.50	-	-	72	72	1	1-50	72.00	6.00	-	-	

				M	I	NO	Runs	HS	Avg	100	50	Balls	Runs	Wkts	BB	Avg	RpO	4I	Ct	St
B.J.Lloyd	WalMC	1993	GC	1	1	1	31	31*	-	-	-	36	39	0	-	-	6.50	-	-	
D.Lloyd	Cumb	1984-1985	GC	2	2	0	40	28	20.00	-	-	67	56	0	-	-	5.01	-	-	
G.D.Lloyd	Cumb	2003	GC	1	1	0	123	123	123.00	1	-								-	
D.G.Lock	Oxfsh	1975	GC	2	1	0	0	0	0.00	-	-	114	57	5	3-44	11.40	3.00	-	-	
K.J.Locke	Buck	1999-2003	GC	6	4	0	54	41	13.50	-	-								6	3
M.C.Lomas	LanCB	1999-2001	GC	3	3	0	17	15	5.66	-	-								1	
I.R.Lomax	Wilt	1965-1969	GC	2	2	0	113	63	56.50	-	2	72	34	0	-	-	2.83	-	1	
S.R.L.Long	Suf	1979	GC	2	2	0	12	7	6.00	-	-								-	
M.C.Longmore	Sta	2001-2002	GC	3	3	0	63	40	21.00	-	-								1	
A.G.R.Loudon	KntCB	2001	GC	1	1	0	53	53	53.00	-	1	6	4	0	-	-	4.00	-	-	
H.J.H.Loudon	KntCB	2002-2003	GC	2	2	0	57	38	28.50	-	-	60	58	1	1-58	58.00	5.80	-	-	
J.Love	Oxfsh	9167	GC	1	1	0	7	7	7.00	-	-								-	
J.D.Love	Lin	1990-1991	GC	2	2	0	25	24	12.50	-	-	12	11	0	-	-	5.50	-	-	
	MC	1991-1992	BH	6	6	1	351	81	70.20	-	4								-	
G.E.Loveday	Berk	1988-2000	GC	13	13	0	249	56	19.15	-	1								3	
C.C.Lovell	Corn	1986-1996	GC	3	3	0	8	7	2.66	-	-	216	264	4	2-107	66.00	7.33	-	1	
D.J.Lovell	WalMC	1998-2001	GC	2	2	0	13	8	6.50	-	-								-	
B.M.Lowe	Ches	1964	GC	1	1	0	0	0	0.00	-	-								-	
D.Lowe	Hert	2001	GC	3	3	0	18	9	6.00	-	-								-	
L.Lowe	Sta	1975	GC	1	1	1	7	7*	-	-	-	72	64	0	-	-	5.33	-	1	
S.J.Lowe	Hert	2001	GC	2	2	0	5	5	2.50	-	-								5	1
M.J.Lowrey	MidCB	1999	GC	1	1	0	24	24	24.00	-	-	60	38	1	1-38	38.00	3.80	-	-	
D.J.Lupton	Cumb	1984	GC	1	1	0	0	0	0.00	-	-	36	27	1	1-27	27.00	4.50	-	-	
R.D.Lupton	Here	2000	GC	1	1	0	24	24	24.00	-	-	48	33	2	2-33	16.50	4.12	-	-	
D.F.Lye	Dev	2000-2005	GC	10	9	0	265	121	29.44	1	1	16	9	0	-	-	3.37	-	3	
R.Lynch	Oxfsh	2002-2003	GC	2	2	0	60	39	30.00	-	-	114	90	1	1-49	90.00	4.73	-	-	
S.G.Lynch	Buck	1990	GC	1	1	0	46	46	46.00	-	-	42	52	1	1-52	52.00	7.42	-	1	
A.W.Lyon	Buck	1979-1988	GC	6	5	0	8	4	1.60	-	-	330	214	5	3-71	42.80	3.89	-	1	
D.W.Lyon	Cambsh	1972	GC	1	1	1	0	0*	-	-	-	72	44	1	1-44	44.00	3.66	-	-	
K.P.W.J.McAdam	Buck	1969	GC	1	1	0	1	1	1.00	-	-								-	
B.J.McArdle	Sta	1984-1989	GC	2	2	0	38	37	19.00	-	-	60	63	1	1-40	63.00	6.30	-	-	
M.J.McCague	Here	2002-2004	GC	3	3	2	29	18*	29.00	-	-	126	173	4	2-58	43.25	8.23	-	2	
R.C.A.M.McCarthy	YorCB	2000	GC	2	1	0	1	1	1.00	-	-	120	90	3	2-46	30.00	4.50	-	-	
C.Macconacie	LeiCB	2002	GC	2	2	1	49	25	49.00	-	-	48	39	0	-	-	4.87	-	-	
S.McDonald	WarCB	1999-2001	GC	4	4	0	51	25	12.75	-	-	18	16	0	-	-	5.33	-	-	
G.J.McDougall	Cambsh	2002-2003	GC	2	1	1	6	6*	-	-	-								1	3
M.S.A.McEvoy	Cambsh	1982	GC	1	1	0	52	52	52.00	-	1								-	
	Suf	1985-1990	GC	6	6	0	218	61	36.33	-	2								-	
A.C.McGarry	Suf	2005	GC	1								60	63	1	1-63	63.00	6.30	-	1	
S.C.G.MacGill	Dev	1997-1998	GC	2	2	0	4	4	2.00	-	-	120	59	2	1-29	29.50	2.95	-	-	
A.Machin	Corn	1980	GC	1	1	0	0	0	0.00	-	-	72	23	0	-	-	1.91	-	-	
T.J.Machin	Bed	1977	GC	1	1	0	14	14	14.00	-	-								-	
A.J.Mack	MC	1990-1991	BH	7	1	0	6	6	6.00	-	-	426	283	8	2-22	35.37	3.98	-	1	
A.N.Mackleworth	Sta	1989	GC	1	1	0	2	2	2.00	-	-								-	
	Shr	1997	GC	1	1	0	0	0	0.00	-	-								-	

				M	I	NO	Runs	HS	Avg	100	50	Balls	Runs	Wkts	BB	Avg	RpO	4I	Ct	St
A.E.McKenna	YorCB	1999-2001	GC	5	5	0	57	43	11.40	-	-	48	35	1	1-25	35.00	4.37	-	1	
P.C.McKeown	Ches	2001	GC	1	1	0	30	30	30.00	-	-								-	
P.D.McKeown	Lin	1990-1991	GC	2	2	2	4	3*	-	-	-	144	136	3	3-52	45.33	5.66	-	1	
N.A.S.Mackey	LeiCB	2002	GC	1	1	0	25	25	25.00	-	-								-	
A.I.MacKinlay	EssCB	1999-2001	GC	4	4	2	72	33*	36.00	-	-	219	147	3	1-31	49.00	4.02	-	1	
D.S.Mackintosh	Buck	1972-1975	GC	3	3	0	26	14	8.66	-	-								2	
	MCS	1973	BH	1	1	0	9	9	9.00	-	-								-	
N.R.C.MacLaurin	Hert	1989-1991	GC	3	3	0	45	21	15.00	-	-	12	20	0	-	-	10.00	-	1	
R.A.McLean	NhCB	2000-2002	GC	2	2	2	12	10*	-	-	-	90	53	1	1-21	53.00	3.53	-	-	
C.A.McManus	Norf	1968-1969	GC	2	2	0	26	16	13.00	-	-								2	
	MCN	1975	BH	1	1	0	1	1	1.00	-	-								-	
B.E.McNamara	MidCB	1999	GC	1	1	0	5	5	5.00	-	-	54	40	2	2-40	20.00	4.44	-	3	
N.M.McVicker	Lin	1966-1967	GC	2	2	0	20	16	10.00	-	-	144	103	6	3-42	17.16	4.29	-	1	
I.S.Madray	Lin	1966-1967	GC	2	2	0	59	58	29.50	-	1	18	19	0	-	-	6.33	-	-	
K.R.Maguire	Sta	1984-1986	GC	3	1	1	0	0*	-	-	-	162	127	4	3-64	31.75	4.70	-	-	
D.J.C.Mahadanaarachchi																				
	WalMC	1994	GC	1	1	0	1	1	1.00	-	-								-	
S.I.Mahmood	LanCB	2001	GC	1	1	0	11	11	11.00	-	-	24	37	0	-	-	9.25	-	-	
A.J.Mahoney	Berk	1976	GC	1	1	0	0	0	0.00	-	-	72	32	4	4-32	8.00	2.66	1	-	
Maisam Hasnain	Shr	2002	GC	1	1	0	1	1	1.00	-	-								-	
M.Makin	Ches	2002	GC	1	1	0	4	4	4.00	-	-								-	1
D.J.Makinson	Cumb	1992-1995	GC	3	3	0	32	23	10.66	-	-	192	152	3	2-44	50.66	4.75	-	1	
M.N.Malik	NottCB	2000	GC	1	1	1	1	1*	-	-	-	36	20	0	-	-	3.33	-	-	
P.J.Malkin	Cambsh	1983	GC	1	1	1	10	10*	-	-	-	24	25	0	-	-	6.25	-	-	
S.J.Malone	Dur	1986	GC	1	1	0	6	6	6.00	-	-	72	51	2	2-51	25.50	4.25	-	-	
	MC	1986	BH	3	3	2	2	1*	2.00	-	-	160	95	4	3-26	23.75	3.56	-	-	
	Dor	1987	GC	1	1	0	2	2	2.00	-	-	72	82	1	1-82	82.00	6.83	-	-	
	Wilt	1990	GC	1	1	1	5	5*	-	-	-	55	54	0	-	-	5.89	-	-	
C.J.Malton	Hunt	2000-2001	GC	5	5	1	128	37	32.00	-	-								1	
J.Manger	Oxfsh	1983-1984	GC	2	2	0	26	17	13.00	-	-								-	
Maninder Singh	Shr	1988	GC	1	1	1	3	3*	-	-	-	72	59	1	1-59	59.00	4.91	-	-	
C.Mann	DurCB	2001	GC	1	1	0	7	7	7.00	-	-								1	
J.P.W.Mann	NhCB	2000-2001	GC	2	1	0	5	5	5.00	-	-								-	
	Cambsh	2004	GC	1	1	0	1	1	1.00	-	-								-	
D.Manning	WorCB	1999-2003	GC	8	6	0	169	80	28.16	-	1	107	94	3	2-12	31.33	5.27	-	4	
R.J.Mansfield	SurCB	2001-2002	GC	3	3	0	46	40	15.33	-	-	66	62	0	-	-	5.63	-	-	
M.G.Maranta	Suf	1981	GC	1	1	0	12	12	12.00	-	-	72	40	2	2-40	20.00	3.33	-	-	
K.Marc	Berk	1997	GC	1								54	61	1	1-61	61.00	6.77	-	-	
	MidCB	2000	GC	2	2	1	13	7	13.00	-	-	84	53	1	1-21	53.00	3.78	-	-	
	SurCB	2001	GC	2	2	0	2	2	1.00	-	-	61	56	2	2-31	28.00	5.50	-	1	
	Hert	2002	GC	1	1	0	5	5	5.00	-	-	48	42	1	1-42	42.00	5.25	-	-	
J.G.March	Dur	1972-1973	GC	4	4	0	91	78	22.75	-	1	48	18	1	1-18	18.00	2.25	-	-	
C.P.Marks	Sta	1971-1973	GC	2	2	0	5	3	2.50	-	-	18	10	0	-	-	3.33	-	-	
P.A.Marks	HamCB	2001	GC	2	2	1	22	17*	22.00	-	-								-	
L.J.Marland	WarCB	2002	GC	1	1	0	39	39	39.00	-	-								1	
C.Marples	DerbCB	1999-2000	GC	3	3	0	15	11	5.00	-	-								4	

				M	I	NO	Runs	HS	Avg	100	50	Balls	Runs	Wkts	BB	Avg	RpO	4I	Ct	St
C.V.L.Marques	Hert	1964-1966	GC	2	2	0	23	13	11.50	-	-	54	29	1	1-13	29.00	3.22	-	-	
J.P.Marquet	Norf	2003	GC	1	1	0	4	4	4.00	-	-	60	55	3	3-55	18.33	5.50	-	-	
A.J.Marsh	DerbCB	1999-2001	GC	4	4	0	73	53	18.25	-	1								2	
A.M.Marsh	Dor	1973	GC	1	1	0	1	1	1.00	-	-	72	33	0	-	-	2.75	-	-	
D.Marsh	Shr	1993	GC	1	1	0	0	0	0.00	-	-	66	51	0	-	-	4.63	-	-	
P.M.Marsh	Wilt	1993-2001	GC	2	2	0	3	2	1.50	-	-	90	63	1	1-35	63.00	4.20	-	-	
A.G.Marshall	Wilt	1964-1969	GC	3	3	1	41	31*	20.50	-	-	228	100	3	3-36	33.33	2.63	-	-	
D.Marshall	Lin	1983-1991	GC	4	3	0	9	5	3.00	-	-	288	212	4	2-34	53.00	4.41	-	1	
H.J.H.Marshall	Buck	2003	GC	1	1	1	66	66*	-	-	1								-	
J.A.H.Marshall	Buck	2002-2003	GC	4	4	0	51	24	12.75	-	-								2	
P.A.Marshall	Sta	1984-1985	GC	2	2	0	2	1	1.00	-	-								1	
S.J.Marshall	Ches	2001-2002	GC	2	2	0	7	4	3.50	-	-	96	85	0	-	-	5.31	-	-	
C.P.Martin	Shr	2005	GC	1	1	0	1	1	1.00	-	-								1	
G.R.E.Martin	SurCB	2002	GC	2	2	0	20	13	10.00	-	-								-	
M.H.Martin	Wilt	1964-1965	GC	2	2	0	1	1	0.50	-	-	88	63	2	2-46	31.50	4.29	-	1	
R.J.Maru	HamCB	1999-2001	GC	5	3	1	21	11*	10.50	-	-	240	150	4	2-53	37.50	3.75	-	2	
M.J.Marvell	MC	1996	BH	2	2	0	24	14	12.00	-	-	66	59	2	1-21	29.50	5.36	-	-	
	Shr	2002-2003	GC	3	3	1	47	26	23.50	-	-								-	
B.L.Marvin	Bed	1985	GC	1	1	0	0	0	0.00	-	-	66	56	2	2-56	28.00	5.09	-	-	
M.Maslin	Lin	1966-1976	GC	7	7	2	164	62*	32.80	-	2	318	158	4	3-29	39.50	2.98	-	4	
	MCN	1972-1975	BH	13	13	0	195	47	15.00	-	-	261	153	6	3-33	25.50	3.51	-	7	
	MCE	1976	BH	4	4	1	125	103*	41.66	1	-	179	166	2	1-24	83.00	5.56	-	1	
A.M.Mason	Here	2001	GC	1	1	0	1	1	1.00	-	-								1	
J.Mason	Cumb	2001-2002	GC	2	2	1	16	14	16.00	-	-	24	39	1	1-39	39.00	9.75	-	-	
M.B.Mason	WalMC	2003-2005	GC	3	2	0	2	2	1.00	-	-	132	106	4	2-32	26.50	4.81	-	-	
M.J.G.Mason	Cambsh	2000-2003	GC	5	2	1	0	0*	0.00	-	-	259	154	6	2-34	25.66	3.56	-	1	
R.W.Mason	Cumb	2002-2003	GC	2	2	0	0	0	0.00	-	-								-	
T.J.Mason	Shr	2002-2004	GC	4	3	0	28	18	9.33	-	-	144	86	7	5-17	12.28	3.58	1	2	
K.D.Masters	Cambsh	1996	GC	1	1	1	3	3*	-	-	-	72	52	2	2-52	26.00	4.33	-	-	
	KntCB	1999-2002	GC	12	5	4	9	4*	9.00	-	-	570	281	6	1-10	46.83	2.95	-	1	
B.L.Matthews	Dev	1969-1984	GC	7	7	0	119	66	17.00	-	1								4	
	MCS	1974	BH	1	1	0	6	6	6.00	-	-								-	
R.B.Matthews	Oxfsh	1967-1970	GC	2	1	1	1	1*	-	-	-	121	44	4	2-15	11.00	2.18	-	1	
D.E.Mattocks	Norf	1969-1991	GC	7	7	1	7	2*	1.16	-	-								5	
J.K.Maunders	MidCB	2001	GC	1	1	0	11	11	11.00	-	-	13	18	0	-	-	8.30	-	-	
A.D.Mawson	Cumb	1996-1998	GC	3	3	0	122	77	40.66	-	1								1	
	Suf	2002-2005	GC	3	3	0	67	65	22.33	-	1								-	
B.Mayes	Suf	19870	GC	1	1	1	13	13*	-	-	-	6	6	0	-	-	6.00	-	-	
J.C.Maynard	Norf	1994	GC	1	1	0	0	0	0.00	-	-	72	52	1	1-52	52.00	4.33	-	-	
R.G.J.Meale	Wilt	1983-1984	GC	2	1	0	19	19	19.00	-	-								-	2
K.T.Medlycott	Buck	2005	GC	1	1	1	21	21*	-	-	-								1	
P.Meehan	Wilt	1972-1988	GC	4	4	0	38	20	9.50	-	-	144	158	2	1-61	79.00	6.58	-	-	
T.Mees	WorCB	1999	GC	1								48	34	0	-	-	4.25	-	-	
	WarCB	2001-2001	GC	3	2	1	4	4*	4.00	-	-	150	110	3	3-19	36.66	4.40	-	-	
C.A.Melhuish	Dev	1983	GC	1	1	0	4	4	4.00	-	-								-	
M.A.Meman	Shr	1978	GC	1	1	0	16	16	16.00	-	-	60	22	0	-	-	2.20	-	-	

				M	I	NO	Runs	HS	Avg	100	50	Balls	Runs	Wkts	BB	Avg	RpO	4I	Ct	St
J.A.Mence	Berk	1965	GC	1	1	0	22	22	22.00	-	-								-	
M.D.Mence	MCS	1973-1975	BH	6	6	0	92	50	15.33	-	1	247	212	0	-	-	5.14	-	-	
	Berk	1976-1979	GC	2	2	0	46	44	23.00	-	-	144	62	0	-	-	2.58	-	-	
A.J.Mercer	LanCB	2002	GC	2								120	49	6	4-26	8.16	2.45	1	-	
D.J.M.Mercer	Wilt	1983-1988	GC	3	3	0	16	13	5.33	-	-								2	
	Berk	1989-1994	GC	4	4	0	70	45	17.50	-	-								3	
	Bed	1998-2001	GC	10	9	1	98	39*	12.25	-	-								5	
I.P.Mercer	Norf	1965-1970	GC	4	4	0	81	31	20.25	-	-	12	16	0	-	-	8.00	-	1	
R.A.D.Mercer	Dur	1977-1986	GC	9	9	2	47	23	6.71	-	-								1	2
	MCN	1979	BH	2	1	0	0	0	0.00	-	-								-	
R.P.Merriman	Dor	1986-1990	GC	3	3	0	53	25	17.66	-	-	18	32	2	2-32	16.00	10.66	-	-	
	Cambsh	1991-1997	GC	2	2	0	11	11	5.50	-	-								-	
W.G.Merry	Hert	1977-1991	GC	9	8	4	32	11	8.00	-	-	522	299	12	3-27	24.91	3.43	-	2	
	MCW	1978	BH	2	1	0	3	3	3.00	-	-	132	51	5	3-19	10.20	2.31	-	1	
	MC	1984-1987	BH	11	7	3	25	8	6.25	-	-	504	288	5	2-37	57.60	3.42	-	-	
J.H.Merryweather	Wilt	1964-1973	GC	5	5	5	6	4*	-	-	-	276	123	9	3-41	13.66	2.67	-	3	
	MCS	1972	BH	4	1	1	0	0*	-	-	-	246	174	9	3-22	19.33	4.24	-	2	
B.Metcalf	WalMC	1993	GC	1	1	0	30	30	30.00	-	-								-	
A.A.Metcalfe	Cumb	1998-2003	GC	10	10	1	415	138	46.11	1	3	6	3	1	1-3	3.00	3.00	-	4	
C.P.Metson	WalMC	2000-2004	GC	9	5	2	10	4	3.33	-	-								11	7
J.D.Meyer	WorCB	2000	GC	1	1	0	7	7	7.00	-	-	60	42	1	1-42	42.00	4.20	-	-	
D.B.Middleton	WorCB	2001	GC	2	1	0	7	7	7.00	-	-								3	
A.Mildenhall	Wilt	1989-1990	GC	2	2	0	5	3	2.50	-	-	90	77	1	1-32	77.00	5.13	-	-	
A.J.T.Miller	Hert	1988	GC	1	1	0	44	44	44.00	-	-								-	
C.A.Miller	Suf	1993-1996	GC	3	3	1	13	7	6.50	-	-	216	199	6	2-61	33.16	5.52	-	1	
D.R.Miller	Dor	1999	GC	1	1	0	41	41	41.00	-	-								-	
G.Miller	Ches	1992-1994	GC	3	3	0	13	9	4.33	-	-	199	95	3	2-29	31.66	2.86	-	-	
	MC	1993	BH	1	1	1	22	22*	-	-	-	66	29	1	1-29	29.00	2.63	-	-	
G.V.Miller	Cambsh	1982-1986	GC	3	3	0	30	21	10.00	-	-								1	
J.N.Miller	Nmb	2001	GC	1	1	0	19	19	19.00	-	-								-	
M.G.Miller	Dor	1999-2003	GC	7	6	0	150	81	25.00	-	1								6	2
R.S.Miller	Dor	1968	GC	1	1	1	15	15*	-	-	-	6	6	0	-	-	6.00	-	-	
R.T.P.Miller	HamCB	1999-2002	GC	8	7	1	128	34	21.33	-	-	396	291	8	3-26	36.37	4.40	-	2	
F.W.Millett	Ches	1964-1968	GC	4	4	0	69	35	17.25	-	-	270	139	5	2-56	27.80	3.08	-	3	
	MCN	1972-1973	BH	8	8	2	111	33*	18.50	-	-	281	188	3	2-26	62.66	4.01	-	1	
G.Millman	Bed	1967-1968	GC	3	3	1	126	54*	63.00	-	1								1	1
K.D.Mills	Lin	2001	GC	1	1	0	36	36	36.00	-	-	60	39	1	1-39	39.00	3.90	-	-	
R.A.Milne	Cambsh	1987-1991	GC	2	2	0	2	2	1.00	-	-								1	
S.A.Milner	MCN	1975	BH	4	3	2	13	9*	13.00	-	-	258	163	2	1-15	81.50	3.79	-	-	
M.E.Milton	Buck	1984-1985	GC	2	2	0	75	42	37.50	-	-	108	58	2	1-13	29.00	3.22	-	-	
M.Milward	Sta	1978	GC	1								72	44	0	-	-	3.66	-	-	
R.J.Minter	KntCB	2001-2002	GC	2	1	0	1	1	1.00	-	-	90	45	7	6-8	6.42	3.00	1	-	
E.A.Mitchell	Dev	2002	GC	1	1	0	10	10	10.00	-	-	12	20	0	-	-	10.00	-	-	
M.G.Mixer	Dor	2003	GC	1								42	35	0	-	-	5.00	-	1	
T.Mohamed	Suf	1979-1980	GC	3	3	0	108	85	36.00	-	1								-	
	MC	1980	BH	4	4	0	112	63	28.00	-	1								-	

				M	I	NO	Runs	HS	Avg	100	50	Balls	Runs	Wkts	BB	Avg	RpO	4I	Ct	St
I.Mohammad	GloCB	2000	GC	2	2	0	53	53	26.50	-	1	42	38	1	1-38	38.00	5.42	-	1	
Mohammad Akhtar	EssCB	2003	GC	1	1	0	71	71	71.00	-	1	60	46	2	2-46	23.00	4.60	-	-	
S.Mohammad Ali	WalMC	1999	GC	1	1	0	14	14	14.00	-	-	60	43	3	3-43	14.33	4.30	-	2	
N.Mohammed	Cambsh	1994-2001	GC	5	5	1	118	54*	29.50	-	1	152	100	2	1-17	50.00	3.94	-	1	
	MidCB	1999	GC	1	1	0	3	3	3.00	-	-	12	9	0	-	-	4.50	-	-	
S.Mohammed	Cambsh	1994-1999	GC	6	6	0	36	14	6.00	-	-								-	
C.M.Mole	SusCB	1999-2002	GC	5	5	1	172	66	43.00	-	1								3	
	Dev	2003-2005	GC	4	4	0	44	40	11.00	-	-								1	2
D.Mongia	Sta	2004	GC	1	1	0	31	31	31.00	-	-	60	42	2	2-42	21.00	4.20	-	3	
G.Monkhouse	Cumb	1987	GC	1	1	0	27	27	27.00	-	-	54	34	0	-	-	3.77	-	0	
S.Monkhouse	Sta	1989	GC	1	1	0	11	11	11.00	-	-	72	66	0	-	-	5.50	-	1	
R.D.Montgomerie	Oxfsh	1967-1972	GC	3	3	0	96	64	32.00	-	1								-	
H.I.Moore	Lin	1971-1976	GC	5	4	0	61	31	15.25	-	-	6	4	1	1-4	4.00	4.00	-	-	
	MCN	1973-1974	BH	4	4	0	51	30	12.75	-	-	42	34	0	-	-	4.85	-	1	
J.D.Moore	Sta	1971-1978	GC	6	6	1	79	49*	15.80	-	-								-	
	MCN	1975	BH	4	3	0	39	28	13.00	-	-	6	3	0	-	-	3.00	-	2	
	MCE	1977	BH	2	2	0	10	6	5.00	-	-								-	
S.Moore	EssCB	2000-2001	GC	4	4	2	20	9*	10.00	-	-	211	129	5	2-25	25.80	3.66	-	1	
S.O.Moore	DerbCB	1999-2002	GC	2	2	0	22	13	11.00	-	-	120	113	4	2-46	28.25	5.65	-	1	
T.I.Moore	Norf	1965-1970	GC	4	4	2	4	2	2.00	-	-	286	171	10	6-48	17.10	3.58	1	0	
	MCN	1972-1973	BH	8	7	6	20	9*	20.00	-	-	479	298	8	2-32	37.25	3.73	-	1	
	MCE	1976	BH	1	1	0	0	0	0.00	-	-	66	56	1	1-56	56.00	5.09	-	-	
D.J.Mordaunt	Berk	1965-1976	GC	4	4	0	144	60	36.00	-	2	219	132	3	3-24	44.00	3.61	-	2	
B.H.D.Mordt	Berk	2004-2005	GC	2	2	0	44	43	22.00	-	-								-	
G.Morgan	Suf	1984-1988	GC	5	5	0	51	40	10.20	-	-								1	
H.J.Morgan	Dev	1996	GC	1	1	0	34	34	34.00	-	-								-	
J.R.Morgan	SusCB	2000-2002	GC	7	4	1	10	5	3.33	-	-	336	224	10	4-55	22.40	4.00	1	1	
L.N.Morgan	KntCB	2001-2003	GC	3	3	1	66	27	33.00	-	-								1	
M.Morgan	Bed	1977-1985	GC	3	3	0	32	13	10.66	-	-	18	16	0	-	-	5.33	-	-	
M.J.Morgan	Buck	2000	GC	1	1	0	2	2	2.00	-	-								1	
T.G.A.Morley	Bed	1970-1973	GC	3	2	1	3	2*	3.00	-	-	204	128	6	3-52	21.33	3.76	-	-	
D.M.Morrell	Norf	1992	GC	1	1	0	6	6	6.00	-	-								-	
G.R.Morris	Nmb	1986-1994	GC	3	2	0	76	47	38.00	-	-								1	
J.C.Morris	Berk	2002-2003	GC	2	1	0	17	17	17.00	-	-	24	9	0	-	-	2.25	-	-	
S.E.Morris	WalMC	2002-2004	GC	4	4	1	56	46	18.66	-	-								-	
I.S.Morton	Suf	2002-2005	GC	3	3	1	98	42*	49.00	-	-	54	88	0	-	-	9.77	-	2	
J.Moss	Berk	2001	GC	2	2	0	28	28	14.00	-	-	120	88	5	3-52	17.60	4.40	-	-	
G.W.Moulds	DerbCB	2001	GC	2	1	0	18	18	18.00	-	-	84	47	3	2-19	15.66	3.35	-	1	
J.R.Moyes	Cumb	1984-1989	GC	6	6	0	53	37	8.83	-	-								2	
J.R.Moyes	Cumb	2001	GC	1	1	0	12	12	12.00	-	-								-	
G.J.Muchall	DurCB	2001	GC	1	1	0	19	19	19.00	-	-	12	11	0	-	-	5.50	-	2	
Mudassar Nazar	Ches	1981-1988	GC	5	5	0	90	32	18.00	-	-	288	133	5	2-26	26.60	2.77	-	-	
	MC	1985	BH	2	2	0	22	13	11.00	-	-	94	62	1	1-56	62.00	3.95	-	-	
G.J.Mumford	Shr	2001-2002	GC	4	4	2	42	13*	21.00	-	-								2	1
M.K.Munday	Corn	2001	GC	1								30	39	1	1-39	39.00	7.80	-	-	

				M	I	NO	Runs	HS	Avg	100	50	Balls	Runs	Wkts	BB	Avg	RpO	4I	Ct	St
J.C.T.Murch	Hert	2003	GC	1	1	0	24	24	24.00	-	-	60	67	0			6.70	-	-	
A.J.Murphy	Ches	1995-1999	GC	4	4	2	34	18	17.00	-	-	216	142	6	4-48	23.66	3.94	1	-	
	MC	1997	BH	3	3	2	2	1*	2.00	-	-	180	149	2	2-39	74.50	4.96	-	-	
O.T.Murrain	LeiCB	2001	GC	2	1	0	0	0	0.00	-	-	96	82	0	-	-	5.12	-	-	
K.S.Murray	Berk	1986-1992	GC	2	2	0	1	1	0.50	-	-								-	
S.N.Murray	Bed	2000	GC	1	1	0	6	6	6.00	-	-								-	
T.J.Murrills	MCS	1979	BH	1	1	0	27	27	27.00	-	-								-	
T.J.Murtagh	SurCB	2001	GC	1	1	0	11	11	11.00	-	-	48	40	1	1-40	40.00	5.00	-	1	
Mushtaq Mohammad																				
	Shr	1984-1985	GC	3	3	0	108	80	36.00	-	1	180	104	3	3-26	34.66	3.46	-	2	
P.Mustard	DurCB	2000-2003	GC	6	5	1	47	33	11.75	-	-								7	3
K.R.Mustow	Oxfsh	1996-2001	GC	4	4	0	29	13	7.25	-	-								-	
A.J.S.D.Mutucumarana																				
	Hunt	2001	GC	1	1	0	29	29	29.00	-	-	6	0	0	-	-	0.00	-	-	
S.D.Myles	Sta	1992-1994	GC	3	3	0	138	71	46.00	-	2	58	45	1	1-15	45.00	4.65	-	-	
	MC	1994-1996	BH	8	7	1	205	57	34.16	-	2	159	178	3	2-54	59.33	6.71	-	2	
	Berk	1995-2002	GC	6	6	2	143	81	35.75	-	1	264	192	10	4-8	19.20	4.36	1	1	
A.Mynett	YorCB	1999	GC	2	2	0	38	37	19.00	-	-								1	
Nadeem Khan	DurCB	2002	GC	1	1	0	5	5	5.00	-	-	60	35	1	1-35	35.00	3.50	-	-	
Naeem Akhtar	Corn	1999	GC	1	1	0	7	7	7.00	-	-	60	51	1	1-51	51.00	5.10	-	-	
	DerbCB	2002	GC	1	1	0	6	6	6.00	-	-	60	40	3	3-40	13.33	4.00	-	1	
R.S.Nagra	Here	2001-2002	GC	3	3	0	154	105	51.33	1	-	54	48	0	-	-	5.33	-	1	
J.K.H.Naik	LeiCB	2002	GC	2	1	0	1	1	1.00	-	-	114	75	0	-	-	3.94	-	-	
A.P.Nambiar	Oxfsh	2003	GC	1	1	0	0	0	0.00	-	-								-	
G.R.Napier	EssCB	2000	GC	1	1	0	79	79	79.00	-	1	42	37	1	1-37	37.00	5.28	-	-	
K.J.Nash	Wilt	2000-2005	GC	6	4	1	29	17	9.66	-	-	317	224	8	4-46	28.00	4.23	1	-	
M.A.Nash	Shr	1984-1985	GC	3	2	1	47	36*	47.00	-	-	216	103	2	1-16	51.50	2.86	-	1	
Nasim Khan	Cambsh	2002	GC	1	1	1	47	47*	-	-	-								-	
Nasim-ul-Ghani	Sta	1971-1978	GC	5	5	0	134	85	26.80	-	1	360	191	1	1-46	191.00	3.18	-	-	
Naved-ul-Hasan	Here	2002	GC	1	1	0	25	25	25.00	-	-	53	49	4	4-49	12.25	5.54	1	1	
S.P.Naylor	Buck	2000-2001	GC	2	2	0	9	7	4.50	-	-	114	108	1	1-31	108.00	5.68	-	2	
	Berk	2002-2005	GC	4	3	1	42	23	21.00	-	-	174	104	4	3-28	26.00	3.58	-	1	
E.P.Neal	Hert	1981-1988	GC	5	5	0	70	52	14.00	-	1	138	102	0	-	-	4.43	-	3	
S.N.Neal	NottCB	1999	GC	1	1	0	7	7	7.00	-	-								-	
F.W.Neate	Berk	1965-1979	GC	4	4	0	57	38	14.25	-	-								3	
M.Neave	NhCB	2001	GC	1	1	0	11	11	11.00	-	-	24	38	0	-	-	9.50	-	-	
A.Needham	Hert	1989-1991	GC	3	3	0	50	35	16.66	-	-	210	114	2	2-50	57.00	3.25	-	-	
R.D.Nelson	MidCB	2000-2002	GC	3	2	1	7	5*	7.00	-	-	138	99	0	-	-	4.30	-	-	
C.J.Nevin	HamCB	1999	GC	3	3	0	147	88	49.00	-	2	18	26	0	-	-	8.66	-	-	
P.M.New	Berk	1983-1986	GC	4	4	0	25	13	6.25	-	-	280	152	6	3-58	25.33	3.25	-	1	
T.J.New	LeiCB	2001-2002	GC	2	2	0	9	6	4.50	-	-								-	
M.J.Newbold	WalMC	1994-2001	GC	8	8	0	203	35	25.37	-	-								-	
O.J.Newby	LanCB	2002	GC	2	1	1	3	3*	-	-	-	110	104	1	1-45	104.00	5.67	-	1	
J.J.Newell	SusCB	1999	GC	1	1	1	9	9*	-	-	-	42	33	0	-	-	4.71	-	-	
K.Newell	WalMC	2003-2005	GC	3	3	1	18	10	9.00	-	-	114	112	2	2-36	56.00	5.89	-	1	
M.Newell	SusCB	1999	GC	1	1	0	92	92	92.00	-	1								1	

				M	I	NO	Runs	HS	Avg	100	50	Balls	Runs	Wkts	BB	Avg	RpO	4I	Ct	St
J.J.Newman	Wilt	1983-1989	GC	5	5	1	102	62	25.50	-	1								3	
P.G.Newman	Dur	1990	GC	1	1	0	0	0	0.00	-	-	60	30	1	1-30	30.00	3.00	-	-	
	Sta	1991-1995	GC	5	5	2	73	28*	24.33	-	-	298	196	2	1-29	98.00	3.94	-	-	
	MC	1992-1998	BH	13	13	3	116	33	11.60	-	-	691	391	15	4-29	26.06	3.39	1	-	
	Norf	1996-2003	GC	12	8	2	40	15	6.66	-	-	630	366	12	4-23	30.50	3.48	1	5	
R.J.Newman	Dev	2003	GC	1								60	48	3	3-48	16.00	4.80	-	-	
S.A.Newman	SurCB	2001	GC	3	3	0	100	49	33.33	-	-								1	
D.G.Nicholls	Sta	1976-1978	GC	3	3	1	21	13*	10.50	-	-	216	182	5	3-44	36.40	5.05	-	-	
	MC	1982	BH	2	2	0	17	15	8.50	-	-	132	74	9	6-43	8.22	3.36	1	-	
P.J.Nicholson	MC	1997-1998	BH	10	9	0	50	15	5.55	-	-								8	
	Nmb	1999-2005	GC	8	6	1	42	18*	8.40	-	-								2	4
J.E.M.Nicolson	Corn	1995	GC	1	1	0	38	38	38.00	-	-								-	
B.P.F.Nolan-Stone	HamCB	2001	GC	1															-	
D.P.Norman	Cambsh	1989-2000	GC	7	7	1	58	14	9.66	-	-								-	
J.S.G.Norman	Cambsh	1998-2000	GC	3	3	0	19	7	6.33	-	-								-	
J.W.Norris	HamCB	2002	GC	1															1	
M.J.North	DurCB	2000-2003	GC	6	6	1	171	69*	34.20	-	1	264	178	5	4-26	35.60	4.04	1	2	
P.D.North	Wilt	1993	GC	1	1	0	0	0	0.00	-	-	72	44	1	1-44	44.00	3.66	-	-	
K.Norton	Nmb	1971-1977	GC	3								112	54	2	1-13	27.00	2.89	-	1	
L.H.Nurse	Berk	2000-2003	GC	7	7	0	182	81	26.00	-	1								3	
M.D.Nurton	Oxfsh	1970-1987	GC	11	11	1	312	70	31.20	-	3								1	
	MCS	1974-1979	BH	7	7	1	69	22	11.50	-	-	60	27	1	1-27	27.00	2.70	-	1	
	MCW	1977-1978	BH	8	8	0	180	51	22.50	-	2	222	122	4	2-29	30.50	3.29	-	-	
	MC	1982	BH	1	1	0	36	36	36.00	-	-								-	
S.Oakes	Lin	1996-2003	GC	12	8	2	34	21	5.66	-	-	594	410	13	2-16	31.53	4.14	-	-	
	MC	1997-1998	BH	2	2	0	5	5	2.50	-	-	120	133	3	3-37	44.33	6.65	-	2	
J.F.M.O'Brien	Ches	1987-1995	GC	8	8	6	61	14*	30.50	-	-	432	290	11	4-40	26.36	4.02	1	5	
N.T.O'Brien	MCE	1977-1978	BH	8	8	0	72	31	9.00	-	-	438	193	9	4-15	21.44	2.64	1	3	
	MCN	1979	BH	4	3	0	16	15	5.33	-	-	186	120	1	1-65	120.00	3.87	-	1	
	Ches	1981-1989	GC	9	9	0	134	28	14.88	-	-	486	278	2	1-16	139.00	3.43	-	3	
	MC	1981-1989	BH	13	11	1	156	51*	15.60	-	1	429	243	10	3-19	24.30	3.39	-	4	
A.P.O'Connor	Shr	2001-2005	GC	6	4	2	8	7*	4.00	-	-	251	196	5	2-27	39.20	4.68	-	1	
S.C.Oddy	LanCB	2001	GC	2	2	0	3	3	1.50	-	-	90	46	2	2-27	23.00	3.06	-	-	
S.P.O'Donnell	Nmb	1989	GC	1	1	0	44	44	44.00	-	-	72	33	1	1-33	33.00	2.75	-	-	
S.Ogilby	Ches	2001-2004	GC	4	3	1	37	36	18.50	-	-								8	1
S.Ogrizovic	Shr	1983-1984	GC	3	2	0	19	14	9.50	-	-	168	120	3	2-44	40.00	4.28	-	1	
	MC	1984	BH	1	1	1	4	4*	-	-	-	66	21	2	2-21	10.50	1.90	-	-	
A.G.B.Old	Dur	1972-1973	GC	4	4	1	78	39	26.00	-	-	258	119	2	1-23	59.50	2.76	-	1	
	MCN	1973-1975	BH	4	4	0	69	25	17.25	-	-	234	129	2	1-13	64.50	3.30	-	-	
C.M.Old	Nmb	1986-1987	GC	2	1	0	1	1	1.00	-	-	144	107	2	1-34	53.50	4.45	-	1	
M.Olive	Dev	1987	GC	1	1	0	9	9	9.00	-	-								-	
P.R.Oliver	Shr	1974	GC	1	1	0	2	2	2.00	-	-								1	
	Sta	1988-1990	GC	3	3	0	45	28	15.00	-	-								-	
	MC	1988-1989	BH	6	6	0	125	48	20.83	-	-								-	
R.M.Oliver	Dev	1983-1985	GC	3	3	3	57	33*	-	-	-								2	

				M	I	NO	Runs	HS	Avg	100	50	Balls	Runs	Wkts	BB	Avg	RpO	4I	Ct	St
M.W.C.Olley	Hert	1985-1989	GC	5	5	1	64	20	16.00	-	-								3	
	Cambsh	1991-1994	GC	3	2	1	26	20*	26.00	-	-								1	
G.Onions	DurCB	2003-2003	GC	1	1	0	5	5	5.00	-	-	60	59	2	2-59	29.50	5.90	-	-	
L.J.O'Reilly	Hert	1999	GC	3								162	151	2	1-39	75.50	5.59	-	-	
	MidCB	2001	GC	1								18	18	0	-	-	6.00	-	-	
P.J.O'Reilly	Hert	2001-2002	GC	4	3	3	10	10*	-	-	-	144	97	2	2-54	48.50	4.04	-	-	
S.J.O'Shaughnessy																				
	Cumb	1994-2003	GC	12	11	1	207	50	20.70	-	1	258	229	6	2-22	38.16	5.32	-	1	
M.P.O'Shea	WalMC	2005	GC	1	1	0	0	0	0.00	-	-								1	
W.M.Osman	Hert	1974-1986	GC	10	10	0	224	54	22.40	-	1								6	
	MCW	1978	BH	4	4	0	76	62	19.00	-	1	4	2	0	-	-	3.00	-	-	
	MCS	1979	BH	4	4	1	27	20	9.00	-	-								-	
	MC	1982-1985	BH	13	13	0	174	44	13.38	-	-								1	
D.R.O'Sullivan	Dur	1974-1977	GC	3	3	0	25	17	8.33	-	-	162	70	1	1-26	70.00	2.59	-	-	
M.J.O'Sullivan	Berk	1999-2001	GC	2	1	0	20	20	20.00	-	-	96	48	1	1-12	48.00	3.00	-	3	
G.V.Othen	Shr	1974-1976	GC	2	2	0	4	3	2.00	-	-	120	69	4	4-34	17.25	3.45	1	-	
D.G.Ottley	Hert	1976-1986	GC	8	8	1	127	54*	18.14	-	1	2	4	0	-	-	12.00	-	3	
	MCW	1976-1978	BH	10	9	0	94	34	10.44	-	-	3	6	0	-	-	12.00	-	2	
	MCS	1979	BH	2	1	0	34	34	34.00	-	-								1	
D.M.Owen	Buck	1997	GC	1								72	81	1	1-81	81.00	6.75	-	1	
J.E.H.Owen	DerbCB	2002	GC	1	1	0	48	48	48.00	-	-								1	
S.C.Owen	Sta	1973	GC	2	1	0	6	6	6.00	-	-								5	1
P.J.Oxley	Berk	1990-1996	GC	6	5	2	112	49	37.33	-	-	246	262	7	5-87	37.42	6.39	1	-	
R.J.Pack	NhCB	1999-2000	GC	2	1	1	2	2*	-	-	-	120	72	2	2-41	36.00	3.60	-	1	
	Bed	2002	GC	2								82	21	6	3-1	3.50	1.53	-	1	
D.B.K.Page	Shr	1990	GC	1	1	0	0	0	0.00	-	-	30	24	0	-	-	4.80	-	-	
	Sta	1992	GC	1	1	1	6	6*	-	-	-	54	46	1	1-46	46.00	5.11	-	-	
J.R.Page	Bed	2000	GC	1	1	0	61	61	61.00	-	1								1	
A.P.Palladino	EssCB	2002-2003	GC	2	1	0	16	16	16.00	-	-	113	90	3	3-56	30.00	4.77	-	1	
R.J.Pannell	SomCB	2001	GC	1	1	0	12	12	12.00	-	-	60	21	3	3-21	7.00	2.10	-	1	
C.L.Park	Dor	2001-2004	GC	2	2	0	58	35	29.00	-	-								-	
	NhCB	2002	GC	1	1	0	3	3	3.00	-	-								1	
B.Parker	Nmb	2000-2005	GC	7	7	0	211	108	30.14	1	1								3	
I.J.Parker	Cambsh	1982	GC	1	1	0	2	2	2.00	-	-	72	55	0	-	-	4.58	-	-	
L.C.Parker	WarCB	2001-2002	GC	2	2	1	23	17	23.00	-	-	12	11	0	-	-	5.50	-	1	
G.S.Parkin	LeiCB	2002-2002	GC	1								60	62	1	1-62	62.00	6.20	-	-	
I.C.Parkin	DerbCB	1999-2002	GC	6	6	2	89	23*	22.25	-	-	337	212	10	5-24	21.20	3.77	1	4	
O.T.Parkin	Dor	1992-1993	GC	2	1	0	0	0	0.00	-	-	48	54	0	-	-	6.75	-	-	
A.W.Parkin-Coates																				
	Lin	2004	GC	1	1	0	2	2	2.00	-	-	36	34	0	-	-	5.66	-	-	
M.E.Parkinson	LanCB	1999	GC	1	1	0	20	20	20.00	-	-	12	16	0	-	-	8.00	-	-	
	Cambsh	2000	GC	1	1	1	5	5*	-	-	-	12	15	0	-	-	7.50	-	-	
M.E.Parlane	Norf	2002	GC	2	2	0	10	9	5.00	-	-								3	
M.M.Parmar	Oxfsh	2003	GC	1	1	0	1	1	1.00	-	-								-	
D.S.Parrott	Oxfsh	1972	GC	1	1	0	1	1	1.00	-	-								1	
C.J.Parry	Buck	1970-1972	GC	4	2	0	10	10	5.00	-	-	90	87	4	3-61	21.75	5.80	-	-	

				M	I	NO	Runs	HS	Avg	100	50	Balls	Runs	Wkts	BB	Avg	RpO	4I	Ct	St
D.J.Parry	Ches	1985	GC	1								55	32	0	-	-	3.49	-	-	
D.R.Parry	Cambsh	1982-1986	GC	3	3	0	70	43	23.33	-	-	204	121	0	-	-	3.55	-	-	
D.D.Parsana	Dur	1978	GC	1	1	1	48	48*	-	-	-	30	40	0	-	-	8.00	-	-	
D.J.Parsons	Cumb	1984	GC	1	1	0	13	13	13.00	-	-	6	18	0	-	-	18.00	-	-	
G.R.Parsons	Corn	1970	GC	1	1	0	6	6	6.00	-	-								1	
K.J.Parsons	SomCB	1999-2002	GC	5	5	1	125	65	31.25	-	1								2	
M.Parsons	SomCB	2002	GC	1	1	0	0	0	0.00	-	-	60	70	3	3-70	23.33	7.00	-	-	
T.Parton	Shr	1988-2004	GC	9	9	1	141	51*	17.62	-	1								4	
D.K.Pashley	Sta	1997	GC	1	1	0	5	5	5.00	-	-								-	
G.D.T.Paskins	Buck	2000-2005	GC	6	5	0	55	25	11.00	-	-								2	1
A.S.Patel	Dur	1981-1991	GC	12	12	3	237	59	26.33	-	1	246	185	3	3-34	61.66	4.51	-	3	
	MC	1986	BH	2	2	0	50	35	25.00	-	-								-	
B.Patel	NottCB	2001	GC	1	1	0	6	6	6.00	-	-	48	38	0	-	-	4.75	-	-	
C.M.Patel	MidCB	1999	GC	1	1	0	2	2	2.00	-	-	42	30	2	2-30	15.00	4.28	-	-	
D.Patel	Cumb	1995	GC	1	1	0	0	0	0.00	-	-								-	
D.B.Patel	WorCB	1999	GC	1	1	1	19	19*	-	-	-	42	36	1	1-36	36.00	5.14	-	-	
D.N.Patel	Sta	1987	GC	1	1	0	0	0	0.00	-	-	72	26	2	2-26	13.00	2.16	-	-	
H.V.Patel	Sta	1989	GC	1	1	0	63	63	63.00	-	1								-	
	Here	1995-2003	GC	12	12	0	196	68	16.33	-	1								4	
K.Patel	WorCB	2001-2001	GC	1															1	
K.N.Patel	Sta	1995-1996	GC	2	2	0	1	1	0.50	-	-								-	
N.G.Patel	LeiCB	1999-2002	GC	7	7	1	139	62*	23.16	-	1	234	194	4	2-30	48.50	4.97	-	-	
S.Patel	MidCB	2002	GC	1	1	0	4	4	4.00	-	-								-	
S.S.Patel	Berk	1999-2005	GC	11	8	1	104	53*	14.85	-	1	345	257	7	2-28	36.71	4.46	-	7	
A.D.Patterson	Bed	2003	GC	1	1	0	38	38	38.00	-	-								1	
M.W.Patterson	Bed	2002-2005	GC	3	1	0	0	0	0.00	-	-	123	110	5	3-39	22.00	5.36	-	3	
S.A.Patterson	YorCB	2002	GC	2	1	1	1	1*	-	-	-	104	88	4	3-11	22.00	5.07	-	-	
I.Pattison	DurCB	2000-2003	GC	5	5	2	68	48*	22.66	-	-	150	130	3	1-25	43.33	5.20	-	3	
D.A.Paveling	EssCB	2001-2002	GC	2	2	0	15	11	7.50	-	-								-	
C.J.Payne	MCS	1975	BH	2	2	0	7	5	3.50	-	-								-	
D.E.Paynter	NhCB	2001	GC	1	1	0	104	104	104.00	1	-	36	46	0	-	-	7.66	-	-	
D.J.Peacock	HamCB	2002	GC	1	1	0	8	8	8.00	-	-	24	19	1	1-19	19.00	4.75	-	1	
L.R.Peacock	Lin	1999	GC	1	1	1	2	2*	-	-	-	54	37	0	-	-	4.11	-	-	
	Hunt	2001-2002	GC	4	4	1	14	8	4.66	-	-	192	167	7	3-65	23.85	5.21	-	1	
A.M.Pearce	Corn	2002-2003	GC	4	4	0	57	28	14.25	-	-								-	
C.J.Pearce	WorCB	2003-2003	GC	1	1	0	5	5	5.00	-	-	12	20	0	-	-	10.00	-	1	
R.Pearman	Bed	1973	GC	1	1	0	2	2	2.00	-	-								-	
	MCS	1973	BH	4	4	0	8	4	2.00	-	-								-	
	MCN	1974-1975	BH	5	5	0	69	41	13.80	-	-								-	
T.J.Pearman	Hert	2003	GC	1	1	1	4	4*	-	-	-								-	
T.Pearsall	Sta	1975-1978	GC	3	3	0	49	34	16.33	-	-								1	
	MCN	1979	BH	2	2	0	17	9	8.50	-	-								-	
A.S.Pearson	Bed	1982-1985	GC	2	2	0	43	39	21.50	-	-								1	
D.J.Pearson	Cumb	1994-2000	GC	10	10	0	136	30	13.60	-	-								4	
J.A.Pearson	GloCB	2001	GC	2	2	0	7	7	3.50	-	-	18	29	1	1-29	29.00	9.66	-	-	

				M	I	NO	Runs	HS	Avg	100	50	Balls	Runs	Wkts	BB	Avg	RpO	4I	Ct	St
K.Pearson	MCE	1976-1977	BH	8	8	0	170	74	21.25	-	1								1	
	Nmb	1977-1989	GC	6	6	0	153	61	25.50	-	1								2	
	MCN	1979	BH	2	2	0	6	6	3.00	-	-	1	1	0	-	-	6.00	-	-	
K.Pearson	Here	1999-2002	GC	8	7	2	115	35	23.00	-	-	150	121	4	2-18	30.25	4.84	-	-	
S.Pearson	LeiCB	2001	GC	1	1	0	12	12	12.00	-	-								-	
I.G.Peck	Bed	1977-1985	GC	2	2	0	6	5	3.00	-	-								-	
M.J.Peck	Suf	1990-1995	GC	2	2	0	49	49	24.50	-	-								1	
G.S.Peddy	Oxfsh	2003	GC	1	1	0	0	0	0.00	-	-	60	39	1	1-39	39.00	3.90	-	-	
N.D.Peel	Ches	1992-1996	GC	4	4	0	0	0	0.00	-	-	258	196	4	2-45	49.00	4.55	-	-	
D.B.Pennett	Cumb	1997-2002	GC	11	9	3	86	51*	14.33	-	1	622	397	19	4-20	20.89	3.82	1	3	
	MC	1998	BH	5	5	2	71	39*	23.66	-	-	192	203	5	3-97	40.60	6.34	-	-	
	Ches	2003-2004	GC	2	2	0	26	21	13.00	-	-	111	114	3	2-44	38.00	6.16	-	-	
C.T.Peploe	MidCB	2001	GC	1								54	32	1	1-32	32.00	3.55	-	-	
D.J.Pepperell	Dor	1992	GC	1	1	0	6	6	6.00	-	-								-	
B.S.Percy	Buck	1990-2001	GC	8	8	1	59	19	8.42	-	-	126	83	3	1-2	27.66	3.95	-	2	
G.C.Perkins	Suf	1966	GC	1								72	31	0	-	-	2.58	-	-	
J.R.Perkins	Berk	2001-2005	GC	4	4	0	36	22	9.00	-	-								2	
C.T.Perren	Ches	2003-2004	GC	2	2	0	18	16	9.00	-	-	44	38	0	-	-	5.18	-	-	
S.M.Perrin	Wilt	1993-2001	GC	5	5	0	65	34	13.00	-	-								2	3
A.Perry	SusCB	2002	GC	1	1	0	4	4	4.00	-	-								-	
A.H.D.Perry	HamCB	1999-2002	GC	6	5	0	41	16	8.20	-	-								1	
B.J.Perry	Shr	1974-1984	GC	5	5	1	79	43	19.75	-	-	186	107	7	4-39	15.28	3.45	1	2	
	MCN	1975	BH	1	1	1	8	8*	-	-	-								1	
D.C.Perry	Shr	1983	GC	1	1	0	5	5	5.00	-	-	48	30	2	2-30	15.00	3.75	-	-	
S.P.Perryman	Sta	1988	GC	1	1	1	1	1*	-	-	-	72	34	1	1-34	34.00	2.83	-	-	
Pervez Iqbal	DerbCB	2000	GC	1	1	0	6	6	6.00	-	-	60	30	1	1-30	30.00	3.00	-	-	
Pervez Mir	Norf	1982-1985	GC	4	4	0	105	55	26.25	-	1	272	152	4	3-43	38.00	3.35	-	1	
V.D.Philander	Dev	2004	GC	2	2	0	23	15	11.50	-	-	120	93	2	1-25	46.50	4.65	-	1	
S.D.Philbrook	Cumb	1986	GC	1	1	1	14	14*	-	-	-								-	
N.Phillips	Berk	1979	GC	1	1	0	21	21	21.00	-	-								-	
C.A.Pickett	Buck	1965-1970	GC	4	3	1	10	5	5.00	-	-	276	156	7	4-20	22.28	3.39	1	3	
J.K.Pickup	Ches	1981-1985	GC	4	3	2	11	6*	11.00	-	-								1	2
P.J.Pickworth	Nmb	1984	GC	1	1	0	5	5	5.00	-	-								-	
E.P.Picton	Dev	1979-1980	GC	3	3	1	21	17	10.50	-	-								-	
A.R.K.Pierson	Cambsh	1992	GC	1	1	0	1	1	1.00	-	-	72	23	0	-	-	1.91	-	-	
D.R.Pike	Wilt	1989	GC	1	1	0	3	3	3.00	-	-	72	40	2	2-40	20.00	3.33	-	-	
V.J.Pike	Dor	1998-2001	GC	5	5	1	71	45	17.75	-	-	312	185	9	5-10	20.55	3.55	1	2	
D.G.Pilch	Norf	1965-1983	GC	5	5	0	22	11	4.40	-	-	204	180	9	3-15	20.00	5.29	-	-	
	MCN	1974-1975	BH	3	3	1	30	20*	15.00	-	-	126	89	2	1-38	44.50	4.23	-	-	
R.Pilgrim	NottCB	2001	GC	1	1	1	6	6*	-	-	-								-	
R.W.Pineo	Suf	2001-2002	GC	6	3	2	18	11*	18.00	-	-	264	176	7	3-38	25.14	4.00	-	1	
D.J.Pipe	WorCB	2000-2001	GC	2	1	0	56	56	56.00	-	1								3	
D.J.Pipes	Lin	2000-2002	GC	5	5	3	14	6*	7.00	-	-	202	173	3	3-24	57.66	5.13	-	1	
N.D.Pishos	Hunt	2000	GC	2	2	0	38	38	19.00	-	-	84	55	3	2-17	18.33	3.92	-	2	
R.J.Pitcher	Berk	1995	GC	1	1	1	16	16*	-	-	-	38	32	0			5.05	-	-	

				M	I	NO	Runs	HS	Avg	100	50	Balls	Runs	Wkts	BB	Avg	RpO	4I	Ct	St
G.Plaskitt	Lin	1967-1974	GC	5	3	0	3	2	1.00	-	-	351	207	7	3-61	29.57	3.53	-	1	
	MCN	1972	BH	1	1	0	4	4	4.00	-	-	66	36	1	1-36	36.00	3.27	-	-	
B.W.W.Platt	Shr	2002	GC	1	1	0	8	8	8.00	-	-	60	15	2	2-15	7.50	1.50	-	-	
S.Platt	WarCB	1999-2001	GC	5	5	0	65	22	13.00	-	-								2	3
S.G.Plumb	MC	1980-1992	BH	47	45	5	827	63	20.67	-	2	1411	1030	17	2-3	60.58	4.37	-	8	
	Norf	1982-1995	GC	10	10	0	153	57	15.30	-	1	588	355	5	1-36	71.00	3.62	-	2	
	Lin	1997-2000	GC	5	5	0	125	52	25.00	-	1	60	26	4	4-16	6.50	2.60	1	-	
L.E.Plunkett	DurCB	2002-2003	GC	2	1	0	3	3	3.00	-	-	84	87	4	3-63	21.75	6.21	-	1	
B.W.Poll	Buck	1969-1979	GC	8	6	2	69	23	17.25	-	-								6	1
	MCS	1972	BH	2	1	0	4	4	4.00	-	-								-	1
L.G.Pollard	LeiCB	1999-2001	GC	3	2	0	2	2	1.00	-	-	168	152	5	2-33	30.40	5.42	-	1	
	Bed	2003	GC	2	2	1	17	14	17.00	-	-	120	80	3	2-41	26.66	4.00	-	-	
M.L.Pollard	Nmb	2001-2005	GC	3	2	1	10	6	10.00	-	-	156	79	2	1-18	39.50	3.03	-	-	
P.R.Pollard	Lin	2003	GC	2	2	0	56	40	28.00	-	-								4	
S.P.Pollard	Corn	2001	GC	1	1	0	0	0	0.00	-	-								-	
G.A.Pollock	LeiCB	1999	GC	1	1	0	46	46	46.00	-	-	30	41	0	-	-	8.20	-	1	
R.H.Pomphrey	Hert	1974-1981	GC	6	6	0	54	22	9.00	-	-								1	
	MCS	1979	BH	1	1	0	2	2	2.00	-	-								-	
A.M.Ponder	Cambsh	1967-1983	GC	5	5	0	75	57	15.00	-	1								5	
I.L.Pont	MC	1983	BH	3	2	1	18	13*	18.00	-	-	161	101	1	1-42	101.00	3.76	-	1	
	Nmb	1989	GC	1	1	0	0	0	0.00	-	-	60	62	1	1-62	62.00	6.20	-	-	
	Lin	1990	GC	1	1	0	1	1	1.00	-	-	72	52	1	1-52	52.00	4.33	-	-	
A.K.Poole	Suf	2001	GC	2	1	0	0	0	0.00	-	-	47	27	2	1-13	13.50	3.44	-	1	
N.S.Poonia	WarCB	2002	GC	1	1	0	17	17	17.00	-	-								-	
S.C.Pope	Hunt	1999	GC	1	1	0	69	69	69.00	-	1	36	31	0	-	-	5.16	-	-	
	Corn	2000-2003	GC	8	8	0	294	74	36.75	-	3	402	253	9	2-16	28.11	3.77	-	2	
S.P.Pope	GloCB	1999-2001	GC	5	4	0	22	15	5.50	-	-								10	1
J.J.Porter	SurCB	2002	GC	1	1	0	96	96	96.00	-	1	60	51	4	4-51	12.75	5.10	1	1	
S.R.Porter	Oxfsh	1975-1987	GC	8	6	0	55	44	9.16	-	-	486	408	9	3-58	45.33	5.03	-	2	
J.K.Potter	Hunt	1999	GC	1	1	1	30	30*	-	-	-								-	
J.R.Potter	Oxfsh	1975	GC	2	2	1	94	75*	94.00	-	1								-	
L.Potter	Sta	1995-2001	GC	8	8	1	211	105*	30.14	1	-	372	192	9	4-9	21.33	3.09	1	5	
	MC	1995-1998	BH	8	7	0	197	47	28.14	-	-	389	245	9	4-23	27.22	3.77	1	8	
J.Potts	Ches	1992-1993	GC	2	2	0	1	1	0.50	-	-	144	81	1	1-34	81.00	3.37	-	-	
H.Pougher	Lin	1967-1988	GC	4	4	0	112	54	28.00	-	1								1	
J.C.A.Powell	Ches	2001	GC	1	1	1	6	6*	-	-	-	54	45	1	1-45	45.00	5.00	-	-	
K.H.A.Powell	MidCB	2001-2002	GC	4	4	0	66	42	16.50	-	-	227	161	7	3-34	23.00	4.25	-	3	
M.G.Powell	Norf	1995	GC	2	2	0	38	37	19.00	-	-	120	103	1	1-60	103.00	5.15	-	1	
	MC	1996	BH	2	2	0	11	11	5.50	-	-	81	68	0	-	-	5.03	-	-	
R.D.Powell	Cambsh	2001	GC	1	1	0	16	16	16.00	-	-								2	1
N.V.Prabhu	Here	2000-2001	GC	2	1	0	24	24	24.00	-	-								-	
G.J.Pratt	DurCB	2001	GC	1	1	0	32	32	32.00	-	-								-	
B.P.Price	Corn	2001-2003	GC	7	7	0	184	74	26.28	-	2								2	
C.L.Price	Sta	1973	GC	2	2	0	64	52	32.00	-	1								-	
H.J.Price	Lin	1971	GC	2	1	0	0	0	0.00	-	-	120	97	3	2-47	32.33	4.85	-	-	

				M	I	NO	Runs	HS	Avg	100	50	Balls	Runs	Wkts	BB	Avg	RpO	4I	Ct	St
S.J.Price	Here	1998-1999	GC	3	3	1	37	19*	18.50	-	-								-	
	MidCB	2001-2002	GC	4	4	0	97	85	24.25	-	1								1	
P.J.Prichard	Berk	2002-2005	GC	5	5	2	119	51*	39.66	-	1								-	
A.P.Pridgeon	Shr	1991	GC	1	1	0	4	4	4.00	-	-	65	21	0	-	-	1.93	-	-	
N.Priestley	Lin	1983-1990	GC	2	2	0	78	54	39.00	-	1								-	1
	MC	1986-1989	BH	6	6	0	95	37	15.83	-	-								4	2
N.Prigent	Wilt	1993	GC	1	1	1	14	14*	-	-	-	72	38	2	2-38	19.00	3.16	-	-	
T.H.E.Prime	Cumb	2001	GC	2	2	0	9	9	4.50	-	-								-	
I.D.Prior	Suf	1966	GC	1	1	0	41	41	41.00	-	-								1	
M.J.Prior	SusCB	2000	GC	1	1	0	3	3	3.00	-	-								-	
S.M.Priscott	GloCB	2001	GC	1	1	0	5	5	5.00	-	-	60	24	2	2-24	12.00	2.40	-	-	
	Dev	2002	GC	1	1	0	7	7	7.00	-	-								1	
C.S.Pritchard	Dev	1991-1994	GC	4	2	1	1	1*	1.00	-	-								2	
L.R.Prittipaul	HamCB	1999	GC	3	3	0	66	30	22.00	-	-	156	125	4	2-53	31.25	4.80	-	3	
A.J.Procter	Dev	2000-2005	GC	10	10	6	114	29*	28.50	-	-	582	421	14	3-26	30.07	4.34	-	1	
J.Proud	YorCB	2000-2001	GC	3	3	0	7	6	2.33	-	-								1	
C.J.Proudman	Bed	1985	GC	1	1	1	14	14*	-	-	-	72	40	0	-	-	3.33	-	-	
G.D.Puckle	SurCB	2001	GC	1	1	0	5	5	5.00	-	-	60	46	2	2-46	23.00	4.60	-	-	
A.C.Puddle	WalMC	1993-1994	GC	2	2	0	6	5	3.00	-	-								2	
A.J.Pugh	Dev	1990-2005	GC	18	18	2	271	54	16.93	-	1	192	172	7	2-4	24.57	5.37	-	10	
N.J.Pullen	LeiCB	1999-2002	GC	7	7	1	225	88	37.50	-	2	389	267	21	5-41	12.71	4.11	3	5	
B.F.S.Purchase	Corn	1999	GC	1	1	0	38	38	38.00	-	-								1	
I.C.Purdy	Nmb	2003	GC	1	1	0	6	6	6.00	-	-								-	
J.R.Purvis	Nmb	1987-1989	GC	2	1	0	0	0	0.00	-	-	84	64	1	1-42	64.00	4.57	-	-	
R.A.Pybus	Suf	1986	GC	1	1	0	4	4	4.00	-	-	24	27	0	-	-	6.75	-	-	
R.A.Pyman	Dor	1991-1999	GC	5	4	0	24	23	6.00	-	-	258	225	2	1-47	112.50	5.23	-	-	
R.M.Pyrah	YorCB	2001-2002	GC	4	4	0	106	27	26.50	-	-	102	98	7	5-50	14.00	5.76	1	2	
Qasim Umar	Cumb	1984-1985	GC	2	1	0	6	6	6.00	-	-								-	
N.V.Radford	Here	1997-1998	GC	2	2	1	42	25*	42.00	-	-	114	88	3	2-64	29.33	4.63	-	1	
	MC	1997	BH	4	4	1	37	14	12.33	-	-	234	156	4	3-52	39.00	4.00	-	1	
T.A.Radford	Berk	1999	GC	1	1	0	4	4	4.00	-	-								-	
D.F.Ralfs	Cambsh	1994-1999	GC	6	6	3	39	14*	13.00	-	-	342	269	4	2-69	67.25	4.71	-	-	
J.T.Ralph	Shr	1999-2005	GC	11	9	1	329	102*	41.12	1	2	66	28	2	2-19	14.00	2.54	-	5	
S.Ramadhin	Lin	1971	GC	2	1	0	0	0	0.00	-	-	144	89	1	1-21	89.00	3.70	-	-	
A.Ramage	MC	1984	BH	2	2	2	37	23*	-	-	-	108	45	1	1-34	45.00	2.50	-	-	
G.Ramsden	YorCB	2002	GC	1								36	25	1	1-25	25.00	4.16	-	1	
S.K.Ranasinghe	MidCB	2000-2002	GC	6	6	0	210	75	35.00	-	1	312	195	2	1-29	97.50	3.75	-	1	
D.W.Randall	Suf	1996-2000	GC	2	2	0	43	39	21.50	-	-								1	
S.J.Randall	NottCB	1999	GC	1	1	0	1	1	1.00	-	-	60	43	0	-	-	4.30	-	-	
G.S.Randhawa	WarCB	2001	GC	1	1	0	13	13	13.00	-	-								-	
P.L.Ranells	Shr	1978-1985	GC	2	2	1	13	13	13.00	-	-	136	107	3	3-38	35.66	4.72	-	-	
R.K.Rao	MidCB	2000-2002	GC	4	4	0	77	49	19.25	-	-	37	42	0	-	-	6.81	-	-	
S.Rashid	Bed	2001-2005	GC	7	3	3	13	9*	-	-	-	350	285	15	4-30	19.00	4.88	2	2	
P.A.Rawden	Lin	1994-1997	GC	3	3	0	21	21	7.00	-	-	24	25	0	-	-	6.25	-	1	
M.J.Rawnsley	Here	2003-2004	GC	2	1	0	61	61	61.00	-	1	100	52	3	3-8	17.33	3.12	-	-	
P.W.E.Rawson	Suf	1984	GC	1	1	0	28	28	28.00	-	-	72	26	1	1-26	26.00	2.16	-	-	

				M	I	NO	Runs	HS	Avg	100	50	Balls	Runs	Wkts	BB	Avg	RpO	4I	Ct	St
B.Read	Corn	1970	GC	1	1	0	0	0	0.00	-	-	72	30	1	1-30	30.00	2.50	-	-	
C.M.W.Read	Dev	1995-1997	GC	3	2	0	40	37	20.00	-	-								1	1
M.J.Record	Dev	1991	GC	1	1	1	8	8*	-	-	-	36	32	0	-	-	5.33	-	-	
P.A.Redfarn	Cambsh	1983-1989	GC	3	3	0	30	21	10.00	-	-								1	
V.C.Reed	Cambsh	1975	GC	1	1	0	8	8	8.00	-	-	72	26	0	-	-	2.16	-	-	
G.P.Rees	WalMC	2003-2005	GC	3	3	0	38	15	12.66	-	-								1	
L.Reeves	LeiCB	2000-2001	GC	3	2	0	6	5	3.00	-	-								1	
B.W.Reidy	Cumb	1984-1989	GC	6	6	0	49	33	8.16	-	-	358	209	6	2-27	34.83	3.50	-	2	
C.C.Remy	MidCB	2000-2001	GC	3	3	0	54	28	18.00	-	-	24	31	0	-	-	7.75	-	1	
J.P.Rendell	GloCB	1999-2002	GC	4	2	1	7	4*	7.00	-	-	240	146	7	3-36	20.85	3.65	-	-	
A.P.Rennocks	LeiCB	2001-2002	GC	3	2	2	5	3*	-	-	-	144	84	3	1-23	28.00	3.50	-	3	
S.J.Renshaw	Ches	1994-2004	GC	5	4	0	12	7	3.00	-	-	247	207	10	3-50	20.70	5.02	-	2	
	Sta	2005	GC	1	1	0	1	1	1.00	-	-	60	42	0	-	-	4.20	-	-	
A.C.Revill	Berk	1965	GC	1	1	0	0	0	0.00	-	-	12	6	1	1-6	6.00	3.00	-	-	
G.Reynolds	LanCB	2001	GC	1	1	0	2	2	2.00	-	-	60	28	1	1-28	28.00	2.80	-	-	
G.D.Reynolds	Dor	1990-2000	GC	7	7	1	134	60	22.33	-	1								2	
J.Rhodes	Dev	1995-2001	GC	3								144	137	1	1-64	137.00	5.70	-	-	
G.S.Rice	Cambsh	1982-1988	GC	3	3	1	4	4	2.00	-	-	216	166	2	1-31	83.00	4.61	-	1	
J.M.Rice	Wilt	1983-1984	GC	2	2	1	76	75*	76.00	-	1	132	125	2	2-57	62.50	5.68	-	-	
K.G.Rice	Dev	1985-1991	GC	6	6	0	167	107	27.83	1	-	36	34	0	-	-	5.66	-	-	
P.C.Rice	Suf	1979-1981	GC	4	4	0	62	45	15.50	-	-								-	
A.C.Richards	EssCB	1999-2003	GC	6	6	0	172	64	28.66	-	2								4	
D.M.Richards	Wilt	1964-1965	GC	2	2	0	11	11	5.50	-	-								1	
I.M.Richards	Dur	1982	GC	1	1	0	9	9	9.00	-	-								1	
M.A.E.Richards	Dev	2002-2005	GC	3	2	1	11	11*	11.00	-	-	180	116	6	4-22	19.33	3.86	1	-	
A.Richardson	Sta	1996-1998	GC	3	3	0	3	3	1.00	-	-	168	116	1	1-48	116.00	4.14	-	-	
	MC	1998	BH	3	2	1	2	1*	2.00	-	-	72	48	1	1-16	48.00	4.00	-	-	
A.R.Richardson	Dor	1987	GC	1	1	0	0	0	0.00	-	-								-	
C.A.Richardson	Lin	1966-1974	GC	4	3	1	75	31	37.50	-	-								-	
M.H.Richardson	Buck	2001	GC	1	1	0	62	62	62.00	-	1								-	
R.A.Richardson	Ches	1968	GC	2	2	0	38	20	19.00		-								1	
T.W.Richings	Dor	1992-1998	GC	4	4	1	128	74*	42.66	-	1								-	
C.D.Ricks	Oxfsh	1985	GC	1	1	0	17	17	17.00	-	-	54	49	0	-	-	5.44	-	-	
N.A.Riddell	Dur	1973-1990	GC	20	20	1	347	52	18.26	-	1								4	
	MCE	1976-1978	BH	9	9	1	205	109*	25.62	1	-								1	
	MCN	1979	BH	4	4	1	84	47*	28.00	-	-								-	
	MC	1981-1986	BH	21	21	1	462	74	23.10	-	3	5	8	0	-	-	9.60	-	11	
J.A.Ridge	Wilt	1969-1973	GC	3	3	0	12	10	4.00	-	-	66	78	0	-	-	7.09	-	-	
P.F.Ridgway	Sta	1995-1996	GC	2	1	1	47	47*	-	-	-	120	103	5	4-62	20.60	5.15	1	1	
D.A.Ridley	Dor	1983-1989	GC	3	3	0	18	10	6.00	-	-								2	
G.N.S.Ridley	Oxfsh	1970-1972	GC	2	2	0	1	1	0.50	-	-	30	26	0	-	-	5.20	-	1	
	MCS	1972	BH	4	4	0	42	29	10.50	-	-	198	86	2	1-22	43.00	2.60	-	-	
P.K.Riley	NottCB	2002	GC	1	1	0	2	2	2.00	-	-								-	
M.J.R.Rindel	Buck	1998-1999	GC	3	3	0	90	46	30.00	-	-	84	75	1	1-56	75.00	5.35	-	2	
	WorCB	2001	GC	1	1	0	5	5	5.00	-	-	60	54	1	1-54	54.00	5.40	-	-	
	Sta	2002	GC	1	1	0	13	13	13.00	-	-	52	21	4	4-21	5.25	2.42	1	-	

				M	I	NO	Runs	HS	Avg	100	50	Balls	Runs	Wkts	BB	Avg	RpO	4I	Ct	St
P.J.Ringwood	Norf	1983	GC	1	1	0	19	19	19.00	-	-								1	
S.W.D.Rintoul	Dor	1989-2003	GC	10	9	1	184	55	23.00	-	1								1	
W.Ritzema	Nmb	2003	GC	1	1	0	6	6	6.00	-	-								-	
A.Roberts	YorCB	2002	GC	1	1	0	1	1	1.00	-	-	24	22	1	1-22	22.00	5.50	-	-	
A.R.Roberts	Bed	1997-2005	GC	16	13	1	379	113	31.58	1	1	714	498	25	5-28	19.92	4.18	4	4	
	MC	1998	BH	2	2	0	41	25	20.50	-	-	36	31	0	-	-	5.16	-	2	
B.Roberts	Cambsh	1992	GC	1	1	0	9	9	9.00	-	-	72	32	1	1-32	32.00	2.66	-	1	
C.M.Roberts	WalMC	2005	GC	1	1	0	10	10	10.00	-	-	26	22	1	1-22	22.00	5.07	-	-	
D.J.Roberts	NhCB	2001	GC	2	2	0	54	40	27.00	-	-								1	
	Bed	2002	GC	2	2	1	43	31*	43.00	-	-								2	
	Corn	2003	GC	1	1	0	0	0	0.00	-	-								1	
G.M.Roberts	Here	2002	GC	1	1	0	12	12	12.00	-	-	60	35	1	1-35	35.00	3.50	-	-	
I.C.Roberts	Dev	1980	GC	1								42	11	0	-	-	1.57	-	-	
J.S.Roberts	Shr	1988-1989	GC	2								144	80	1	1-52	80.00	3.33	-	2	
L.A.Roberts	Here	2001	GC	1	1	0	10	10	10.00	-	-	36	36	2	2-36	18.00	6.00	-	-	
M.J.Roberts	Buck	1988-1993	GC	4	4	1	94	54	31.33	-	1								-	
	MC	1990-1995	BH	17	17	0	451	121	26.52	1	1								6	
S.A.Roberts	Here	2002-2004	GC	3	2	0	5	3	2.50	-	-	138	92	5	3-36	18.40	4.00	-	-	
T.E.Roberts	Berk	1984-1985	GC	2	2	0	10	7	5.00	-	-	138	112	2	2-42	56.00	4.86	-	-	
T.W.Roberts	Bed	2003	GC	1	1	0	48	48	48.00	-	-								-	
B.D.Robinson	Bed	1968	GC	2	1	0	8	8	8.00	-	-								-	
D.J.Robinson	Dor	1973	GC	1	1	0	2	2	2.00	-	-								-	
G.Robinson	Lin	1966-1983	GC	8	8	0	264	132	33.00	1	-	3	4	0	-	-	8.00	-	8	
	MCN	1972-1979	BH	18	18	2	205	51	12.81	-	2								10	1
	MCE	1976-1978	BH	11	11	0	131	37	11.90	-	-	96	56	1	1-46	56.00	3.50	-	6	
J.D.Robinson	Bed	1994	GC	1	1	0	67	67	67.00	-	1	66	72	0	-	-	6.54	-	1	
J.M.Robinson	WorCB	1999	GC	1	1	0	15	15	15.00	-	-								1	
M.Robinson	Shr	2005	GC	1	1	0	0	0	0.00	-	-	7	7	0	-	-	6.00	-	-	
M.F.D.Robinson	Here	1995	GC	1	1	0	15	15	15.00	-	-	48	73	0	-	-	9.12	-	-	
	MC	1996	BH	3	3	0	14	7	4.66	-	-	132	133	5	3-75	26.60	6.04	-	1	
R.J.Robinson	Suf	1978-1989	GC	8	8	2	95	40*	15.83	-	-	432	286	8	3-59	35.75	3.97	-	3	
W.G.Robson	Nmb	1977	GC	2	1	1	15	15*	-	-	-								1	
D.J.Rock	Suf	2000	GC	1	1	0	7	7	7.00	-	-								-	
R.G.Rodger	Ches	1982	GC	1	1	0	16	16	16.00	-	-	42	13	0	-	-	1.85	-	-	
E.C.Rodgers	Cambsh	2003	GC	1	1	0	23	23	23.00	-	-	24	41	0	-	-	10.25	-	-	
J.P.Rodham	MidCB	2002	GC	2	2	0	27	23	13.50	-	-	93	54	4	4-23	13.50	3.48	1	1	
B.Roe	MCS	1973	BH	1	1	0	18	18	18.00	-	-								-	
P.M.Roebuck	Dev	1993-2001	GC	9	8	3	200	83	40.00	-	1	534	276	11	3-37	25.09	3.10	-	2	
C.J.Rogers	Norf	1991-2003	GC	17	17	2	490	139*	32.66	1	2	192	171	6	3-26	28.50	5.34	-	8	
	MC	1998	BH	5	5	0	34	11	6.80	-	-								2	
C.J.L.Rogers	Shr	2003	GC	1	1	0	49	49	49.00	-	-								-	
	Wilt	2005	GC	1	1	0	3	3	3.00	-	-								-	
R.J.Rollins	Cambsh	2001-2003	GC	4	4	1	104	50	34.66	-	1								2	
	Hunt	2002	GC	1	1	0	10	10	10.00	-	-								-	
T.E.Rollock	KntCB	2003	GC	1	1	0	5	5	5.00	-	-	60	28	1	1-28	28.00	2.80	-	-	
P.W.Romaines	Dur	1979-1980	GC	3	3	0	64	48	21.33	-	-								-	

				M	I	NO	Runs	HS	Avg	100	50	Balls	Runs	Wkts	BB	Avg	RpO	4I	Ct	St
L.Ronchi	HamCB	2002	GC	1	1	0	78	78	78.00	-	1								-	
D.J.Rooney	Cumb	2003	GC	1	1	1	11	11*	-	-	-	58	47	0	-	-	4.86	-	-	
G.R.J.Roope	Berk	1983-1988	GC	5	5	0	128	40	25.60	-	-	216	154	2	1-32	77.00	4.27	-	1	
	MC	1985-1988	BH	13	13	1	229	53*	19.08	-	1	30	30	0	-	-	6.00	-	9	
C.Roper	Dor	1968	GC	1	1	0	0	0	0.00	-	-								-	
F.A.Rose	Here	2003-2004	GC	2	2	0	17	15	8.50	-	-	102	76	7	5-19	10.85	4.47	1	-	
W.Rose	Norf	1965-1970	GC	2	2	0	2	2	1.00	-	-	72	35	0	-	-	2.91	-	-	
P.G.Roshier	Buck	1991-1993	GC	3	3	1	34	32	17.00	-	-	204	165	2	1-40	82.50	4.85	-	1	
T.K.Rosier	Bed	1968-1973	GC	3	3	0	82	52	27.33	-	1	210	125	5	3-22	25.00	3.57	-	-	
	MCS	1973	BH	2	2	0	22	19	11.00	-	-	108	102	0	-	-	5.66	-	2	
N.W.Round	WorCB	1999-2003	GC	3	3	0	58	32	19.33	-	-	60	49	0	-	-	4.90	-	1	
	Here	2000-2001	GC	5	5	1	160	66	40.00	-	1	60	53	2	2-28	26.50	5.30	-	1	
J.G.C.Rowe	KntCB	2002	GC	1	1	0	30	30	30.00	-	-								-	
R.J.Rowe	Wilt	1999-2005	GC	8	8	1	181	47	25.85	-	-								2	
M.Rowell	Oxfsh	2002	GC	1	1	0	5	5	5.00	-	-	30	26	2	2-26	13.00	5.20	-	-	
C.N.Rowlands	Hunt	1999-2001	GC	6	3	3	10	6*	-	-	-	300	184	7	2-32	26.28	3.68	-	3	
C.F.B.P.Rudd	Dev	1984-1985	GC	2	2	0	41	30	20.50	-	-	132	86	1	1-42	86.00	3.90	-	-	
R.K.Rudd	MCN	1973	BH	1	1	0	1	1	1.00	-	-	66	46	1	1-46	46.00	4.18	-	-	
W.D.Rudge	GloCB	2001-2002	GC	2	2	1	4	3	4.00	-	-	72	75	0	-	-	6.25	-	-	
L.J.Rushworth	DurCB	2001	GC	1	1	0	12	12	12.00	-	-	18	17	0	-	-	5.66	-	-	
S.N.Ruskin	Hert	2001	GC	2	2	1	14	8*	14.00	-	-	108	101	3	2-73	33.66	5.61	-	-	
E.P.Russell	Wilt	1964	GC	1	1	0	8	8	8.00	-	-								1	
T.P.Russell	Buck	1985-1993	GC	3	3	0	36	23	12.00	-	-								1	
W.E.Russell	Berk	1976	GC	1	1	0	4	4	4.00	-	-								-	
D.J.Rutherford	Nmb	1999-2003	GC	7	5	1	40	14*	10.00	-	-	360	273	4	2-33	68.25	4.55	-	1	
A.E.H.Rutter	Norf	1965	GC	1	1	0	7	7	7.00	-	-								-	
C.Rutterford	Suf	1966-1984	GC	8	6	4	57	22*	28.50	-	-	486	205	7	3-14	29.28	2.53	-	-	
	MCE	1978	BH	3	3	0	1	1	0.33	-	-	180	121	4	2-16	30.25	4.03	-	-	
Saad Janjua	EssCB	2002-2003	GC	2	2	0	128	91	64.00	-	1	108	113	2	2-78	56.50	6.27	-	-	
J.L.Sadler	YorCB	1999	GC	1	1	0	9	9	9.00	-	-								-	
A.Saeed	EssCB	1999-2001	GC	3	2	1	25	25*	25.00	-	-	168	106	5	2-33	21.20	3.78	-	2	
M.J.Saggers	Norf	1996	GC	1	1	0	0	0	0.00	-	-	60	56	0	-	-	5.60	-	-	
	MC	1996	BH	5	5	3	58	34*	29.00	-	-	246	247	5	2-49	49.40	6.02	-	2	
M.L.Saggers	Cambsh	1982-1983	GC	2	2	0	7	6	3.50	-	-								1	
C.F.Sains	EssCB	2000	GC	1	1	1	2	2*	-	-	-	18	31	0	-	-	10.33	-	-	
N.Sajjad	WarCB	1999-2002	GC	8	8	1	31	13	4.42	-	-	408	210	13	3-21	16.15	3.08	-	5	
R.D.Salmon	Sta	1992	GC	1	1	0	0	0	0.00	-	-								2	
E.K.Sample	Cumb	1985-1992	GC	3	2	0	5	4	2.50	-	-	200	151	7	4-58	21.57	4.53	1	-	
P.J.Sampson	SurCB	2000	GC	1	1	1	4	4*	-	-	-	60	26	0	-	-	2.60	-	1	
I.E.W.Sanders	Dor	1986	GC	1	1	0	2	2	2.00	-	-	24	20	0	-	-	5.00	-	-	
G.D.Sandford	Bed	1991-2000	GC	8	6	1	56	26	11.20	-	-								3	5
	Hunt	2001-2002	GC	4	2	0	24	20	12.00	-	-								2	5
N.F.Sargeant	MidCB	2000	GC	2	2	0	12	6	6.00	-	-								1	
D.G.Savage	Norf	1991	GC	1	1	0	1	1	1.00	-	-								-	
R.R.Savage	Wilt	1988-1993	GC	2	2	0	58	32	29.00	-	-								2	
L.Savident	Dor	2003	GC	1								48	54	1	1-54	54.00	6.75	-	-	

				M	I	NO	Runs	HS	Avg	100	50	Balls	Runs	Wkts	BB	Avg	RpO	4I	Ct	St
T.E.Savill	NottCB	2001	GC	2	2	2	50	35*	-	-	-	111	90	1	1-45	90.00	4.86	-	1	
G.J.Saville	Norf	1968-1969	GC	2	2	0	81	73	40.50	-	1								1	
G.P.Savin	Oxfsh	1989-2002	GC	11	10	1	223	41	24.77	-	-	618	399	8	3-33	49.87	3.87	-	5	
J.R.Savin	Wilt	1964-1973	GC	3	3	0	21	18	7.00	-	-	162	111	1	1-46	111.00	4.11	-	1	
S.Sawney	Dor	1989-1991	GC	2	2	0	10	8	5.00	-	-	86	86	1	1-71	86.00	6.00	-	1	
P.R.Sawyer	Buck	1997-2005	GC	10	9	1	196	50	24.50	-	1	42	58	3	2-55	19.33	8.28	-	6	
M.Saxelby	Ches	1996	GC	1	1	0	23	23	23.00	-	-								-	
	NottCB	2000	GC	1	1	0	23	23	23.00	-	-								-	
G.Scarratt	Dur	1972	GC	1	1	0	4	4	4.00	-	-								-	
M.G.Scothern	Cumb	1988-1997	GC	6	6	3	54	23*	18.00	-	-	422	352	7	3-29	50.28	5.00	-	2	
	MC	1995	BH	1	1	0	1	1	1.00	-	-	36	51	0	-	-	8.50	-	1	
A.W.Scott	Dur	1985	GC	2	1	0	7	7	7.00	-	-	108	74	2	2-45	37.00	4.11	-	-	
B.J.M.Scott	MidCB	1999	GC	1	1	0	11	11	11.00	-	-								-	
D.A.Scott	KntCB	2002	GC	1	1	0	7	7	7.00	-	-	33	40	1	1-40	40.00	7.27	-	-	
G.M.Scott	DurCB	2001-2002	GC	3	3	0	130	100	43.33	1	-	174	107	4	2-32	26.75	3.68	-	2	
M.A.Scott	HamCB	1999	GC	3	3	1	56	30*	28.00	-	-								1	
M.P.Scott	Wilt	1972	GC	1	1	0	0	0	0.00	-	-								-	
M.S.Scott	WorCB	1999	GC	1	1	0	16	16	16.00	-	-								-	
P.J.Scott	NottCB	2001	GC	1								42	28	1	1-28	28.00	4.00	-	-	
R.J.Scott	Dor	1983-1998	GC	3	3	0	28	14	9.33	-	-	96	113	1	1-89	113.00	7.06	-	-	
S.P.Scott	Nmb	1986-1987	GC	2	1	1	0	0*	-	-	-	102	85	2	2-55	42.50	5.00	-	-	
T.J.A.Scriven	Buck	1988-1999	GC	9	8	1	57	33	8.14	-	-	540	392	9	3-61	43.55	4.35	-	2	
M.E.Scrutton	Suf	1966	GC	1	1	0	14	14	14.00	-	-	72	45	1	1-45	45.00	3.75	-	-	
C.P.Seal	Suf	1999-2001	GC	7	6	2	100	41	25.00	-	-	86	79	2	1-6	39.50	5.51	-	1	
J.P.Searle	Wilt	2000-2001	GC	3	2	0	8	7	4.00	-	-	119	89	4	3-40	22.25	4.48	-	1	
L.A.Sears	HamCB	1999	GC	3	3	0	46	23	15.33	-	-	78	87	0	-	-	6.69	-	1	
K.G.Sedgbeer	SomCB	1999-2002	GC	4	4	1	74	37	24.66	-	-	168	111	2	1-29	55.50	3.96	-	1	
	Hunt	2000	GC	2	2	0	29	25	14.50	-	-	18	18	0	-	-	6.00	-	3	
R.J.Sellers	Nmb	2001	GC	1	1	0	1	1	1.00	-	-								-	
A.J.Sexton	Dor	2000	GC	2	2	0	35	34	17.50	-	-								1	
R.J.Sexton	DerbCB	2002	GC	1	1	1	1	1*	-	-	-								1	
A.C.H.Seymour	Corn	1995	GC	1	1	0	0	0	0.00	-	-	72	35	0	-	-	2.91	-	2	
	Suf	1999-2000	GC	2	2	0	31	22	15.50	-	-	24	37	0	-	-	9.25	-	-	
S.A.Seymour	Berk	1997-2001	GC	6	5	0	90	30	18.00	-	-								2	
D.Shackleton	Dor	1973	GC	1	1	1	18	18*	-	-	-	72	11	4	4-11	2.75	0.91	1	1	
J.H.Shackleton	Dor	1990-1998	GC	6	3	2	3	2	3.00	-	-	372	163	1	1-18	163.00	2.62	-	-	
B.M.Shafayat	NottCB	2000-2001	GC	2	2	0	40	36	20.00	-	-								-	
R.M.Shafayat	NottCB	1999	GC	1	1	0	1	1	1.00	-	-	36	36	0	-	-	6.00	-	-	
I.H.Shah	Nmb	1999-2003	GC	2	1	0	3	3	3.00	-	-	60	64	1	1-64	64.00	6.40	-	1	
Shahid Nazir	Nmb	2002-2003	GC	3	3	1	34	22*	17.00	-	-	156	93	1	1-39	93.00	3.57	-	1	
A.Shankar	Bed	2005	GC	1	1	0	27	27	27.00	-	-								-	
A.J.Shantry	NhCB	2002	GC	1	1	0	15	15	15.00	-	-	42	21	2	2-21	10.50	3.00	-	-	
B.K.Shantry	Dor	1983-1986	GC	2	2	0	9	6	4.50	-	-	128	80	0	-	-	3.75	-	-	
	Shr	1990-1993	GC	2	2	1	8	4*	8.00	-	-	102	83	4	2-36	20.75	4.88	-	-	
T.N.Shardlow	Wilt	1990-2005	GC	6	4	0	28	12	7.00	-	-								5	1
S.Sharma	NottCB	2002	GC	1	1	0	1	1	1.00	-	-								-	

				M	I	NO	Runs (bat)	HS	Avg (bat)	100	50	Balls	Runs (bowl)	Wkts	BB	Avg (bowl)	RpO	4I	Ct	St
C.J.Sharp	EssCB	1999	GC	1	1	0	13	13	13.00	-	-	18	8	0	-	-	2.66	-	-	
K.Sharp	Shr	1993-1997	GC	2	2	0	17	14	8.50	-	-	60	50	0	-	-	5.00	-	1	
	MC	1994-1996	BH	6	6	0	170	71	28.33	-	1								-	
M.A.Sharp	Cumb	1994-2003	GC	16	11	8	48	17	16.00	-	-	789	416	19	3-8	21.89	3.16	-	4	
	MC	1995-1998	BH	18	15	8	67	16*	9.57	-	-	922	556	13	2-17	42.76	3.61	-	6	
S.Sharp	Cumb	1986-1994	GC	6	6	1	201	75	40.20	-	1								-	
	MC	1990	BH	2	2	1	11	11*	11.00	-	-	18	26	0	-	-	8.66	-	1	
T.G.Sharp	Corn	1999-2003	GC	9	9	0	263	61	29.22	-	2	84	71	2	2-33	35.50	5.07	-	2	
P.J.Sharpe	Norf	1982	GC	1	1	0	0	0	0.00	-	-								-	
P.S.Sharpe	Norf	1965	GC	1	1	0	0	0	0.00	-	-	78	38	1	1-38	38.00	2.92	-	-	
T.J.Sharpe	Dor	2000	GC	1	1	0	0	0	0.00	-	-	60	56	1	1-56	56.00	5.60	-	-	
D.A.Shaw	Berk	1990-1995	GC	4	4	1	103	57	34.33	-	1	26	20	0	-	-	4.61	-	-	
G.Shaw	DurCB	1999-2000	GC	4	4	1	26	14*	8.66	-	-	42	64	2	1-27	32.00	9.14	-	2	
J.W.Shaw	NottCB	1999	GC	1	1	0	32	32	32.00	-	-	60	34	0	-	-	3.40	-	-	
	Here	2001	GC	1								54	49	3	3-49	16.33	5.44	-	-	
K.G.Shaw	Suf	2002	GC	3	2	1	34	34*	34.00	-	-	66	82	3	2-79	27.33	7.45	-	2	
P.F.Shaw	Sta	1993-2004	GC	12	12	1	310	62	28.18	-	2								3	
S.M.Shearman	Buck	1992-1993	GC	2	2	0	23	15	11.50	-	-								3	
G.J.J.Sheen	KntCB	1999-2001	GC	5	4	1	70	45	23.33	-	-	162	146	7	2-31	20.85	5.40	-	-	
K.P.Sheeraz	Shr	1999	GC	1	1	0	2	2	2.00	-	-	60	38	1	1-38	38.00	3.80	-	1	
R.J.Shenton	Ches	2001	GC	2	1	0	29	29	29.00	-	-	30	12	1	1-12	12.00	2.40	-	1	
G.F.Shephard	WarCB	2001	GC	2	2	2	88	73*	-	-	1	72	22	1	1-14	22.00	1.83	-	2	
G.Sheppard	Wilt	1993	GC	1	1	1	2	2*	-	-	-	24	41	0	-	-	10.25	-	-	
J.Shepperd	Norf	1965-1968	GC	2	2	0	6	4	3.00	-	-	150	108	4	3-23	27.00	4.32	-	4	
Z.A.Sher	MC	1996	BH	1	1	0	14	14	14.00	-	-	29	20	3	3-20	6.66	4.13	-	-	
	Bed	1997-1999	GC	5	4	3	74	47*	74.00	-	-	192	230	5	2-77	46.00	7.18	-	1	
	Buck	2001-2005	GC	8	7	3	165	55*	41.25	-	1	397	348	13	3-23	26.76	5.25	-	1	
D.Sherrington	DurCB	1999	GC	3	1	1	2	2*	-	-	-								4	1
A.L.Shillinglaw	Ches	1964-1968	GC	4	4	2	65	23*	32.50	-	-	270	128	6	2-21	21.33	2.84	-	4	
A.M.Shimmons	Shr	1997-2004	GC	11	8	2	67	23	11.16	-	-	522	388	13	3-30	29.84	4.45	-	3	
J.A.Ship	WarCB	2001	GC	1	1	0	5	5	5.00	-	-								-	
S.Shipp	NottCB	2000	GC	1	1	1	2	2*	-	-	-	30	17	1	1-17	17.00	3.40	-	-	
P.A.Shippey	Cambsh	1964-1972	GC	5	5	0	41	37	8.20	-	-								1	
	MCN	1972	BH	4	4	0	7	5	1.75	-	-								-	
S.W.Shippey	Cambsh	1964-1967	GC	2	2	0	2	2	1.00	-	-								-	
D.C.Shirazi	HamCB	2000-2002	GC	4	3	0	117	101	39.00	1	-				-				-	
C.E.Shreck	Corn	1999-2002	GC	7	3	1	11	9	5.50	-	-	360	298	12	5-19	24.83	4.96	1	2	
D.G.Shurben	Nmb	2005	GC	1	1	0	37	37	37.00	-	-								-	
C.J.Siddall	YorCB	2000	GC	1	1	0	5	5	5.00	-	-	18	26	0	-	-	8.66	-	-	
R.J.Sillence	Wilt	1999-2000	GC	4	3	0	89	82	29.66	-	1	96	75	4	3-47	18.75	4.68	-	-	
S.Simmonds	SusCB	1999	GC	1	1	1	14	14*	-	-	-	48	50	2	2-50	25.00	6.25	-	-	
P.C.P.Simmonite	Ches	1994	GC	1	1	0	2	2	2.00	-	-								-	
M.L.Simmons	Berk	1979-1995	GC	12	11	1	154	34	15.40	-	-	60	43	2	2-43	21.50	4.30	-	2	
P.V.Simmons	Dur	1989-1990	GC	2	2	0	47	33	23.50	-	-	96	71	1	1-43	71.00	4.43	-	-	
	WalMC	2000-2002	GC	9	9	2	266	82	38.00	-	3	468	353	11	3-34	32.09	4.52	-	4	
R.G.Simons	Hert	1964-1966	GC	2	2	0	14	7	7.00	-	-								2	2

				M	I	NO	Runs	HS	Avg	100	50	Balls	Runs	Wkts	BB	Avg	RpO	4I	Ct	St
D.P.Simpkins	Wilt	1984-1993	GC	5	5	1	117	48	29.25	-	-	198	123	2	2-33	61.50	3.72	-	2	
D.W.Simpkins	Wilt	1969-1973	GC	2	2	0	7	5	3.50	-	-								1	1
P.A.Simpkins	Berk	1966	GC	2								144	87	3	2-54	29.00	3.62	-	-	
R.R.Simpson	Ches	1983	GC	1	1	0	1	1	1.00	-	-								-	
T.A.Simpson	MidCB	2000	GC	1	1	0	3	3	3.00	-	-								-	
A.E.Skeggs	Hert	2003	GC	1	1	0	3	3	3.00	-	-	48	83	0	-	-	10.37	-	-	
R.J.Skone	WalMC	2002	GC	1								60	54	0	-	-	5.40	-	-	
R.P.Skyrme	Here	1995-1997	GC	2	2	0	17	10	8.50	-	-	72	78	2	2-78	39.00	6.50	-	3	
J.K.E.Slack	Buck	1969	GC	1	1	0	6	6	6.00	-	-								1	
D.N.F.Slade	Shr	1974-1978	GC	3	3	0	86	54	28.66	-	1	186	69	1	1-18	69.00	2.22	-	2	
	MCN	1974	BH	1	1	0	34	34	34.00	-	-	66	31	0	-	-	2.81	-	-	
	MCE	1976	BH	3	3	0	64	42	21.33	-	-	150	88	1	1-28	88.00	3.52	-	1	
O.M.Slipper	SurCB	2000	GC	1	1	0	26	26	26.00	-	-	24	18	0	-	-	4.50	-	-	
L.P.Sluman	Berk	1985	GC	1	1	1	12	12*	-	-	-	72	53	1	1-53	53.00	4.41	-	-	
A.M.Small	Dev	1999	GC	2	2	0	84	52	42.00	-	1								-	
D.Smit	DerbCB	1999-2002	GC	5	5	0	94	38	18.80	-	-								3	
A.C.Smith	MC	1993-1994	BH	2								132	63	4	3-40	15.75	2.86	-	1	
	WalMC	1993-2004	GC	4	2	0	8	6	4.00	-	-	212	124	5	2-20	24.80	3.50	-	3	
A.M.Smith	Wilt	1964-1969	GC	3	3	0	46	34	15.33	-	-	156	83	1	1-46	83.00	3.19	-	1	
B.Smith	SusCB	1999	GC	1	1	0	16	16	16.00	-	-								1	
C.W.Smith	Buck	1965	GC	1	1	0	0	0	0.00	-	-	60	32	3	3-32	10.66	3.20	-	-	
D.E.Smith	Buck	1974-1987	GC	6	5	0	112	54	22.40	-	1	3	1	0	-	-	2.00	-	4	
D.J.Smith	Ches	1968	GC	2	2	0	1	1	0.50	-	-	132	72	1	1-44	72.00	3.27	-	1	
D.M.Smith	Hert	1989-1991	GC	3	3	0	79	39	26.33	-	-	78	53	1	1-26	53.00	4.07	-	2	
D.T.Smith	Cumb	1994	GC	1	1	0	17	17	17.00	-	-								-	
G.Smith	DurCB	1999-2001	GC	7	4	2	20	9*	10.00	-	-	348	211	10	2-35	21.10	3.63	-	1	
G.C.Smith	HamCB	2000	GC	1	1	0	4	4	4.00	-	-								-	
G.J.Smith	Hert	1969	GC	2	2	0	1	1	0.50	-	-	114	53	1	1-12	53.00	2.78	-	-	
J.Smith	Bed	1967-1973	GC	6	5	2	21	8	7.00	-	-	384	250	5	2-41	50.00	3.90	-	1	
	MCS	1973	BH	4	4	1	70	50	23.33	-	1	168	123	1	1-20	123.00	4.39	-	-	
J.A.Smith	Shr	1976-1985	GC	3	3	0	14	10	4.66	-	-	216	113	5	3-40	22.60	3.13	-	-	
	MC	1982	BH	2	2	1	23	17	23.00	-	-	104	49	4	4-8	12.25	2.82	1	-	
J.D.Smith	LeiCB	1999-2000	GC	2	2	1	13	11	13.00	-	-								1	
J.G.D.Smith	Dur	1982	GC	1	1	0	3	3	3.00	-	-	72	61	1	1-61	61.00	5.08	-	1	
K.B.Smith	LeiCB	2001	GC	1	1	0	8	8	8.00	-	-								-	
L.K.Smith	Wilt	1993	GC	1	1	0	73	73	73.00	-	1								-	
M.E.Smith	Hert	2001	GC	2	2	0	23	18	11.50	-	-	96	78	3	3-43	26.00	4.87	-	-	
M.W.Smith	Oxfsh	1967	GC	1	1	0	12	12	12.00	-	-								-	
N.Smith	Ches	1988-1989	GC	3	3	0	5	5	1.66	-	-								5	
N.M.K.Smith	Shr	2004	GC	1	1	0	2	2	2.00	-	-	18	3	0	-	-	1.00	-	-	
P.B.Smith	Oxfsh	1967-1975	GC	5	4	2	81	34*	40.50	-	-	233	110	3	2-40	36.66	2.83	-	1	
P.C.Smith	MidCB	2002	GC	1															-	1
R.Smith	Cumb	2001	GC	1	1	0	3	3	3.00	-	-								-	
R.A.Smith	EssCB	2000-2002	GC	3	3	0	27	11	9.00	-	-								1	
T.D.Smith	Oxfsh	2001	GC	2	1	0	12	12	12.00	-	-								-	
T.M.Smith	Suf	2002-2005	GC	4	4	0	55	37	13.75	-	-	204	177	4	2-37	44.25	5.20	-	1	

				M	I	NO	Runs	HS	Avg	100	50	Balls	Runs	Wkts	BB	Avg	RpO	4I	Ct	St
T.S.Smith	Hert	1983-1990	GC	8	8	2	104	36	17.33	-	-	390	244	3	2-31	81.33	3.75	-	6	
	MC	1984	BH	4	3	2	7	4*	7.00	-	-	150	127	0	-	-	5.08	-	1	
	Cambsh	1994-2004	GC	11	9	1	41	19	5.12	-	-	612	351	8	3-35	43.87	3.44	-	2	
W.A.Smith	Wilt	1972-1973	GC	2	2	0	14	12	7.00	-	-								-	
	MCS	1972	BH	4	4	0	36	18	9.00	-	-								2	
A.C.Smyth	WarCB	2000	GC	1	1	0	21	21	21.00	-	-	12	32	1	1-32	32.00	16.00	-	-	
J.S.Snashall	SusCB	2001	GC	2	2	0	59	56	29.50	-	1								-	
W.E.Sneath	Bed	1999-2003	GC	10	5	2	6	4	2.00	-	-	486	359	16	4-38	22.43	4.43	1	-	
A.M.Snell	Corn	1995-1996	GC	2	2	2	13	10*	-	-	-								2	
S.D.Snell	HamCB	2001	GC	1	1	0	3	3	3.00	-	-								1	
D.R.Snellgrove	LanCB	1999-2002	GC	5	5	0	33	18	6.60	-	-	130	93	5	3-23	18.60	4.29	-	-	
J.Snowden	KntCB	2001	GC	1															-	
A.E.Snowdon	Corn	1986	GC	1	1	0	9	9	9.00	-	-	72	97	0	-	-	8.08	-	-	
M.T.Snowdon	Corn	1975	GC	1	1	0	4	4	4.00	-	-	51	30	0	-	-	3.52	-	-	
D.W.Soakell	Dur	1973-1973	GC	2	2	1	46	36	46.00	-									-	
J.W.Solanky	Dev	1969	GC	1	1	0	3	3	3.00	-	-	72	41	1	1-41	41.00	3.41	-	-	
H.F.G.Southwell	SusCB	2000-2001	GC	3	3	1	46	36	23.00	-	-	36	39	3	3-39	13.00	6.50	-	-	
C.R.Soza	Berk	1996	GC	1	1	0	10	10	10.00	-	-								-	
J.Sparrow	EssCB	1999	GC	1								54	42	2	2-42	21.00	4.66	-	-	
M.P.Speight	Nmb	2002-2003	GC	2	2	0	53	30	26.50	-	-								-	
A.J.Spencer	Wilt	1984	GC	1								72	82	4	4-82	20.50	6.83	1	-	
I.S.Spencer	Ches	2003	GC	1	1	0	3	3	3.00	-	-								3	
B.L.Spendlove	DerbCB	2001	GC	2	2	0	69	55	34.50	-	1								1	
R.A.Spiers	Sta	1991-1994	GC	3	3	2	22	13*	22.00	-	-	144	127	0	-	-	5.29	-	-	
J.A.S.Spires	WarCB	2001	GC	1								60	33	1	1-33	33.00	3.30	-	-	
W.Spooner	NottCB	1999	GC	1	1	1	3	3*	-	-	-	46	46	0	-	-	6.00	-	-	
A.J.Squire	Suf	1993-2001	GC	4	4	0	46	29	11.50	-	-								1	
R.C.Staddon	Dev	1969	GC	1	1	0	1	1	1.00	-	-								-	
D.M.Stamp	Norf	1990-1991	GC	2	2	0	24	18	12.00	-	-								2	
J.A.Standen	MCS	1972	BH	2	2	0	18	16	9.00	-	-	132	109	3	2-41	36.33	4.95	-	-	
T.C.M.Standing	Ches	1992-1993	GC	2	2	0	16	14	8.00	-	-								1	
K.Standring	Bed	1994	GC	1	1	1	14	14*	-	-	-	66	67	1	1-67	67.00	6.09	-	-	
E.J.Stanford	KntCB	1999-2001	GC	7	6	1	26	13	5.20	-	-	288	211	10	3-29	21.10	4.39	-	1	
C.Stanley	Nmb	1994-2000	GC	3	1	0	0	0	0.00	-	-	192	135	3	2-66	45.00	4.21	-	1	
N.A.Stanley	Bed	1994-2003	GC	13	13	1	295	69	24.58	-	2	348	275	9	3-48	30.55	4.74	-	6	
S.F.Stanway	Buck	1997-2005	GC	12	5	5	6	2*	-	-	-	582	334	9	2-30	37.11	3.44	-	4	
B.R.F.Staunton	GloCB	2001-2002	GC	4	4	0	106	56	26.50	-	1	60	54	1	1-54	54.00	5.40	-	3	
J.M.Steadman	Bed	2002-2003	GC	4	2	0	37	21	18.50	-	-								2	
M.G.Stear	Berk	1988-1992	GC	5	4	3	46	23	46.00	-	-	252	155	2	1-39	77.50	3.69	-	-	
M.G.Stedman	Bed	1982	GC	1	1	0	7	7	7.00	-	-								-	
M.H.Steed	NhCB	2001-2002	GC	4	4	2	12	5	6.00	-	-	36	36	0	-	-	6.00	-	-	
	Bed	2003-2005	GC	3	3	0	43	22	14.33	-	-	72	55	0	-	-	4.58	-	1	
S.A.Steel	Suf	1996	GC	1								60	62	1	1-62	62.00	6.20	-	-	
A.S.Steele	NhCB	1999	GC	1	1	0	23	23	23.00	-	-								-	
D.S.Steele	Bed	1985	GC	1	1	0	0	0	0.00	-	-	72	29	0	-	-	2.41	-	1	
H.K.C.Steele	Cambsh	1972	GC	1	1	0	0	0	0.00	-	-	6	10	0	-	-	10.00	-	1	

				M	I	NO	Runs	HS	Avg	100	50	Balls	Runs	Wkts	BB	Avg	RpO	4I	Ct	St
M.V.Steele	Sta	1998	GC	1	1	0	24	24	24.00	-	-								-	
W.F.Stelling	Berk	1999	GC	2	2	2	79	76*	-	-	1	102	42	3	3-18	14.00	2.47	-	-	
J.C.J.Stephens	Corn	1999-2003	GC	9	8	5	97	31*	32.33	-	-	507	325	13	3-54	25.00	3.84	-	3	
P.J.Stephens	Corn	1986	GC	1	1	0	54	54	54.00	-	1								-	
H.W.Stephenson	Dor	1968	GC	1	1	0	16	16	16.00	-	-								-	
M.G.Stephenson	Cambsh	1972-1992	GC	7	4	1	15	8*	5.00	-	-	334	216	3	1-42	72.00	3.88	-	4	
M.E.Stevens	Berk	1986-1991	GC	5	2	0	34	23	17.00	-	-								2	1
P.J.Stevens	SusCB	1999-2002	GC	8	8	0	172	62	21.50	-	1	18	18	0	-	-	6.00	-	11	1
B.Stewart	Nmb	2000	GC	1	1	0	2	2	2.00	-	-	60	58	1	1-58	58.00	5.80	-	-	
K.D.E.Stewart	HamCB	1999	GC	3	2	0	2	2	1.00	-	-	156	131	7	3-52	18.71	5.03	-	-	
D.A.Stiff	YorCB	2001	GC	1								30	27	1	1-27	27.00	5.40	-	-	
C.J.Stockdale	Cumb	1986-1992	GC	5	5	0	86	51	17.20	-	1								-	
	MC	1988-1989	BH	5	5	0	61	25	12.20	-	-								-	
D.C.Stockings	Norf	1968	GC	1	1	0	3	3	3.00	-	-								1	
P.L.B.Stoddart	Buck	1965	GC	1	1	0	0	0	0.00	-	-								1	
J.S.Stoker	Dur	1974	GC	2	2	0	13	9	6.50	-	-	144	60	3	3-16	20.00	2.50	-	1	
I.W.E.Stokes	Sta	1997-1998	GC	2	2	0	22	18	11.00	-	-								-	
C.Stone	Dor	1983-1990	GC	5	5	1	65	32*	16.25	-	-	294	171	3	2-44	57.00	3.48	-	-	
S.A.Stoneman	Ches	1998-2001	GC	4	4	2	87	34*	43.50	-	-	216	151	2	2-35	75.50	4.19	-	-	
	Dev	2002	GC	1	1	0	2	2	2.00	-	-	42	47	0	-	-	6.71	-	1	
T.C.Stonock	Nmb	2003	GC	1	1	0	16	16	16.00	-	-								-	
D.B.Storer	Lin	1990-1994	GC	3	3	0	29	28	9.66	-	-	30	17	1	1-17	17.00	3.40	-	1	
L.R.F.Stoughton	MidCB	2001	GC	1	1	0	2	2	2.00	-	-								-	
N.A.Stovold	GloCB	2001	GC	3	3	0	111	75	37.00	-	1	48	58	1	1-33	58.00	7.25	-	-	
N.C.Stovold	GloCB	2000-2001	GC	5	5	0	86	33	17.20	-	-								2	
T.V.Strange	Oxfsh	1970	GC	1	1	1	2	2*	-	-	-	54	21	0	-	-	2.33	-	-	
K.H.Stride	Sta	1975-1978	GC	4	2	1	1	1*	1.00	-	-	288	164	9	3-66	18.22	3.41	-	-	
	MCN	1975	BH	1								66	32	0	-	-	2.90	-	-	
P.F.J.Strong	Buck	1993	GC	1	1	0	42	42	42.00	-	-								-	
P.C.Strydom	Hunt	2002	GC	1	1	0	37	37	37.00	-	-	60	22	2	2-22	11.00	2.20	-	-	
I.C.D.Stuart	Dor	1987-1999	GC	2	2	1	32	23*	32.00	-	-	102	54	0	-	-	3.17	-	-	
L.G.Stubbs	Hert	1969-1971	GC	3	3	0	32	18	10.66	-	-								1	
J.P.Stuck	Suf	1978	GC	1	1	0	0	0	0.00	-	-								-	
P.D.Stuckey	Dor	1968	GC	1	1	0	6	6	6.00	-	-	24	11	0	-	-	2.75	-	-	
M.J.Sturgeon	Suf	1986	GC	1	1	0	0	0	0.00	-	-								-	
P.M.Such	Cambsh	2002	GC	1								60	37	3	3-37	12.33	3.70	-	-	
M.E.Sullivan	Buck	1998	GC	1	1	1	14	14*	-	-	-	12	24	0	-	-	12.00	-	-	
J.Sunley	Lin	1966-1976	GC	4	4	0	26	14	6.50	-	-	18	14	2	1-5	7.00	4.66	-	1	
	MCE	1976-1977	BH	4	4	1	45	15	15.00	-	-	6	2	0	-	-	2.00	-	-	
A.V.Suppiah	SomCB	2002	GC	1	1	0	70	70	70.00	-	1	60	36	0	-	-	3.60	-	2	
	Dev	2003-2005	GC	4	4	0	72	36	18.00	-	-	102	108	2	1-24	54.00	6.35	-	-	
D.Surridge	Hert	1983-1993	GC	8	4	1	7	3*	2.33	-	-	443	272	5	3-61	54.40	3.68	-	2	
	MC	1983-1986	BH	13	7	4	10	3*	3.33	-	-	695	380	13	4-26	29.23	3.28	1	2	
M.D.R.Sutliff	LeiCB	1999-2002	GC	4	4	0	107	97	26.75	-	1								-	1
	GloCB	2001	GC	1	1	0	24	24	24.00	-	-								-	

				M	I	NO	Runs	HS	Avg	100	50	Balls	Runs	Wkts	BB	Avg	RpO	4I	Ct	St
J.A.Sutton	Ches	1964-1986	GC	8	8	1	84	18	12.00	-	-	427	193	5	3-29	38.60	2.71	-	1	
	MCN	1975	BH	1	1	0	54	54	54.00	-	1	66	27	1	1-27	27.00	2.45	-	1	
C.A.Swallow	Suf	2001-2005	GC	6	4	1	49	29*	16.33	-	-	144	167	1	1-62	167.00	6.95	-	1	
P.J.Swanepoel	YorCB	2001-2002	GC	4	4	2	59	28*	29.50	-	-	216	139	8	3-9	17.37	3.86	-	1	
	Cambsh	2004	GC	1	1	0	5	5	5.00	-	-	60	42	3	3-42	14.00	4.20	-	-	
A.J.Swann	NhCB	2000	GC	1	1	0	40	40	40.00	-	-	18	16	0	-	-	5.33	-	-	
R.Swann	Nmb	1971	GC	1	1	0	11	11	11.00	-	-								-	
	Bed	1991	GC	1	1	0	7	7	7.00	-	-	24	12	0	-	-	3.00	-	-	
	NhCB	1999	GC	1	1	0	19	19	19.00	-	-	30	50	2	2-50	25.00	10.00	-	-	
P.A.Swannell	Hunt	1999-2002	GC	2	2	0	17	12	8.50	-	-	90	66	1	1-28	66.00	4.40	-	-	
	Cambsh	2004	GC	1	1	0	5	5	5.00	-	-	30	44	0	-	-	8.80	-	-	
P.Swanwick	Sta	1971	GC	1	1	1	1	1*	-	-	-								1	
M.Swarbrick	Dor	1998-2003	GC	5	4	0	40	24	10.00	-	-								-	
P.D.Swart	Cambsh	1975	GC	1	1	0	12	12	12.00	-	-								-	
	MCN	1975	BH	1	1	0	14	14	14.00	-	-	60	53	2	2-53	26.50	5.30	-	-	
N.T.Swetman	WalMC	2004	GC	1	1	0	4	4	4.00	-	-	60	41	1	1-41	41.00	4.10	-	-	
M.Swift	Wilt	1999	GC	1	1	0	17	17	17.00	-	-	60	60	0	-	-	6.00	-	-	
J.W.Swinburne	Shr	1976	GC	1	1	0	16	16	16.00	-	-	60	34	0	-	-	3.40	-	-	
G.R.Swinney	SomCB	1999	GC	1	1	0	5	5	5.00	-	-	48	28	0	-	-	3.50	-	1	
J.F.Sykes	Dur	1990	GC	1	1	0	4	4	4.00	-	-	36	16	1	1-16	16.00	2.66	-	-	
J.P.J.Sylvester	MC	1996-1997	BH	6	6	0	63	30	10.50	-	-								-	
	Berk	1997	GC	1	1	0	22	22	22.00	-	-	54	59	2	2-59	29.50	6.55	-	-	
	Here	1998-2000	GC	2	2	0	59	53	29.50	-	1	24	10	0	-	-	2.50	-	1	
	WalMC	1999-2002	GC	9	9	1	165	37	20.62	-	-	186	182	5	2-37	36.40	5.87	-	2	
R.W.Sylvester	WalMC	1999-2002	GC	12	10	0	294	73	29.40	-	3	48	42	0	-	-	5.25	-	2	
S.A.Sylvester	Hert	1999-2000	GC	4	1	0	0	0	0.00	-	-	216	138	3	2-31	46.00	3.83	-	2	
M.J.Symington	Nmb	2003-2005	GC	2	2	0	18	14	9.00	-	-	36	39	0	-	-	6.50	-	-	
K.T.Talboys	Oxfsh	1967	GC	1	1	0	1	1	1.00	-	-								-	
D.A.Tall	Dev	1992	GC	1	1	0	23	23	23.00	-	-	18	12	0	-	-	4.00	-	-	
J.M.Tandy	WorCB	2000-2001	GC	2	2	0	1	1	0.50	-	-								-	
I.J.Tansley	Ches	1985-1988	GC	3	3	0	35	18	11.66	-	-								1	
A.G.Tapp	Cambsh	2000	GC	2	1	1	4	4*	-	-	-	78	37	3	3-17	12.33	2.84	-	-	
Tauseef Ali	EssCB	2002-2003	GC	2	2	0	65	65	32.50	-	1	102	126	4	4-66	31.50	7.41	1	1	
B.V.Taylor	Wilt	1999	GC	1								60	43	0	-	-	4.30	-	-	
C.G.Taylor	GloCB	1999	GC	1	1	0	0	0	0.00	-	-								1	
D.K.Taylor	Oxfsh	2001	GC	1	1	0	1	1	1.00	-	-	60	60	0	-	-	6.00	-	-	
	Buck	2002	GC	2	2	0	154	140	77.00	1	-								1	
	Berk	2004	GC	1	1	0	2	2	2.00	-	-	12	15	0	-	-	7.50	-	-	
G.M.Taylor	Ches	1981	GC	1	1	0	10	10	10.00	-	-								-	
J.L.Taylor	Wilt	1999-2002	GC	5	5	1	117	49	29.25	-	-	12	19	1	1-19	19.00	9.50	-	3	
J.P.Taylor	Sta	1989-1990	GC	2	2	0	14	9	7.00	-	-	144	148	0	-	-	6.16	-	-	
	Norf	2002	GC	2	2	1	20	10*	20.00	-	-	97	87	4	2-28	21.75	5.38	-	-	
M.Taylor	Dev	1984-1987	GC	2	2	0	17	12	8.50	-	-	132	149	1	1-52	149.00	6.77	-	1	
M.Taylor	LanCB	2000	GC	2	1	0	5	5	5.00	-	-	120	52	1	1-22	52.00	2.60	-	2	
N.R.Taylor	Dor	1989-1991	GC	3	3	0	17	10	5.66	-	-	204	145	3	2-25	48.33	4.26	-	-	
	MC	1989-1992	BH	14	4	2	19	14	9.50	-	-	852	548	18	3-38	30.44	3.85	-	1	

				M	I	NO	Runs	HS	Avg	100	50	Balls	Runs	Wkts	BB	Avg	RpO	4I	Ct	St
N.S.Taylor	Norf	1990	GC	1	1	0	0	0	0.00	-	-	24	32	0	-	-	8.00	-	-	
P.M.Taylor	Bed	1967	GC	1	1	0	25	25	25.00	-	-								-	
S.K.Taylor	Norf	1992	GC	1	1	0	0	0	0.00	-	-								-	
T.J.Taylor	Ches	1981	GC	1	1	0	1	1	1.00	-	-	60	28	1	1-28	28.00	2.80	-	-	
K.Teasdale	Ches	1985-1987	GC	3	3	0	72	46	24.00	-	-								-	
C.M.B.Tetley	MidCB	2001	GC	1	1	0	1	1	1.00	-	-	60	48	0	-	-	4.80	-	-	
M.C.Theedom	Dev	1999-2002	GC	4	3	2	28	19*	28.00	-	-	150	125	5	5-18	25.00	5.00	1	-	
J.E.Theunissen	Berk	2003	GC	1	1	0	16	16	16.00	-	-	30	41	1	1-41	41.00	8.20	-	-	
J.Thewlis	Nmb	1971-1977	GC	2	2	0	26	19	13.00	-	-								-	
M.J.Thewlis	Nmb	1994	GC	1	1	0	0	0	0.00	-	-	48	59	1	1-59	59.00	7.37	-	1	
A.C.Thomas	NottCB	2001	GC	2	1	1	7	7*	-	-	-								1	1
	Sta	2005	GC	1	1	0	21	21	21.00	-	-	59	55	2	2-55	27.50	5.59	-	-	
A.W.Thomas	Buck	1998-2005	GC	4	3	1	20	9	10.00	-	-	222	192	5	3-47	38.40	5.18	-	-	
C.Thomas	Hert	1983	GC	1	1	0	2	2	2.00	-	-								-	
D.R.Thomas	Norf	1984-1999	GC	12	12	2	256	70*	25.60	-	2	450	361	13	3-34	27.76	4.81	-	2	
	MC	1990-1995	BH	8	7	2	95	49*	19.00	-	-	354	286	8	3-34	35.75	4.84	-	2	
G.M.Thomas	Corn	1995-2003	GC	12	12	0	115	44	9.58	-	-	48	56	0	-	-	7.00	-	3	
K.O.Thomas	Cambsh	1991	GC	1	1	0	2	2	2.00	-	-	24	22	0	-	-	5.50	-	-	
K.P.T.Thomas	NottCB	1999	GC	1	1	0	28	28	28.00	-	-								-	
M.D.Thomas	Oxfsh	1980-1981	GC	2	2	0	22	15	11.00	-	-								-	
M.W.Thomas	Norf	1996-1999	GC	4	4	0	35	26	8.75	-	-	229	182	1	1-53	182.00	4.76	-	-	
P.A.Thomas	Here	1999-2001	GC	5	3	0	14	7	4.66	-	-	270	252	5	2-50	50.40	5.60	-	1	
	Shr	1992	GC	1	1	1	12	12*	-	-	-	48	54	0	-	-	6.75	-	-	
P.A.Thomas	Ches	2001	GC	1								48	48	2	2-48	24.00	6.00	-	-	
P.D.Thomas	Bed	1991-1994	GC	2	2	0	8	4	4.00	-	-	72	71	1	1-71	71.00	5.91	-	-	
P.W.Thomas	Norf	1983	GC	1	1	0	0	0	0.00	-	-	60	35	2	2-35	17.50	3.50	-	-	
B.J.Thompson	Oxfsh	1999-2001	GC	4	4	0	129	42	32.25	-	-	42	36	2	2-36	18.00	5.14	-	-	
G.Thompson	NhCB	1999	GC	1								18	13	1	1-13	13.00	4.33	-	1	
J.Thompson	Wilt	1989-1990	GC	2	2	0	41	34	20.50	-	-	114	76	0	-	-	4.00	-	-	
J.G.Thompson	GloCB	2002	GC	1	1	0	1	1	1.00	-	-								-	
M.J.Thompson	Nmb	1999	GC	1	1	0	21	21	21.00	-	-	53	63	0	-	-	7.13	-	-	
P.L.Thorn	Wilt	1983-1984	GC	2	2	0	15	15	7.50	-	-	102	79	1	1-47	79.00	4.64	-	-	
C.W.A.Thornely	Cambsh	1988	GC	1	1	1	11	11*	-	-	-								-	
N.D.Thornicroft	YorCB	2001	GC	1								30	19	0	-	-	3.80	-	-	
N.J.Thurgood	Dor	1999-2004	GC	5	4	0	29	22	7.25	-	-								1	
C.J.Tibbett	MCS	1979	BH	1	1	0	1	1	1.00	-	-								1	
J.K.Tierney	Dev	1985-1991	GC	5	5	0	43	26	8.60	-		318	252	5	3-47	50.40	4.75	-	-	
M.S.Tiffin	Nmb	1989-1992	GC	2	2	1	51	49*	51.00	-	-								2	
H.W.Tilly	Hert	1964-1971	GC	5	5	0	55	36	11.00	-	-	264	132	6	2-8	22.00	3.00	-	-	
M.A.Tilt	Shr	2000-2005	GC	7	4	1	4	3	1.33	-	-								8	4
P.J.Timmis	Sta	1971-1973	GC	3	3	1	8	8*	4.00	-	-	174	76	3	2-9	25.33	2.62	-	-	
R.T.Timms	SomCB	2002	GC	1	1	1	38	38*	-	-	-								-	
J.Tindale	Dur	1988	GC	1	1	0	30	30	30.00	-	-	30	17	0	-	-	3.40	-	-	
M.R.Tipping	Norf	1988	GC	1	1	0	12	12	12.00	-	-								-	
P.A.Tipton	Ches	1982-1983	GC	2	2	0	7	5	3.50	-	-								2	
J.G.Tizzard	Dor	2001	GC	1	1	0	0	0	0.00	-	-	5	14	0	-	-	16.80	-	-	

				M	I	NO	Runs	HS	Avg	100	50	Balls	Runs	Wkts	BB	Avg	RpO	4I	Ct	St
P.A.Todd	MC	1986-1987	BH	8	8	0	279	107	34.87	1	1								1	
J.G.Tolchard	Dev	1969-1983	GC	5	5	0	49	24	9.80	-	-								2	
	MC	1980-1983	BH	12	12	0	259	54	21.58	-	1								3	
R.C.Tolchard	Dev	1978-1984	GC	6	6	1	77	40	15.40	-	-								-	
	MCS	1979	BH	4	3	1	15	14*	7.50	-	-								-	
C.M.Tolley	NottCB	2001	GC	2	2	0	112	78	56.00	-	1	106	69	1	1-38	69.00	3.90	-	-	
J.R.Tolliday	Dev	1978-1979	GC	2	2	0	10	10	5.00	-	-								-	
K.P.Tomlins	Wilt	1993	GC	1	1	0	28	28	28.00	-	-	72	51	2	2-51	25.50	4.25	-	-	
J.A.Tomlinson	HamCB	2000	GC	1	1	0	4	4	4.00	-	-	60	17	0	-	-	1.70	-	-	
	Wilt	2001	GC	1	1	0	0	0	0.00	-	-	42	29	1	1-29	29.00	4.14	-	-	
S.C.B.Tomlinson	Dev	2001	GC	1	1	0	30	30	30.00	-	-	48	38	2	2-38	19.00	4.75	-	-	
G.J.Toogood	Shr	1992	GC	1	1	0	1	1	1.00	-	-	72	47	6	6-47	7.83	3.91	1	-	
	Cambsh	1995	GC	1	1	0	0	0	0.00	-	-	72	66	0	-	-	5.50	-	-	
C.D.M.Tooley	KntCB	1999	GC	1	1	0	24	24	24.00	-	-								-	
T.D.Topley	Norf	1984-1985	GC	2	2	0	10	9	5.00	-	-	138	81	3	2-37	27.00	3.52	-	-	
D.A.Toseland	Corn	1975-2000	GC	5	4	2	46	39	23.00	-	-	348	181	7	3-27	25.85	3.12	-	-	
M.A.Tournier	NottCB	2002	GC	1	1	0	25	25	25.00	-	-	60	33	2	2-33	16.50	3.30	-	-	
D.E.J.Townsend	Dev	1993	GC	1	1	0	29	29	29.00	-	-								-	
G.T.J.Townsend	Dev	1994-2001	GC	11	11	0	249	60	22.63	-	1								2	
	MC	1996	BH	2	2	0	12	10	6.00	-	-								-	
A.D.Towse	Lin	1996	GC	1	1	0	30	30	30.00	-	-	72	47	1	1-47	47.00	3.91	-	-	
	WalMC	1998-2004	GC	11	9	3	114	30*	19.00	-	-	639	311	18	3-19	17.27	2.92	-	1	
S.J.Trafford	Sta	1976	GC	1	1	0	1	1	1.00	-	-								-	
R.C.Travers	SomCB	2001	GC	1								42	26	2	2-26	13.00	3.71	-	-	
D.J.Traylor	Dev	1969	GC	1	1	0	4	4	4.00	-	-								-	
G.R.Treagus	Dor	2000-2004	GC	7	6	0	104	76	17.33	-	1	233	220	1	1-44	220.00	5.66	-	-	
J.C.Tredwell	KntCB	2000-2001	GC	6	5	0	166	71	33.20	-	2	234	169	3	1-31	56.33	4.33	-	1	
P.D.Trego	SomCB	1999-2001	GC	2	2	0	11	11	5.50	-	-	96	63	4	2-21	15.75	3.93	-	-	
C.R.Trembath	Wilt	1987	GC	1	1	0	4	4	4.00	-	-	30	34	0	-	-	6.80	-	-	
C.T.Tremlett	HamCB	2000	GC	1	1	0	10	10	10.00	-	-	48	35	2	2-35	17.50	4.37	-	-	
P.C.Trend	Lin	1997-2000	GC	5	5	0	94	52	18.80	-	1								5	1
M.O.Trenwith	Corn	1975-1980	GC	2	2	1	14	14*	14.00	-	-	144	72	5	3-51	14.40	3.00	-	-	
M.R.Trevor	LeiCB	2002	GC	2	1	0	2	2	2.00	-	-	64	51	0	-	-	4.78	-	-	
D.J.Trigger	KntCB	1999-2003	GC	10	7	2	56	18*	11.20	-	-	528	387	14	3-53	27.64	4.39	-	1	
R.I.Trotman	SomCB	1999	GC	1	1	0	2	2	2.00	-	-	48	30	2	2-30	15.00	3.75	-	-	
A.J.Trott	Bed	1997-2005	GC	11	9	2	178	41*	25.42	-	-	234	234	4	1-17	58.50	6.00	-	-	
K.Trotter	Dur	1989	GC	1	1	0	4	4	4.00	-	-	72	60	2	2-60	30.00	5.00	-	1	
J.O.Troughton	WarCB	1999-2001	GC	4	4	1	222	115*	74.00	1	1	130	83	7	4-23	11.85	3.83	1	2	
J.Trower	Lin	2000-2004	GC	10	9	0	219	76	24.33	-	2	24	26	0	-	-	6.50	-	2	
S.D.Trower	Lin	2001	GC	1	1	1	1	1*	-	-	-	30	6	3	3-6	2.00	1.20	-	-	
C.J.Trudgeon	Corn	1980	GC	1	1	0	9	9	9.00	-	-								-	
J.F.Trueman	DerbCB	2002	GC	1	1	0	24	24	24.00	-	-	60	49	0	-	-	4.90	-	1	
G.Trump	Dev	1969	GC	1	1	0	1	1	1.00	-	-	72	42	1	1-42	42.00	3.50	-	-	
K.D.Tudge	WalMC	2005	GC	1	1	0	4	4	4.00	-	-	30	31	0	-	-	6.20	-	-	
N.R.K.Turk	SusCB	2002	GC	1	1	0	20	20	20.00	-	-	12	21	0	-	-	10.50	-	-	
K.B.Turnbull	Dur	1972	GC	1	1	0	0	0	0.00	-	-								-	

				M	I	NO	Runs	HS	Avg	100	50	Balls	Runs	Wkts	BB	Avg	RpO	4I	Ct	St
D.R.Turner	Wilt	1990	GC	1	1	0	18	18	18.00	-	-								-	
	MC	1991	BH	1	1	0	15	15	15.00	-	-								-	
J.B.Turner	Buck	1969-1979	GC	8	8	0	254	88	31.75	-	3								4	
	MCS	1972-1975	BH	8	8	0	126	56	15.75	-	1								5	
	MCW	1976	BH	4	4	0	18	17	4.50	-	-								-	
M.A.Turner	Hunt	1999-2000	GC	2	1	0	5	5	5.00	-	-	84	45	1	1-20	45.00	3.21	-	-	
M.J.Turner	Shr	1999	GC	1	1	0	0	0	0.00	-	-								-	
S.Turner	Cambsh	1987-1994	GC	4	4	1	23	7	7.66	-	-	262	98	1	1-23	98.00	2.24	-	-	
	MC	1988	BH	1	1	0	2	2	2.00	-	-	36	21	0	-	-	3.50	-	-	
R.C.Turpin	Dev	1986-1990	GC	4	4	1	59	29*	19.66	-	-								2	
S.J.Turrill	Dor	1986-1987	GC	2	2	0	6	6	3.00	-	-	30	39	0	-	-	7.80	-	-	
A.Tutt	KntCB	1999-2002	GC	10	5	2	10	5*	3.33	-	-	411	276	9	3-16	30.66	4.02	-	1	
T.A.Tweats	Sta	2000	GC	2	2	0	12	10	6.00	-	-								-	
A.N.W.Tweedie	Here	1999	GC	2	1	0	0	0	0.00	-	-	90	81	3	2-27	27.00	5.40	-	-	
S.A.Twigg	Cumb	2002	GC	2	2	0	74	63	37.00	-	1								1	
	Ches	2003-2004	GC	2	2	0	75	68	37.50	-	1								-	
P.H.Twizell	Nmb	1984	GC	1	1	1	9	9*	-	-	-	72	45	1	1-45	45.00	3.75	-	-	
R.G.Twose	Dev	1988	GC	1	1	0	56	56	56.00	-	1	60	48	1	1-48	48.00	4.80	-	1	
R.P.Twose	Dev	1988	GC	1	1	0	1	1	1.00	-	-	6	14	0	-	-	14.00	-	-	
P.N.Unsworth	LanCB	2001	GC	1	1	0	6	6	6.00	-	-	60	34	1	1-34	34.00	3.40	-	1	
K.E.A.Upashantha	Ches	2002	GC	1	1	1	59	59*	-	-	1	54	54	2	2-54	27.00	6.00	-	-	
B.C.Usher	DurCB	1999-2000	GC	6	5	2	61	32	20.33	-	-	230	180	6	2-30	30.00	4.69	-	-	
C.G.van der Gucht	HamCB	1999	GC	3	2	0	4	3	2.00	-	-	144	95	5	3-35	19.00	3.95	-	-	
R.S.van der Knaap	Berk	1976	GC	1	1	1	12	12*	-	-	-	61	20	1	1-20	20.00	1.96	-	-	
J.van Geloven	Nmb	1971	GC	1	1	1	60	60*	-	-	1	60	65	0	-	-	6.50	-	-	
M.van Jaarsveld	Suf	2003	GC	1	1	0	21	21	21.00	-	-	60	50	0	-	-	5.00	-	3	
D.W.Varey	Ches	1988-1992	GC	4	4	0	29	17	7.25	-	-								1	
	MC	1988	BH	1	1	0	5	5	5.00	-	-								-	
R.N.R.Vartan	Hert	1990	GC	1	1	0	10	10	10.00	-	-								1	
D.B.Vengsarkar	Sta	1985	GC	1	1	0	4	4	4.00	-	-								-	
J.F.Venter	WorCB	1999	GC	1	1	0	42	42	42.00	-	-	60	33	1	1-33	33.00	3.30	-	-	
D.R.Vincent	Cambsh	1986	GC	1	1	0	6	6	6.00	-	-								-	
L.Vincent	Suf	2005	GC	1	1	0	0	0	0.00	-	-	42	55	0	-	-	7.85	-	-	
M.F.Voss	Hert	1991	GC	1	1	0	2	2	2.00	-	-								-	
R.H.Wacey	Hert	1964-1976	GC	5	5	1	26	12*	6.50	-	-	240	130	5	2-21	26.00	3.25	-	-	
J.R.Wade	NhCB	2001	GC	2	2	0	50	38	25.00	-	-	12	37	0	-	-	18.50	-	1	
R.H.Wade	Wilt	1999-2002	GC	4	4	0	70	28	17.50	-	-	78	77	1	1-53	77.00	5.92	-	2	
G.G.Wagg	WarCB	2000-2002	GC	2	2	0	21	21	10.50	-	-	90	52	3	3-35	17.33	3.46	-	-	
M.C.Wagstaffe	MCS	1974	BH	1	1	0	1	1	1.00	-	-	42	19	0	-	-	2.71	-	-	
	Dev	1978-1980	GC	3	3	0	44	21	14.66	-	-	124	76	2	2-48	38.00	3.67	-	-	
	Dor	1983	GC	1	1	1	34	34*	-	-	-	2	6	0	-	-	18.00	-	1	
A.C.Waite	Buck	1965-1970	GC	4	3	2	8	8	8.00	-	-	252	163	2	1-46	81.50	3.88	-	1	
R.P.Waite	DurCB	2001-2003	GC	2	2	0	6	6	3.00	-	-	69	74	4	2-25	18.50	6.43	-	1	
J.R.Wake	Bed	1985-1991	GC	2	2	0	39	37	19.50	-	-	72	47	1	1-47	47.00	3.91	-	1	
P.G.Wakefield	Ches	1983	GC	1	1	0	13	13	13.00	-	-								-	
J.A.Wakeling	NottCB	1999	GC	1	1	0	5	5	5.00	-	-								-	

				M	I	NO	Runs	HS	Avg	100	50	Balls	Runs	Wkts	BB	Avg	RpO	4I	Ct	St
A.G.Wakely	Bed	2005	GC	1	1	0	3	3	3.00	-	-								1	
S.R.Walbridge	Dor	1992-2003	GC	7	4	1	19	11	6.33	-	-	322	252	1	1-34	252.00	4.69	-	-	
J.E.P.Walford	Bed	2005	GC	1	1	0	27	27	27.00	-	-								-	
A.J.Walker	YorCB	1999-2000	GC	3	3	1	57	30*	28.50	-	-	138	86	0	-	-	3.73	-	-	
J.R.Walker	Norf	1999-2003	GC	6	6	1	103	76	20.60	-	1								2	
N.G.E.Walker	Hert	2001-2003	GC	2	2	0	13	12	6.50	-	-	104	114	4	3-49	28.50	6.57	-	2	
P.D.Walker	Dev	1978	GC	1	1	0	2	2	2.00	-	-	72	40	0	-	-	3.33	-	-	
S.Wall	Cumb	1987-1989	GC	3	2	0	12	11	6.00	-	-	186	140	3	3-24	46.66	4.51	-	-	
G.Wallen	MCW	1977-1978	BH	8	8	1	123	49*	17.57	-	-								1	
	Dev	1978-1988	GC	7	7	0	209	104	29.85	1	-								1	
C.D.Walsh	Cambsh	2000	GC	1	1	0	0	0	0.00	-	-								-	
M.J.Walshe	Hert	1993	GC	1	1	0	1	1	1.00	-	-	72	67	2	2-67	33.50	5.58	-	-	
A.P.Walton	KntCB	2000	GC	3	3	0	13	8	4.33	-	-	98	89	4	3-31	22.25	5.44	-	1	
R.T.Walton	Corn	1995	GC	1	1	0	39	39	39.00	-	-								2	
T.C.Walton	Cambsh	2001	GC	1	1	0	4	4	4.00	-	-								-	
Waqar Mohammad																				
	WarCB	2001	GC	1	1	0	2	2	2.00	-	-	24	20	0	-	-	5.00	-	-	
A.J.Ward	Buck	2003	GC	1															-	
D.C.Ward	DerbCB	1999-2000	GC	2	2	2	23	22*	-	-	-	102	78	4	2-31	19.50	4.58	-	-	
D.M.Ward	MC	1998	BH	3	3	0	60	33	20.00	-	-								-	
	Hert	1999-2003	GC	7	7	1	189	83*	31.50	-	1	6	6	0	-	-	6.00	-	1	
M.J.P.Ward	Norf	1996	GC	1	1	0	0	0	0.00	-	-								-	
S.Ward	Dur	1987	GC	1								36	13	0	-	-	2.16	-	-	
T.W.Ward	Dev	1987-1993	GC	4	4	0	37	17	9.25	-	-	262	249	5	3-60	49.80	5.70	-	4	
J.H.Wardle	Cambsh	1964-1967	GC	4	4	0	29	19	7.25	-	-	227	107	5	2-21	21.40	2.82	-	-	
S.N.Warman	Lin	1990-2001	GC	9	9	1	195	39	24.37	-	-								3	
C.J.Warn	Suf	2001-2005	GC	7	7	3	136	52*	34.00	-	1								11	2
A.E.Warner	WorCB	2000	GC	1	1	0	0	0	0.00	-	-	60	37	0	-	-	3.70	-	-	
G.S.Warner	Sta	1976-1986	GC	4	4	0	127	56	31.75	-	2								1	
N.A.Warren	WarCB	2001	GC	1	1	0	0	0	0.00	-	-	36	29	0	-	-	4.83	-	2	
P.M.Warren	Dev	1997-2001	GC	4	1	1	12	12*	-	-	-	156	128	3	1-24	42.66	4.92	-	-	
	WalMC	1999	GC	1								60	46	0	-	-	4.60	-	-	
A.G.Warrington	MCS	1973-1975	BH	7	7	0	103	44	14.71	-	-								1	
	Suf	1978-1981	GC	5	5	0	44	18	8.80	-	-								2	
Wasim Raja	Dur	1979-1987	GC	6	6	0	158	53	26.33	-	2	318	227	3	2-50	75.66	4.28	-	1	
J.A.Waterhouse	Sta	1988-1996	GC	3	3	0	76	52	25.33	-	1								2	
H.T.Waters	WalMC	2005	GC	1	1	0	8	8	8.00	-	-	30	13	0	-	-	2.60	-	-	
S.N.V.Waterton	Oxfsh	1989-1994	GC	4	4	0	158	92	39.50	-	1								2	1
	MC	1990-1992	BH	5	5	0	57	25	11.40	-	-								3	
M.Watkinson	Ches	1982	GC	1	1	0	6	6	6.00	-	-	21	23	0	-	-	6.57	-	-	
A.G.M.Watson	Dor	1973	GC	1	1	0	2	2	2.00	-	-	72	39	3	3-39	13.00	3.25	-	1	
D.J.Watson	DerbCB	1999	GC	1	1	0	19	19	19.00	-	-								-	
	Suf	2005	GC	1	1	0	6	6	6.00	-	-								1	
J.M.Watson	Dur	1964	GC	2	1	1	2	2*	-	-	-	78	63	0	-	-	4.84	-	-	
M.A.Watts	Wilt	1987-1988	GC	2	2	1	10	7*	10.00	-	-	132	154	1	1-57	154.00	7.00	-	1	
P.W.Watts	Berk	1966	GC	2	2	0	9	5	4.50	-	-	66	82	2	1-17	41.00	7.45	-	-	

				M	I	NO	Runs	HS	Avg	100	50	Balls	Runs	Wkts	BB	Avg	RpO	4I	Ct	St
S.J.Watts	Bed	2003-2005	GC	2	2	2	7	4*	-	-	-	54	50	0	-	-	5.55	-	-	
S.D.Weale	MidCB	1999	GC	1	1	1	9	9*	-	-	-	60	24	1	1-24	24.00	2.40	-	-	
J.R.Weaver	Shr	1990-1991	GC	2	2	0	6	6	3.00	-	-							-	2	
S.Webb	Lin	2002	GC	2	2	1	62	55	62.00	-	1							-	-	
P.J.Webley	Bed	1971	GC	1	1	0	4	4	4.00	-	-							-	-	
T.Webley	SomCB	2001-2002	GC	2	2	0	12	8	6.00	-	-							-	1	
A.J.Webster	Sta	1985-1988	GC	4	4	0	34	30	8.50	-	-	288	179	7	4-38	25.57	3.72	1	-	
	MC	1986-1988	BH	6	5	0	29	12	5.80	-	-	336	244	4	2-31	61.00	4.35	-	-	
L.C.Weekes	Lin	1997	GC	1	1	0	8	8	8.00	-	-	36	39	0	-	-	6.50	-	-	
	YorCB	1999	GC	1	1	0	0	0	0.00	-	-	22	27	0	-	-	7.36	-	1	
N.P.Weekes	SusCB	2001	GC	1	1	0	5	5	5.00	-	-	60	51	1	1-51	51.00	5.10	-	1	
P.E.Wellings	Sta	1998-2000	GC	4	4	1	54	28*	18.00	-	-	82	45	4	2-9	11.25	3.29	-	1	
	MidCB	2001-2002	GC	4	4	0	175	60	43.75	-	2	84	53	3	2-19	17.66	3.78	-	1	
B.M.Wellington	SomCB	1999	GC	1	1	1	5	5*	-	-	-	18	17	0	-	-	5.66	-	-	
G.E.Welton	Lin	2004	GC	1	1	0	60	60	60.00	-	1							-	-	
D.A.Wenlock	Sta	1985	GC	1	1	0	0	0	0.00	-	-	72	45	0	-	-	3.75	-	-	
J.C.Went	EssCB	2003	GC	1	1	0	1	1	1.00	-	-	60	64	1	1-64	64.00	6.40	-	-	
B.West	Bed	2000	GC	1	1	1	1	1*	-	-	-	38	34	1	1-34	34.00	5.36	-	-	
F.M.Westcott	Dur	1967-1968	GC	2	2	0	47	47	23.50	-	-							-	1	
S.A.Westley	Suf	1978-1983	GC	6	6	1	96	28	19.20	-	-							-	11	
M.J.Weston	Here	1995	GC	1	1	0	9	9	9.00	-	-	72	40	0	-	-	3.33	-	-	
M.P.Weston	Dur	1972	GC	2	2	0	11	11	5.50	-	-							-	-	
I.J.Westwood	WarCB	2001-2002	GC	4	4	0	78	55	19.50	-	1	180	139	2	1-28	69.50	4.63	-	1	
R.D.Whalley	LanCB	2001	GC	1	1	0	5	5	5.00	-	-							-	1	
D.M.Wheatman	Cumb	2000-2001	GC	4	3	1	9	8*	4.50	-	-	120	75	2	2-23	37.50	3.75	-	-	
M.R.Whitaker	Norf	1969	GC	1	1	1	2	2*	-	-	-	42	20	0	-	-	2.85	-	-	
G.G.Whitbread	Hunt	1999	GC	1	1	1	3	3*	-	-	-							-	1	
A.P.White	Oxfsh	1994	GC	1	1	0	7	7	7.00	-	-	12	19	0	-	-	9.50	-	-	
B.H.White	Wilt	1965-1990	GC	9	9	0	79	29	8.77	-	-							-	1	
	MCS	1972-1974	BH	6	6	0	54	25	9.00	-	-							-	1	
C.C.E.White	EssCB	2002	GC	1								60	34	2	2-34	17.00	3.40	-	-	
D.G.White	LanCB	1999	GC	1	1	0	1	1	1.00	-	-	18	15	0	-	-	5.00	-	-	
G.A.White	Cumb	2002	GC	1	1	0	0	0	0.00	-	-	30	28	1	1-28	28.00	5.60	-	1	
G.W.White	Dev	1992-1993	GC	2	2	0	11	11	5.50	-	-	72	45	1	1-45	45.00	3.75	-	2	
J.W.White	GloCB	1999-2002	GC	7	5	1	58	29	14.50	-	-	379	172	11	4-14	15.63	2.72	1	-	
M.R.White	Bed	1994-1998	GC	3	3	1	8	6*	4.00	-	-	182	132	2	1-35	66.00	4.35	-	-	
R.H.White	Bed	1967	GC	1	1	0	0	0	0.00	-	-	72	41	1	1-41	41.00	3.41	-	1	
S.P.White	Hert	2001-2003	GC	5	5	1	59	31*	14.75	-	-	264	220	6	2-32	36.66	5.00	-	2	
J.D.Whitney	Shr	2005	GC	1	1	0	39	39	39.00	-	-	36	26	1	1-26	26.00	4.33	-	-	
J.P.Whittaker	Ches	2001-2004	GC	4	2	1	31	27	31.00	-	-	224	125	12	4-45	10.41	3.34	1	4	
P.K.Whittaker	Norf	1984-1985	GC	2	2	1	5	4*	5.00	-	-	102	30	1	1-5	30.00	1.76	-	1	
C.M.Whyborn	Cambsh	1997	GC	1	1	0	7	7	7.00	-	-	66	62	1	1-62	62.00	5.63	-	1	
C.Wicks	Lin	1988	GC	1	1	0	12	12	12.00	-	-							-	-	
P.S.Widdowson	LeiCB	2000	GC	1	1	0	11	11	11.00	-	-	24	12	1	1-12	12.00	3.00	-	-	
S.Widdup	YorCB	2002	GC	3	3	0	140	90	46.66	-	1							-	2	
K.M.Wijesuriya	Suf	1996-1999	GC	2	2	1	171	109*	171.00	1	1	30	40	0	-	-	8.00	-	-	

				M	I	NO	Runs	HS	Avg	100	50	Balls	Runs	Wkts	BB	Avg	RpO	4I	Ct	St
J.R.Wileman	Lin	1994-1997	GC	2	2	0	15	14	7.50	-	-								2	
	SurCB	1999-2001	GC	2	2	0	28	15	14.00	-	-	42	17	1	1-17	17.00	2.42	-	-	
J.S.Wilkinson	Dur	1973-1985	GC	12	8	2	28	8	4.66	-	-	791	417	13	5-24	32.07	3.16	1	2	
	MCE	1977-1978	BH	7	7	3	7	4	1.75	-	-	396	182	9	3-23	20.22	2.75	-	-	
	MCN	1979	BH	4	3	2	4	3*	4.00	-	-	189	99	3	1-15	33.00	3.14	-	1	
M.O.Wilkinson	Norf	2003-2003	GC	1	1	0	0	0	0.00	-	-								1	
R.Wilkinson	YorCB	2001-2002	GC	4	4	0	55	36	13.75	-	-	186	147	5	2-38	29.40	4.74	-	-	
E.G.Willcock	Corn	1970-1986	GC	5	5	0	79	43	15.80	-	-								5	
K.J.Willcock	Corn	1995-1996	GC	2	2	0	26	25	13.00	-	-	144	95	2	1-43	47.50	3.95	-	1	
D.R.Willetts	Here	2004	GC	1															-	
F.T.Willetts	Corn	2980	GC	1	1	0	1	1	1.00	-	-								1	
P.Willey	Nmb	1992	GC	1	1	0	10	10	10.00	-	-	18	19	0	-	-	6.33	-	-	
A.R.Williams	Shr	1992	GC	1	1	0	6	6	6.00	-	-								-	
A.S.Williams	Cumb	2001	GC	1	1	0	19	19	19.00	-	-								-	
C.Williams	EssCB	2002	GC	1	1	0	7	7	7.00	-	-	24	24	0	-	-	6.00	-	-	
C.D.Williams	Bed	1982	GC	1	1	1	20	20*	-	-	-	72	47	0	-	-	3.91	-	-	
D.R.Williams	Cumb	2001-2003	GC	2	2	0	20	16	10.00	-	-								2	
G.D.Williams	Sta	1991	GC	1	1	0	7	7	7.00	-	-	72	41	0	-	-	3.41	-	-	
	WorCB	2000	GC	1	1	1	6	6*	-	-	-	48	42	0	-	-	5.25	-	-	
G.G.Williams	GloCB	2002	GC	1	1	0	17	17	17.00	-	-	48	57	0	-	-	7.12	-	-	
G.J.Williams	WorCB	2001-2003	GC	5	1	1	0	0*	-	-	-	213	141	5	3-61	28.20	3.97	-	-	
J.C.Williams	SomCB	2000	GC	1	1	0	10	10	10.00	-	-								-	
J.J.Williams	Dev	2001-2002	GC	2	2	0	45	40	22.50	-	-								1	2
J.M.Williams	Buck	1972	GC	1	1	0	0	0	0.00	-	-								-	
K.C.Williams	Nmb	1984-1992	GC	3	3	0	56	33	18.66	-	-	216	129	3	2-52	43.00	3.58	-	-	
N.F.Williams	Corn	2000	GC	1	1	1	8	8*	-	-	-	53	37	0	-	-	4.18	-	-	
O.C.W.Williams	LeiCB	2002-2002	GC	2	2	0	7	4	3.50	-	-								-	
R.J.Williams	Oxfsh	1996-2003	GC	5	5	0	55	22	11.00	-	-								2	
S.Williams	Wilt	1989-1990	GC	2	2	0	11	11	5.50	-	-								-	
S.L.Williams	Cambsh	1995-1996	GC	2	2	0	22	13	11.00	-	-								1	
	KntCB	1999-2000	GC	6	6	2	130	45*	32.50	-	-								3	
S.M.Williams	Corn	1995-2000	GC	4	4	0	151	52	37.75	-	1								1	
D.Williamson	Shr	2001-2002	GC	2	2	0	51	49	25.50	-	-	54	35	1	1-18	35.00	3.88	-	-	
J.G.Williamson	Dur	1964-1968	GC	4	3	0	4	2	1.33	-	-	242	128	7	4-13	18.28	3.17	1	-	
S.M.Willis	Dev	1992-1994	GC	3	3	0	102	42	34.00	-	-								1	
W.P.Willis	Lin	1974-1976	GC	3	1	0	31	31	31.00	-	-	150	114	1	1-29	114.00	4.56	-	2	
G.R.Willott	Sta	2001-2003	GC	2	1	0	4	4	4.00	-	-	78	68	3	2-47	22.66	5.23	-	1	
C.M.Willoughby	Berk	2000	GC	2	1	0	0	0	0.00	-	-	120	54	2	2-27	27.00	2.70	-	1	
A.Willows	Dor	1991-1995	GC	4	2	0	26	14	13.00	-	-	90	79	0	-	-	5.26	-	-	
P.J.Wilshaw	NottCB	2002	GC	1	1	0	0	0	0.00	-	-								1	
	Sta	2005	GC	1	1	0	20	20	20.00	-	-								1	
A.G.Wilson	Cumb	1984	GC	1	1	0	10	10	10.00	-	-								-	
A.R.Wilson	Cambsh	1964-1967	GC	4	2	1	1	1*	1.00	-	-	144	72	3	3-14	24.00	3.00	-	-	
A.R.Wilson	Cumb	1996	GC	1	1	0	10	10	10.00	-	-	48	22	1	1-22	22.00	2.75	-	-	
D.Wilson	DurCB	2002-2003	GC	2	2	2	19	19*	-	-	-								2	2

				M	I	NO	Runs	HS	Avg	100	50	Balls	Runs	Wkts	BB	Avg	RpO	4I	Ct	St
D.G.Wilson	Cambsh	2000-2001	GC	5	4	1	44	22*	14.66	-	-	144	133	6	3-30	22.16	5.54	-	2	
	Hunt	2002	GC	1	1	0	29	29	29.00	-	-	12	22	0	-	-	11.00	-	-	
E.J.Wilson	Cambsh	2003	GC	1	1	0	33	33	33.00	-	-								-	
E.J.Wilson	WarCB	2002	GC	1								54	25	0	-	-	2.77	-	-	
	Lin	2003-2004	GC	2								91	126	1	1-85	126.00	8.30	-	-	
G.B.Wilson	Lin	1996	GC	1	1	0	1	1	1.00	-	-								2	2
J.R.Wilson	Dor	2002-2003	GC	2	1	1	0	0*	-	-	-	108	76	4	2-36	19.00	4.22	-	-	
K.J.Wilson	Dor	2001	GC	2	2	0	0	0	0.00	-	-	66	55	1	1-41	55.00	5.00	-	-	
R.Wilson	Wilt	1983	GC	1	1	1	9	9*	-	-	-	18	12	0	-	-	4.00	-	-	
N.J.Wilton	Berk	2002	GC	2	1	0	5	5	5.00	-	-								5	
J.B.Windows	Nmb	1999-2005	GC	9	8	2	144	52*	24.00	-	1	118	136	3	2-17	45.33	6.91	-	-	
H.M.Winfield	Lin	1971	GC	2	1	0	14	14	14.00	-	-								-	
D.C.Wing	Cambsh	1964-1986	GC	9	7	2	19	11*	3.80	-	-	562	302	13	4-40	23.23	3.22	1	2	
	MCN	1972-1975	BH	12	9	3	36	9	6.00	-	-	660	321	5	2-31	64.20	2.91	-	3	
	MCE	1976-1977	BH	6	4	0	14	12	3.50	-	-	366	199	7	3-31	28.42	3.26	-	2	
	MC	1980	BH	1	1	1	2	2*	-	-	-	48	25	0	-	-	3.12	-	-	
A.R.Wingfield Digby																				
	Dor	1986-1992	GC	5	4	2	34	23*	17.00	-	-	336	272	2	1-30	136.00	4.85	-	-	
	MC	1989	BH	1								66	22	1	1-22	22.00	2.00	-	-	
V.P.Winn	Hunt	1999-2000	GC	3	3	0	97	50	32.33	-	1								-	
A.Winstone	SusCB	2001	GC	1								54	62	0	-	-	6.88	-	-	
D.A.Winter	Wilt	1999-2001	GC	5	5	1	73	37*	18.25	-	-								-	
D.A.J.Wise	Oxfsh	1985-1993	GC	7	6	1	104	68	20.80	-	1								1	
I.A.Wishart	MCN	1979	BH	1	1	0	0	0	0.00	-	-	42	25	0	-	-	3.57	-	-	
J.P.Wolstenholme	NhCB	2000	GC	1	1	0	10	10	10.00	-	-								-	
M.A.Wolstenholme																				
	NhCB	1999-2001	GC	5	2	0	20	18	10.00	-	-	242	177	9	5-41	19.66	4.38	1	1	
D.R.Womble	Sta	1997-2005	GC	11	10	1	151	49	16.77	-	-	384	401	6	3-42	66.83	6.26	-	1	
B.Wood	Ches	1986-1989	GC	4	4	0	50	40	12.50	-	-	288	172	6	4-56	28.66	3.58	1	1	
J.Wood	Dur	1991	GC	1	1	0	1	1	1.00	-	-	60	82	0	-	-	8.20	-	-	
J.R.Wood	Berk	1994-2005	GC	13	13	1	339	88	28.25	-	3	89	66	4	2-14	16.50	4.44	-	2	
M.J.Wood	Dev	2000-2003	GC	2	2	0	56	43	28.00	-	-								-	
N.T.Wood	Ches	2001	GC	1	1	0	50	50	50.00	-	1								-	
S.L.Wood	Ches	1966-1968	GC	3	3	0	57	49	19.00	-	-								-	
	MCN	1975	BH	2	2	0	31	31	15.50	-	-								-	
J.D.Woodford	MCN	1975	BH	1	1	0	5	5	5.00	-	-	12	17	0	-	-	8.50	-	-	
	Nmb	1977	GC	1	1	1	56	56*	-	-	1	36	16	2	2-16	8.00	2.66	-	1	
M.C.Woodman	Dev	1988-1995	GC	6	3	0	9	8	3.00	-	-	402	210	3	1-16	70.00	3.13	-	1	
P.J.Woodroffe	Buck	1999-2003	GC	5	2	1	31	16*	31.00	-	-	228	146	7	2-18	20.85	3.84	-	-	
D.C.Woods	Oxfsh	1991-1994	GC	3	2	0	21	14	10.50	-	-								-	
M.D.Woods	Cumb	1984-1992	GC	7	6	1	110	36	22.00	-	-	336	274	4	2-33	68.50	4.89	-	2	
J.R.Woodward	Hunt	2000-2001	GC	4	4	0	40	30	10.00	-	-								-	
P.B.Wormwald	Shr	1988-1991	GC	4	4	1	42	16	14.00	-	-	207	157	5	2-85	31.40	4.55	-	1	
D.J.L.Worrad	Dor	2002-2004	GC	2	2	0	28	17	14.59	-	-	78	60	3	2-31	20.00	4.61	-	-	
A.Worthy	DurCB	2000-2003	GC	4	4	0	193	74	48.25	-	3								2	
	Nmb	2005	GC	1	1	0	0	0	0.00	-	-								-	

				M	I	NO	Runs	HS	Avg	100	50	Balls	Runs	Wkts	BB	Avg	RpO	4I	Ct	St
A.J.Wright	Hunt	2002	GC	1	1	0	6	6	6.00	-	-								-	
A.S.Wright	LeiCB	1999-2001	GC	3	3	0	181	112	60.33	1	1	36	32	0	-	-	5.33	-	-	
	Lin	2004	GC	1	1	1	14	14*	-	-	-								-	
E.Wright	Norf	1982	GC	1								54	19	0	-	-	2.11	-	-	
G.D.Wright	Sta	2001	GC	1	1	0	1	1	1.00	-	-								-	
H.J.W.Wright	Suf	1985-1989	GC	4	3	0	38	16	12.66	-	-	180	127	4	3-29	31.75	4.23	-	3	
J.D.W.Wright	Hert	1974-1981	GC	2	2	1	33	19	33.00	-	-	144	86	1	1-38	86.00	3.58	-	-	
J.P.Wright	Here	1995	GC	1	1	0	20	20	20.00	-	-								-	
	WorCB	1999-2001	GC	5	4	0	80	45	20.00	-	-	198	123	10	5-21	12.30	3.72	1	4	
L.J.Wright	LeiCB	2001	GC	1	1	0	16	16	16.00	-	-								-	
L.W.Wright	Hert	1964	GC	1	1	0	7	7	7.00	-	-								-	
M.C.G.Wright	Hert	1986-1989	GC	4	4	0	58	36	14.50	-	-								-	
M.J.W.Wright	MidCB	2001	GC	1	1	0	5	5	5.00	-	-	24	13	1	1-13	13.00	3.25	-	-	
N.P.G.Wright	Hert	1983-1991	GC	7	7	0	67	17	9.57	-	-	7	11	1	1-2	11.00	9.42	-	-	
T.A.Wright	Dev	2002-2003	GC	2	1	0	6	6	6.00	-	-	18	19	1	1-19	19.00	6.33	-	1	
T.M.Wright	Norf	1965	GC	1	1	1	1	1*	-	-	-	78	69	0	-	-	5.30	-	1	
S.C.Wundke	Ches	1982-1998	GC	2	2	0	10	10	5.00	-	-	41	21	0	-	-	3.07	-	-	
J.G.Wyatt	Dev	1993-1995	GC	3	3	0	24	15	8.00	-	-	42	55	1	1-25	55.00	7.85	-	3	
S.J.Wyatt	Berk	2001	GC	1	1	0	8	8	8.00	-	-								-	
A.P.A.Wykes	Cambsh	1987-1989	GC	3	1	1	0	0*	-	-	-	151	78	5	3-36	15.60	3.09	-	1	
R.M.Wyld	NottCB	2000-2002	GC	3	3	0	19	8	6.33	-	-	114	113	1	1-67	113.00	5.94	-	1	
M.E.Wynn	Bed	1970	GC	1	1	0	35	35	35.00	-	-								-	
M.H.Yardy	SusCB	1999-2000	GC	3	3	0	28	15	9.33	-	-	108	90	1	1-46	90.00	5.00	-	4	
C.J.Yates	HamCB	2000-2001	GC	2	2	0	23	23	11.50	-	-	90	39	4	3-17	9.75	2.60	-	-	
K.C.Yates	Cambsh	1964	GC	1	1	0	5	5	5.00	-	-								-	
S.C.Yates	Ches	1985-1986	GC	2	2	0	26	20	13.00	-	-								1	
D.I.Yeabsley	Dev	1969-1987	GC	9	7	5	34	22*	17.00	-	-	572	315	6	2-15	52.50	3.30	-	1	
	MCS	1972-1979	BH	16	15	9	90	21*	15.00	-	-	868	406	14	3-21	29.00	2.80	-	3	
	MCW	1976-1978	BH	12	9	6	27	7	9.00	-	-	708	305	12	3-25	25.41	2.58	-	1	
	MC	1980	BH	4	2	1	13	9	13.00	-	-	210	136	4	2-28	34.00	3.88	-	-	
R.S.Yeabsley	Dev	1990	GC	1	1	0	2	2	2.00	-	-	72	77	0	-	-	6.41	-	-	
D.L.York	Shr	1974	GC	1	1	0	1	1	1.00	-	-	72	34	1	1-34	34.00	2.83	-	-	
S.E.York	Buck	1975	GC	1	1	1	73	73*	-	-	1								-	
M.Youll	Nmb	1971-1977	GC	3	3	1	65	36*	32.50	-	-								1	
O.S.Youll	Nmb	1994-1999	GC	2	2	1	82	65	82.00	-	1								-	
E.J.Young	Bed	1997	GC	1	1	1	30	30*	-	-	-								-	
D.J.Young	MidCB	2002	GC	2	2	0	32	22	16.00	-	-								2	
I.Young	Dur	1990	GC	1	1	0	0	0	0.00	-	-	37	47	0	-	-	7.62	-	-	
S.Young	Bed	2001-2003	GC	7	6	2	184	78*	46.00	-	2	364	154	5	1-12	30.80	2.53	-	2	
S.H.Young	Dur	1964-1972	GC	5	3	0	38	22	12.66	-	-	346	116	12	4-13	9.66	2.01	2	3	
W.Young	Hunt	2000	GC	2	2	1	16	15	16.00	-	-	102	62	3	3-22	20.66	3.64	-	1	
M.E.Younger	Nmb	1984-1994	GC	5	5	1	123	57	30.75	-	1	204	151	2	2-32	75.50	4.44	-	-	